Contemporary Perspectives on Reading and Spelling

With contributions from leading international researchers, *Contemporary Perspectives on Reading and Spelling* offers a critique of current thinking on the research literature into reading, reading comprehension and spelling. Each chapter in this volume provides an account of empirical research that challenges aspects of accepted models and widely accepted theories about reading and spelling.

This book develops the argument for a need to incorporate more complexity into popular accounts of written language development and disability, challenging the idea that the development of a universal theory of written language development is currently attainable. The arguments within the book are explored in three parts:

- overarching debates in reading and spelling
- reading and spelling across languages
- written language difficulties and approaches to teaching.

Opening up the existing debates, and incorporating psychological theory and the politics surrounding the teaching and learning of reading and spelling, this edited collection offers some challenging points for reflection about how the discipline of psychology as a whole approaches the study of written language skills.

Highlighting many new perspectives, this book forms essential reading for all researchers and practitioners with a focus on the development of reading and spelling skills.

Clare Wood is Reader in Developmental Psychology at Coventry University, UK.

Vincent Connelly is Senior Lecturer in Psychology at Oxford Brookes University, Oxford, UK.

New Perspectives on Learning and Instruction

Editor in Chief – Mien Segers (Leiden University and Maastricht University – The Netherlands)
Assistant Editor – Isabel Raemdonck (Leiden University – The Netherlands)

Editorial Board Members
David Gijbels (University of Antwerp – Belgium)
Sanna Järvelä (University of Oulu – Finland)
Margareta Limon (Autonoma University of Madrid – Spain)
Karen Littleton (The Open University – UK)
Wolff-Michael Roth (University of Victoria – Canada)

Advisory Board Members
Costas Constantinou (University of Cyprus, Cyprus)
Valéria Csépe (Hungarian Academy of Sciences – Hungary)
Sibel Erduran (University of Bristol – UK)
Sylvia Rojas-Drummond (UNAM – Mexico)
Martin Valcke (Ghent University – Belgium)
Lieven Verschaffel (Katholieke Universiteit Leuven – Belgium)
Kate Wall (Newcastle University – UK)
Marold Wosnitza (Murdoch University – Australia)

New Perspectives on Learning and Instruction is published by Routledge in conjunction with EARLI (European Association for Research on Learning and Instruction). This series publishes cutting-edge international research focusing on all aspects of learning and instruction in both traditional and non-traditional educational settings. Titles published within the series take a broad and innovative approach to topical areas of research, are written by leading international researchers and are aimed at a research and postgraduate student audience.

Also available:

Transformation of Knowledge Through Classroom Interaction
Edited by Baruch Schwarz, Tommy Dreyfus and Rina Hershkowitz

Forthcoming title:

Researching and Understanding Educational Networks
Edited by Robert McCormick, Patrick Carmichael, Richard Proctor and Alison Fox

Contemporary Perspectives on Reading and Spelling

Edited by
Clare Wood and Vincent Connelly

Routledge
Taylor & Francis Group

LONDON AND NEW YORK

First published 2009
by Routledge
2 Park Square, Milton Park, Abingdon, Oxon OX14 4RN

Simultaneously published in the USA and Canada
by Routledge
270 Madison Avenue, New York, NY 10016

Routledge is an imprint of the Taylor & Francis Group, an informa business

Typeset in Galliard by Taylor & Francis Books
Printed and bound in Great Britain by
CPI Antony Rowe, Chippenham, Wiltshire

British Library Cataloguing in Publication Data
A catalogue record for this book is available from the British Library

Library of Congress Cataloging in Publication Data
Contemporary perspectives on reading and spelling / edited by Clare Wood and
Vincent Connelly.
    p. cm.
    1. Reading–Cross-cultural studies. 2. Language and languages–Orthography and
spelling. I. Wood, Clare Patricia. II. Connelly, Vincent.
    LB1050.C623 2009
    418'.4071–dc22

                                                                    2008048237

ISBN 10: 0-415-49716-7 (hbk)
ISBN 10: 0-415-49717-5 (pbk)
ISBN 10: 0-203-87783-7 (ebk)

ISBN 13: 978-0-415-49716-9 (hbk)
ISBN 13: 978-0-415-49717-6 (pbk)
ISBN 13: 978-0-203-87783-8 (ebk)

Contents

Figures and tables

Figures

Tables

Contributors

Selma Babayiğit is a Senior Lecturer in the Faculty of Health and Life Sciences at the University of the West of England (Bristol), UK.

Ruth H. Bahr is an Associate Professor in the Department of Communication Sciences and Disorders at the University of South Florida in Tampa, USA.

Virginia Berninger is Professor of Educational Psychology at the University of Washington, USA.

Kate Cain is Reader in Language and Cognitive Development in the Department of Psychology, Lancaster University, UK.

Vincent Connelly is Senior Lecturer in the Department of Psychology, Oxford Brookes University, UK.

Sarah Critten is a Lecturer in the School of Psychology at the University of Hertfordshire, UK.

Lynne G. Duncan is a Lecturer in the School of Psychology at the University of Dundee, UK.

Claire M. Fletcher-Flinn is Associate Professor in the Department of Education Studies and Professional Practice, College of Education, University of Otago, New Zealand.

Vincent Goetry is a specialist in literacy development and dyslexia, and scientific collaborator of the Unité de Recherche en Neurosciences Cognitives (UNESCOG) and Laboratoire Cognition, Langage et Développement (LCLD), Université Libre de Bruxelles, Belgium.

Andrew J. Holliman is a Postdoctoral Fellow in the Faculty of Children and Health at the Institute of Education, University of London, UK.

Shahrzad Irannejad is a PhD candidate in the School of Applied Child Psychology at the Department of Educational and Counselling Psychology, McGill University, Montreal, Canada.

Rhona S. Johnston is Professor of Psychology in the Department of Psychology at the University of Hull, UK.

Nenagh Kemp is a Lecturer in the School of Psychology at the University of Tasmania, Australia.

Régine Kolinsky is Senior Research Associate at the Belgian National Funds for Scientific Research (FNRS) and Director of the Unité de Recherche en Neurosciences Cognitives (UNESCOG), Université Libre de Bruxelles, Belgium.

Annukka Lehtonen is a postdoctoral researcher in the Department of Psychiatry at the University of Oxford, UK.

Phil D. Liu is a doctoral candidate in the Department of Psychology at the Chinese University of Hong Kong.

Sarah Logan is Lecturer in the Department of Psychology at the University of Hull, UK.

Catherine McBride-Chang is Professor in the Department of Psychology and Director of the Developmental Centre at the Chinese University of Hong Kong.

Michael F. McKay, retired, formerly Professor and Head of Department of Psychology, Australian Catholic University, Melbourne, Australia.

Morag MacLean is a Senior Lecturer in the Department of Psychology, Oxford Brookes University, UK.

Philippe Mousty is Lecturer in the Faculty of Psychological and Educational Sciences, and member of the Laboratoire Cognition, Langage et Développement (LCLD), Université Libre de Bruxelles, Belgium.

Karen J. Pine is Professor of Developmental Psychology at the University of Hertfordshire, UK.

Robert Savage is an Associate Professor and William Dawson Scholar in the Department of Educational and Counselling Psychology, Faculty of Education, McGill University, Montreal, Canada.

Kieron Sheehy is Senior Lecturer in the Centre for Childhood, Development and Learning at the Open University, UK.

Elaine R. Silliman is Professor of Communication Sciences and Disorders and Cognitive and Neural Science at the University of South Florida, Tampa, USA.

G. Brian Thompson is a Senior Research Associate in the Faculty of Education at Victoria University of Wellington, Wellington, New Zealand.

Jennifer Thomson is Assistant Professor in Education, Harvard Graduate School of Education, USA.

Xiuli Tong is a Postdoctoral Fellow in the Department of Psychology at the Chinese University of Hong Kong.

Lesly Wade-Woolley is Associate Professor of Education at Queen's University at Kingston, Ontario, Canada.

Joyce E. Watson is an Honorary Research Fellow in the School of Psychology, University of St Andrews, UK.

Clare Wood is Reader in Developmental Psychology at Coventry University, UK.

Introduction

Contemporary perspectives on reading and spelling

Clare Wood and Vincent Connelly

There are many good texts that offer a comprehensive overview of theoretical ideas in reading and writing. It is easy to assume from such excellent accounts that although there are some areas that are still contested, much of the evidence regarding how children learn to read and write fits together reasonably well. This volume, whilst not seeking to underplay the significance of existing theories, argues that the work into written language acquisition is far from done. The current models of reading and spelling development only take us so far in understanding these highly complex and interrelated processes, and interventions developed on these models therefore only offer a partial solution to written language difficulties.

The book is organised into three main parts. Part 1 is concerned with overarching issues about the nature of reading and spelling processes. The purpose of this part is to open up a discussion of existing accounts of reading and spelling acquisition. That is, our favoured models focus on the development of segmental phonological awareness and the skills of decoding and recoding text by learning and applying phoneme–grapheme correspondences. Such discussions primarily focus on the constituents of single syllables, with the assumption that polysyllabic word reading is a relatively simple matter of decoding each syllable in turn, and spelling is about acquiring grapheme–phoneme correspondences and learning exceptional spellings. However, this conceptualisation of reading and spelling may be seen as problematic for a number of reasons.

The first issue with this type of model is that it is somewhat light on the detail of where segmental phonological awareness comes from. That is, although it has been argued and assumed that phonemic awareness at least is the result of explicit tuition in the alphabetic principle this claim is not universally agreed, and there is evidence that phonological awareness can develop independently of and prior to reading tuition. Whether or not we accept that such development is possible, the fact remains that many children fail to acquire phonological awareness despite years of tuition in phonics. Why? What is distinctive about these children?

The first three chapters in this book suggest that the answer to this question might lie in the skills that developmentally precede phonological awareness. According to Thomson in Chapter 2, it may be that these children have difficulties in auditory processing, whereas in Chapter 1, Wood, Wade-Woolley and Holliman argue more specifically that such children may have a relative insensitivity to speech rhythm. The idea of speech rhythm being implicated in reading development is not a new one, insofar as it has been linked to reading comprehension and reading fluency in the past. However, the idea of suprasegmental phonology underpinning the acquisition of segmental forms is more novel and offers the beginnings of a model for understanding multisyllabic word reading, something that Lynne Duncan in Chapter 3 develops further and argues is essential to the development of a model that can explain reading development in alphabetic languages.

In Chapter 4, Kate Cain discusses the characteristics, causes and correlates of poor reading comprehension, providing an enlightening account of this group of children who are now beginning to receive more research attention, thanks to her work and that of others central to this area. The chapters on spelling in this part also highlight issues around existing models. For example in Chapter 5, Nenagh Kemp shows us that while children are very sensitive to orthographic and morphological information from an earlier age than we might have thought, adults, on the other hand, appear not to have developed a full understanding of the more complex relations and conventions in spelling. Critten and Pine in Chapter 6 also address the theme of children's competence at spelling and relate this competence to more general theories of cognition. By situating spelling as another cognitive domain and using methods that reflect this approach the authors argue that they have gained more access to the underlying cognitive mechanisms in spelling. Bahr, Silliman and Berninger in Chapter 7 illustrate a new way to classify and use misspellings using a linguistically based approach to inform theory and practice.

Part 2 moves to a discussion of the research evidence which relates to our understanding of reading and spelling in languages other than English. That is, the models of reading and spelling that dominate are primarily based on research that has been conducted with children learning to read English. However, as both Babayiğit and Lehtonen observe (in chapters 8 and 9, respectively), the significance of phoneme awareness in accounts of literacy development and reading failure is open to debate, as this will be influenced by the transparency of the orthography and other variables, such as print experience. The issue of bilingualism is also raised in this part in Chapter 10 by Goetry, Kolinsky and Mousty, who examine the impact of being schooled in a language that is very different to the one that you speak, and considers whether knowledge of different languages is compartmentalised or integrated. In Chapter 11, MacLean describes a novel approach to studying understanding of spelling 'rules' in two different languages: picking up on some of the ideas about the significance of children's self-reports as a means of understanding their spelling strategies, MacLean describes work that she and colleagues have done using the children's game 'hangman' as a basis for interrogating the children's understandings. Then in Chapter 12, Tong, Liu and McBride-Chang broaden the discussion to encompass learning to read and writing in a symbolic script, which has other features that make it distinct from English as well. They describe work comparing children learning to read in Hong Kong with those learning on mainland China, which introduces the theme for the third and final part of the book: the impact of teaching methods on what is learned.

Approaches to teaching reading and spelling is a controversial and highly political area. For example, the high-profile media presence of international comparisons of literacy achievement such as PISA and PIRLS and local but influential pressure groups has made many governments look again at the Teaching of Reading. In 2005 the UK Parliament instituted an inquiry into teaching children to read (House of Commons Education and Skills Committee, 2005) that led to changes in the UK literacy curriculum which were directly influenced by recent psychological studies, including research reported in Chapter 13 by Rhona Johnston and colleagues. In Australia a similar inquiry was also concluded (DEST, 2005). These pressures have led to an ever-growing influence of psychological theories on classroom interventions.

The political pressures surrounding the teaching of reading to special populations of children who are diagnosed with dyslexia or who have severe learning difficulties are even more acute. Here, as well, psychological theories of reading are being applied to the design of interventions in the classroom across the globe. Some see this trend as a welcome change in the role of psychology in the classroom (National Reading Panel, 2000). Others are less convinced (Allington, 2002). However, it is acknowledged that difficulties in learning to read are likely to be strongly associated with individual difficulties in responding to methods of teaching reading in the classroom (Vellutino *et al.*, 2004).

Therefore, it is increasingly important that we take stock of some of the issues raised by psychological research about teaching reading to children and particularly for those children with written language difficulties. Johnston, Watson and Logan tackle the debates about synthetic phonics teaching by detailing their work on their recent synthetic phonics interventions. The authors take a strong stand for the benefits of their programmes and extend their recent reported work by providing additional data on attitudes to reading and reading comprehension. This extension, according to the authors, provides a riposte to the claims that synthetic phonics does not provide more general benefits to readers beyond word recognition.

The Johnston *et al.* work has been highly cited and influential. However, psychologists are generally less successful at incorporating the teaching of reading into models or accounts of the development of reading. Given that we now acknowledge the differences that teaching programmes can make in the speed of acquisition of key reading skills, it is interesting that little research has been conducted into how reading teaching may influence the reading of words itself. Chapter 14 by Connelly and colleagues reports on this area and details some surprising effects. For instance, they comment on recent work showing that skilled adult readers make pronunciations of unknown words based on how they originally were taught to read. This challenges some current models of how children learn to read and indeed adult models of reading skill. The authors also report on studies that challenge assumptions made about the way instruction may influence reading progress. For example, in one of the studies summarised it is reported that the quantity of children's 'sounding out' in the classroom is not directly related to success in pronouncing words while frequent exposure in print to whole words in one method of instruction is directly related to success at reading sub word components. It is clear from this research that models of reading development need to consider how a child is being taught in order to fully capture how children learn to read. This aspect of the external environment does influence not just speed of reading progress but may also influence reading strategies.

The final two chapters in this part deal with psychological theory and psychologically derived interventions for children with dyslexia and severe learning difficulties. Chapter 15, by Irannejad and Savage, deals with the cerebellar deficit theory of developmental dyslexia and whether such a deficit can be addressed through programmes of remediation. The authors provide an overview of this account of developmental dyslexia and show how influential this unique theory has been in recent years. They then provide a critique of various aspects of the theory while acknowledging its originality and its close links with other theories of developmental dyslexia. The authors conclude that there is not enough current evidence for a cerebellar deficit directly contributing to the development of dyslexia and therefore caution should be used in developing interventions based on the theory.

The book concludes with a discussion of an area of research which really challenges the way in which teaching reading is frequently approached; that is, when teaching children with severe learning difficulties (SLD, i.e. children with very low IQ – we use the term 'learning difficulties' in the UK sense, rather than as the North American term for dyslexic-type difficulties). The final chapter (16) details an approach to teaching reading to children with SLD that builds on the local feature hypothesis of early word recognition. Sheehy and Holliman show that applying principles from psychology allows these children who can struggle to read any words at all to make some progress. However, there is room for considerably more research in this area and the authors leave us with many questions about how we can help these children progress beyond reading just a few words.

Overall, the book raises a number of themes including: what can we learn about reading and spelling by locating them in their proper developmental context? What does reading and spelling in other languages tell us about the acquisition process? Does the way in which you are taught to read really matter? How do young readers acquire multisyllabic word reading? What methodological approaches might help us to better understand reading and spelling development? We hope that you agree that this collection offers some challenging points for reflection about how we as a discipline approach the study of written language skills.

References

Allington, R.L. (2002). *Big brother and the National Reading Curriculum: How ideology trumped evidence.* Portsmouth, NH: Heinemann.

DEST (2005). *Teaching reading. National inquiry into the teaching of literacy.* Department of Education, Science and Training: Canberra, ACT. Retrieved 2 October 2008 at: http://www.dest.gov.au/nitl/report.htm

House of Commons Education and Skills Committee (2005). *Teaching children to read.* Eighth Report of Session 2004-05. London: The Stationery Office. Retrieved 2 October 2008 at: http://www.publications.parliament.uk/pa/cm200405/cmselect/cmeduski/121/121.pdf

National Reading Panel (2000). *Teaching children to read: an evidence-based assessment of the scientific research literature on reading and its implications for reading instruction: Reports of the subgroups.* Rockville, MD: National Institute of Child Health and Human Development. Retrieved 31 August 2007 at: http://www.nichd.nih.gov/publications/nrp/report.cfm

Vellutino, F.R., Fletcher, J.M., Snowling, M.J., & Scanlon, D.M. (2004). 'Specific reading disability (dyslexia): What have we learned in the past four decades?' *Journal of Child Psychology and Psychiatry, 45,* 2-40.

Part 1

Overarching debates in reading and spelling

Chapter 1

Phonological awareness

Beyond phonemes

Clare Wood, Lesly Wade-Woolley and Andrew J. Holliman

Current models of reading development emphasise segmental phonological aware-ness as the basis for success in reading and spelling development. This chapter explores the possibility that suprasegmental phonology may have a contribution to make in explaining both the origins of segmental phonological awareness in begin-ning readers, but also polysyllabic word reading in more experienced readers. The chapter reviews the evidence suggesting a link between decoding skills and sensitivity to aspects of speech rhythm. These accounts build to a model, which explains the possible contribution of speech rhythm to reading development.

Phonological deficits and reading difficulties

One of the most frequently cited explanations of reading difficulties is the *phonologi-cal deficit hypothesis* (Stanovich, 1986; Stanovich & Siegel, 1994). According to this theory, developmental reading difficulties are characterised by poor or underspecified phonological representations. The quality of these representations are such that when children learn to read and write they experience delays in acquiring the letter-sound correspondences necessary for reading in an alphabetic language.

Although questions over the extent to which there is evidence of a causal link between phonological deficits and reading difficulties have been raised (Castles & Coltheart, 2004), there is extensive evidence that children with reading difficulties demonstrate deficits on tasks that have a phonological component relative to children of the same age, and in some instances, relative to younger, typically reading children who are at the same level of reading skill as they are (see Snowling, 2000, for review). The question, however, remains 'Why do children with reading difficulties have phonological deficits?'

The answer to this question could be simply a case of individual differences. As with all learned abilities, some children are less able, less skilled, less fluent than their peers in a particular domain. In this sense, it is therefore possible that children with reading difficulties are just the unlucky ones in terms of phonological competence. However, there is the question of whether there are also deficits in the underlying layer of skills and abilities that developmentally precede or are associated with pho-nological skills. If we find no relationship between phonological deficits and other more fundamental skills, then this would suggest that phonological deficits are char-acteristic, and perhaps causal, of reading difficulties. However, phonological deficits may equally be the expression of more fundamental difficulties in cognitive development. If we could find the origins of the phonological deficit in skills that developmentally precede the development of segmental phonological awareness, this could expand possibilities for early identification and intervention.

The idea that if a child experiences difficulties perceiving speech this might impact on the quality of the phonological representations that the child goes on to form was explored by Wood and Terrell (1998). However, as they noted, the literature concerned with children's speech perception is mixed (see McBride-Chang, 1995). While some studies reported that children with reading difficulties showed deficits in speech perception (Brady *et al.*, 1983; De Weirdt, 1988; Freeman & Beasley, 1978; Godfrey *et al.*, 1981; Hurford, 1991; Reed, 1989; Tallal, 1980; Werker & Tees, 1987), others did not (Snowling *et al.*, 1986; Pennington *et al.*, 1990). This has led Snowling (2000) to conclude that the phonological impairments of children with dyslexia are not the result of perceptual difficulties, but of difficulties in the encoding and retrieval of phonological representations.

However, a closer examination of the papers reviewed by McBride-Chang (1995) revealed that many of the papers reporting to assess speech perception were actually presenting children with tasks of phoneme discrimination. For instance, the speech perception tasks in De Weirdt (1988) and in Werker and Tees (1987) required children to discriminate between phonemes such as /pa/-/ta/ and /ba/-/da/ respectively. It was therefore not surprising that children with reading difficulties, known to experience difficulties with phonemic awareness in particular, were found to be deficient on such tasks. As a result, Wood and Terrell (1998) turned their attention to a specific component of speech perception that seemed to be less of a direct measure of phoneme discrimination: that of spoken word recognition.

Spoken word recognition and speech rhythm

Fluent speech contains no reliable acoustic cues that indicate where one word ends and the next word begins. The question of how infants come to break fluent speech down into component units of meaning was one that Wood and Terrell (1998) felt might hold the key to the quality of a child's phonological representations. A review of the literature on spoken word recognition revealed one theory that offered a plausible account of how children may come to bootstrap their way into spoken word recognition from infancy. This was the model outlined by Cutler and Mehler (1993). They suggest that children are born with a *periodicity bias* that predisposes them to 'tune in' to the rhythmic characteristics of their first language. This information enables them to make initial attempts at segmentation as rhythmic information appears to provide a rough indicator of word boundaries. For example, English is a stress-timed language. This means that, roughly speaking, equal amounts of time elapse between the occurrence of stressed syllables in natural speech (this contrasts with syllable-timed languages, such as French, in which equal amounts of time elapse between syllables). Content words in English tend to begin with stressed (or 'strong') syllables. As a result, sensitivity to stressed syllables in speech would provide a child with a basis for segmenting speech into units of meaning.

However, a notable characteristic of linguistic stress is that phoneme identification appears to be much easier in stressed as opposed to unstressed syllables. For example, Chiat (1983), reporting on the speech errors of a phonologically delayed child, observed that the prosodic features of speech were, for that child at least, central to his ability to articulate the appropriate representation of the word. The 5-year-old child showed that although he had difficulties with segmental phonology, he was sensitive to the prosodic features of speech, and that sensitivity influenced his ability to produce the correct phonological form of the word he was trying to say. Chiat (1983: 292) argued that: 'segmental features are not independent of prosodic features in lexical representations ... Lexical representations are not, then, strings of phonemes on which stress is marked, but prosodic structures on which segmental features are specified'.

Wood and Terrell (1998) hypothesised that children who have poorly specified phonological representations may also show evidence of insensitivity to speech rhythm. To test this they matched a group of children who were delayed in their reading attainment to typically developing readers on either chronological age or reading age. They then tested their reading, spelling and phonological awareness, as well as their ability to accurately perceive time-compressed speech and their sensitivity to metrical stress. To assess metrical stress sensitivity, sentences were recorded and low pass filtered until no phonemes could be identified and only the intonation pattern of the utterance could be discerned. The children were then presented with two entirely different sentences. One of them shared the same metrical pattern as the original, whereas the other differed in rhythm from the filtered sentence by just one syllable. The children were asked to indicate which of the two sentences was 'the same' as the filtered sentence. It was found that the children who were delayed in their reading development were significantly worse than chronological age matched controls on both the speech perception and speech rhythm measures. Crucially, unlike the difference in speech perception performance, the difference in speech rhythm was found to exist after individual differences in vocabulary were controlled.

Since the publication of Wood and Terrell (1998) there has been increased interest in the possible contribution of prosodic processing to reading acquisition and phonological decoding. It should be noted that the contribution of prosodic sensitivity to reading comprehension is well established (e.g. see Kuhn & Stahl, 2003). However, Wood and Terrell's study signalled a possible contribution of prosodic sensitivity to word reading ability (decoding) that had not been found previously.

Some predictions

If speech rhythm and related aspects of prosodic sensitivity *are* important for reading, then a number of research predictions should be supported by the data obtained by studies in this area.

I Individuals with reading difficulties will be insensitive to speech rhythm relative to typically developing readers.

There should be clear evidence of a deficit in sensitivity to, or processing of, or representation of, speech rhythm in individuals with reading difficulties. The question of whether such a deficit is specific to individuals with reading difficulties or simply indicative of a developmental delay also needs consideration.

2 Speech rhythm sensitivity should be associated with reading ability in typically developing readers.

If sensitivity to speech rhythm is important for reading development then it should also be associated with reading success as much as it is with reading failure. Studies therefore need to demonstrate an association between measures of reading attainment and speech rhythm sensitivity in typically developing populations.

3 Speech rhythm should be linked to reading ability regardless of the language spoken.

Wood and Terrell (1998) specifically examined sensitivity to metrical stress as their measure of speech rhythm. However, other measures of speech rhythm that are less closely associated with the features of a specific language are possible (e.g. overall intonation patterns), and other languages have other elements that are characteristic of speech rhythm. It is therefore important to consider whether the results found by Wood and Terrell are peculiar to stress-timed languages.

4 There will be associations between speech rhythm sensitivity and segmental phonological awareness.

This prediction directly tests one of the suggestions made by Wood and Terrell (1998); namely, that sensitivity to speech rhythm may be a necessary prerequisite for successful reading development. If this is the case we should expect to find evidence of an association between segmental phonological awareness and prosodic sensitivity. Ideally, there should be longitudinal evidence of an association between speech rhythm and phonological awareness.

5 Speech rhythm sensitivity should be linked to skilled reading.

Finally, we should expect to find that sensitivity to speech rhythm will be associated not just with young children acquiring literacy, but also with skilled reading in an adult sample. If it is, we can say with some confidence that representation of suprasegmental phonology is a key component of reading processes, rather than merely enabling young children to bootstrap their way into segmental phonology.

The sections that follow review the evidence available to date in relation to each of these predictions in turn, before offering a synthesis of this literature in the form of a potential model that accounts for the mechanisms through which reading may be influenced by sensitivity to the prosodic features of speech.

Reading difficulties and speech rhythm

The initial Wood and Terrell (1998) study identified a deficit in children who were experiencing a delay in their reading development: none of the children in the sample had been identified as experiencing developmental dyslexia, although that did not necessarily mean that none of the children had dyslexia, merely that they had not yet had an assessment. Another important feature of the sample was that the children in the reading difficulties group represented a broad age range, which also meant that the children were potentially in different stages of reading development.

Subsequent studies of speech rhythm sensitivity have used more focused samples and have been concerned with children formally identified as experiencing dyslexia. The most notable examples of such work have looked at children's sensitivity to amplitude envelope onsets or 'rise time'. Goswami *et al.* (2002) considered whether the perception of auditory signals in the rhythm of speech can facilitate word segmentation and subsequent phonological awareness and reading. According to Goswami *et al.*, the acoustic beats in the speech stream (marked by the peak in amplitude in the speech signal) correspond with vowel location, which mark onset–rime boundaries. They speculated that children with dyslexia may be less sensitive to amplitude modulation beat detection. In line with expectations, dyslexic children were found to be significantly less sensitive to rise time than non-dyslexic controls. Additionally, sensitivity to amplitude modulation predicted 25 per cent unique variance in reading and spelling after age, non-verbal IQ and vocabulary had been accounted for, which suggests that sensitivity to speech rhythm and the associated auditory characteristics may be related to phonological awareness and subsequent reading development. These findings have been replicated in an adult sample where adult dyslexics were also found to have rise-time deficits (Pasquini *et al.*, 2007).

There is also evidence that 3-year-old children who are at risk of developing dyslexia also show reduced sensitivity to speech rhythm relative to same-age controls. De Bree *et al.* (2006) administered a word stress task to 49, 3-year-old children who had a close relative with dyslexia and 28 controls. The non-words used in this task varied from 2 to 4 syllables in length and contained either regular, irregular, highly irregular, or prohibited stress patterns. It was found that the children at risk were significantly less able to repeat the non-words that contained prohibited or irregular (but legitimate) stress patterns relative to their same-age controls. This suggests that not only is rhythmic sensitivity a characteristic that can discriminate between children as young as 3-years-old, but also the results imply that speech rhythm deficits are a characteristic which may be part of the inherited profile of difficulties.

Both Kitzen (2001) and Thomson *et al.* (2006) have found similar results in samples of young adults who have reading difficulties. Kitzen (2001) investigated whether prosodic insensitivity was related to reading disability. Thirty young adults with a history of reading difficulties were gathered along with 30 adults without a history of reading difficulties, and these two groups were compared on their performance on two prosodic sensitivity tasks. For the first task, participants had to discriminate between two phonemically similar phrases (e.g. hotrod and hot-rod), which differed only in terms of their prosodic characteristics. In the second task, participants had to match a nonsense phrase (a 'DEEdee' phrase) to the correct word or phrase based on its prosodic patterns. It was found that adults with a history of reading difficulties were outperformed by the controls on both prosodic sensitivity tasks. The Deedee task alone also predicted unique variance in oral text reading accuracy, oral text reading comprehension and oral text non-word reading.

Thomson *et al.* (2006) recruited undergraduates with dyslexia, aged between 18 and 31, and matched them on age, verbal IQ and non-verbal IQ to controls. All participants completed phoneme deletion, rapid automatised naming and digit span tasks in addition to tasks which assessed whether participants had adequate hearing, and could discriminate between tones of different durations and intensity (loudness). They were also presented with two rise-time tasks, which required participants to listen to two dinosaurs roaring and identify which one had the 'sharpest' beat or sounded sharpest at the beginning. Two non-speech rhythm tasks were also administered: one which assessed whether participants could discriminate between stimuli of different tempos, and another which assessed whether a participant could tap in time with a metronome beat. Significant differences between the two groups were found in terms of the speech rhythm tasks and there was evidence of within-individual variability on the metronome tapping task. Dyslexic participants were also observed to have significantly worse performance on the tone duration and intensity discrimination tasks. Significant partial correlations (controlling for IQ) were observed between a subset of the rise–time, auditory discrimination and metronome variables and reading and spelling ability (but not phonemic awareness). These results suggest that rhythmic insensitivity continues to persist into adulthood and also continues to be implicated in reading and spelling attainment.

Speech rhythm in typical reading development

One of the challenges in this area is the production of speech rhythm sensitivity measures that are appropriate for use with children, especially very young children, yet this is essential if we intend to use sensitivity to speech rhythm as an early assessment of children at risk of reading difficulties. In an attempt to address this need, Wood (2006) developed a measure that was designed to be appropriate for use with pre-school children. The task needed to make sense to the children, and to minimise the memory load as far as possible. Wood therefore devised a task in which the children were introduced to 'Blueberry', a little blue toy dog, and the children were shown a line drawing of some rooms in Blueberry's house. The children were told that Blueberry was a very messy dog, and he had lost some things, and the children's task was to help him to find them. So, in the baseline condition, the children simply had to point to the item in the picture that corresponded to the item that was spoken (e.g. 'sofa'). In further sessions, the children were introduced to Blueberry's friends, who were also looking for the things in Blueberry's house. However, each of his friends had a different speech impediment which meant that they mispronounced the words in specific ways. The main mispronunciation of interest was one in which the metrical stress pattern of the word was reversed, such that 'sofa' was pronounced 's'far'. To solve this task, the children had to recognise from the practice item that the stress pattern of the word had been switched and apply their understanding of metrical stress to retrieve the correct representation of the word. However, Wood was also interested to see how the children performed on this condition relative to other types of mispronunciation which also related to the different features that are affected by a change in metrical stress. So, the children were also exposed to items that had the two vowel sounds changed (but without changing the stress), had the lexical stress changed (but without any vowel reduction) and had one vowel sound changed (but without changing the stress and retaining a reduction in the second vowel). Wood found that performance on the stress reversal condition of this task was the only one of the four types of word manipulation to be significantly related to reading attainment. It was further found that the stress reversal condition of this task was able to predict significant variance in spelling ability after controlling for phonological awareness. These findings suggest that sensitivity to stress in speech may be an important component related to successful early reading development.

Holliman *et al.* (2008) adopted the stress reversal condition of the mispronunciations task and administered it to 44, 5- to 6-year-old children to investigate whether stress sensitivity could predict significant variance in reading attainment after controlling for age, vocabulary and phonological awareness. It was found that stress sensitivity was able to account for unique variance in reading, which adds weight to the developing argument that speech rhythm sensitivity (stress sensitivity in particular) is a necessary component for successful reading development, which persists even after accounted for phonological processing skills.

Holliman *et al.* (submitted) further simplified the mispronunciations task: instead of children having to locate the mispronounced word from a line drawing of a house, they had to locate the mispronounced word from a choice of four pictures all of which began with the same letter and letter sound and were matched on word frequency. This study explored the relatedness of speech and non-speech rhythm. Speech rhythm sensitivity was found to be significantly correlated with receptive non-speech rhythm sensitivity, but not productive non-speech rhythm sensitivity. Moreover, a series of hierarchical regression analyses revealed that while sensitivity to speech rhythm and sensitivity to receptive non-speech rhythm were able to predict a significant amount of unique variance in reading attainment once age, vocabulary, phonological awareness, memory, and non-speech rhythm had been controlled, productive non-speech rhythm was unable to predict unique variance in reading attainment once phonological awareness and speech rhythm had been controlled. The findings are suggestive of some degree of overlap between the processing of speech and non-speech rhythm at a receptive, perceptual level. The major finding from this study was that stress sensitivity was able to predict significant variance in reading attainment after controlling for age, vocabulary, memory, phonological awareness and non-speech rhythm. Although the authors do not dispute the relationship between speech rhythm sensitivity and phonological processing, the mere fact that speech rhythm sensitivity was able to account for additional, unique variance in reading attainment suggests that stress sensitivity may have an independent relationship with reading development. However, more theoretical explanation is required in order to account for this relationship.

As we have seen, sensitivity to speech rhythm may be assessed at the level of an individual word (lexical stress) or phrase (metrical stress), although there is necessarily some overlap between these forms. In an attempt to assess phrase-level sensitivity to speech rhythm, Whalley and Hansen (2006) used a variation on the 'Deedee task' from Kitzen (2001). Children's performance on this task accounted for significant variance in reading comprehension after controlling for word reading accuracy, phonological awareness and general rhythmic sensitivity. Whalley and Hansen (2006) also used Kitzen's (2001) Compound Noun task to assess prosody at a word level. Children's performance on this task accounted for significant variance in word identification accuracy. These findings also suggest that speech rhythm sensitivity has a unique relationship with reading attainment, independently of phonological processing.

Speech rhythm and phonological awareness

One of the difficulties with assessing the question of whether phonological awareness development may be dependent in some may on a sensitivity to, or representation of, speech rhythm is the fact that many measures of speech rhythm require the processing of phonemic information at some level, and so phonemic awareness needs to be controlled in any analyses. There are two exceptions to this observation, however: the beat detection (rise-time) task developed by Goswami *et al.* (2002), and the sentence matching task developed by Wood and Terrell (1998). Goswami (2002) theorised that children less sensitive to beat detection would have inferior phonological processing skills. Indeed, Goswami *et al.* (2002) found significant, positive correlations between beat detection and phonological processing (RAN, phonological memory, and phonological awareness) after age and IQ had been controlled. Performance on the beat detection task was also able to predict unique variance in the phonological processing tasks after controlling for age, non-verbal IQ and vocabulary. On the basis of these findings, Goswami (2002) argued that beat detection may underlie the development of phonological awareness.

Wood (2006) revisited the data from Wood and Terrell's (1998) study to investigate whether sensitivity to stress, as measured by the sentence matching task that used low-pass filtered sentences, could predict variance in segmental phonological awareness. It was found that sensitivity to stress predicted significance variance in phonological processing skills (phoneme deletion and rhyme detection), which is suggestive of a link between sensitivity to stress (suprasegmental phonology) and phonological awareness (segmental phonology). However, more studies are required to explore the link between segmental and suprasegmental phonology using speech rhythm tasks that are not reliant stimuli that include segmental phonology.

Reading in languages other than English

The potential relationships between speech rhythm and reading related processes addressed previously have also been addressed in languages other than English, although the current body of research is only beginning to accumulate. This topic is important for theoretical development because every language is specified for rhythmic timing in some way. Languages also differ in the way in which orthography represents information related to speech rhythm, and this can have an impact on reading development and skilled reading.

One way in which languages differ is the underlying timing unit used for marking speech rhythm. For example, English, Dutch and Greek are stress-timed languages, while languages such as French and Finnish are syllable-timed languages. The chief difference between stress- and syllable-timed languages is the unit of rhythm that is perceived by the listener to be evenly spaced. In syllable-timed languages, the rhythmic unit is the syllable and all syllables are perceived to be of equal duration. In stress-timed languages, on the other hand, the stressed syllables in an utterance are equally paced, with varying numbers of unstressed syllables (often with reduced vowels) intervening. Even in syllable-timed languages, syllables may have greater or lesser emphasis. For example, French typically has stress on the final syllable, while Finnish assigns stress to the initial syllable. Likewise, the stressed syllable in all stress-assigning languages is marked by the same characteristics: relatively greater duration and amplitude, and higher fundamental frequency than unstressed syllables.

As Wood and Terrell (1998) pointed out, one key factor that relates speech rhythm to reading could be the language processing necessary for vocabulary development. In this case, one might expect that difficulties processing speech rhythm would be apparent in language acquisition processes. The previously cited study by de Bree *et al.* (2006) supports this, as Dutch-speaking preschoolers who were at familial risk of dyslexia made more stress-related errors than typically developing peers when repeating pseudowords. Importantly, this performance decrement was noticeable primarily when the items to be repeated differed from the typical stress pattern found in Dutch. If acquisition of word stress, which is lexically distinctive in Dutch, is delayed in some children, it could result in the phonological processing problems that are the hallmark of reading disability. De Bree and colleagues argue that this impairment leads to phonological representations that are poorly specified, especially for those Dutch words which do not follow canonical stress assignment rules, affecting vocabulary development and reading development simultaneously.

If processing of speech rhythm is necessary for the development of reading-related language skills, then one may make a cross-linguistic prediction for children learning a second language, where first and second language differs as a result of typological speech rhythm differences. For example, Goetry *et al.* (2006) report a study involving 6-year-old monolingual children who were native speakers of French or native speakers of Dutch, plus same-age bilingual children (Dutch speakers schooled in French and French speakers schooled in Dutch). Using a paradigm piloted by Dupoux *et al.* (2001), Goetry *et al.* showed that Dutch children were better able than French children at discriminating minimal pairs that differed only as a function of stress placement (e.g. TApu – taPU). The authors attributed this difference to the fact that speech rhythm is syllable-timed in French but stress-timed in Dutch. However, in the performance of French children who had received formal instruction in Dutch, but not in that of Dutch children schooled in French, sensitivity to speech rhythm was longitudinally correlated with reading in Grade 1 and Grade 2, suggesting that second-language learners may invoke prosodic knowledge when reading in a stress-timed language. Moreover, a relationship between speech rhythm and vocabulary in speakers of Dutch is evident in this study, echoing the findings remarked upon earlier: a significant correlation between receptive vocabulary and speech rhythm sensitivity was observed in native speakers of Dutch; and in French children schooled in Dutch, a similar relationship was evident between speech rhythm sensitivity and the degree of L2-dominance (better lexical competence in Dutch over French).

Findings of differences between syllable- and stress-timed languages are not to be taken as implying that sensitivity to speech rhythm is necessarily relevant only in the latter. Using the amplitude modulation 'beat detection' paradigm discussed earlier, Goswami and her colleagues (Muneaux *et al.*, 2004) demonstrated that 11-year-old French dyslexic children performed more poorly at the beat perception task than chronological-age matched peers. In addition, beat perception displayed strong explanatory power in reading, rime awareness and rapid naming. These results were similar to those found with native speakers of English, and this suggests that basic auditory processes which may be related to the processing of speech rhythm do not depend on whether the language is stress- or syllable-timed.

As mentioned earlier, one of the acoustic correlates of linguistic stress is duration. Finnish, a syllable-timed language, uses duration to determine phoneme quantity, which is lexically contrastive (e.g. /mato/ means *worm* while /mat:o/ means carpet). Lyytinen *et al.* (1995) report that reading-disabled children make many errors reading and spelling words such as these, despite the fact that Finnish marks phoneme quantity explicitly in the orthography. In a study with 6-month-old Finnish infants at familial risk of dyslexia, Richardson *et al.* (2003) examined categorical perception of phoneme duration. They manipulated the duration of the pseudoword *ata* incrementally by inserting into each one a silent closure at the dental stop that increased by 20 milliseconds per item, so that the occlusion was 95 msec at the shortest and 255 msec at the longest. Over the course of these stimuli, the perception of the stimulus changed from *ata* /ata/ to atta /at:a/. Using a conditioned head-turn procedure commonly used in infant studies, Richardson *et al.* determined that at-risk infants perceived the shift from *ata* to *atta* at a later point than did control infants. Similar results were observed with an age-appropriate task for the infants' parents; dyslexic parents required longer duration to shift from *ata* to *atta*. The relevance of this study is twofold: first, it demonstrates that sensitivity to an acoustic correlate of speech rhythm is related to reading ability, and second, it shows that this relationship does not necessarily depend on whether the language is stress- or syllable-timed.

An additional consideration for languages other than English is the degree to which indicators of lexical stress are marked orthographically. In both Greek and Spanish, diacritics are used to signal the placement of lexical stress. Greek requires stress to be marked in every word longer than one syllable, while Spanish has a system of diacritic use for stress assignment that is extremely predictable from a simple set of rules. Gutierrez-Palma and Reyes (2007) showed that the ability to discriminate minimal pairs based on stress in two-item sequences was related to the ability of Spanish children aged 7–8 years to decode pseudowords. Interestingly, the authors suggest that sensitivity to prosodic sensitivity may be related to decoding through fluency, since the most frequent type of errors in pseudoword decoding involved false starts and pauses between syllables. Since Spanish employs a shallow and consistent orthography, it is reasonable to suppose that decoding errors in unfamiliar or non-words are less likely to be due to faulty grapheme-phoneme conversion and more likely to slow or effortful computation of stress assignment. Since the rules for stress assignment in Spanish depend on syllable structure, final consonant, and presence or absence of the diacritic, readers who are less sensitive to speech rhythm may struggle to integrate the multiple sources of information for proper stress placement.

In Greek, the use of the diacritic is obligatory for proper spelling, but this does not mean that the diacritic is always used by readers to assign stress in reading. Protopapas *et al.* (2006) showed that Greek children in grade seven did not always make use of the stress indicator provided by the diacritic when decoding pseudowords, and they were less likely to use the diacritic to guide stress placement when the words were difficult to decode. Furthermore, poor readers were more likely than good readers to make errors that involved improper stress assignment. Protopapas *et al.* (2006) asked Greek children in grades 7–9 to read pseudowords with and without diacritics to determine possible sources of information for stress placement decisions. The errors made by participants in this study were suggestive of a lexical strategy, where stress was assigned to a given syllable by analogy with a real Greek word that resembled the pseudoword. The errors were also consistent with a default metrical frame that assigned stress to the penultimate syllable, in addition to the use of the diacritic. The authors suggest that use of the diacritic is resource-demanding during the relatively challenging task of decoding pseudowords. Accordingly, as reading skill increases, adult readers of Greek are less challenged by reading non-words and they are much more likely to profit from the stress information conveyed by diacritics when they are available (Protopapas *et al.*, 2006).

Taken together, the Spanish and Greek findings suggest that there are multiple sources of information that can be recruited to assist stress placement when reading, even in languages where stress is overtly marked. In English, where stress is never overtly marked, there is evidence from eye movements during silent reading that the number of stressed syllables in a word affects reading time. Ashby and Clifton (2005) showed that skilled readers took longer to read and re-fixated more often on words with two stressed syllables (e.g. *OStenTAtious*) than on words matched for length and frequency, but with one stressed syllable (e.g. prePOSterous). Ashby and Clifton argue that readers construct a phonological representation during silent reading, and that computation of the appropriate stress contour is part of that process. That this effect was observed for both low and high frequency words suggests that the effect reflects processing at a late stage of word recognition; the reader's eyes remain on the word until phonological units for lexical access have been assembled. The suggestion that stress assignment accompanies lexical access is consistent with the finding of lexical effects in Greek stress assignment, suggesting that whether or not languages mark stress overtly with a diacritic, the placement of word stress may occur in the later stages of word recognition, in both oral and silent reading.

Skilled reading

Skilled adult reading and prosodic sensitivity has yet to be fully explored at the present time. However, there is some evidence of an association in the scant evidence that we do have. For example, as we have seen, Ashby and Clifton (2005) found evidence of a link between reading speed and presence of stressed syllables through the study of eye movements. What is needed now are dedicated studies to examine skilled adult readers' performance on measures of speech rhythm and their performance on a range of challenging reading and spelling tasks to enable a fuller consideration of whether or not speech rhythm sensitivity continues to play a role in literacy into adulthood, and if so, with respect to what aspects of reading (e.g. polysyllabic word decoding, spelling of morphologically complex words).

A possible model

Although there is a need for more work in key areas of speech rhythm and reading development, there is now sufficient data to begin to integrate these findings into a single model which attempts to map and explain the contribution of speech rhythm to reading development. In this section we outline a series of routes via which sensitivity to speech rhythm might contribute to reading and spelling attainment.

The first pathway begins with the suggestion that children are born with a periodicity bias (Cutler & Mehler, 1993) which enables them to tune into the rhythmic characteristics of their first language. This enables them to bootstrap their way into spoken word recognition. Spoken word recognition contributes to individual differences in vocabulary development. Vocabulary development, it has been suggested, in turn contributes to phonological awareness development via the Lexical Restructuring Hypothesis (Metsala & Walley, 1998). The development of phonological awareness, in turn, promotes the development of reading and spelling abilities through the well-documented theoretical routes (Adams, 1990) (see Figure 1.1).

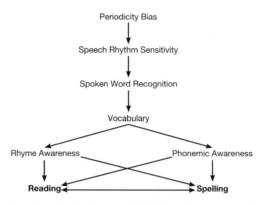

Figure 1.1 Pathway 1 – Speech rhythm sensitivity contributes to reading via spoken word recognition and vocabulary growth.

The second pathway is concerned with the finding that there is an association between rhyme awareness and speech rhythm (see Figure 1.2). Consistent with the suggestions from Wood and Terrell (1998) and Goswami (2003), it is suggested that rhythmic sensitivity necessarily centres on awareness of the peak of loudness associated with the vowel, and the quality of that vowel sound. Thus, in being sensitive to vowel occurrence, a child's attention is directed to the onset-rime boundary, and that onset-rime awareness contributes to reading development through highlighting phonemic similarities across words (and possibly also through the provision of an orthographic analogy strategy for some readers).

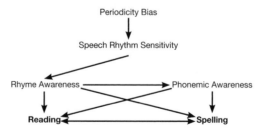

Figure 1.2 Pathway 2 – Speech rhythm sensitivity contributes to speech rhythm via onset–rime awareness.

Another possible pathway suggested by Wood and Terrell (1998) is via a phonemic awareness route. As noted, phoneme identification appears to be easier in stressed rather than unstressed syllables. Therefore, it is possible that children who become sensitive to stress go on to also become skilled in the manipulation of stress in order to gain insights into the phonemic structure of ambiguous syllables. This, in turn, could promote phonemic awareness, thereby promoting reading and spelling development (see Figure 1.3).

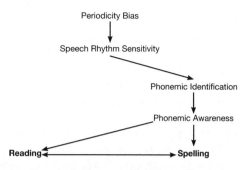

Figure 1.3. Pathway 3 – Speech rhythm sensitivity contributes to reading by facilitating phoneme identification in speech

However, the evidence also suggests another, more intriguing contribution of speech rhythm sensitivity to reading development. According to this pathway, sensitivity to speech rhythm makes a direct contribution to reading development, and that contribution is independent of its contribution via vocabulary development and phonological awareness (see Figure 1.4). It is possible that this additional variance could be accounted for by the well-documented contribution of prosodic factors to reading comprehension and fluency (Kuhn & Stahl, 2003). However, given the young age of some of the participants of the studies that demonstrated this independent relationship, it would seem unlikely that much of this variance could be explained through these variables. It seems more likely that this additional variance could be linked to the need for lexical stress to be assigned during the reading of polysyllabic words. As has been noted (e.g. Duncan, Chapter 3 this volume; Protopapas *et al.*, 2006; Wade-Woolley & Wood, 2006), this aspect of word reading is one that has been neglected by many models of reading ability. Given that children are required to read polysyllabic words very early in their school career, this oversight should be addressed.

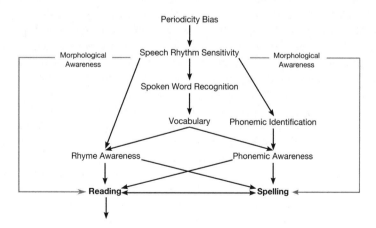

Figure 1.4 Pathway 4 – Speech rhythm sensitivity contributes to reading and spelling via morphological awareness

Once we look at multisyllabic words, there are at least two productive areas for further exploration. One involves the near-obligatory vowel reduction that is characteristic of English phonology. As stressed syllables tend to have full vocalic realization, unstressed syllables frequently contain vowels that have become schwa or reduced in other ways. It is possible that, as well as having other decoding skills, good readers are those who implicitly grasp this alternation of strong and weak syllables and can apply this knowledge to decoding longer, unfamiliar words (see Duncan, Chapter 3 this volume).

A related area of investigation is morphology. The relationship between morphological awareness and reading has received a substantial amount of attention from researchers, and there is mounting evidence that morphological awareness is a predictor of both decoding and reading comprehension (Carlisle, 2000; Carlisle & Stone, 2005; Singson *et al.*, 2000). Morphology is related to speech rhythm in English in at least two ways. First, stress in compound words is different from the constituent words in citation form; the word *man* in *snowman* is shorter and of slighter amplitude than it would be in the list *snow, man*. Attention to speech rhythm information can signal important grammatical information about a word, which may be recruited to boost reading performance. Morphological knowledge may also be related to reading through reading with appropriate prosodic phrasing. In a study with Hebrew-speaking fourth graders, Ravid and Mashraki (2007) showed that morphological knowledge moderated the relationship between prosodic reading (rendering expressive reading that aligned with adult models) and reading comprehension.

Another way in which morphology can be related to reading is through the effect that some suffixes have on stress placement in morphologically complex words. Certain suffixes (e.g. -ity, -al) in derived words have the ability to pull main stress from its position in the stem to the syllable before the suffix (e.g. *AC*tive – ac*TIV*ity), while other suffixes are stress neutral, leaving word stress in derivations on the same syllable that was stressed in the stem (*HAP*py – *HAP*piness). Jarmulowicz (2002) demonstrated that young children were able to place stress on the syllable that would be predicted by theory using derived words with stress-shifting suffixes. Children aged 7 and 9 heard pairs of both pseudowords and real words, both members of each pair ending in a stress-shifting suffix. Each pair consisted of a word or pseudoword that was segmentally identical, but one member had stress in the location that theory predicts based on the suffix (e.g. auth*OR*ity; klo*R I*pity) while the other kept stress on the same syllable where it occurs in the stem (e.g. *A U*thority; *KLO*ripity); participants were required to choose which of the two items sounded better. Jarmulowicz showed that children made judgements that accorded with the morphological rules for stress assignment for both real and pseudowords, with performance on less frequent suffixes being less accurate than that for more frequent suffixes, and that this was developmental, with older children more accurate than younger children. This shows that implicit knowledge of stress assignment driven by morphology is an underlying linguistic competence that develops over time.

Given this relationship between speech rhythm and morphological knowledge, one might expect to see a relationship between morphological awareness and prosodic sensitivity. Indeed, Clin and Wade-Woolley (2007) found such a relationship in children aged 9–13 years; in this study they observed that prosodic sensitivity measured by a sentence matching task similar to that of Wood and Terrell (1998) predicted 16 per cent of variance in morphological awareness after controlling for vocabulary, non-verbal intelligence, memory and phonemic awareness. They also found zero-order correlations between prosodic sensitivity and various reading measures ranging from 0.39 to 0.46. Once morphological awareness was added to a regression equation along with the predictors above, however, the relationships between prosodic sensitivity and reading were attenuated to non-significant levels, suggesting that the relationship of reading to speech rhythm is mediated by morphological awareness. In another study, and using a similar paradigm to that of Jarmulowicz, Wade-Woolley (2007) showed that adult readers' sensitivity to the morphological rules of stress assignment was significantly related to word reading and pseudoword decoding. Taken together, these studies provide evidence to validate further research into the relationship between morphological knowledge and sensitivity to speech rhythm to further our understanding of reading, especially of longer, morphologically complex words.

Conclusion

This chapter has argued that studying speech rhythm can extend and contribute to our understanding of reading development and reading failure. In particular, we are excited by its potential to underpin theorising about how polysyllabic word reading is realised in different languages, as current models of word reading are vague about how novice readers progress from decoding single syllable words to phonologically and morphologically complex ones. Measures of productive speech rhythm are also implicated in reading development through their contribution to fluent and expressive reading and text comprehension and phonemic awareness.

References

Adams, M.J. (1990). *Beginning to read: thinking and learning about print*. Cambridge: MIT Press.

Ashby, J., & Clifton Jr, C. (2005). 'The prosodic property of lexical stress affects eye movements during silent reading'. *Cognition, 96*, 89–100.

Brady, S., Shankweiler, D., & Mann, V. (1983). 'Speech perception and memory coding in relation to reading ability'. *Journal of Experimental Psychology, 35*, 345–367.

Carlisle, J.F. (2000). 'Awareness of the structure and meaning of morphologically complex words: Impact on reading'. *Reading and Writing, 12*, 169–190.

Carlisle, J.F. & Stone, C.A. (2005). 'Exploring the role of morphemes in word reading. *Reading Research Quarterly, 40*, 428–449.

Castles, A. & Coltheart, M. (2004). 'Is there a causal link from phonological awareness to success in learning to read?' *Cognition, 91*, 77–111.

Chiat, S. (1983). 'My *mikey's* right and *my key's* wrong: the significance of stress and word boundaries in a child's output system'. *Cognition, 14*, 275–300.

Clin, E. & Wade-Woolley, L. (2007). 'Investigating the role of prosody in the development of fluent reading'. Poster presented at the annual meeting of the Society for the Scientific Study of Reading, Prague, CZ, July.

Cutler, A., & Mehler, J. (1993). 'The periodicity bias'. *Journal of Phonetics, 21*, 103–108.

De Bree, E., Wijnen, F. & Zonneveld, W. (2006). 'Word stress production in three-year-old children at risk of dyslexia'. *Journal of Research in Reading, 29*, 304–317.

De Weirdt, W. (1988). 'Speech perception and frequency discrimination in good and poor readers'. *Applied Psycholinguistics, 9*, 163–183.

Dupoux, E., Peperkamp, S., & Sebastián-Gallés, N. (2001) 'A robust method to study stress "deafness"'. *Journal of the Acoustical Society of America, 110*, 1606–1618.

Freeman, B.A. & Beasley, D.S. (1978). 'Discrimination of time-altered sentential approximations and monosyllables by children with reading problems'. *Journal of Speech and Hearing Research, 21*, 497–506.

Godfrey, J.J., Syrdal-Lasky, A.K., Millay, K., & Knox, C.M. (1981). 'Performance of dyslexic children on speech perception tests'. *Journal of Experimental Child Psychology, 32*, 401–424.

Goetry, V., Wade-Woolley, L., Kolinsky, R. & Mousty, P. (2006). 'The role of stress processing abilities in the development of bilingual reading'. *Journal of Research in Reading, 29*, 349–362.

Goswami, U. (2002). 'Phonology, reading development, and dyslexia: A cross-linguistic perspective'. *Annals of Dyslexia, 52*, 141–163.

—— (2003). 'How to beat dyslexia'. *The Psychologist, 16*, 462–465.

Goswami, U., Thomson, J.M., Richardson, U., Stainthorp, R., Hughes, D., Rosen, S., *et al.* (2002). 'Amplitude envelope onsets and developmental dyslexia: a new hypothesis'. *Proceedings of the National Academy of Sciences, 99*, 10911–10916.

Gutierrez-Palma, N. & Reyes, A.P. (2007). 'Stress sensitivity and reading performance in Spanish: a study with children'. *Journal of Research in Reading, 30*, 157–168.

Holliman, A.J., Wood, C. & Sheehy, K. (2008). 'Sensitivity to speech rhythm explains individual differences in reading ability independently of phonological awareness'. *British Journal of Developmental Psychology, 26*(3), 357–367.

Holliman, A.J., Wood, C. & Sheehy, K. (submitted). 'The contribution of sensitivity to speech rhythm and non-speech rhythm to early reading development'.

Hurford, D. (1991). 'The possible use of IBM-compatible computers and digital-to-analog conversion to assess children for reading disabilities and to increase their phonemic awareness'. *Behavior Reseach Methods, Instruments, & Computers, 23*, 319–323.

Jarmulowicz, L.D. (2002). 'English derivational suffix frequency and children's stress judgments'. *Brain and Language, 81*, 192–204.

Kitzen, K. (2001). 'Prosodic sensitivity, morphological ability, and reading ability in young adults with and without childhood histories of reading difficulty'. Unpublished doctoral dissertation, University of Colombia, Colombia.

Kuhn, M.R. & Stahl, S.A. (2003). 'Fluency: a review of developmental and remedial practices'. *Journal of Educational Psychology, 95*, 3–21.

Lyytinen, H., Leinonen,S., Nikula, M., Richardson, U., Aro, M. & Leiwo, M. (1995) 'In search of the core features of dyslexia – Observations concerning ortho-graphically highly regular Finnish language'. In V.W. Berninger (ed) *The Varieties of Orthographic Knowledge II* (pp. 177–204). Kluwer Academic Publisher, Dordrecht, The Netherlands.

McBride-Chang, C. (1995). 'Phonological processing, speech perception, and reading disability: An integrative review'. *Educational Psychologist, 30*, 109–121.

Metsala, J.L., and Walley, A.C. (1998). 'Spoken vocabulary growth and the segmental restructuring of lexical representations: Precursors to phonemic awareness and early reading ability'. In J.L. Metsala & L.C. Ehri (eds), *Word recognition in beginning literacy* (pp. 89–120). 'London: Laurence Erlbaum'.

Muneaux, M., Ziegler, J.C., Truc, C., Thomson, J., & Goswami, U. (2004). 'Deficits in beat perception and dyslexia: Evidence from French'. *NeuroReport, 15*, 1255–1259.

Pasquini, E.S., Corriveau, K.H. & Goswami, U. (2007) 'Auditory processing of ampli-tude envelope rise time in adults diagnosed with developmental dyslexia'. *Scientific Studies of Reading, 11*(3), 259–286.

Pennington, B.F., Van Orden, G.C., Smith, S.D., Green, P.A. & Haith, M.M. (1990). 'Phonological processing skills and deficits in adult dyslexics'. *Child Development, 61,* 1753–1778.

Protopapas, A., Gerakaki, S. & Alexandri, S. (2006). 'Lexical and default stress assignment in reading Greek'. *Journal of Research in Reading, 29,* 418–432.

Ravid, D. & Mashraki, Y.E. (2007) 'Prosodic reading, reading comprehension and morphological skills in Hebrew-speaking fourth graders'. *Journal of Research in Reading, 30,* 140–156.

Reed, M.A. (1989). 'Speech perception and the discrimination of brief auditory cues in reading disabled children'. *Journal of Experimental Child Psychology, 48,* 270–292.

Richardson, U., Leppänen, P.H.T., Leiwo, M. & Lyytinen, H. (2003) 'Speech perception of infants with high familial risk for dyslexia differ at the age of 6 months'. *Developmental Neuropsychology, 23,* 385–397.

Singson, M., Mahoney, D. & Mann, V. (2000). 'The relation between reading ability and morphological skills: evidence from derivational suffixes'. *Reading and Writing, 12,* 219–252.

Snowling, M.J. (2000). *Dyslexia* (2nd edn). 'Boston, MA: Blackwell'.

Snowling, M., Goulandris, N., Bowlbey, M. & Howell, P. (1986). 'Segmentation and speech perception in relation to reading skill: a developmental analysis'. *Journal of Experimental Child Psychology, 41,* 489–507.

Stanovich, K.E. (1986). 'Matthew effects in reading: some consequences of individual differences in the acquisition of literacy'. *Reading Research Quarterly, 21,* 360–364.

Stanovich, K.E. & Siegel, L.S. (1994) 'Phenotype performance profile of children with reading disabilities: A regression-based test of the phonological-core variable-difference model'. *Journal of Educational Psychology, 86,* 24–53.

Tallal, P. (1980). 'Auditory temporal perception, phonics, and reading disabilities in children'. *Brain and Language, 9,* 182–198.

Thomson, J.M., Fryer, B., Maltby, J. & Goswami, U. (2006). 'Auditory and motor rhythm awareness in adults with dyslexia'. *Journal of Research in Reading, 29,* 334–344.

Wade-Woolley, L. (2007). 'Stress assignment and derivational morphology in skilled reading'. Paper presented at the annual meeting of the Society for the Scientific Study of Reading, Prague, CZ, July.

Wade-Woolley, L., & Wood, C. (eds) (2006). 'Prosodic sensitivity and reading development' (Special issue). *Journal of Research in Reading, 29*(3).

Werker, J.F. & Tees, R.C. (1987). 'Speech perception in severely disabled and average reading children'. *Canadian Journal of Psychology, 41,* 48–61.

Whalley, K. & Hansen, J. (2006). 'The role of prosodic sensitivity in children's reading development'. *Journal of Research in Reading, 29,* 288–303.

Wood, C. (2006). 'Metrical stress sensitivity in young children and its relationship to phonological awareness and reading'. *Journal of Research in Reading, 29,* 270–287.

Wood, C. & Terrell, C. (1998). 'Poor readers' ability to detect speech rhythm and perceive rapid speech'. *British Journal of Developmental Psychology, 16,* 397–413.

Chapter 2

Auditory processing and developmental dyslexia

Throwing the baby out with the bathwater?

Jennifer Thomson

Our understanding of developmental dyslexia has progressed substantially in the past few decades. Once a contentious diagnosis, the understanding that dyslexia arises from a core phonological deficit is now widely accepted. However, phonological awareness itself depends on cognitive processes such as sensory perception, short-term memory, long-term memory and executive function (Snowling, 2000). The associations between these skills and reading ability have been subject to intensive research, often fraught with debate. Most researched are sensory abilities. Proposed sensory causes of the phonological deficit in developmental dyslexia include a magnocellular impairment in both the visual and auditory systems (e.g. Stein & Talcott, 1999); a general sensory processing deficit (Ramus, 2003), a deficit in cerebellar functioning (Nicolson *et al.*, 1995) and deficits in basic auditory temporal processing (Goswami *et al.*, 2002; Tallal, 1980, 2004).[1] Debate has been intensified by attempts to find a 'one-deficit-fits-all' answer to reading difficulties. This is particularly true of research focusing on auditory perception and reading relationships: the focus of this chapter.

Auditory perception – the key to phonological deficits?

A first hypothesis: the Rapid Auditory Processing Deficit (RAPD)

As early as 1937, through the studies of Orton, links were being made between literacy difficulties and more basic perceptual anomalies. However, it was not until Tallal's studies during the 1970s and 1980s, that the hypothesis of auditory processing as a central causal factor in dyslexia was systematically explored. Although Tallal's specific hypothesis has been increasingly questioned (see Rosen, 2003), her work has been extremely influential due to the subsequent research it generated.

Using a paradigm developed in her studies of children with Specific Language Impairment (SLI; Tallal & Piercy, 1973), Tallal's investigation centred on temporal order judgement (TOJ), through an activity known as the Repetition Task. In this task, two sounds were presented in pairs, at varied inter-stimulus intervals (ISIs). The listener was asked to press associated buttons in the order heard. The same stimuli were also presented in a same–different judgement paradigm. In a study involving dyslexic children (Tallal, 1980), whilst all children performed at or near ceiling with long ISIs (≥428ms), at shorter ISIs (≤305ms) 8 out of the 20 dyslexic children demonstrated performance deficits in both the Repetition and same–different judgement tasks. Parallel studies of children with SLI (Tallal & Piercy, 1973, 1974) showed widespread difficulties for this group of children in short ISI conditions, as well as greater difficulty than their controls in discriminating between /ba/ and /da/ stimuli. Taking these findings as a whole, Tallal and Piercy concluded that both children with SLI and dyslexia evinced an auditory deficit specific to the perception of rapidly changing or brief sounds.

Discrimination between many phonemic contrasts is dependent upon processing frequency, formant transitions and voice onset times occurring within very brief temporal windows. The accompanying assumption was that failure to perceive these features might lead to degraded phonological encoding. In the dyslexia study (Tallal, 1980), high correlations (r_s = 0.81) between the number of errors in a phonic reading test and the number of errors in responding to the rapidly presented auditory stimuli were taken as evidence to support this supposition: a basic perceptual mechanism may compromise the development of stable phonological representations, which in turn leads to the phonological processing and literacy difficulties observed in dyslexia. This viewpoint has become known as the 'Rapid Auditory Processing Deficit' (RAPD) hypothesis.

Challenges to the RAPD hypothesis

A major claim of Tallal's 1980 study was that dyslexic children have a specific difficulty with processing rapidly presented or brief acoustic stimuli. However, this argument has been refuted. First, studies have attempted to replicate Tallal's original findings using the Repetition Task with dyslexics. Although the first replication by Reed (1989) obtained supportive results, further studies have failed to find relationships between non-verbal temporal processing and phonological skills or reading (Bretherton & Holmes, 2003). A second problem stems from the methodological pitfalls of using a non-adaptive presentation format for psychoacoustic testing. This format consistently yields ceiling effects for control groups. It also lacks reliability and sensitivity in comparison to adaptive procedures, which reduces the validity of subsequent findings (De Martino et al., 2001; Heiervang et al., 2002; Rey et al., 2002). Third, further studies have found that as long as performances at long inter-stimuli intervals are not at ceiling, the difficulties dyslexic children demonstrate are not limited to short ISIs alone (Marshall et al., 2001; Nittrouer, 1999; Reed, 1989; Waber et al., 2001). In a study where the Repetition Task was applied to children entering school (Share et al., 2002), it was only at long ISIs that those later identified as having reading difficulties differed from those who went on to read normally. There have also been a number of findings where other tasks involving 'rapid' auditory processing have not yielded performance differences between dyslexic children and their controls, for example, detection of short tones following a masker (forward masking; Rosen & Manganari, 2001). Conversely, studies examining 'non-rapid' auditory phenomena, such as detection of amplitude modulations occurring at rates as low as 4Hz have found robust group differences (Lorenzi et al., 2000).

Another challenge for the RAPD is the purported link between non-speech deficits and speech perception. Although not directly tested by Tallal and colleagues, their assertion was that non-speech deficits observed on the temporal order judgement task would directly relate to difficulties in the temporal ordering of speech sounds, required for successful literacy acquisition. Thirty years later, evidence for this assertion remains limited. Reed's (1989) replication examined dyslexic children's ability to process speech sounds differing only in the rate of formant transition within a brief time window. Although a group deficit was found for both tasks in the dyslexic group, unfortunately, the relationship between non-speech and speech deficits was not directly tested. Bretherton and Holmes (2003) went further, exploring dyslexic children's performance on speech processing, phonological processing and literacy tasks in terms of whether they were strong or weak performers on Tallal's repetition paradigm. Poor non-speech performance did not necessarily relate to speech processing or literacy deficits, questioning the hypothesis of a causal connection. Mody *et al.* (1997) studied a group of poor readers who were actively selected on the basis of poor discrimination performance in a synthetic speech task involving the phonetically similar syllables /ba/ and /da/. Of note, however, was the absence of a deficit for the children in discriminating between carefully created non-speech analogues of these stimuli. The analogues featured identical second and third formant transitions, assumed to be the acoustic signature of dyslexic children's difficulties, which would accordingly link speech and non-speech findings (see also Serniclaes *et al.*, 2001). Thus, no study has yet convincingly linked observed non-speech auditory perceptual deficits to their purported speech equivalents.

Auditory processing deficits and developmental paradigms

Returning to our question of why certain individuals have a phonological deficit: can underlying auditory perceptual deficits serve as a convincing answer? In a review of the literature by Franck Ramus (2003), he estimates that the actual reported incidence of auditory deficits is around 40 per cent. In addition, an easily identifiable locus of auditory perceptual weakness, with clear links to speech perception and literacy, remains to be found. Ramus concludes that auditory processing deficits are neither necessary nor sufficient in explaining the phonological deficits of dyslexia. Yet calling off the search here is a disservice to the 40 per cent of individuals who *do* have co-occurring auditory processing and reading difficulties. How can we explain this relationship in theoretical terms, as well as intervene effectively with these individuals for whom an auditory processing deficit may well be limiting their reading progress?

In order to answer these questions, it is first necessary to look at wider philosophies shaping developmental psychology in the past few decades. Until recently, cognitive neuropsychology has been a dominant framework for conceptualizing development and developmental difficulties. A primary way in which this approach builds models of normal cognitive processing is to study highly selective deficits in brain-damaged individuals (usually adults), in order to show the relative independence of the processes implicated. The idea of dissociation is key; thus if a patient has a poor ability to name things, but preserved irregular word reading, one would surmise an independence in cognitive processing for these skills (Breen & Warrington, 1995).

Whilst this approach has been useful for building models of adult cognition, there are caveats in applying the same logic to a child's still-developing cognitive system. There is evidence for interaction between systems such as language and executive function, as well as interaction between representational systems, altering the developmental course of all systems involved (Karmiloff-Smith, 2006, 2007). Independent, or modular processes are thus posited to emerge over the course of development, rather than being the initial state (Karmiloff-Smith, 2006). As Dorothy Bishop (1997: 1) noted: 'Changes in the nature of representations and in the relationships between components of a developing system mean that cross-sectional data at a single point in development may be misleading indicators of the primary deficit.'

Bishop goes on to give the example of a study by Bernstein and Stark (1985) where language-impaired children originally studied by Tallal *et al.* (1981) were followed up several years later. In the original study the children were found to have significant deficits in discriminating tone pairs at short inter-stimulus intervals. When followed up, these children were impaired on a test of sentence comprehension; however, the aforementioned deficit in tone pair discrimination was no longer present. If these children had just been tested once at the second time point and dissociation logic was applied, one might conclude that the receptive language problems were not caused by an auditory difficulty. However, forearmed with the information from the first testing point, our conclusion might be quite different – a slow-maturing auditory perceptual system might result in lasting effects on the language system, even after ceiling scores on a specific auditory test are reached.

The cognitive neurospychological approach has contributed enormously to our understanding of reading. Investigations generated to test or refine the applicability of the dual-route model of reading (Coltheart *et al.*, 2001), for example, have expedited understanding of the multiple processes in play. However, in the case of auditory processing and developmental dyslexia, such an approach may be holding back our understanding of both areas of cognition. As the following sections will elaborate, by taking a more developmentally sensitive approach we may be better positioned to understand how the two interact.

Developmentally sensitive design I: longitudinal studies of auditory perception and literacy

When children with reading difficulties are assessed on their auditory perceptual ability, generally a subgroup demonstrates impaired auditory processing skills. However, there is not yet consensus on which aspects of auditory processing are most related to reading difficulty and which subgroup of children this will affect. Pedagogically, this is not satisfactory. If current assessment tools only show a subgroup to be affected and we do not know which auditory skills are related to reading, we cannot use auditory processing ability as a basis for diagnosis or intervention. This also leaves theories of dyslexia incomplete, as the importance of auditory perception in acquiring well-specified phonological representations cannot be ruled in or out.

One way to move beyond this position is to be more developmental in our thinking. Rather than drawing conclusions and building theories from findings at one point in a child's immensely dynamic developmental trajectory, researchers need to grapple with this complexity. The first step is to look at developmental changes that occur within the skill domains of interest. Taking auditory perception as an example, evidence from both behavioural (Allen *et al.*, 1989; Fischer & Hartnegg, 2004; Wightman *et al.*, 1989) and electrophysiological (Bruneau *et al.*, 1997; Ceponiene *et al.*, 2002; Gilley *et al.*, 2005) psychoacoustic research already tells us that auditory processing undergoes significant developmental changes during infancy and childhood. Having more understanding of how auditory processing skills develop over time and how these changes relate to language and literacy development will help us make more sense of individual differences.

Arguably the most ambitious study to explore the development and interaction of auditory processing and language and literacy is the Finnish Jyväskylä Longitudinal Study of Dyslexia (JLD). In this study approximately 100 children born to families with a dyslexic parent (and at least one other member among his/her close relatives) have been followed from birth, together with a similar number of unaffected children (see Lyytinen *et al.*, 2004a, 2004b). In order to assess auditory processing in newborns, Lyytinen and colleagues employed brain-related measures, specifically, a technique that allows pre-attentive neural responses to auditory stimuli to be measured – event-related potential (ERP) recording. Measurements were taken both when the infants were one to six weeks old and then again at six months old. The most robust finding across these studies, which looked at responses to both speech syllables and pseudowords, was differential hemispheric activation between groups. Whilst the at-risk group showed right hemisphere dominance, the control group demonstrated responses largely over the left hemisphere (Lyytinen *et al.*, 2005).

As well as suggesting the existence of processing differences present from birth in individuals at risk of reading disabilities, the JLD is also starting to shed light on how these differences are related to subsequent language and literacy development. In one sub-study carried out with newborns (at risk for familial dyslexia, N = 26; control infants, N = 23) synthetic consonant-vowel syllables were presented with equal probability and an early processing ERP response, the N1, was measured. Results found that responses to /ga/ around 600ms in the at-risk newborns had a slower polarity shift from the major positive peak to the later negative deflection, especially over the right hemisphere (Guttorm *et al.*, 2001). Using data from subsequent assessment phases, analyses showed that this at-risk response pattern in the right hemisphere was related to significantly poorer receptive language skills across both groups at the age of 2.5 years. The similar ERP pattern in the left hemisphere was associated with poorer verbal memory skills at the age of 5 years.

Another research group that has used ERPs to explore longitudinal relationships between auditory processing skills from birth and later reading skills is that of Dennis and Victoria Molfese (Molfese, 2000; Molfese *et al.*, 2002; Molfese & Molfese, 2002), who have followed a cohort in the rural Midwest of the USA. Unlike the infants in the JLD, the participants in this study were not initially selected on the basis of a family history of reading difficulites. The Molfeses also looked at N1 responses to speech and non-speech syllables. In early investigations they found relationships between the N1 waveform from newborn ERPs and language abilities at 3 and 5 years old (Molfese & Molfese, 2000) as well as reading ability at age 8 (Molfese, 2000; Molfese *et al.*, 2001). More recently, the same group reported a study in which ERP recordings were taken annually for a group of 109 children between the ages of 1 and 8 years (Espy *et al.*, 2004). Peak amplitude and latency data were collected. Intriguingly, it was the *change* in N1 waveform between the ages of 1 and 4 years that differentiated average and poor readers. As the authors note, these findings suggest that it is not just brain make-up at birth that determines later cognitive proficiency, but rather the *development* of brain-based perceptual skills, which creates the subsequent foundations for higher order skills such as reading and spelling. This development will itself be dependent upon factors such as the child's exposure to sound, their emotional readiness for learning and the development of other skills, such as motor skills, which allow sounds to be dynamically experienced. Such findings make hypotheses built from single time point measurement look increasingly inadequate.

Developmentally sensitive design II: in the beginning was the phoneme?

If auditory perception development *before* the age of 4 years is predicting later reading ability, then logically, inter-individual variation in auditory perceptual acuity will result in inter-individual variability in phonological representation development during this period as well. So what phonological representation development is occurring? The exact nature of fully developed phonological representations is not yet completely understood. It is generally assumed that their internal structure corresponds to the hierarchy of units developed in phonological theory. Language contains a finite number of elements that can be combined contrastively. In phonology these elements are provided by the peaks and troughs of energy or stricture within the speech stream. Across languages, syllables are units of relative prominence and within each syllable the point of maximal acoustical energy is provided by the obligatory vowel. In English, a syllable can then be divided into an onset and a rime, the latter containing the vowel (nucleus) and an optional coda (for example, c-ot). In many other languages, syllables divide into the units of nucleus and coda. Onsets, nuclei and coda can all be either simple or complex depending upon whether they contain single or multiple phonemes. Phonemes are the smallest sound units used contrastively to signal meaning differences within a language.

Understanding the process of phonological representation establishment has been a notoriously difficult area of enquiry for two main reasons. First, due to their inherent abstractness, phonological representations cannot be investigated directly. Second, because spoken word recognition and production are a universal human necessity, phonological representations are being established from the earliest stages of infancy – this again makes investigation more difficult. It does not make it impossible however, and by exploring infant behaviour using tools such as preferential-looking patterns and responses to novelty, a great deal has been learnt. Finally, there is an important distinction between the phonological contrasts infants can perceive, and what they represent.

We know, for example, that infants can discriminate the phonological contrasts of their own language by the age of 2 months (Kuhl, 1987) and are sensitive to language-specific vowel prototypicality by 6 months (Kuhl *et al.*, 1992). Such studies have indicated perceptual abilities in infancy previously assumed not possible, and shown that processing limitations attributed to infancy are sometimes an artefact of investigative insensitivity.

However, knowing that infants can perceive and distinguish phonological detail at the finest level is not evidence that they are also encoding such detail to long-term phonological representations. This point is well illustrated by Stager and Werker (1997). Using a release-from-habituation task, these researchers found that 14-month-old infants failed to discriminate between the minimal pair 'bih' and 'dih' when presented as referents; however, in an accompanying discrimination task where the syllables were not linked to referential targets, the children succeeded in the task.

In a subsequent word learning study of 14, 17 and 20 month olds, Werker *et al.*, (2002) showed that by 17 months children could represent newly learnt words in enough detail to distinguish slight differences. Werker *et al.* attributed this developmental change to the reaching of a critical vocabulary threshold, triggering finer-grain phonological encoding.

The idea that vocabulary growth drives phonological representation specificity is also central to the Lexical Restructuring Theory (Metsala & Walley, 1998; Walley, 1993). In this theory, Walley and colleagues suggest that in infancy and early childhood phonological representations are initially holistic in form, with increasingly detailed levels of representation developing primarily in response to vocabulary growth. Despite the intuitive appeal of this idea and the preliminary evidence we have of a representational 'shift' around the time of an infant's vocabulary spurt (see also, Locke, 1997), more recent research suggests this cannot be the whole story. Most notable is the work of Swingley and Aslin (2000, 2002), who examined the looking behaviour of toddlers between 18 and 24 months when asked to direct their gaze at one of two pictures, the name of one being either pronounced accurately (e.g. 'dog') or mispronounced (e.g. 'tog'). On average the toddlers looked at a target picture more when its name was pronounced correctly than when it was mispronounced. The size of this effect, however, was not related to age or vocabulary size. This finding was also replicated with 14-month-old infants in subsequent studies (Bailey & Plunkett, 2002; Swingley & Aslin, 2002).

Thus, we have strong evidence for the sophistication of infants' phonological perception skills, with emerging evidence that this has direct relevance to the representation of first words. Vocabulary growth appears to play a role in phonological representation specification, although more work is needed to fully elucidate the developmental mechanism. Another factor that may be important to phonological representation development in infancy is statistical learning. Work by Jenny Saffran and colleagues (Saffran, 2003; Saffran *et al.*, 1996) has shown that infants have the ability to abstract and retain phonological information concerning speech categories and word boundaries through statistical learning of occurrence probabilities. In one study Saffran *et al.* (1996) exposed 8-month-old infants to a spoken nonsense language in which the only cues to word boundaries were the sequential probabilities of syllable sequences. Following a brief exposure infants were successfully able to discriminate 'words' of the nonsense language from syllable sequences spanning word boundaries.

An equally powerful cue is that provided by prominence information, which contributes to the perceived rhythm of the language. Mehler and colleagues have shown that newborn infants are able to discriminate languages on the basis of their rhythmic properties (Mehler & Christophe, 1995; Mehler *et al.*, 1998; Nazzi *et al.*, 1998). Jusczyk and Thompson (1978) found that aged between 1 and 4 months, infants can detect changes in rhythmic patterns of strong and weak syllables, whilst by 9 months English infants demonstrate a listening bias for the predominant strong–weak syllable rhythm of English (Jusczyk *et al.*, 1993).

Following on from Saffran *et al.*'s work, Curtin *et al.* (2005) investigated the role of syllable stress in the phonological representations for words that are developed by young infants. Using a connectionist model, they showed that stress combines additively with phoneme transitional probabilities in the process of word segmentation.

Curtin *et al.* (2005) then used a habituation paradigm to explore whether the early phonological representations of infants aged 7 months encoded lexical stress as well as phonetic information. Infants were exposed to nonsense words embedded in sentences. The nonsense words were made up of identical segments, but either had the lexical stress typical of English (DObita), or atypical stress (doBIta). The results showed that the infants represented these nonsense words as distinct lexical items on the basis of whether they contained initial or medial stress. This work also concurs with that of Morgan and Saffran (1995) who found that at 6 months infants relied predominantly on rhythmic regularity to segment speech, whilst by 9 months infants are able to integrate this 'suprasegmental' information with segmental cues.

To review, with auditory perception development *before* the age of 4 years predicting later reading ability, it was asked here what concomitant *development* is occurring within phonological representations during the same pre-school period. The answer appears to be a gradual progression from the use of larger phonological units for segmentation and representation to smaller segmental units. This latter stage is also facilitated by the act of learning to read (Perfetti *et al.*, 1987). Relating this to our overarching question of why some children have phonological deficits, a developmental approach would suggest exploring the causal pathway from auditory perception to *syllable* processing, then to phonemic processing and lastly to phonic decoding. Yet most of the extant research has bypassed the syllabic step, looking directly at auditory perceptual links to phoneme-level processing and/or reading. As an initial strategy, focusing upon auditory processing associations with the phonological processing level most directly related to phonics is vital. Yet having ascertained that the collected findings from such investigations have not provided firm conclusions, and hypothesizing that more basic units of phonological representation development may play a role in determining reading progress, a longer range perspective becomes imperative.

Auditory perception and syllable-level processing

What are the auditory parameters that provide segmentation cues at the level of the syllable and word? Rather than auditory changes occurring in the time window of 10s of milliseconds, sensitivity to phonological information at the syllable level depends partly on sensitivity to longer modulations within the 'temporal envelope' of speech. The speech signal contains modulations of both frequency and amplitude. Both of these modulations can occur at varied rates. The modulations signalling syllable-level information are generally believed to be amplitude modulations below 4Hz (i.e. a modulation rate of less than four cycles per second) (Drullman *et al.*, 1994; Houtgast & Steenken, 1985). Shannon *et al.* (1995) have also shown that amplitude modulation at these low rates, as opposed to spectral frequency cues, is the critical factor determining speech intelligibility for adult listeners.

Two studies by Lorenzi *et al.* (Lorenzi *et al.*, 2000; Rocheron *et al.*, 2002) have examined amplitude modulation sensitivity in dyslexic children. In the first of these, Lorenzi *et al.* (2000) examined AM detection thresholds in 8–14-year-old children with dyslexia (n = 6). They found that the detection thresholds of dyslexic children at 4Hz particularly, but also at 1024Hz, were much higher (poorer) than for a group of normally reading control children, as well as a group of normally reading adults. They found no difference between groups in the detection of 16, 64 or 256Hz AM. Interestingly, the normally reading child and adult groups did not differ significantly from one another in any of their detection thresholds. In this study Lorenzi *et al.* (2000) also looked at the dyslexic children's ability to identify synthetically manipulated speech sounds in which the spectral information was degraded, leaving predominantly amplitude envelope information. Here both the normally reading and dyslexic children performed more poorly than the normally reading adults. However, whilst the normally reading children showed an improvement in performance across sessions, the dyslexic children did not. These findings suggest that whilst typically developing children have acquired basic sensitivity to amplitude modulation, sophisticated usage of this information in processing degraded speech is not immediately adult-like. For dyslexic children, in whom basic amplitude modulation detection is weaker, it is considerably more difficult to use this information when processing degraded speech, and so a performance gap is found in comparison to same-age peers.

In their second study, Lorenzi *et al.* attempted to replicate these findings and extend their investigation to the measurement of AM discrimination thresholds (Rocheron *et al.*, 2002). Whilst detection tasks necessitate being aware of a modulation within a sound as opposed to no modulation, discrimination tasks use supra-threshold degrees of modulation and require the listener to distinguish between modulations of varying depth or rate. Assessing 10–15-year-old children with both 4 and 128Hz AM stimuli, the authors found higher detection thresholds for the dyslexics (n = 10) at both modulation frequencies, though again the deficit was strongest at 4Hz in the detection task. In terms of discrimination thresholds, a group difference occurred for rate and depth discrimination at 128Hz AM condition. The dyslexic children did not differ significantly from the controls in an intensity discrimination control task using the same experimental presentation, thus ruling out procedural reasons for the group differences.

The findings of Lorenzi *et al.* suggest reduced AM detection sensitivity in both dyslexic children and adults, especially for the lower modulation rates characteristic of speech (Lorenzi *et al.*, 2000; Rocheron *et al.*, 2002). Lorenzi *et al.* proposed that this reduced sensitivity might produce an 'internal smoothing' (Rocheron *et al.*, 2002: 4) of auditory representations, which could lead to a reduced information-carrying capacity of such envelope cues.

Being able to detect amplitude modulations will allow one to attune to the rhythm of the speech stream, determined by the presence of syllables. This is crucial in allowing subsequent fine-grained sub-syllabic analysis to occur. Music, speech rhythm or tempo provides the scaffolding structure within which more 'micro' acoustic information is carried (Fraisse, 1963). In dyslexic individuals, despite the slightly mixed results, it appears that there is a reduced sensitivity to this basic amplitude modulation structure. It also appears that this deficit is not restricted to rapid amplitude modulation changes, but rather the strongest results so far implicate modulation detection ability when the modulation rate is slow, that is when amplitude is changing relatively slowly as a function of time. This suggests that dyslexic individuals have difficulty processing auditory information when the dynamic information provided by the signal as a function of time is reduced. This hypothesis is quite different to the early ideas of researchers such as Tallal (1980), who argued that when dyslexic individuals are faced with changing acoustic information within a short time window, they manifest processing difficulties.

However, the two hypotheses are not mutually exclusive. Amplitude fluctuations represent a speech macro-structure that is distinct from the rapid frequency or spectral changes investigated by Tallal and colleagues. We know that frequency discrimination skills have a long maturational course and that spectral information is important for identifying fine-structure within speech. We also know that speech perception in general is a dynamic process and that as children develop, the perceptual weighting of cues such as noise spectra vs. formant transitions, employed in phoneme identification, appears to change (Nittrouer & Miller, 1997). Therefore, when the auditory skills of school-age children are investigated, if we assume that dyslexic children may have manifested auditory processing differences from earlier in development, which affected macro-structure speech perception, further 'downstream' effects on micro-structure perception, such as rapid frequency discrimination, could be predicted.

Despite the value of Lorenzi *et al.*'s findings, their work does not provide the testable explanatory framework for the causal pathway between syllable-level auditory processing, phonological representation and literacy acquisition. Work by Goswami and colleagues, however, has attempted to provide such a framework.

Amplitude rise time, phonological processing and literacy

In normal speech, the amplitude modulations that occur will not be completely regular, but rather will show variability both across and within speakers. One way in which amplitude modulations can vary, as well as in the overall length, is how quickly the maximum amplitude is reached, the amplitude rise time, as well as how rapidly the amplitude modulation decays. Amplitude rise time is a particularly salient cue in that it combines both amplitude change as well as a duration parameter, two important cues to speech prosody. Rise time variation has various important linguistic consequences. As well as acting as a segmental cue to manner of articulation, for example the voiceless affricate-fricative distinction (/t$\sum$/ and /$\sum$/ in the initial consonants of 'chop' and 'shop'; Howell & Rosen, 1983), amplitude rise time is also used in syllabification (Mermelstein, 1975 cf. Rosen, 1992) and the demarcation of linguistic units (vowel, syllable or word; Rosen, 1992). This latter role is important when considering the segmentation task tackled by infants. The importance of amplitude rise times to speech processing has also been elaborated in the work of Scott (1998), who has shown that amplitude envelope rise times in speech correlate with the vowel onset within any syllable.

Goswami and colleagues have carried out three cross-sectional studies with children that explore the role of auditory rise time sensitivity in developmental dyslexia (Goswami *et al.*, 2002; Richardson *et al.*, 2004; Muneaux *et al.*, 2004). In all of these studies, sensitivity to rise time was tested using non-speech stimuli; because the speech signal is infinitely complex in its interplay of amplitude, frequency and durational cues, non-speech stimuli are more amenable to manipulation of single variables. Continua of pure tone stimuli were created in which the rate of amplitude modulation remained constant, whilst the rise time of the modulations varied (see Figure 2.1). The stimuli were presented through adaptive threshold-seeking programmes using both a categorization paradigm (Goswami *et al.*, 2002; Muneaux *et al.*, 2004) as well as a discrimination paradigm (Richardson *et al.*, 2004). In Goswami *et*

(a)

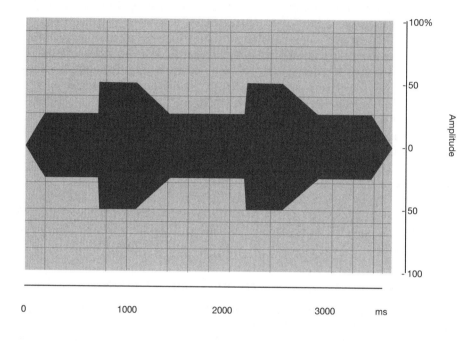

0   1000   2000   3000   ms

(b)

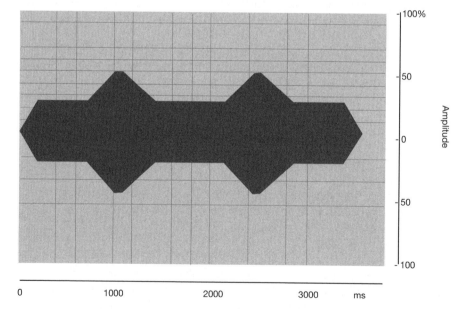

0   1000   2000   3000   ms

Figure 2.1. Schematic depiction of amplitude modulating stimuli with (a) a short rise time and (b) a long rise time (used in Richardson *et al.*, 2004). Time is on the x axis and amplitude on the y axis.

al.'s initial study (2002), performance in a rise time categorization task accounted for 25 per cent unique variance in children's concurrent reading and spelling ability (after controlling for age, non-verbal IQ and vocabulary). Rise time categorization also accounted for unique variance in each of the core triad of phonological processing tasks known to be compromised in dyslexia: phonological short-term memory, rapid automatized naming and phonological (rime) awareness. Such a finding is exciting for the support it offers developmental models of reading difficulties, demonstrating relationships between syllable-level auditory processing, phonological processing *and* literacy.

In Richardson *et al.* (2004), a threshold-based rise time discrimination task was also administered to English dyslexic children. A 2IFC (two interval, forced choice) design was used. In this paradigm the listener hears two sounds in each trial. Rather than making a categorical judgement (e.g. 'has this sound got a "beat" in it?'), a comparative judgement is made – 'which sound has the clearer beat?' Using this mode of presentation, rise time sensitivity accounted for a significant 13 per cent of unique variance in a rhyme oddity task after controlling for age, verbal and non-verbal IQ and vocabulary, and for 8, 11 and 13 per cent of significant unique variance in reading, spelling and non-word reading respectively. The Richardson *et al.* (2004) study also found that sensitivity to durational differences in non-word syllables was equally predictive of these three outcome variables, accounting for 10, 8 and 12 per cent of the unique variance respectively. Interestingly, the key difference in this study between 'long' and 'short' syllables was the length of the intra-syllable silence gap, clearly indicating that rapid dynamic speech cues are not the only factor to consider. The stimulus scale is also based on that used by the Finnish JLD study to differentiate at-risk and non-risk groups (Richardson *et al.*, 2003), suggesting that perception of this cue is important for phonological representation across languages (see also Muneaux *et al.*, 2004).

These cross-sectional findings are highly promising. Additional studies that have examined the profile of adults with dyslexia highlight considerable developmental continuity in the relationships between syllable-level auditory processing and literacy, even in relatively compensated individuals studying at university (Pasquini *et al.*, 2007; Thomson *et al.*, 2006; see Chapter 1 in this volume). Both pedagogically and theoretically however, the most informative findings will come from the longitudinal studies now underway. The ultimate goal of any research into reading precursors must be to trace the development of a precursor skill from its earliest manifestation to the point of reading instruction and understand both its influence on other skills as well as how the skill itself can be influenced by both intrinsic (e.g. cognitive) and extrinsic (environmental) factors. By starting to understand this dynamic process, both researchers and educators will be in a better position to optimize the developmental process for children in whom it is compromised.

Where next?

The question asked at the beginning of this chapter was why children with dyslexia have a phonological deficit. A hypothesis put forward was that for at least a subgroup of this population, auditory perception was a limiting factor. A theoretical framework is put forward in which both initial and later phonological representation development are considered in the etiology of dyslexia, which means a greater consideration of syllabic processing than has hereto occurred. This in turn requires more sophisticated means of measuring syllable processing skills, going beyond the default syllable clapping test. More widely, there is a pressing need for theorists to consider more than one developmental time point when trying to model the phonological deficit in dyslexia.

This chapter ends with some recommendations for future research. Because we have established that a 'one-size-fits-all' solution will not provide all the answers, work focusing upon auditory processing should be carried out in the context of research exploring other factors that will affect phonological representation development such as attentional, memory and motor skills as well as quality and quantity of environmental input:

First, more work is needed to investigate individual variation in auditory processing ability. Having ascertained different auditory parameters associated with phonological processing at the syllable or phoneme level, it is necessary to look at individual trajectories – what are the reading profiles of children who show auditory perceptual weaknesses which may affect both syllable and segmental processing? How does this differ from those who have more specific auditory limitations? How time-sensitive are these relationships? Useful in this regard will be utilization of approaches such as dynamic systems modelling, which can represent associations between multiple variables at multiple stages of development (van Geert & Steenbeek, 2005).

Second, armed with knowledge concerning individual trajectories, we can explore the efficacy of training different auditory parameters and consequent effects on reading progress. Does auditory training improve either phonological processing or reading ability; should it be combined with more direct literacy instruction? Are there optimal ages for such pedagogy? Although some informative studies already exist that ask some of these questions (Agnew et al., 2004; Macaruso et al., 2006; Strehlow et al., 2006; Valentine et al., 2006), more systematic study is needed. Another possibility is that the subgroup of children found to have auditory perceptual weaknesses are the 2–6 per cent of children, described by Torgesen (2000), from the 16 per cent most at risk of reading failure, that remain poor readers despite concentrated exposure to such instruction. Clearly a key priority for future research is to understand how we can help this 'treatment resistant' group (Torgesen, 2000).

Third, it is important to consider children's native language within this research. Languages have different rhythms, which we know newborn infants are already sensitive to (Mehler et al., 1988; Nazzi et al., 1998). Diversity of rhythms may mean that different auditory parameters play greater or lesser roles in segmentation across languages. English, for example, has a predominant weak–strong syllable–stress rhythm pattern (Chomsky & Halle, 1991), which, as acknowledged in the work of Goswami and colleagues (2002), will make sensitivity to the abruptness of a syllable onset a advantage in syllable segmentation. In contrast, languages such as Finnish or Estonian (both Finno-Ugric languages) have less distinction between strong and weak syllables and other acoustic cues, such as durational differences, may have a greater role (Lehiste & Fox, 1992). This may result in particular sensitivity to certain auditory parameters, which then result in language–specific relationships between auditory perception and phonological processing. Preliminary work by Thomson et al. (2007) comparing English and Finnish-speaking individuals supports this hypothesis, and is being investigated further. This work will also have direct implications for understanding learner differences amongst populations learning to read in a language that is not their native tongue.

Note

1 Note that many of these causal theories are not mutually exclusive.

References

Agnew, J.A., Dorn, C., & Eden, G.F. (2004). 'Effect of intensive training on auditory processing and reading skills'. *Brain and Language, 88*, 21–25.

Allen, P., Wightman, F., Kistler, D., & Dolan, T. (1989). 'Frequency resolution in children'. *Journal of Speech & Hearing Research, 32*, 317–322.

Bailey, T.M. & Plunkett, K. (2002). 'Phonological specificity in early words'. *Cognitive Development, 17*, 1265–1282.

Bernstein, L.E. & Stark, R.E. (1985). 'Speech perception development in language-impaired children: a 4-year follow-up study'. *Journal of Speech & Hearing Disorders, 50*, 21–30.

Bishop, D.V.M. (1997). 'Cognitive neuropsychology and developmental disorders: uncomfortable bedfellows'. *Quarterly Journal of Experimental Psychology A: Human Experimental Psychology, 50*, 899–923.

Breen, K. & Warrington, E.K. (1995). 'Impaired naming and preserved reading: a complete dissociation'. *Cortex, 31*, 583–588.

Bretherton, L. & Holmes, V.M. (2003). 'The relationship between auditory temporal processing, phonemic awareness, and reading disability'. *Journal Experimental Child Psychology, 84*, 218–243.

Bruneau, N., Roux, S., Guerin, P., & Barthelemy, C. (1997). 'Temporal prominence of auditory evoked potentials (N1 wave) in 4–8-year-old children'. *Psychophysiology, 34*, 32–38.

Ceponiene, R., Rinne, T., & Naatanen, R. (2002). 'Maturation of cortical sound processing as indexed by event-related potentials'. *Clinical Neurophysiology, 113*, 870–882.

Chomsky, N. & Halle, M. (1991). *The sound pattern of English.* Cambridge, MA: MIT Press.

Coltheart, M., Rastle, K., Perry, C., Langdon, R., & Ziegler, J. (2001). 'DRC: a dual route cascaded model of visual word recognition and reading aloud'. *Psychological Review, 108*, 204–256.

Curtin, S., Mintz, T.H., & Christiansen, M.H. (2005). 'Stress changes the representational landscape: evidence from word segmentation'. *Cognition, 96*, 233–262.

De Martino, S., Espesser, R., Rey, V., & Habib, M. (2001). 'The "temporal processing deficit" hypothesis in dyslexia: new experimental evidence'. *Brain and Cognition, 46*, 104–108.

Drullman, R., Festen, J.M., & Plomp, R. (1994). 'Effect of temporal envelope smearing on speech reception'. *Journal of the Acoustical Society of America, 95*, 1053–1064.

Espy, K.A., Molfese, D.L., Molfese, V.J., & Modglin, A. (2004). 'Development of auditory event-related potentials in young children and relations to word-level reading abilities at age 8 years'. *Annals of Dyslexia, 54*, 9–38.

Fischer, B. & Hartnegg, K. (2004). 'On the development of low-level auditory discrimination and deficits in dyslexia'. *Dyslexia, 10*, 105–118.

Fraisse, P. (1963). *The psychology of time.* New York: Harper and Row.

Gilley, P.M., Sharma, A., Dorman, M., & Martin, K. (2005). 'Developmental changes in refractoriness of the cortical auditory evoked potential'. *Clinical Neurophysiology, 116*, 648–657.

Goswami, U., Thomson, J., Richardson, U., Stainthorp, R., Hughes, D., Rosen, S., *et al.* (2002). 'Amplitude envelope onsets and developmental dyslexia: a new hypothesis'. *Proceedings of the National Academy of Sciences of the United States of America 99*, 10911–10916.

Guttorm, T.K., Leppanen, P.H., Richardson, U., & Lyytinen, H. (2001). 'Event-related potentials and consonant differentiation in newborns with familial risk for dyslexia'. *Journal of Learning Disability, 34*, 534–544.

Heiervang, E., Stevenson, J., & Hugdahl, K. (2002). 'Auditory processing in children with dyslexia'. *Journal of Child Psychology and Psychiatry, 43*, 931–938.

Houtgast, T. & Steenken, H.J.M. (1985). 'A review of the MTF concept in room acoustics and its use for estimating speech intelligibility in auditoria'. *Journal of the Acoustical Society of America, 77*, 1069–1077.

Howell, P. & Rosen, S. (1983). 'Perception of rise time and explanations of the affricate/fricative contrast'. *Speech Communication, 2*, 164–166.

Jusczyk, P.W. & Thompson, E. (1978). 'Perception of a phonetic contrast in multisyllabic utterances by 2-month-old infants'. *Perception & Psychophysics, 23*, 105–109.

Jusczyk, P.W., Cutler, A., & Redanz, N. J. (1993). 'Infants' preference for the predominant stress patterns of English words'. *Child Development, 64*, 675–687.

Karmiloff-Smith, A. (2006). 'The tortuous route from genes to behavior: a neuroconstructivist approach'. *Cognitive, Affective & Behavioral Neuroscience, 6*, 9–17.

—— (2007). 'Atypical epigenesis'. *Developmental Science, 10*, 84–88.

Kuhl, P.K. (1987). 'Perception of speech and sound early in infancy'. In P. Salapatek & L. Cohen (eds), *Handbook of infant perception* (Vol. 2, pp. 275–382). 'New York: Academic Press'.

Kuhl, P.K., Williams, K.A., Lacerda, F., & Stevens, K.N. (1992). 'Linguistic experience alters phonetic perception in infants by 6 months of age'. *Science, 255*(5044), 606–608.

Lehiste, I. & Fox, R.A. (1992). 'Perception of prominence by Estonian and English listeners'. *Language and Speech, 35*, 419–434.

Locke, J.L. (1997). 'A theory of neurolinguistic development'. *Brain and Language, 58*, 265–326.

Lorenzi, C., Dumont, A., & Fullgrabe, C. (2000). 'Use of temporal envelope cues by children with developmental dyslexia'. *Journal of Speech, Language, and Hearing Research, 43*, 1367–1379.

Lyytinen, H., Ahonen, T., Eklund, K., Guttorm, T., Kulju, P., Laakso, M.L., *et al.* (2004a). 'Early development of children at familial risk for dyslexia: follow-up from birth to school age'. *Dyslexia, 10*, 146–178.

Lyytinen, H., Eklund, K., Erskine, J., Guttorm, T., Laakso, M.-L., Leppänen, P., *et al.* (2004b). 'Development of children at familial risk for dyslexia before school age'. *Enfance, 56*, 289–309.

Lyytinen, H., Guttorm, T.K., Huttunen, T., Hämäläinen, J., Leppänen, P.H.T., & Vesterinen, M. (2005). 'Psychophysiology of developmental dyslexia: a review of findings including studies of children at risk for dyslexia'. *Journal of Neurolinguistics, 18*, 167–195.

Macaruso, P., Hook, P.E., & McCabe, R. (2006). 'The efficacy of computer-based supplementary phonics programs for advancing reading skills in at-risk elementary students'. *Journal of Research in Reading, 29*, 162–172.

Marshall, C.M., Snowling, M.J., & Bailey, P.J. (2001). 'Rapid auditory processing and phonological ability in normal readers and readers with dyslexia'. *Journal of Speech, Language, and Hearing Research, 44*, 925–940.

Mehler, J. & Christophe, A. (1995). *Maturation and learning of language in the first year of life*. Cambridge, MA: MIT Press.

Mehler, J., Jusczyk, P., Lambertz, G., & Halsted, N. (1988). 'A precursor of language acquisition in young infants'. *Cognition, 29,* 143–178.

Mehler, J., Pallier, C., Christophe, A., Sabourin, M., Craik, F., & Robert, M. l. (1998). *Language and cognition.* Hove: Psychology Press/Erlbaum (UK) Taylor & Francis.

Metsala, J.L. & Walley, A.C. (1998). *Spoken vocabulary growth and the segmental restructuring of lexical representations: precursors to phonemic awareness and early reading ability.* Mahwah, NJ: LEA.

Mody, M., Studdert-Kennedy, M., & Brady, S. (1997). 'Speech perception deficits in poor readers: auditory processing or phonological coding?' *Journal of Experimental Child Psychology, 64*(2), 199–231'.

Molfese, D.L. (2000). 'Predicting dyslexia at 8 years of age using neonatal brain responses'. *Brain and Language, 72,* 238–245.

Molfese, D.L. & Molfese, V.J. (2000). 'The continuum of language development during infancy and early childhood: electrophysiological correlates'. In C. Rovee-Collier, L.P. Lewis, H. Hayne (eds), *Progress in infancy research: Vol. 1* (pp. 251–287). Mahwah, NJ: Lawrence Erlbaum.

Molfese, V.J. & Molfese, D.L. (2002). 'Environmental and social influences on reading skills as indexed by brain and behavioral responses'. *Annals of Dyslexia, 52,* 121–137.

Molfese, V.J., Molfese, D.L., & Modglin, A.A. (2001). 'Newborn and preschool predictors of second-grade reading scores: an evaluation of categorical and continuous scores'. *Journal of Learning Disabilities, 34*(6), 545–554.

Molfese, D.L., Molfese, V.J., Key, S., Modglin, A., Kelley, S., & Terrell, S. (2002). 'Reading and cognitive abilities: longitudinal studies of brain and behavior changes in young children'. *Annals of Dyslexia, 52,* 99–119.

Morgan, J.L. & Saffran, J.R. (1995). 'Emerging integration of sequential and suprasegmental information in preverbal speech segmentation'. *Child Development, 66,* 911–936.

Muneaux, M., Ziegler, J.C., Truc, C., Thomson, J., & Goswami, U. (2004). 'Deficits in beat perception and dyslexia: evidence from French'. *Neuroreport: For Rapid Communication of Neuroscience Research, 15,* 1255–1259.

Nazzi, T., Bertoncini, J., & Mehler, J. (1998). 'Language discrimination by newborns: toward an understanding of the role of rhythm'. *Journal of Experimental Psychology: Human Perception and Performance, 24,* 756–766.

Nicolson, R.I., Fawcett, A.J., & Dean, P. (1995). 'Time estimation deficits in developmental dyslexia: evidence of cerebellar involvement'. *Proceedings. Biological Sciences, 259*(1354), 43–47.

Nittrouer, S. (1999). 'Do temporal processing deficits cause phonological processing problems?' *Journal of Speech, Language, and Hearing Research, 42,* 925–942.

Nittrouer, S. & Miller, M.E. (1997). 'Predicting developmental shifts in perceptual weighting schemes'. *Journal of the Acoustical Society of America, 101,* 2253–2266.

Orton, S.T. (1937). *Reading, writing and speech problems in children.* New York: W.W. Norton.

Pasquini, E.S., Corriveau, K.H., & Goswami, U. (2007). 'Auditory processing of amplitude envelope rise time in adults diagnosed with developmental dyslexia'. *Scientific Studies of Reading, 11,* 259–286.

Perfetti, C.A., Beck, I., Bell, L.C., & Hughes, C. (1987). 'Phonemic knowledge and learning to read are reciprocal: a longitudinal study of first grade children'. *Merrill-Palmer Quarterly, 33,* 283–319.

Ramus, F. (2003). 'Developmental dyslexia: specific phonological deficit or general sensorimotor dysfunction? *Current Opinion in Neurobiology, 13,* 212–218'.

Reed, M.A. (1989). 'Speech perception and the discrimination of brief auditory cues in reading disabled children'. *Journal of Experimental Child Psychology, 48,* 270–292.

Rey, V., De Martino, S., Espesser, R., & Habib, M. (2002). 'Temporal processing and phonological impairment in dyslexia: effect of phoneme lengthening on order judgment of two consonants'. *Brain and Language, 80*, 576–591.

Richardson, U., Leppänen, P.H.T., Leiwo, M., & Lyytinen, H. (2003). 'Speech perception of infants with high familial risk for dyslexia differ at the age of 6 months'. *Developmental Neuropsychology, 23*, 385–397.

Richardson, U., Thomson, J.M., Scott, S.K., & Goswami, U. (2004). 'Auditory processing skills and phonological representation in dyslexic children'. *Dyslexia, 10*, 215–233.

Rocheron, I., Lorenzi, C., Füllgrabe, C., & Dumont, A. (2002). 'Temporal envelope perception in dyslexic children'. *Neuroreport, 13*, 1683–1687.

Rosen, S. (1992). 'Temporal information in speech: acoustic, auditory and linguistic aspects'. *Philosophical transactions of the Royal Society of London. Series B, Biological Sciences, 336*(1278), 367–373.

—— (2003). 'Auditory processing in dyslexia and specific language impairment: Is there a deficit? What is its nature? Does it explain anything? *Journal of Phonetics, 31*, 509–527'.

Rosen, S. & Manganari, E. (2001). 'Is there a relationship between speech and nonspeech auditory processing in children with dyslexia?' *Journal of Speech, Language, and Hearing Research, 44*, 720–736'.

Saffran, J.R. (2003). 'Statistical language learning: mechanisms and constraints'. *Current Directions in Psychological Science, 12*, 110–114.

Saffran, J.R., Aslin, R.N., & Newport, E.L. (1996). 'Statistical learning by 8-month-old infants'. *Science, 274*(5294), 1926–1928.

Scott, S.K. (1998). 'The point of P-centres'. *Psychological Research/Psychologische Forschung, 61*, 4–11.

Serniclaes, W., Sprenger-Charolles, L., Carré, R., & Demonet, J.F. (2001). 'Perceptual discrimination of speech sounds in developmental dyslexia'. *Journal of Speech, Language, and Hearing Research, 44*(2), 384–399.

Shannon, R.V., Zeng, F.G., Kamath, V., & Wygonski, J. (1995). 'Speech recognition with primarily temporal cues'. *Science, 270*(5234), 303–304.

Share, D.L., Jorm, A.F., Maclean, R., & Matthews, R. (2002). 'Temporal processing and reading disability'. *Reading and Writing, 15*, 151–178.

Snowling, M.J. (2000). *Dyslexia* (2nd edn). 'Boston, MA: Blackwell'.

Stager, C.L. & Werker, J.F. (1997). 'Infants listen for more phonetic detail in speech perception than in word-learning tasks'. *Nature, 388*(6640), 381–382.

Stein, J. & Talcott, J. (1999). 'Impaired neuronal timing in developmental dyslexia: the magnocelluar hypothesis'. *Dyslexia, 5*, 59–77.

Strehlow, U., Haffner, J., Bischof, J.R., Gratzka, V., Parzer, P., & Resch, F. (2006). 'Does successful training of temporal processing of sound and phoneme stimuli improve reading and spelling?' *European Child & Adolescent Psychiatry, 15*, 19–29.

Swingley, D. & Aslin, R.N. (2000). 'Spoken word recognition and lexical representation in very young children'. *Cognition, 76*, 147–166.

Swingley, D. & Aslin, R.N. (2002). 'Lexical neighborhoods and the word-form representations of 14-month-olds'. *Psychological Science, 13*, 480–484.

Tallal, P. (1980). 'Auditory temporal perception, phonics, and reading disabilities in children'. *Brain and Language, 9*, 182–198.

—— (2004). 'Improving language and literacy is a matter of time'. *Nature Reviews. Neuroscience, 5*(9), 721–728.

Tallal, P. & Piercy, M. (1973). 'Defects of non-verbal auditory perception in children with developmental aphasia'. *Nature, 241*, 468–469.

Tallal, P. & Piercy, M. (1974). 'Developmental aphasia: rate of auditory processing and selective impairment of consonant perception'. *Neuropsychologia, 12*, 83–93.

Tallal, P., Stark, R., Kallman, C., & Mellits, D. (1981). 'A reexamination of some non-verbal perceptual abilities of language-impaired and normal children as a function of age and sensory modality'. *Journal of Speech & Hearing Research, 24,* 351–357.

Thomson, J.M., Fryer, B., Maltby, J., & Goswami, U. (2006). 'Auditory and motor rhythm awareness in adults with dyslexia'. *Journal of Research in Reading, 29*(3), 334–348.

Thomson, J.M., Hämäläinen, J., Richardson, U., & Goswami, U. (2007). 'Beat processing in developmental dyslexia: comparing a stress-timed and syllable-timed language'. Paper presented at the Speech Prosody in Atypical Populations.

Torgesen, J.K. (2000). 'Individual differences in response to early interventions in reading: the lingering problem of treatment resisters'. *Learning Disabilities Research & Practice, 15,* 55–64.

Valentine, D., Hedrick, M.S., & Swanson, L.A. (2006). 'Effect of an auditory training program on reading, phoneme awareness, and language'. *Perceptual & Motor Skills, 103,* 183–196.

van Geert, P. & Steenbeek, H. (2005). 'Explaining after by before: basic aspects of a dynamic systems approach to the study of development'. *Developmental Review, 25,* 408–442.

Waber, D.P., Weiler, M.D., Wolff, P.H., Bellinger, D., Marcus, D.J., Ariel, R., *et al.* (2001). 'Processing of rapid auditory stimuli in school-age children referred for evaluation of learning disorders'. *Child Development, 72,* 37–49.

Walley, A.C. (1993). 'The role of vocabulary development in children's spoken word recognition and segmentation ability'. *Developmental Review, 13,* 286–350.

Werker, J.F., Fennell, C.T., Corcoran, K.M., & Stager, C.L. (2002). 'Infants' ability to learn phonetically similar words: effects of age and vocabulary size'. *Infancy, 3,* 1–30.

Wightman, F., Allen, P., Dolan, T., & Kistler, D. (1989). 'Temporal resolution in children. *Child Development, 60,* 611–624.

Chapter 3

Acquiring complex reading skills

An exploration of disyllabic reading

Lynne G. Duncan

The recent burgeoning of cross-linguistic research in the field of reading and spelling development has exposed how central the English language has been to theorizing about literacy acquisition. Early work by Heinz Wimmer, in particular, brought this to the forefront of discussion with his documentation of differences in the expression of developmental dyslexia in German compared to English (Wimmer & Hummer, 1990; Wimmer, 1993). A process of change initiated by this work has led to more flexible models of reading development in which the concept of orthographic depth (Frost *et al.*, 1987) and related linguistic differences now shape the formulation of the acquisition process (e.g. Ziegler & Goswami, 2005).

As horizons have broadened, one further consequence of a research literature deeply rooted in the English language is the customary restriction of interest to the case of monosyllabic words. The connectionist models which appeared in the 1990s are typical but certainly not isolated examples of this (Seidenberg & McClelland, 1989; Plaut *et al.*, 1996; Harm & Seidenberg, 1999). Traditionally, syllabic or morphemic units, the components of polysyllabic words, featured only in later or higher level phases of developmental models, for example, Frith's (1985) *orthographic* stage or Ehri's (1992) *consolidated* phase. Whilst this line of research has been productive for English, which contains an unusually high proportion of monosyllables (approximately 12 per cent of the English words in the CELEX database are monosyllables), many languages contain few monosyllables and beginning readers encounter mostly polysyllabic words. Even within English early reading texts, the number of polysyllabic words is not negligible (see Table 3.1). This raises the issue of how young children learn to read polysyllabic words.

In the case of monosyllables, there is a longstanding expectation that the lexicon is organized in terms of onset-rime segments which define families or neighbourhoods of rhyming words (Glushko, 1979). One advantage of this organization in English is that the rime unit offers a level of orthographic consistency, which leads to more accurate pronunciation of words than correspondences based on vowel or 'initial consonant plus vowel' segments (Treiman *et al.*, 1995). Accordingly, both dual-route (Patterson & Morton, 1985) and connectionist models of word recognition (Seidenberg & McClelland, 1989) have made reference to this onset-rime level of structure.

One view is that rhyming skills promote an organization in the orthographic lexicon based on the rime unit (Goswami & Bryant, 1990; Goswami, 1993). According to Goswami (1993) 'orthographic analysis is founded in phonological skills' with rhyming skill playing an early and formative role. Recently, Duncan *et al.* (2007)

examined how this view might adapt to the polysyllabic domain by investigating children's conception of rhyme for disyllabic stimuli. Children were asked to play a game in which they produced a rhyme for target monosyllables and then subsequently for disyllables. When the disyllabic stimuli had initial stress, the data showed a strong commitment to a phonological structure composed of an onset plus a unit termed the *superrime*. This is a higher order unit introduced by Berg (1989), which, together with the onset, heads the internal structure of initial-stress disyllables (see Figure 3.1). The superrime itself can be split into a rime unit and a following syllable which retains its internal onset-rime structure.

Awareness of monosyllabic rhyme has been thought to lead to the use of orthographic rime analogies in reading (Goswami & Bryant, 1990; Goswami, 1993). If this link between rhyme and reading holds for disyllabic words, the results of Duncan *et al.* (2007) suggest that orthographic analogies may not always involve the rime unit. For example, it is the superrime, and not the rime unit, which appears to be the source of rhyming similarity for disyllabic words with initial stress. This suggests that if children derive the common spelling patterns from rhyming categories of disyllabic words, it is orthographic units at the level of the superrime which should be represented. Supportive evidence comes from Goswami *et al.* (1998), who investigated analogy use when reading monosyllabic and disyllabic nonwords. Orthographically familiar nonwords shared either a rime (monosyllables) or a superrime (disyllables) with a real word (e.g. cake → dake; comic → bomic). The orthography of these nonwords was then altered to produce structures which maintained the original phonological pattern but were orthographically unfamiliar (e.g. daik; bommick). Goswami *et al.* found speed and accuracy advantages for the orthographically familiar nonwords amongst children with reading ages of 7 years and above. Goswami *et al.* (1997) replicated this finding and extended it to trisyllabic stimuli constructed in a similar manner (e.g. daffodil → taffodil, tafoddyl).

Table 3.1 Occurrence of words of different syllable lengths in reception year texts in the children's printed word database (Stuart *et al.* 2003)

Number of Syllables in Word	Total Number of Words across Reception Reading Schemes	% of Total Words in Reception Reading Schemes
1	672	62.5%
2	341	31.7%
3	55	5.1%
4	5	<0.5%
5	2	<0.5%

Note: Individual reading schemes vary in the proportion of polysyllabic words included at the Reception level.

Experiment 1: orthographic and phonological familiarity in nonword reading[1]

To explore the correspondence between our earlier phonological findings on disyllabic rhyme (Duncan *et al.*, 2007) and the orthographic units used to read disyllables, we based our first experiment on the studies conducted by Goswami and colleagues. We extended the original design to include a manipulation of stress pattern as an adjunct to the main investigation of the effects of orthographic and phonological familiarity. On the basis of Goswami *et al.*'s (1997, 1998) findings, facilitation ought to occur for orthographic familiarity based on the rime unit with monosyllabic stimuli and the superrime with disyllabic stimuli. However, if such orthographic effects are linked to rhyming skills, the results of Duncan *et al.* (2007) suggest that this principle will work well for initial stress words but less well for final stress items, since these latter items do not map preferentially onto an onset plus superrime structure but instead onto a poorly defined or ambiguous structure. Therefore, the expectation is that facilitation should be greater for initial stress than final stress disyllables if familiarity is based on the superrime.

Another motivation for this replication is to investigate whether the original orthographic familiarity effect might have been mediated by differences in ortho- graphic *regularity* between the O+P+ and O–P+ conditions, as items in the former condition tended to contain more familiar graphemes making them more amenable to small-unit decoding than items in the O–P+ condition (cf. 'bicket' vs 'bikket'). Goswami *et al.* (1998) addressed this question by calculating mean positional bigram frequencies for each condition. Although no statistical differences were reported between the O+P+ and O+P– nonword conditions, mean bigram frequency appeared far better matched for the monosyllables than for the disyllables as the mean figure for the O+P+ disyllables was almost twice that of the O–P+ disyllables (1,280 vs. 667). An analysis of covariance to control for the effect of bigram frequency would have eliminated the concern that the large-unit effect of orthographic familiarity was actually being mediated by small-unit processing. This analysis will be conducted on the data from the present study to examine this possibility.

Method

It will be possible to draw a direct link between the present study of reading and this earlier investigation because the 22 participants were the Primary 2 group from Duncan *et al.*'s (2007) Experiment 1.[2] The participants had progressed to Primary 3 and now had a mean chronological age of 7 years 4 months (SD = 4 months). The mean British Ability Scales Word Reading Age for the group was 8 years 9 months (SD = 1 year 2 months). It had been established previously that these children had normal receptive vocabulary skills (Duncan *et al.*, 2007).

The study was based on lists prepared by Goswami *et al.* (1998) for their study of analogy use. The original sets of monosyllables and initial stress disyllables were used with some minor alterations to cater for Scottish accents. A further condition was added containing disyllables with final stress (see Appendix 3.A) to test the link with disyllabic rhyming skills. Lists of words were compiled first of all and then nonword stimuli were constructed to be either (a) orthographically and phonologically similar (O+P+) to their real-word analogues (e.g. dake, bicket, biraffe); or (b) ortho- graphically dissimilar but phonologically similar (O–P+) to the real words (e.g. daik, bikket, biraf). The real words were matched across monosyllabic and disyllabic con- ditions on word frequency ($F < 1$; Carroll *et al.*, 1971) and on mean positional bigram frequency ($F < 1$; Solso & Juel, 1980). Mean positional bigram frequencies were also calculated between nonword categories. Analyses of variance showed that bigram frequency was well matched for nonword type (monosyllables, initial stress disyllables, final stress disyllables), $F < 1$, but less well matched for orthographic similarity (O+P+, O–P+) where the effect was marginal, $F(1, 34) = 3.85$, $p = .058$).

Participants were tested individually. The experiment was run using Cognitive Workshop software (Version 1.6). The stimuli were displayed at the centre of a 12″ LCD computer screen in a white, lower-case font against a black background. After a 500 msec. warning (#####) followed by a 500 msec. delay, a stimulus was presented on the screen for up to 10 sec. The participants were instructed to read the target as quickly and accurately as possible. Reaction times were gathered via the computer software and responses were transcribed by the experimenter to be checked later using a tape recording of the session. The stimuli were presented in three blocks (monosyllables, initial stress disyllables, final stress disyllables), each on a separate occasion. The order of these blocks was randomized across participants. Within each block, the order of the O+P+ and O–P+ nonwords was counterbalanced and the real-word analogues were always presented last in the sequence.

Results

Words: the mean accuracy scores and reaction times are shown in Table 3.2. A repeated measures analysis of variance for word accuracy tested the effect of word type (monosyllable, initial stress disyllable, final stress disyllable), $F1(2, 42) = 7.61$, $p < .01$; $F2(2, 14) = 5.63$, $p < .05$. Word frequency was entered as a covariate in the analysis by items. Newman–Keuls tests indicated that monosyllables and initial stress disyllables were read with similar accuracy but the error rate increased significantly with final stress disyllables.

Missing data due to reading errors and premature triggering of the voice key excluded seven participants from the reaction time analysis with the result that the

Table 3.2 Mean accuracy for word and nonword reading in experiment 1 (Standard Deviations in Parentheses)

	Word Analogues	*Nonwords*	
		O+P+	*O-P+*
Monosyllables	75.00(29.00)	65.17(27.17)	56.00(32.00)
Initial Stress Disyllables	83.33(29.17)	59.17(29.00)	43.17(29.00)
Final Stress Disyllables	62.17(34.50)	38.67(33.17)	31.83(31.17)
Reaction Time (msecs)[#]			
Monosyllables	1084.20 (376.49)	1548.07 (916.09)	1541.27 (715.60)
Initial Stress Bisyllables	1094.27 (343.07)	1751.73(1064.72)	2080.93(1223.70)
Final Stress Bisyllables	1263.40 (343.38)	1721.07 (766.83)	2274.43(1271.00)

[#] N=15

remaining data came from the more advanced readers in the sample. A repeated measures analysis of variance found no significant effect of Word Type on reaction time, $F1(2, 28) = 2.60$, $p > .05$; $F2 (2, 14) = 2.29$, $p > .05$.

Nonwords: nonword naming accuracy was investigated in an analysis of variance with repeated measures on nonword type (monosyllables, initial stress disyllables, final stress disyllables) and orthographic familiarity (O+P+, O–P+). Bigram frequency was entered as a covariate in the analysis by items. Nonword type was significant across participants and items, $F1(2, 42) = 14.36$, $p < .001$; $F2(2, 29) = 6.97$, $p < .01$, and Newman–Keuls tests confirmed that this was due to the greater difficulty of final stress disyllables compared to the other stimuli. The effect of orthographic familiarity (O+P+, O–P+) was significant by participants only, $F1(1, 21) = 15.62$, $p < .01$; $F2(1, 29) = 3.12$, $p > .05$, and did not interact with nonword type, $F1(2, 42) = 1.34$, $p > .05$; $F2 < 1$.

An analysis of variance of the reaction time data revealed that the effect of nonword type was marginal by participants but significant by items, $F1(2, 26) = 3.21$, $p = .057$; $F2(2, 29) = 4.55$, $p < .05$. Newman–Keuls tests showed that monosyllabic nonwords were read faster than either type of disyllabic nonword. The effect of orthographic familiarity was only significant by participants, $F1(1, 13) = 8.07$, $p < .05$; $F2(1, 29) = 2.11$, $p > .05$. The interaction of these factors was not significant $F1 (2, 26) = 2.65$, $p > .05$; $F2(2, 29) = 1.56$, $p > .05$.

Therefore, when bigram frequency was entered as a covariate in the analyses-by-item of the accuracy and reaction time data, the effect of orthographic familiarity failed to attain significance.

Discussion

The participants' accuracy at reading the real words was equivalent for monosyllables and initial stress disyllables (> 75 per cent correct). However, the additional set of final stress disyllables was found to be significantly more difficult in spite of the controls for word and bigram frequency. The pattern of greater difficulty for final stress items was repeated in the nonword reading data, again in spite of controls for bigram frequency. The reaction time data did not show any specific time penalty for reading final stress disyllables other than that associated with disyllabic length: monosyllables were read faster than disyllables for both word and nonword stimuli. This length effect is consistent with the use of a smaller-unit decoding strategy.

The orthographic familiarity of rime and superrime units was also observed to influence reading as O+P+ nonwords tended to be read more accurately than O–P+ nonwords. No statistical evidence emerged to indicate that this effect was weaker with final stress items although the means tended in this direction. Goswami *et al.* (1998) reported somewhat larger familiarity effects amongst a group of 7-year-olds. Their procedure of intermixing the sets of word analogues and nonword stimuli may be responsible for the size of the effect due to the combined influence of phonological priming and orthographic congruence (Savage & Stuart, 1998).

It is important to note, however, that the orthographic familiarity effects that were detectable across the monosyllabic and disyllabic stimuli in the present study were always restricted to the analysis by participants. One interpretation of this is that the advantage for orthographically familiar items may have been mediated by differences in bigram frequency as the analysis-by-items covaried out this factor. Such an interpretation would be more consistent with the use of small-unit rather than large-unit strategies in decoding and would suggest that the studies by Goswami *et al.* (1997, 1998) may have overestimated the effects of large-unit orthographic familiarity by not controlling statistically for bigram frequency.

Experiment 2: superrime frequency in nonword reading[3]

A second experiment was conducted to further examine the size of the units used in decoding. The literature on monosyllabic reading has produced evidence that children are sensitive to rime frequency in word and nonword reading (Treiman *et al.*, 1990; Laxon *et al.*, 1991; Bowey & Hansen, 1994; Leslie & Calhoon, 1995; Bowey & Underwood, 1996; Duncan *et al.*, 2000). For example, Treiman *et al.* (1990) demonstrated that first and third graders read nonwords containing a high frequency rime unit (e.g. tain) more accurately than nonwords containing a low frequency rime (e.g. goan) even though grapheme-phoneme correspondences were carefully matched between conditions.

In Experiment 1, the by-participants analysis suggested that disyllabic nonwords were processed using the onset plus superrime structure since nonwords were easier to read when they contained a familiar rather than an unfamiliar superrime structure. This leads to the prediction that superrimes which are high in frequency should confer a similar advantage over low frequency structures to that shown by the high frequency *rimes* in Treiman *et al.*'s (1990) study.

Nevertheless, one concern about this prediction is that orthographic familiarity and bigram frequency may have been confounded in Experiment 1. This problem arose because our objective had been to replicate the work of Goswami *et al.* (1998), whose method of constructing the O–P+ nonwords produced stimuli which were orthographically dissimilar to the word analogues but did not exclude orthographically strange items (e.g. 'hacksi', 'loffi') with zero frequency superrimes. As the effect of orthographic familiarity did not achieve significance in the by-items analysis which controlled for bigram frequency, it is possible that small-unit decoding strategies may have been mediating the effect in the by-participants analysis. In Experiment 2, our nonword stimuli are selected to respect orthographic conventions in an attempt to produce a closer match in bigram frequency and high frequency superrimes were compared with low but not zero frequency items.

One further caveat to the prediction that frequency effects should emerge for orthographic superrimes is that an analysis of superrime phonological density neighbourhoods by Duncan *et al.* (2007) established that neighbourhoods were sparse for final stress words especially in children's vocabularies. Thus, it will only be possible to manipulate superrime frequency for initial stress disyllables raising the possibility that any benefits from familiar superrimes in disyllabic word recognition may be largely restricted to initial stress items.

Method

The participants were Scottish and were selected randomly from Primary 3 (n = 12) and Primary 4 (n = 12) classes with mean chronological ages of 7 years 6 months

(SD = 5 months) and 8 years 6 months (SD = 5 months), respectively. The mean British Ability Scales Word Reading Age for each group was 9 years 1 month (SD = 1 month) and 10 years 7 months (SD = 2 months) and their mean standardized British Picture Vocabulary Scale scores were 104 (SD = 15) and 108 (SD = 12), respectively.

Nonwords with high or low frequency superrimes were constructed by substituting the onsets of initial stress disyllabic words with a large or small number of orthographic superrime neighbours (see Appendix 3.B). There were 10 stimuli in each condition. The number of superrime neighbours was established by searching the CELEX database and verifying that these words also occurred in the children's word frequency book (Carroll *et al.*, 1971). On average, the superrimes in the high frequency nonwords occurred in 8 words and those in the low frequency nonwords occurred in only 1 word. Mean positional bigram frequencies (Solso & Juel, 1980) were matched between nonword categories, $F(1, 16) = 1.52$, $p > .05$.

Participants were tested individually using the same experimental procedure and computer setup as described in Experiment 1. All of the stimuli were presented in a single session with the order of presentation randomized by the computer software.

Results and discussion

The mean accuracy scores and reaction times are shown in Table 3.3. A mixed analysis of variance conducted on the accuracy scores indicated that the main effect of group (Primary 3, Primary 4) was only significant by-items, $F1(1, 22) = 1.62$, $p > .05$; $F2(1, 16) = 10.54$, $p < .01$. The Primary 3 group was significantly less accurate than the Primary 4 group. There were no significant effects of either superrime frequency, $F1(1, 22) = 2.23$, $p > .05$; $F2 < 1$, or of the interaction between group and superrime frequency, $F1$, $F2 < 1$.

A mixed analysis of variance of the reaction time data also showed a main effect of group restricted to the analysis by-items $F1 < 1$; $F2(1, 16) = 11.04$, $p < .01$. The Primary 3 group was significantly slower than the Primary 4 group. All of the other effects showed $F < 1$ by participants and by items.

Accuracy and speed at reading the nonwords tended to improve with age. However, there was no significant effect of superrime frequency on reading accuracy or reaction time at either age level. This suggests that the presence of a superrime with a high orthographic frequency confers little advantage on nonword reading amongst these age groups.

Table 3.3 Mean accuracy for nonword reading in experiment 2 (Standard Deviations in Parentheses)

Participant Group	Orthographic Superrime Frequency			
	High		Low	
	Accuracy(%)	RT(msecs.)	Accuracy(%)	RT(msecs.)
Primary 3	83.33(23.00)	2127(1599)	80.56(17.11)	2071(1613)
Primary 4	93.56(16.78)	1746(1384)	88.00(15.33)	1776(1059)

General discussion

A case has been made for a direct link between early rhyming skills and the representation of orthographic rime units within monosyllables (Goswami & Bryant, 1990; Goswami, 1993). The aim of the present study was to examine how well this line of reasoning might extend to longer and more complex words. Building on an investigation of rhyming with disyllabic stimuli by Duncan *et al.* (2007) in which the phonological superrime (e.g. 'umble' in 'tumble') emerged as the mediator of rhyme for initial stress disyllables, it seemed reasonable to expect that the superrime might be an important orthographic unit in disyllabic word recognition. This prediction is consistent with previous experimental results reported by Goswami and colleagues (Goswami *et al.*, 1997, 1998). These authors observed that disyllabic nonwords (e.g. 'bicket'), which shared a superrime with real (initial stress) words (e.g. 'ticket'), were read faster and more accurately than matched sets of nonwords that had a phonologically similar but orthographically dissimilar structure (e.g. 'bikket').

Experiment 1 was an attempt to replicate this finding and to extend the design of the original investigation to manipulate stress pattern by including an additional set of disyllabic nonwords constructed from the superrimes of *final stress* words (e.g. 'balloon': 'ralloon', 'riloon'). This new category of stimuli might not be expected to respond so well to superrime familiarity since Duncan *et al.* (2007) showed that rhyme for final stress disyllabic words was more variable and was associated with several different subunits: the superrime, the final syllable *and* the final rime unit. By extension, this might be thought to promote phonological representation of the orthography at all of these levels, diminishing the importance of the superrime for these stimuli.

The outcome revealed that a group of Primary 3 children did indeed read nonwords which shared superrimes with real disyllabic words more accurately than homophonic nonwords with an orthographically dissimilar structure. As these children had taken part in Duncan *et al.*'s (2007) study, it was expected that the salience of superrimes might be weaker in final stress disyllables but this prediction was not supported. Instead the results of the analysis by participants for all of the stimuli were consistent with Goswami *et al.*'s (1998) report of an orthographic familiarity effect. Nevertheless, the outcome of the analysis *by items* cast doubt on the basis of this 'orthographic familiarity' effect. The concern was that the O+P+ nonwords in the experiments of Goswami *et al.* (1997, 1998), which share a superrime with a real word (e.g. 'bicket'), were also more orthographically regular than the O–P+ nonwords (e.g. 'bikket'). Indeed, when mean positional bigram frequency was controlled by entering this as a covariate in the by-items analysis, the effect of orthographic familiarity disappeared. This made it a priority in the second experiment to balance bigram frequency more carefully.

Superrime frequency was manipulated directly in Experiment 2 to establish whether this factor would exert a similar facilitative effect to the influence of rime frequency on children's monosyllabic decoding (e.g. Treiman *et al.*, 1990). However, these investigations did not reveal any evidence that the superrime was a salient orthographic unit for the 7- and 8-year-old participants tested. Nonwords containing a high frequency superrime were read with equivalent speed and accuracy as those containing a low frequency superrime.

Recognition units in disyllabic reading

There may be a number of reasons why we have failed to uncover strong evidence of superrime effects in disyllabic reading. Bowey and Underwood (1996), for example, showed that sensitivity to rime frequency in monosyllables was related to vocabulary size and, as a result, requires time to develop (see also Duncan *et al.*, 2000). Sets of disyllabic words sharing a superrime are likely to occur with lower frequency than sets of rhyming monosyllables given the inverse relationship between length and frequency in the English language. Thus, superrime frequency effects may develop later than rime frequency effects and be present amongst children older than 7 or 8 years. In fact, the experiments of Goswami *et al.* (1997, 1998) contained additional groups of 9-year-old and adult readers, whose more extensive reading experience may have enhanced the overall orthographic familiarity effect.

Nevertheless, an alternative explanation for the dependence of the orthographic familiarity effect on bigram frequency is that the children were relying on the use of smaller-unit decoding strategies. This would suggest that disyllabic reading is not primarily dependent on phonological rhyming skill in the early phases of reading development. Indeed, comparison of the analyses of phonological neighbourhood density published for monosyllables (De Cara & Goswami, 2002) and for disyllables (Duncan *et al.*, 2007), indicates that superrime neighbourhoods are generally sparser than rime neighbourhoods. Moreover, the rhyming structure of initial and final stress disyllables appears fundamentally different: the underlying phonological structure of initial stress items centres around the superrime but the structure of final stress items appears much more variable involving the final syllable and rime unit as well (Berg, 1989; Duncan *et al.*, 2007). Together these factors may make the emergence of an orthographic structure related to rhyme less likely for polysyllabic than for monosyllabic words.

Furthermore, there is an additional advantage of an orthographic organization related to rhyme in monosyllabic reading due to the greater pronunciation accuracy that results from the level of regularity associated with the orthographic rime unit (Treiman *et al.*, 1995). Thus, rather than phonological skills being the driving force behind the organization of the orthographic lexicon, it may be that the salience of the rime unit in reading monosyllables is due in large part to the nature of the English orthography (Treiman *et al.*, 1995; Brown & Deavers, 1999; Duncan *et al.*, 2000). Consistent with this possibility, monosyllabic rime effects have been simulated in several connectionist models by treating such patterns as *emergent* features of coding across smaller level representations (Plaut *et al.*, 1996; Zorzi *et al.*, 1998).

Studies of English and other orthographies which vary in transparency and consistency are needed to establish whether superrimes, syllables or rimes confer any such beneficial effects on the decoding of polysyllabic words. A preliminary investigation of this issue in English by Treiman *et al.* (1995) showed that the addition of polysyllabic words to their monosyllable analysis did not alter their results greatly in that the final rime unit was still associated with more stability in pronunciation than the initial CV structure. This outcome is consistent with Treiman's (1992) suggestion that polysyllabic words are divisible first into their constituent syllables and then into onsets and rimes within each syllable as depicted in Figure 3.2 (cf. Berg's (1989) view of word structure in Figure 3.1), and this manner of representing word

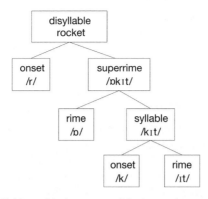

Figure 3.1. Berg's (1989) hierarchical account of the internal structure of a disyllabic word

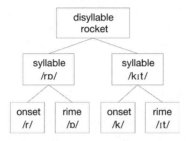

Figure 3.2. Treiman's (1992) hierarchical account of the internal structure of a disyllabic word

structure has been adopted in one of the few connectionist models to have tackled polysyllabic reading (Ans *et al.*, 1998). However, other investigations of naming polysyllabic words have argued against the use of syllabified representations in the pronunciation of English words (Jared & Seidenberg, 1990; Chateau & Jared, 2003), and evidence has been provided instead which indicates that the final vowel and a unit called the body-of-the-BOSS (i.e. 'ead' in 'meadow') offer more reliable orthographic clues to pronunciation (Chateau & Jared, 2003).

As Ziegler and Goswami (2005) observe, the availability of awareness of particular sounds and the consistency of the orthography that is being acquired both seem to interact with the size of the recognition units which emerge in reading. However, the tension between these factors remains to be resolved. Goswami *et al.* (1997, 1998) have suggested that awareness at the level of the rhyme may be especially important for resolving inconsistency in polysyllabic reading in English, but may have a lesser impact in more transparent languages like French and Spanish. Nevertheless, the present results together with those of Duncan *et al.* (2007) do not support a strong link between phonological rhyme and the recognition units used in disyllabic reading in English, at least amongst 7- and 8-year-olds. Whereas the rime unit is beneficial in achieving pronunciation accuracy with respect to the development of monosyllabic reading (Brown & Deavers, 1999; Duncan *et al.*, 2000), it is not clear that the superrime adequately resolves this issue for disyllables. The important thing will be to identify the features that create pronunciation difficulty in polysyllabic reading and to explore whether the adoption of a grain-size appropriate for pronunciation accuracy is driven by phonological or orthographic factors (or a combination of the two). The next section considers how lexical stress is assigned in reading polysyllabic words in English and how early reading skills may adapt to cope with this complexity.

Stress assignment in disyllabic reading

The fact that each English polysyllable has an individual pattern of lexical stress which is essential for its correct identification creates a difficulty that does not arise in monosyllabic reading. The present study demonstrated that lexical stress affected performance in disyllabic reading by reducing accuracy without any time penalty for responses to items with *final* syllable stress. The presence of an effect on accuracy but not on latency has also been described in relation to stress typicality in skilled naming and lexical decision (Kelly *et al.*, 1998; Rastle & Coltheart, 2000; Arciuli & Cupples, 2006). As these effects have been observed in lexical decision as well as in naming tasks, stress appears likely to exert an early effect before the phonological output phase. Ashby and Martin (2008) suggested that skilled readers may activate spoken language representations very early in word recognition which, from what is known of speech production, may mean that suprasegmental information including lexical stress is being activated separately from segmental information (see Wood *et al.*, Chapter 1 in this volume, for a discussion).

Further research is needed to investigate this hypothesis and to establish how mappings between orthography and suprasegmental information may become established during reading acquisition. As Cutler (1989) has noted, disruptions to metrical prosody which result in a full vowel becoming reduced or a reduced vowel becoming full may inhibit lexical access (Cutler & Clifton, 1984). This has been confirmed experimentally with children in the early stages of schooling and sensitivity to stress is linked to phonological awareness and to progress in reading and spelling (Wood & Terrell, 1998; Wood, 2006; Wood *et al.*, Chapter 1 in this volume; Jarmulowicz *et al.*, 2007).

In general, iambic (final syllable) stress is the less frequent stress pattern for English disyllabic words with only 26 per cent of disyllables exhibiting this pattern (Delattre, 1965). As a result, a tendency to assign the more frequent strong–weak stress pattern might be expected in the early phases of reading development. However, a study of reading development by Duncan & Seymour (2003) provided evidence that, by the age of 11 years, children were not simply assigning a default initial stress pattern in reading aloud polysyllabic nonwords but, instead, appeared sensitive to the orthographic structures contained within the nonwords which may serve as correlates of lexical stress.

One such correlate may be the length of the second syllable. Kelly *et al.* (1998) argued that this marks the less typical final syllable stress pattern in English disyllables and demonstrated that adults were sensitive to the fact that longer units like –elle are associated with final syllable stress whereas shorter units like –el are associated with initial stress. Another approach has been to exploit the relationship between affixes and stress. These morphological structures have been incorporated into the non-lexical decoding procedure in a new version of Dual-Route theory for disyllabic reading that shows good agreement with skilled reading performance (Rastle & Coltheart, 2000). In simple terms, the algorithm assigns final stress if the disyllabic word contains a known prefix, and initial stress if the presence of a suffix is detected unless that suffix is stress-taking (e.g. -een). Nevertheless, Rastle and Coltheart acknowledge that the modifications apparently required to simulate disyllabic reading raise several challenges for the Dual–Route model. One question is whether the inclusion of a procedure that assigns phonology at the level of the affix compromises the status of the non-lexical route by introducing lexical or, at least, morphological processing. Another question is how to encode information about lexical stress within the model in a manner that is consistent with what is known about stress in models of speech production (e.g. Levelt *et al.*, 1999; see Ashby and Martin, 2008).

More recent work on this issue highlights the strong association between lexical stress and grammatical category in English as, although only 11 per cent of nouns take final syllable stress, a far higher proportion of verbs (54 per cent) exhibit this stress pattern (Kelly & Bock, 1988). Arciuli and Cupples (2006) explored the orthographic correlates of both stress and grammatical category. Adult naming and lexical decision performance were consistent with the view that the English orthography codes grammatical category and lexical stress simultaneously using cues provided by the orthographic rime unit in the final syllable.

Exactly which of these cues are exploited by children as they learn to assign stress in reading polysyllabic words in English is one of the challenges facing researchers in this field but it seems likely that it is by examining complexities of this kind that we will increase our understanding of the orthographic units that children become sensitive to as reading skills develop. Therefore, if models are to be extended to account for polysyllabic reading, it is important to widen the scope of investigation to consider not just the impact of phonological awareness but also how availability of different units of sound interacts with other aspects of a child's language including lexical stress, syllabic complexity, morphological structure, grammatical class and, of course, orthographic depth.

Cross-linguistic reflections

It is probable that polysyllabic reading presents a particular difficulty for the beginning reader of English due to the nature of the language. English is a stress–timed language, which is characterized by variable lexical stress and complex syllables that contain ambiguous boundaries and reduced vowels. English also has an opaque orthography containing many exceptional spelling patterns.

In other European orthographies with a simpler structure and greater transparency, polysyllabic reading is likely to be more straightforward and an early process of grapheme-to-phoneme decoding may continue to work well if little inconsistency is encountered (Seymour *et al.*, 2003). In deeper orthographies, larger units that resolve inconsistencies are likely to become more salient over time (Treiman *et al.*, 1995; Duncan *et al.*, 2000; Ziegler & Goswami, 2005). Rimes appear to be important in dealing with inconsistency in monosyllabic pronunciation in languages like English and French (Treiman *et al.*, 1995; Peereman & Content, 1997; Brown & Deavers, 1999; Duncan *et al.*, 2000) but it is unclear which large units are most useful for dealing with inconsistency amongst polysyllables. Goswami *et al.* (1997, 1998) addressed this issue by applying the orthographic familiarity paradigm to Greek, French and Spanish, and provided evidence that large-unit (superrime) analogies figure more prominently in polysyllabic decoding in deeper orthographies.

However, the evidence presented here suggests that the influence of bigram frequency in these studies requires further investigation.

Nevertheless, even in transparent orthographies there may be some benefits for reading efficiency in chunking graphemes into larger units such as syllables, especially if these are phonologically salient in the spoken language. In the shallow Finnish orthography, for example, beginning readers are taught to read using texts in which the written words are presented in a syllabified form using hyphens. Furthermore, research on skilled word recognition and naming supports the involvement of syllabic representations in Spanish and German (Carreiras *et al.*, 1993; Conrad & Jacobs, 2004). Sensitivity to syllabic units in skilled reading has also been found in French and seems to emerge amongst French-speaking children from the end of Grade 1 (Colé *et al.*, 1999), in keeping with the early salience of phonological syllables in this language (Duncan *et al.*, 2006).

Finally, while English readers must learn about stress assignment and cope with the reduction of vowels in unstressed syllables, speakers of languages like Finnish, French and Icelandic do not have to confront these complexities because the pattern of stress in each of these languages is fixed and predictable. The effect of such cross-linguistic differences on polysyllabic spelling was documented by Caravolas *et al.* (2003) who observed that poor spellers made more vowel omissions in English than in French due to the particular difficulty of spelling the reduced (schwa) vowels in English unstressed syllables.

Many languages with variable lexical stress contain relatively consistent stress assignment rules or use diacritics in the orthography to mark non-standard stress patterns which seems likely to facilitate the decoding process (e.g. Spanish, Portuguese and Greek). However, like English, Italian has variable stress and contains neither rules nor diacritics to indicate the stress patterns of longer words, and hence, lexical stress constitutes a source of irregularity in this otherwise transparent orthography. When Burani and Arduino (2004) studied how skilled readers of Italian dealt with this problem they found that stress assignment to low frequency words was not accomplished by rule. Instead, it appeared that the adults had built up (implicit) knowledge about the consistency of the stress neighbourhood for longer words. These neighbourhoods were based on overlap within the final two syllables involving a unit that comprised the rime of the penultimate syllable and the final syllable. This outcome is consistent with experimental findings and connectionist models which propose that literacy development entails the gradual acquisition of sensitivity to the complex patterns of statistical regularities between phonology, morphology and orthography that exist in a child's language (e.g. Pacton *et al.*, 2005; Treiman *et al.*, 2006; Gonnerman *et al.*, 2007).

In conclusion, the outcome of this new area of research into the acquisition of complex reading skills will be heavily constrained by the nature of the orthography under scrutiny but the goal in each language is clear, namely, to understand the development of word recognition across the entire lexicon, not just within the subset of *monosyllabic* words, which has been the focus of interest for so long.

Notes

1 Duncan, L.G., Seymour, P.H.K. and Bolik, F. (unpublished data).
2 Plus one class member who had been absent on the previous occasion.
3 Duncan, L.G. and Bruce, A.L. (unpublished data).

References

Ans, B., Carbonnel, S., & Valdois, S. (1998). 'A connectionist multiple-trace memory model for polysyllabic word reading'. *Psychological Review, 105*, 678–723.

Arciuli, J., & Cupples, L. (2006). 'The processing of lexical stress during visual word recognition: Typicality effects and orthographic correlates'. *Quarterly Journal of Experimental Psychology, 59*, 920–948.

Ashby, J., & Martin, A.E. (2008). 'Prosodic phonological representations early in visual word recognition'. *Journal of Experimental Psychology: Human Perception and Performance, 34*, 224–236.

Berg, T. (1989). 'On the internal structure of polysyllabic monomorphemic words: The case for superrimes'. *Studia Linguistica, 43*, 5–32.

Bowey, J.A., & Hansen, J. (1994). 'The development of orthographic rimes as units of word recognition'. *Journal of Experimental Child Psychology, 58*, 465–488.

Bowey, J.A., & Underwood, N. (1996). 'Further evidence that orthographic rime usage in nonword reading increases with word-level reading proficiency'. *Journal of Experimental Child Psychology, 63*, 526–562.

Brown, G.D.A., & Deavers, R.P. (1999). 'Units of analysis in nonword reading: Evidence from children and adults'. *Journal of Experimental Child Psychology, 73*, 208–242.

Burani, C., & Arduino, L.S. (2004). 'Stress regularity or consistency?' Reading aloud Italian polysyllables with different stress patterns'. *Brain and Language Third International Conference on the Mental Lexicon, 90*, 318–325.

Caravolas, M., Bruck, M., & Genesee, F. (2003). 'Similarities and differences in the spelling profiles of English- and French-speaking dyslexic children'. In N. Goulandris (ed.), *Dyslexia: across-linguistic comparison*. London: Whurr Publishers.

Carreiras, M., Alvarez, C.J., & de Vega, M. (1993). 'Syllable frequency and visual word recognition in Spanish'. *Journal of Memory and Language, 32*, 766–780.

Carroll, J.B., Davies, P., & Richman, B. (1971). *Word frequency book*. New York: American Heritage.

Chateau, D., & Jared, D. (2003). 'Spelling-sound consistency effects in disyllabic word naming'. *Journal of Memory and Language, 48*, 255–280.

Colé, P., Magnan, A., & Grainger, J. (1999). 'Syllable-sized units in visual word recognition: Evidence from skilled and beginning readers of French'. *Applied Psycholinguistics, 20*, 507–532.

Conrad, M., & Jacobs, A. (2004). 'Replicating syllable frequency effects in Spanish in German: One more challenge to computational models of visual word recognition'. *Language and Cognitive Processes, 19*, 369–390.

Cutler, A. (1989). 'Auditory lexical access: Where do we start?' In W. Marslen-Wilson (ed.), *Lexical representation and process* (pp. 342–356). Cambridge, MA: MIT Press.

Cutler, A., & Clifton, C.E. (1984). 'The use of prosodic information in word recognition'. In H. Bouma & D.G. Bouwhuis (eds), *Attention and performance X: control of language processes* (pp. 183–196). Hillsdale, NJ: LEA.

De Cara, B., & Goswami, U. (2002). 'Statistical analysis of similarity relations among words: The special status of rimes in English'. *Behaviour Research Methods, Instruments and Computers, 34*, 416–423.

Delattre, P. (1965). *Comparing the phonetic features of English, French, German and Spanish: An interim report*. Heidelberg: Julius Groos Verlag.

Duncan, L.G., & Seymour, P.H.K. (2003). 'How do children read multisyllabic words?' Some preliminary observations'. *Journal of Research in Reading, 26*, 101–120.

Duncan, L.G., Seymour, P.H.K., & Hill, S. (2000). 'A small to large unit progression in metaphonological awareness and reading.' *Quarterly Journal of Experimental Psychology, 53A*, 1081–1104.

Duncan, L.G., Colé, P., Seymour, P.H.K., & Magnan, A. (2006). 'Differing sequences of metaphonological development in French and English'. *Journal of Child Language, 33*, 369–399.

Duncan, L.G., Seymour, P.H.K., & Bolik, F. (2007). 'Rimes and superrimes: An exploration of children's disyllabic rhyming skills'. *British Journal of Psychology, 98*, 199–221.

Ehri, L.C. (1992). 'Reconceptualizing the development of sight word reading and its relationship to recoding'. In P. Gough, L.C. Ehri, & R. Treiman (eds), *Reading acquisition* (pp.107–143). Hillsdale, NJ: LEA.

Frith, U. (1985). 'Beneath the surface of developmental dyslexia'. In K.E. Patterson, J.C. Marshall, & M. Coltheart (eds), *Surface dyslexia: neuropsychological and cognitive studies of phonological reading* (pp. 301–330). Hillsdale, NJ: LEA.

Frost, R., Katz, L., & Bentin, S. (1987). 'Strategies for visual word recognition and orthographical depth: a multilingual comparison'. *Journal of Experimental Psychology, 13*, 104–115.

Glushko, R.J. (1979). 'The organisation and activation of orthographic knowledge in reading aloud'. *Journal of Experimental Psychology: Human Perception and Performance, 5*, 674–691.

Gonnerman, L.M., Seidenberg, M.S., & Andersen, E.S. (2007). 'Graded semantic and phonological similarity effects in priming: Evidence for a distributed connectionist approach to morphology'. *Journal of Experimental Psychology-General, 136*, 323–345.

Goswami, U. (1993). 'Toward an interactive analogy model of reading development: Decoding vowel graphemes in beginning reading'. *Journal of Experimental Child Psychology, 56*, 443–475.

Goswami, U., & Bryant, P.E. (1990). *Phonological skills and learning to read*. Hillsdale, NJ: LEA.

Goswami, U., Porpodas, C., & Wheelwright, S. (1997). 'Children's orthographic representations in English and Greek. *European Journal of Psychology of Education, 12*, 273–292.

Goswami, U., Gombert, J.E., & de Barrera, L.F. (1998). 'Children's orthographic representations and linguistic transparency: Nonsense word reading in English, French, and Spanish'. *Applied Psycholinguistics, 19*, 19–52.

Harm, M.W., & Seidenberg, M.S. (1999). 'Phonology, reading acquisition, and dyslexia: Insights from connectionist models'. *Psychological Review, 106*, 491–528.

Jared, D., & Seidenberg, M.S. (1990). 'Naming multisyllabic words'. *Journal of Experimental Psychology: Human Perception and Performance, 16*, 92–105.

Jarmulowicz, L., Taran, V.L., & Hay, S.E. (2007). 'Third graders' metalinguistic skills, reading skills, and stress production in derived English words'. *Journal of Speech Language and Hearing Research, 50*, 1593–1605.

Kelly, M.H., & Bock, J.K. (1988). 'Stress in time'. *Journal of Experimental Psychology-Human Perception and Performance, 14*, 389–403.

Kelly, M.H., Morris, J., & Verrekia, L. (1998). 'Orthographic cues to lexical stress: Effects on naming and lexical decision'. *Memory & Cognition, 26*, 822–832.

Laxon, V.J., Masterson, J., & Coltheart, V. (1991). 'Some bodies are easier to read: The effect of consistency and regularity on children's reading'. *Quarterly Journal of Experimental Psychology, 43A*, 793–824.

Leslie, L., & Calhoon, A. (1995). 'Factors affecting children's reading of rimes: Reading ability, word frequency, and rime-neighborhood size'. *Journal of Educational Psychology, 87*, 576–586.

Levelt, W.J.M., Roelofs, A., & Meyer, A.S. (1999). 'A theory of lexical access in speech production'. *Behavioral and Brain Sciences, 22,* 1–75.

Pacton, S., Fayol, M., & Perruchet, P. (2005). 'Children's implicit learning of graphotactic and morphological regularities'. *Child Development, 76,* 324–339.

Patterson, K.E., & Morton, J.C. (1985). 'From orthography to phonology: An attempt at an old interpretation'. In K.E. Patterson, J.C. Marshall, & M. Coltheart (eds), *Surface dyslexia: Neuropsychological and cognitive studies of phonological reading* (pp. 335–359). London: LEA.

Peereman, R., & Content, A. (1997). 'Orthographic and phonological neighborhoods in naming: Not all neighbors are equally influential in orthographic space'. *Journal of Memory and Language, 37,* 382–410.

Plaut, D.C., McClelland, J.L., Seidenberg, M.S., & Patterson, K.E. (1996). 'Understanding normal and impaired word reading: Computational principles in quasi-regular domains'. *Psychological Review, 103,* 56–115.

Rastle, K., & Coltheart, M. (2000). 'Lexical and nonlexical print-to-sound translation of disyllabic words and nonwords'. *Journal of Memory and Language, 42,* 342–364.

Savage, R., & Stuart, M. (1998). 'Sublexical inferences in beginning reading: Medial vowel digraphs as functional units of transfer'. *Journal of Experimental Child Psychology, 69,* 85–108.

Seidenberg, M.S., & McClelland, J.L (1989). 'A distributed, developmental model of word recognition and naming'. *Psychological Review, 96,* 523–568.

Seymour, P.H.K., Aro, M., Erskine, J.M., Wimmer, H., Leybaert, J., Elbro, C., *et al.* (2003). 'Foundation literacy acquisition in European orthographies'. *British Journal of Psychology, 94,* 143–174.

Solso, R.L., & Juel, C.L. (1980). 'Positional frequency and versatility of bigrams for two-through nine-letter English words'. *Behavior Research Methods & Instrumentation, 12,* 297–343.

Stuart, M., Dixon, M., Masterson, J., & Gray, B. (2003). 'Children's early reading vocabulary: Description and word frequency lists'. *British Journal of Educational Psychology, 73,* 585–598.

Treiman, R. (1992). 'The role of intrasyllabic units in learning to read and spell'. In P.B. Gough, L.C. Ehri, & R. Treiman (eds), *Reading acquisition* (pp.1–70). Hillsdale, NJ: LEA.

Treiman, R., Fowler, C., Gross, J., Berch, D., & Weatherspoon, S. (1995). 'Syllable structure or word sturcture? Evidence for onset and rime units with disyllabic and trisyllabic stimuli'. *Journal of Memory and Langauges, 34,* 132–155.

Treiman, R., Goswami, U., & Bruck, M. (1990). 'Not all nonwords are alike: Implications for reading development and theory'. *Memory & Cognition, 18,* 559–567.

Treiman, R., Kessler, B., Zevin, J. D., Bick, S., & Davis, M. (2006). 'Influence of consonantal context on the reading of vowels: Evidence from children'. *Journal of Experimental Child Psychology, 93,* 1–24.

Wimmer, H. (1993). 'Characteristics of developmental dyslexia in a regular writing system'. *Applied Psycholinguistics, 14,* 1–33.

Wimmer, H., & Hummer, P. (1990). 'How German-speaking 1st-graders read and spell: Doubts on the importance of the logographic stage. *Applied Psycholinguistics, 11,* 349–368.

Wood, C. (2006). 'Metrical stress sensitivity in young children and its relationship to phonological awareness and reading'. *Journal of Research in Reading, 29,* 270–287.

Wood, C., & Terrell, C. (1998). 'Poor readers' ability to detect speech rhythm and perceive rapid speech'. *British Journal of Developmental Psychology, 16,* 397–413.

Ziegler, J.C., & Goswami, U. (2005). 'Reading acquisition, developmental dyslexia, and skilled reading across languages: A psycholinguistic grain size theory'. *Psychological Bulletin, 131,* 3–29.

Zorzi, M., Houghton, G., & Butterworth, B. (1998). 'The development of spelling-sound relationships in a model of phonological reading. *Language and Cognitive Processes*, *13*, 337–371.

Appendix 3.A

Stimuli for Experiment 1 showing Mean Word Frequency (WF), and Mean Positional Bigram Frequency (BF)*

   * WF from Carroll *et al.* (1971); BF from Solso & Juel (1980)

   # Nonwords used in Goswami *et al.*'s (1998) Experiment 1

Appendix 3.B

Stimuli for Experiment 2 showing Orthographic Superrime Frequency (SF), and Average Positional Bigram Frequency (APBF)*

	High Superrime Frequency			*Low Superrime Frequency*	
	SF	APBF		SF	APBF
datter	14	3400	tiffer	2	1650
hutter	11	3073	penner	1	2449
pumble	10	1277	wentle	1	1488
pender	9	2470	hilver	1	1926
bipper	9	1764	hepper	1	1921
langle	7	1365	bargle	1	1371
micken	5	951	mooden	1	1061
ditten	5	2122	tebble	1	885
hacket	5	1037	lethod	1	876
	Mean SF=8	Mean APBF=1940		Mean SF=1	Mean APBF=1514

* SF is the number of words in the CELEX database containing the orthographic superrime; APBF was calculated using Solso & Juel (1980)

Chapter 4

Children's reading comprehension difficulties

A consideration of the precursors and consequences

Kate Cain

We read to understand, or to begin to understand.

(Manguel, 1997)

The main aim of reading is to understand what we read. To do this, the young reader needs to acquire fluent and accurate word reading skills. Yet, the acquisition of good word reading alone does not guarantee adequate comprehension: a substantial proportion of young children experience significant problems with reading comprehension despite age-appropriate word reading (Yuill & Oakhill, 1991). These poor reading comprehenders often go unnoticed because of their fluent and accurate word reading. What causes their poor comprehension and what are the consequences for their literacy development? Those are the concerns of this chapter.

Comprehension: a brief overview of the process and product

To understand better the reasons why comprehension fails in some young readers, we first need to consider the nature of the comprehension task and the outcome of successful comprehension. Reading comprehension is a dynamic and an interactive process. To understand a written text, the reader needs to recognise each word and retrieve its meaning, combine this information with syntactic knowledge to make meaningful sentences, and integrate the meanings of each sentence to construct a representation of the state of affairs described by the text. This end product of comprehension is a coherent and integrated representation of its meaning, referred to as a mental model (Johnson-Laird, 1983) or situation model (Kintsch, 1998). This model details the causal relations between events, the goals of protagonists, and spatial and temporal information that is relevant to the storyline (Zwaan & Radvansky, 1998). Such representations are not unique to reading comprehension: they are the product of successful comprehension of spoken discourse as well.

Because comprehension happens in real time, the meaning assigned to an individual word or sentence or event will be influenced by the meaning-based representation of the text constructed so far. For example, the meaning of the word 'spade' in 'She picked up the spade' will differ according to the context, for example, 'June was in the garden' or 'June was playing cards'. Likewise, the meaning of the phrase 'Karen spilled the beans' will be interpreted differently when preceded by either 'Karen unpacked the shopping' and 'Karen was chatting with her best friend'. Thus, it is unlikely that the influences of specific skills on comprehension are felt in isolation.

Clearly, reading (and listening) comprehension is a complex process, involving many different skills and sources of knowledge. So why do some young readers fail to develop adequate text comprehension? In this chapter I will examine the text processing and knowledge difficulties that are characteristic of poor comprehenders, evaluate which ones are the most likely sources of reading comprehension difficulties, and consider the wider impacts that such deficits might have on literacy development.

Poor comprehenders: strengths and weaknesses

In this section, I discuss why different skills are important for good text comprehension, describe the characteristics of children with specific reading comprehension difficulties, and review the evidence that these children have problems with comprehension at the word-, sentence-, and text-level. I use the distinction between these three levels of meaning for convenience; readers should bear in mind the influences between them, for example, the sentence or story context can influence understanding of an individual word, as described above. My focus will be on the skills that aid the construction of a meaning-based representation for two reasons: these are the skills essential to successful comprehension; it is in this line of research where findings are most consistent.

What skills do we need to develop to be a successful comprehender?

Word-level knowledge and processing

Good word reading (or decoding) skills support comprehension (Perfetti, 1985). If word reading is fast, accurate, and efficient the reader can devote their processing capacity to making meaning, rather than working out the pronunciation of the individual words on the page. For that reason, many researchers interested in poor comprehension select poor comprehenders who have word reading skills that are equivalent to the same-age good comprehenders, who make up the comparison group (e.g. Cain & Oakhill, 1996; Oakhill, 1982; Stothard & Hulme, 1992).

Some children with reading comprehension difficulties experience deficits in reading certain types of words (Nation & Snowling, 1998a, 1998b). However, poor word reading alone seems to be an inadequate explanation for their language comprehension problems. Children who are selected for poor reading comprehension, are poorer than their peers on measures of listening comprehension, tasks which do not involve the processing of written words (Cain *et al.*, 2000a; Oakhill, 1982; Stothard & Hulme, 1992).

A sentence or longer piece of prose cannot be fully understood if the meanings of key words are not known. Thus, poor vocabulary knowledge is another potential source of poor text comprehension. Good and poor comprehenders have been found to differ on measures of vocabulary knowledge (Nation & Snowling, 1998b). However, it is also possible to identify children with poor text comprehension but adequate vocabulary knowledge (e.g. Cain *et al.*, 2004a; Cain, 1999; Oakhill, 1982, 1984). Reading comprehension difficulties may arise because of deficits in basic word reading or vocabulary skills; for other children poor comprehension is apparent when word reading is intact and vocabulary knowledge comparable with same-age peers. Children with specific reading comprehension difficulties in the presence of age-appropriate word reading and vocabulary knowledge are the focus of my research on poor comprehension and the focus of this chapter. An example of such groups is provided in Table 4.1.

Table 4.1 Characteristics of good and poor comprehenders and a comprehension–age match group

	Poor comprehenders (N=14)	Good comprehenders (N=14)	Comprehension–age match group (N=14)
Chronological age	7,7	7,7	6,7
Sight vocabulary	37.2	37.4	34.2
Word reading accuracy in context	7,9	7,11	6,8
Reading comprehension	6,7	8,1	6,8

Note. Where appropriate, ages are given as years, months. Maximum score for sight vocabulary test is 45.

Sentence-level knowledge and processing

Written and spoken text comprise a set of connected sentences, so a plausible source of reading comprehension difficulties is poor sentence-level skills. If a child fails to grasp the meanings of individual sentences, his/her comprehension of several connected lines of prose will be impaired.

Some children with reading comprehension difficulties have poor syntactic knowledge (Nation et al., 2004; Stothard & Hulme, 1992); others do not (Cain et al., 2005; Cain & Oakhill, 2006; Yuill & Oakhill, 1991). These discrepant findings are surprising because the studies used the same standardised assessment of grammar (TROG: Test for Reception of Grammar, Bishop, 1982). One possibility is that not all children with poor comprehension have the same profile of skill strengths and weaknesses and/or that their grammatical difficulties are very specific. Indeed, using a different task, Nation and colleagues showed that poor comprehenders were less able than good comprehenders at deriving the past tense of irregular verbs, although the two groups performed comparably on regular verbs and 'made-up' irregular verbs (Nation et al., 2005).

Another sentence-level skill that may influence reading comprehension is syntactic awareness. This metalinguistic skill is assessed by tasks that involve the manipulation of spoken sentences, for example word order correction and error detection tasks. Poor comprehenders aged between 8 and 12 years make more errors than their peers on these tasks (Bentin et al., 1990; Nation & Snowling, 2000). However, syntactic awareness should not be taken as a proxy indicator of syntactic knowledge and different measures of syntactic awareness are dependent on different types of knowledge and processes, such as vocabulary, memory, and syntactic knowledge (Cain, 2007).

Anaphors and interclausal connectives are cohesive devices that help the reader to integrate successive clauses and sentences in a text. In this way, they aid sentence comprehension, although they can also extend beyond it. Anaphors include definite and indefinite pronouns, e.g. 'she', 'it', and 'one': 'Bill showed Susan his new squash racquet. She thought it looked rather flash and wanted one too.' Children with poor reading comprehension are less likely to use and process anaphors correctly than their skilled peers. For example, they are less likely to work out the antecedent of a pronoun in order to integrate sentences such as, 'Louise had dinner with Malcolm in a restaurant. She chatted cheerfully with him' (Megherbi & Ehrlich, 2005).

Interclausal connectives include 'before', 'because', and 'although' (and also 'and'). They can be used to signal, amongst other things, the temporal and causal relationship between clauses or sentences. Poor comprehenders are less likely than good comprehenders to select the correct connective in a cloze task (Cain *et al.*, 2005). They are less likely to include causal connectives ('because', 'so') to link events in their narrative productions (Cain, 2003).

Children with specific comprehension difficulties may experience some sentence difficulties at the level of grammar and morphology. The extent of these difficulties requires further exploration. Poor comprehenders demonstrate poor use of linguistic devices that aid cohesion in a text and facilitate the construction of a meaning-based representation of a text. Many of these devices, e.g. pronouns and interclausal connectives, are individual words that serve a grammatical and/or pragmatic function. Thus, impaired knowledge of the relations between clauses and sentences that are signalled by these words may influence understanding of extended text, as well as that of individual sentences.

Discourse-level knowledge and processing

The construction of a coherent and integrated representation of meaning relies on skills other than word- and sentence-level comprehension. To integrate the meanings of individual sentences, readers generate inferences to fill in missing details and use their knowledge about narrative structure and a character's motivations and goals to impose a causal structure on events. Active readers monitor their understanding during reading to identify whether comprehension is adequate and whether additional processing is required. Comprehension occurs in real time and taps memory skills and general knowledge as the reader constructs meaning. I consider these skills in this section.

Inference and integration. Texts are not fully explicit. Authors leave some things unsaid and readers must make links to integrate information between different parts of the text and use their general knowledge to infer – or fill in – missing details. Poor comprehenders make fewer constructive inferences, which involve integrating information from two different sentences in a text, than good comprehenders. They are also less likely to generate simple inferences that involve the integration of information from the text with general knowledge.

In one study by Oakhill (1982), good and poor comprehenders heard short texts such as: 'The boy was chasing the girl. The girl ran into the playground.' The poor comprehenders were subsequently less likely than good comprehenders to falsely 'recognise' the inference: 'The boy ran into the playground' as a sentence that had been presented earlier. After reading a story about a boy cycling to school with the line: 'John ran over some broken bottles and had to walk the rest of the way', poor comprehenders are less likely to infer that John had to walk because the broken glass had caused a puncture (Oakhill, 1984).

The poor comprehenders' difficulties in these studies did not simply arise because of poor memory: they were able to recall literal detail from the texts (Oakhill, 1982) and their inference making difficulties were apparent even when the text was available to search through (Oakhill, 1984). More recent work also finds that poor comprehenders' difficulties with inference making are not in line with their memory for explicit details in a text (Bowyer-Crane & Snowling, 2005).

Comprehension monitoring. When constructing a coherent representation of a text's meaning that integrates elements from different parts of the text and incorporates general knowledge, readers have to monitor their understanding. If the current element cannot be integrated with the model built so far, a reader can take remedial action, such as rereading or generating an inference.

A common method to study how well a reader monitors their comprehension is the error detection task paradigm. Short texts are presented that contain different types of error (see Table 4.2 for examples). These might be elements that are either inconsistent with a previous element in the text – an internal inconsistency – or with general knowledge – an external inconsistency. Another type of error is a nonsense word. These tasks indicate how well the reader is evaluating his/her understanding: a nonsense word will only be detected if the reader strives to understand each sentence; an inconsistency can only be detected if the reader attempts to integrate each new piece of information into the model constructed so far. Nine- to ten-year-old children with poor reading comprehension have difficulties with error detection, particularly with the detection of inconsistencies (Oakhill *et al.*, 2005).

Ehrlich (1996) manipulated the consistency between anaphors and their antecedents to look at comprehension monitoring of expository texts. She found that good comprehenders aged 12 to 15 years old were more likely than poor comprehenders to detect inconsistent anaphors. Good comprehenders spend longer than poor comprehenders reading parts of a text that contain inconsistent anaphors and they are more likely to look back at previous parts of the text when an inconsistent anaphor is encountered (Ehrlich *et al.*, 1999). This work suggests that good comprehenders are more likely to spot inconsistencies than poor comprehenders *as they read*, and that they are more likely to engage in additional processing to try to resolve the inconsistency and make sense of the text.

Table 4.2 Examples of tasks to assess comprehension monitoring and the ability to structure stories

---

Comprehension monitoring text containing internal inconsistencies (from Cain, Oakhill, & Bryant, 2004)

Last night Jill walked home through the woods.
She had just been to the cinema with her friends.
* There was no moonlight, so Jill could hardly see her way.
She walked along the path.
* The moon was so bright that it lit the way.
Jill lives at the other side of the wood.
* denotes lines containing inconsistent information

Short 6-line story used in story anagram task (adapted from Stein & Glenn, 1982)
Once there was a skinny mouse called Tom.
Tom found a big box of cornflakes in the kitchen.
Tom was hungry and wanted to eat some.
Tom nibbled a hole in the corner of the box and slipped inside.
Tom ate every single cornflake.
Tom was very full and went to sleep.

Knowledge and use of story structure. Narrative is the principle genre in children's early literacy experience. It is common to children through books, static and animated cartoons, some poetry, televised programmes and films. Narratives comprise a set of goal-directed actions and causally related events. It is clear how the ability to understand, and also produce, such sequences taps the same processes needed to construct an integrated and coherent situation model.

Poor comprehenders demonstrate deficits on several different measures that involve structuring elements in a story. When asked to produce an oral story from a topic prompt, e.g. 'Pirates', poor comprehenders are less likely than good comprehenders to produce a sequence of causally related events (Cain & Oakhill, 1996). When a goal-directed prompt is provided, e.g. 'How the pirates lost their treasure', they produce better-structured stories (Cain, 2003). These studies suggest that poor comprehenders lack the knowledge or planning skills to produce a goal or end-point for a narrative (see also Cragg & Nation, 2006). Their difficulties extend beyond production tasks. Poor comprehenders are less able than good comprehenders to sequence a jumbled set of six short sentences into a coherent story (Cain & Oakhill, 2006). They are also poor at discriminating between the main point, the setting and the main event of stories (Yuill & Oakhill, 1991).

Summary. Children with reading comprehension difficulties experience deficits in a range of skills and aspects of knowledge that are important for constructing coherent and integrated representations of meaning. Many of these tasks have been administered aurally, indicating a difficulty that extends beyond the processing of written text.

Memory and general knowledge

Memory. Memory underpins reading comprehension. Many of the skills involved in successful comprehension and the construction of a coherent and integrated representation of a text's meaning described above are dependent on the storage and coordination of information in memory. When constructing a representation of a text's meaning, the reader must continuously process new information and integrate this knowledge into the unfolding meaning-based representation stored in memory. Access to that memory-based representation is required in later assessments of comprehension, such as answering questions or recall. As a consequence, the type of memory that is most consistently related to measures of reading comprehension, and which has been of most interest to researchers of reading comprehension, is working memory: the type of memory that enables readers to store and process information simultaneously and retrieve for later recall.

Working memory capacity is correlated with children's and adults' reading and listening comprehension (Cain *et al.*, 2004a; Daneman & Merikle, 1996). Interest has focused on working memory, because poor comprehenders' short-term memory store appears to be intact. Their ability to store and recall a string of words or digits is similar to that of good comprehenders with comparable word reading skills (Cain, 2006; Cain *et al.*, 2004b; Cain *et al.*, 2000b; Stothard & Hulme, 1992; Yuill *et al.*, 1989). In contrast, poor comprehenders are impaired on a variety of memory assessments that require the simultaneous storage and processing of digits (e.g. Yuill *et al.*, 1989 and words/sentences Cain *et al.*, 2004b; de Beni & Palladino, 2000).

The importance of working memory is further demonstrated by studies that have manipulated the processing load in the task. When the working memory demands of a task are high, poor comprehenders have greater problems. For example, they do more poorly on inference tasks when they have to integrate information over several lines of text (Cain *et al.*, 2004a) and similarly in comprehension monitoring tasks when there are several lines of text between the anaphor and its antecedent (Ehrlich *et al.*, 1999; Yuill & Oakhill, 1988). However, working memory cannot fully explain performance on these tasks: working memory and key skills such as inference and integration and comprehension monitoring explain separate but partially overlapping variance in reading comprehension skill (Cain *et al.*, 2004a).

General knowledge. Knowledge is clearly important for inference making because a reader can only make an inference if they have the requisite vocabulary or background knowledge. Poor comprehenders fail to make inferences, such as inferring that a bike was ridden if a child pedalled home, even though they know they know that bikes are pedalled (Cain & Oakhill, 1999). With colleagues, I have also investigated knowledge deficits as a source of poor inference making by teaching children a new knowledge base – information about an imaginary planet – to try to make 'all things equal' to groups of good and poor comprehenders. The procedure was originally developed by Barnes and colleagues (e.g. Barnes *et al.*, 1996).

Children were first taught a set of facts about an imaginary planet, called Gan. For example, 'The flowers on Gan are hot like fire'; 'The ponds on Gan are filled with orange juice'. After ensuring that the knowledge base was fully learned, children listened to a multi-episode story followed by questions. Some of the questions assessed their ability to generate inferences and, in order to draw each inference, children had to incorporate information from the knowledge base with a story premise. For example, in one episode the characters cry 'ouch' when they walk across some flowers; this part of the story only makes sense if the reader incorporates the knowledge that the flowers on Gan are hot like fire. Memory for the knowledge base was assessed at the end of the story and only responses to the inference questions for which the knowledge base item was recalled were included in the final analysis. This procedure enabled strict control for any individual differences in general knowledge. Even when knowledge was controlled for in this way, poor comprehenders generated fewer inferences than did the good comprehenders (Cain *et al.*, 2001).

Summary. There is now a large body of evidence that poor comprehenders have poor working memory, which may influence their ability to construct meaning-based representations of text. Although poor comprehenders may lack some specific knowledge, such as knowledge about the narrative genre, there is no evidence that their inference deficits arise because they lack specific world knowledge. An individual's memory capacity and how readily s/he is able to activate relevant general knowledge will influence how easily s/he can process and make sense of text during reading, and the speed and quality of integration and inference.

Investigating the causes of poor comprehension

Thus far, we have considered the characteristics of poor comprehenders. The next section examines which, if any, of the skills that are associated with reading comprehension level are *causally* related to it. The identification of causal factors can inform our theoretical models of the independence and interrelations between different skills in the acquisition of reading comprehension and is crucial to the development of interventions to help children with comprehension difficulties. Here, I present an overview of research investigating the causes of poor reading comprehension.

Cross-sectional designs

It is easy to see why inference and integration are fundamental to good comprehension and, for that reason, there has been more interest in exploring the direction of causality between inference ability and reading comprehension level than other text-level skills. Poor comprehenders not only generate fewer inferences than same-age skilled comprehenders, they also generate fewer inferences than a younger group matched for absolute comprehension level (Cain & Oakhill, 1999). This comprehension-age match (CAM) design is analogous in its logic to the reading-age match design (see Cain et al., 2000a). It incorporates a group of normally developing comprehenders selected so that their comprehension skill is at the *same absolute level* as that of the older poor comprehenders, but is normal for their age. An example of the characteristics of three such groups is provided in Table 4.1, above.

This design cannot be used to establish causality, but it can rule out a causal link in one direction, for example from comprehension ability to the skill in question. This finding that the poor comprehenders made fewer inferences than the CAM group rules out the possibility that weak inference making skills are a consequence of poor comprehension. The alternative explanation, that weak inference making is a likely cause of reading comprehension difficulties, is supported by the findings from training studies.

Poor comprehenders can be trained to make inferences by looking for 'clue' words in a text (Yuill & Joscelyne, 1988). Such training does not benefit good comprehenders, suggesting that the poor comprehenders benefited because they lacked strategic knowledge about how to generate inferences. In another training study, some children were given the clue word training and another group were trained to generate questions during reading that would help them to think about and test their ongoing comprehension. A third group practised rapid word decoding (Yuill & Oakhill, 1988). The inference and question generation training led to improvements on a standardised assessment of reading comprehension; the rapid word decoding improved the ability to decode words with speed, but did not benefit comprehension. McGee and Johnson (2003) report similar benefits from inference and question generation training.

There are no studies to my knowledge in which children have successfully been trained to monitor their comprehension. Yuill and Oakhill (1991) report little success training such skills and work by Paris and colleagues to teach children to be 'a reading detective' has failed to obtain transfer effects to a standardised measure of comprehension (e.g. Paris & Jacobs, 1984; Paris et al., 1986). However, poor comprehenders' monitoring skills improve when their interest levels are increased (de Sousa & Oakhill, 1996). Further, in Yuill and Oakhill's (1988) study, children who made gains were taught both to generate inferences and to evaluate their understanding of a text; the latter is effectively comprehension monitoring. It may be that comprehension monitoring can only be improved with an additional hook, be it interest level or a new strategy to implement, that helps children to become more actively engaged in processing text and constructing meaning.

Children with comprehension difficulties are poor on a range of measures to assess their knowledge about stories: they produce more poorly structured narratives and fail to identify the main point of a story. In two studies described earlier, I sought to determine whether their story production deficits were the result of their poor comprehension or a potential cause of it using a CAM design (Cain, 2003; Cain & Oakhill, 1996).

These studies revealed that poor comprehenders produced more poorly structured stories than the CAM group when their stories were prompted by a topic. When given a picture sequence to narrate or a goal-directed title, performance improved (Cain & Oakhill, 1996). This pattern of findings rules out the possibility that reading-comprehension level determines the ability to structure stories, because the two groups were matched for absolute comprehension level; instead, it indicates that the ability to structure stories is a potential cause of poor comprehension.

Longitudinal designs

It is clear from the work discussed so far that a wide range of cognitive and language-specific skills are involved in reading comprehension and are potential causes of poor comprehension. For that reason, the design of a longitudinal study to investigate the skills that underpin and facilitate reading comprehension is a difficult task. Essential skills should be included and the influence of possibly extraneous variables controlled to determine the specific role of key skills. The researcher faces a difficult choice: s/he rarely has unlimited resources and, therefore, needs to select carefully which measures to include to make best use of the time with each participant. We are fortunate that the results from several recent studies provide a complementary picture and support the findings of the CAM and training studies described above.

Different skills influence the development of word reading and reading comprehension: phonological skills are related to growth in word reading and comprehension of words, sentences, and text are related to growth in reading comprehension (de Jong & van der Leij, 2002; Muter *et al.*, 2004). De Jong and van der Leij included the autoregressive effect of reading comprehension in their analyses – that is, they took early comprehension ability into account and then identified which skills explained growth in comprehension over and above comprehension ability at the start of their study. This is an important statistical control to include in the analysis of longitudinal data that can help to identify key skills and clarify the relations between variables. By including a measure of early comprehension skills, it is possible to determine which, if any, skills facilitate comprehension development, for example vocabulary or inference skills.

Colleagues and I used this control procedure in an analysis of a longitudinal study of children's reading comprehension development from 8 to 11 years (Oakhill & Cain, under review). Similar to de Jong and van der Leij (2002), we found a dissociation between the skills that influenced growth in word reading and those that influenced growth in reading comprehension. These patterns are presented in Figures 4.1 and 4.2: only significant variables are included. These data indicate that comprehension level and growth are not simply determined by word reading skills.

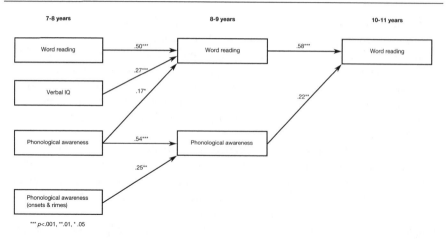

Figure 4.1 Path diagram to show the relations between language and cognitive skills at age 7–8 years and word reading accuracy at 10–11 years

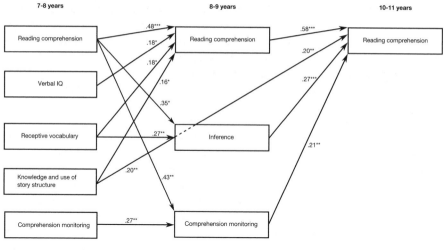

Figure 4.2 Path diagram to show the relations between language and cognitive skills at age 7–8 years and reading comprehension at 10–11 years

Of particular interest is the finding that the component skills of comprehension discussed above – inference making, comprehension monitoring, and knowledge about story structure – were predictive of comprehension development over and above the autoregressive effects of comprehension and also measures of verbal IQ, word reading, and vocabulary knowledge (see Figure 4.2). Thus, although basic word level and language skills are obviously important to comprehension and its development, other skills that aid the construction of meaning have a considerable influence.

Summary

Different methods for investigating the skills that drive comprehension development and, therefore, the skill impairments that lead to comprehension difficulties provide converging evidence that the skills that aid the construction of a coherent representation of the meaning of a text are causally implicated in comprehension failure in young children. Studies using the comprehension-age match design reveal that inference and integration and the ability to impose a causally coherent structure on a story are more likely to be a cause rather than a product of poor reading comprehension. Poor comprehenders benefit from training in specific inference skills and self-questioning to monitor comprehension during reading. Longitudinal research indicates that three skills: inference and integration, comprehension monitoring, and the ability to structure narratives, drive the development of comprehension over and above comprehension level at outset and also vocabulary, word reading, and verbal IQ. These data strongly suggest that comprehension failure can arise for a variety of reasons and that the skills that aid the construction of meaning are fundamental to successful comprehension.

What are the consequences of poor comprehension?

In this section, I consider the consequences of poor comprehension. Two issues are addressed. First the persistence of a reading comprehension impairment. Reading comprehension deficits might be transitory, arising because of a developmental delay in a skill that enables reading comprehension, such as word reading, or key meaning-making skill. If so, some children who do poorly on a measure of reading or listening comprehension relative to their chronological or language age at one time point might 'grow out' of their deficit over time without the need for any intervention. On the other hand, if problems are persistent, we need to focus our attention on the development of effective interventions. The second issue to be considered is the wider implications of poor comprehension. How do weak comprehension skills affect the development of other language skills, and what are the educational implications of being a poor comprehender?

The persistence of poor comprehension

There are a handful of studies in which the progress of poor comprehenders has been tracked across time. Cornoldi and colleagues identified a group of poor comprehenders when they were aged 11 years and tested their abilities two years later (Cornoldi *et al.*, 1996). Of the original sample of 12 children, 5 no longer showed signs of impaired comprehension. Levorato *et al.* (2004) report an even better 'recovery' rate: 67 per cent of a sample of 8-year-old poor comprehenders and 54 per cent of a sample of 10-year-old poor comprehenders did not show a poor comprehender profile when retested eight months later. In a large-scale developmental study, the reading ability of children in Grades 1–3 was monitored over a three-year period (Aarnoutse *et al.*, 2001). At outset, children were identified as being poor, average, and good performers on measures of decoding, reading comprehension, vocabulary and spelling. The group differences in reading comprehension ability got smaller over time.

These statistics are very encouraging at first glance: not all poor comprehenders appear to have a persistent problem; for many, their problems resolve without any specific instruction. Examination of the selection criteria in these studies indicates that many of the children may have had general, rather than specific, reading comprehension difficulties. The good and poor comprehenders in these studies were not matched for word reading ability, for example the good and poor comprehenders in Levorato *et al.*'s study differed on measures of word reading accuracy and speed at the start of the study. Although word reading ability and reading comprehension are underpinned by separate skills and may be dissociated, word efficiency will limit reading comprehension in young readers (Hoover & Gough, 1990). Thus, improvements in word reading may have led to gains in reading comprehension in these samples.

We find a very different incidence of persistence when we look at children classified as poor comprehenders who are matched to same-age peers for word reading. I monitored the progress of two groups of good and poor comprehenders who did not differ in word reading ability when aged 8 (Cain & Oakhill, 2006). Three years later, a comparison of the children available for assessment (19 poor comprehenders and 17 good comprehenders) showed a significant difference on a standardised measure of reading comprehension and only one of the poor comprehenders obtained an age-appropriate reading comprehension score. This study indicates that children with poor comprehension in the presence of good word reading skills may require comprehension-targeted interventions to remediate their comprehension difficulties. More studies of this nature are required to provide an accurate estimate of the persistence of specific comprehension problems.

The wider implications of a comprehension deficit

Many children with specific reading comprehension difficulties may remain poor comprehenders without appropriate intervention. What about other aspects of their literacy and learning? Being a poor comprehender may influence the development of other skills, not only text comprehension. The Matthew Effect refers to the phenomenon that young children with word reading difficulties do not catch up with their peers and fall even further behind in key literacy skills over time (Stanovich, 1986). Readers who read more get more practice in word reading and comprehension. They will also come across, and therefore learn, more information about the world and different topic areas (Stanovich, 1993). Children who fail to understand adequately what they read are likely to read less or certainly to read less challenging books. Thus, we might expect poor comprehenders to show reduced growth in their word reading, vocabulary, and other information that can be learned through text, over time, relative to good comprehenders.

There is some evidence that good and poor comprehenders differ in their out-of-school literacy (Cain, 1996), although group differences are not found on all measures of literacy activities (Cain *et al.*, 2000a). There is no strong evidence to date that poor comprehension in itself leads to depressed word reading development (Cain & Oakhill, 2006). The developmental relationships between appear to be more complex than this. A small-scale study has found that poor comprehenders with weak cognitive abilities make less progress in reading comprehension across a three-year period than their peers; poor comprehenders with weak vocabulary made smaller gains in word reading (Cain & Oakhill, 2006). It has been noted that the evidence for Matthew Effects in other areas of reading development is inconclusive (see Scarborough, 2005, for a review) and this may be because the relations between language and literacy skills are complex, as the analysis of poor comprehenders shows.

There may be other consequences of poor comprehension. Recent work has indicated the importance of inference in vocabulary learning from text for young readers (e.g. Cain *et al.*, 2004; Cain *et al.*, 2003). One possibility is that poor comprehenders, who generally have poor inference skills, may suffer from slow vocabulary growth. In a similar way, knowledge growth may suffer.

In terms of wider educational implications, poor comprehenders do more poorly than the good comprehenders on national assessments of English, Maths, and Science three years later (Cain & Oakhill, 2006). Thus, the consequences of a comprehension difficulty extend beyond understanding of written narrative, the genre typically used to assess comprehension in this age group. Poor performance on measures of maths ability and knowledge and reasoning about science indicate more general learning difficulties on a range of topics. This finding will not be surprising to many researchers in the field of reading comprehension. The construction of an adequate situation model enables the reader to learn from the text and to apply that knowledge in other situations, because the information has been integrated with existing knowledge structures (e.g. Kintsch, 1998).

Conclusions

The studies reviewed in this chapter collate a large body of knowledge about reading comprehension difficulties and identify some important areas for future research. Reading comprehension is a complex task and measures of this skill are correlated with a wide range of language and literacy variables. For that reason, remediation of poor comprehenders will be best informed by a profile of a child's strengths and weaknesses.

In terms of our knowledge about specific reading comprehension difficulties, there is widespread evidence that children can experience specific reading comprehension difficulties in the presence of age-appropriate word reading and vocabulary knowledge and these children's comprehension difficulties are evident for spoken, as well as written, text. Children with specific reading comprehension difficulties are poor on many skills that aid the construction of a situation model of a text. There is converging evidence that meaning-making skills, such as inference, comprehension monitoring, and skill in structuring stories, are causally implicated in the development of comprehension over and above basic language abilities. Further, there is evidence that, without specific intervention, children with specific comprehension difficulties do not spontaneously improve and may perform more poorly than peers on a range of educational assessments, which tap abilities that extend beyond the traditional notion of reading comprehension.

Comprehension of words, sentences, and text does not occur in isolation: our current understanding of the text will influence our interpretation of new information, including the meanings of individual words such as homonyms; the amount of relevant general knowledge a reader brings to a text may influence the adequacy or ease of his/her understanding; and some grammatical features influence more than single sentence comprehension. The interactive nature of comprehension has not been investigated in many studies to date (although see Gernsbacher, 1990) and is clearly an important area for future research. The interactive nature of different levels of text suggests that we are unlikely to identify single discrete deficits at the word-, sentence-, or text-level of processing in our search to understand comprehension difficulties.

When we consider the interactive nature of comprehension we must include how the quality of text comprehension will influence learning and the acquisition of knowledge. Although research with 8- to 10-year-old poor comprehenders does not point to general knowledge deficits as a source of their inference making difficulties, relevant background knowledge may become more important for understanding different curriculum areas in older children and comprehension skills may influence a reader's ability to learn information and vocabulary from text (e.g. Kintsch, 1998). Thus, poor comprehension may lead to restricted growth in knowledge, which may adversely affect future comprehension.

When we consider the product of our research efforts to date, it is fair to say that we now have a detailed understanding of the skills and processes that are important for successful reading comprehension and which are impaired in children with reading comprehension difficulties. We are now beginning to understand the sources of poor reading comprehension and the possible consequences of a reading comprehension impairment.

References

Aarnoutse, C., van Leeuwe, J., Voeten, M., & Oud, H. (2001). 'Development of decoding, reading comprehension, vocabulary and spelling during the elementary school years'. *Reading and Writing, 14*, 61–89.

Barnes, M.A., Dennis, M., & Haefele-Kalvaitis, J. (1996). 'The effects of knowledge availability and knowledge accessibility on coherence and elaborative inferencing in children from six to fifteen years of age'. *Journal of Experimental Child Psychology, 61*, 216–241.

Bentin, S., Deutsch, A., & Liberman, I.Y. (1990). 'Syntactic competence and reading ability in children'. *Journal of Experimental Child Psychology, 48*, 147–172.

Bishop, D. (1982). *Test for reception of grammar*. Manchester: Chapel Press.

Bowyer-Crane, C., & Snowling, M. (2005). 'Assessing children's inference generation: What do tests of reading comprehension measure?' *British Journal of Educational Psychology, 75*, 189–201.

Cain, K. (1996). 'Story knowledge and comprehension skill'. In C. Cornoldi & J. Oakhill (eds), *Reading comprehension difficulties: processes and remediation* (pp.167–192). Mahwah, NJ: LEA.

—— (1999). 'Ways of reading: How knowledge and use of strategies are related to reading comprehension'. *British Journal of Developmental Psychology, 17*, 293–309.

—— (2003). 'Text comprehension and its relation to coherence and cohesion in children's fictional narratives'. *British Journal of Developmental Psychology, 21*, 335–351.

—— (2006). 'Individual differences in children's memory and reading comprehension: an investigation of semantic and inhibitory deficits'. *Memory, 14*, 553–569.

—— (2007). 'Syntactic awareness and reading ability: is there any evidence for a special relationship?' *Applied Psycholinguistics, 28*, 679–694.

Cain, K., & Oakhill, J. (1996). 'The nature of the relationship between comprehension skill and the ability to tell a story'. *British Journal of Developmental Psychology, 14*, 187–201.

Cain, K., & Oakhill, J.V. (1999). 'Inference making and its relation to comprehension failure'. *Reading and Writing, 11*, 489–503.

Cain, K., & Oakhill, J. (2006). 'Profiles of children with specific reading comprehension difficulties'. *British Journal of Educational Psychology, 76*, 683–696.

Cain, K., & Oakhill, J. (in preparation). 'Early reading experience and its relation to language and literacy development'

Cain, K., Oakhill, J.V., & Bryant, P.E. (2000a). 'Investigating the causes of reading comprehension failure: The comprehension-age match design'. *Reading and Writing, 12*, 31–40.

Cain, K., Oakhill, J.V., & Bryant, P.E. (2000b). 'Phonological skills and comprehension failure: A test of the phonological processing deficit hypothesis'. *Reading and Writing, 13*, 31–56.

Cain, K., Oakhill, J.V., Barnes, M.A., & Bryant, P.E. (2001). 'Comprehension skill, inference making ability and their relation to knowledge'. *Memory and Cognition, 29*, 850–859.

Cain, K., Oakhill, J.V., & Elbro, C. (2003). 'The ability to learn new word meanings from context by school-age children with and without language comprehension difficulties'. *Journal of Child Language, 30*, 681–694.

Cain, K., Oakhill, J.V., & Bryant, P.E. (2004a). 'Children's reading comprehension ability: Concurrent prediction by working memory, verbal ability, and component skill'. *Journal of Educational Psychology, 96*, 671–681.

Cain, K., Oakhill, J., & Lemmon, K. (2004b). 'Individual differences in the inference of word meanings from context: The influence of reading comprehension, vocabulary knowledge, and memory capacity'. *Journal of Educational Psychology, 96*, 671–681.

Cain, K., Patson, N., & Andrews, L. (2005). 'Age- and ability-related differences in young readers' use of conjunctions'. *Journal of Child Language, 32*(4), 877–892.

Cornoldi, C., de Beni, R., & Pazzaglia, F. (1996). 'Profiles of reading comprehension difficulties: An analysis of single cases'. In C. Cornoldi & J. Oakhill (Eds.), *Reading comprehension difficulties: processes and intervention*. Mahwah, NJ: LEA.

Cragg, L., & Nation, K. (2006). 'Exploring written narrative in children with poor reading comprehension'. *Educational Psychology, 26*, 55–72.

Daneman, M., & Merikle, P.M. (1996). 'Working memory and language comprehension: A meta-analysis'. *Psychonomic Bulletin and Review, 3*, 422–433.

de Beni, R., & Palladino, P. (2000). 'Intrusion errors in working memory tasks: Are they related to reading comprehension ability?' *Learning and Individual Differences, 12*, 131–143.

de Jong, P.F., & van der Leij, A. (2002). 'Effects of phonological abilities and linguistic comprehension on the development of reading'. *Scientific Studies of Reading, 6*, 51.

de Sousa, I., & Oakhill, J.V. (1996). 'Do levels of interest have an effect on children's comprehension monitoring importance?' *British Jounal of Educational Psychology, 66*, 471–482.

Ehrlich, M.F. (1996). 'Metacognitive monitoring in the processing of anaphoric devices in skilled and less-skilled comprehenders'. In C. Cornoldi & J. Oakhill (eds), *Reading comprehension difficulties: processes and intervention* (pp. 221–249). Mahwah, NJ: LEA.

Ehrlich, M.F., Remond, M., & Tardieu, H. (1999). 'Processing of anaphoric devices in young skilled and less skilled comprehenders: Differences in metacognitive monitoring'. *Reading and Writing, 11*, 29–63.

Gernsbacher, M.A. (1990). *Language comprehension as structure building*. Hillsdale, NJ: Lawrence Erlbaum.

Hoover, W.A., & Gough, P.B. (1990). 'The simple view of reading'. *Reading and Writing, 2*, 127–160.

Johnson-Laird, P.N. (1983). *Mental models: towards a cognitive science of language, inference, and consciousness*. Cambridge: Cambridge University Press.

Kintsch, W. (1998). *Comprehension: a paradigm for cognition*. New York: Cambridge University Press.

Levorato, M.C., Nesi, B., & Cacciari, C. (2004). 'Reading comprehension and comprehension of idiomatic expressions: A developmental study'. *Brain and Language, 91,* 303–314.

McGee, A., & Johnson, H. (2003). 'The effect of inference training on skilled and less skilled comprehenders'. *Educational Psychology, 23,* 49–59.

Manguel, A. (1997). *A history of reading*. Bath: Flamingo.

Megherbi, H., & Ehrlich, M.F. (2005). 'Language impairment in less skilled comprehenders: The on-line processing of anaphoric pronouns in a listening situation'. *Reading and Writing, 18,* 715–753.

Muter, V., Hulme, C., Snowling, M., & Stevenson, J. (2004). 'Phonemes, rimes, vocabulary and grammatical skills as foundations of early reading development: Evidence from a longitudinal study'. *Developmental Psychology, 40,* 665–681.

Nation, K., & Snowling, M.J. (1998a). 'Individual differences in contextual facilitation: Evidence from dyslexia and poor reading comprehension'. *Child Development, 69,* 996–1011.

Nation, K., & Snowling, M.J. (1998b). 'Semantic processing and the development of word-recognition skills: Evidence from children with reading comprehension difficulties'. *Journal of Memory and Language, 39,* 85–101.

Nation, K., & Snowling, M.J. (2000). 'Factors influencing syntactic awareness skills in normal readers and poor comprehenders'. *Applied Psycholinguistics, 21,* 229–241.

Nation, K., Clarke, P., Marshall, C.M., & Durand, M. (2004). 'Hidden language impairments in children: Parallels between poor reading comprehension and specific language impairment?' *Journal of Speech, Language, and Hearing Research, 47,* 199–211.

Nation, K., Snowling, M.J., & Clarke, P. (2005). 'Production of the English past tense by children with language comprehension impairments'. *Journal of Child Language, 32,* 117–137.

Oakhill, J.V. (1982). 'Constructive processes in skilled and less-skilled comprehenders' memory for sentences'. *British Journal of Psychology, 73,* 13–20.

—— (1984). 'Inferential and memory skills in children's comprehension of stories'. *British Journal of Educational Psychology, 54,* 31–39.

Oakhill, J., & Cain, K. (under review). 'The precursors of reading comprehension and word reading in young readers: Evidence from a four-year longitudinal study'.

Oakhill, J.V., Hartt, J., & Samols, D. (2005). 'Levels of comprehension monitoring and working memory in good and poor comprehenders. *Reading and Writing, 18,* 657–713.

Paris, S.G., & Jacobs, J.E. (1984). 'The benefits of informed instruction for children's reading awareness and comprehension skills'. *Child Development, 55,* 2083–2093.

Paris, S.G., Saarnio, D.A., & Cross, D.R. (1986). 'A metacognitive curriculum to promote children's reading and learning'. *Australian Journal of Psychology, 38,* 107–123.

Perfetti, C.A. (1985). *Reading ability*. New York: Oxford University Press.

Scarborough, H. (2005). 'Developmental relationships between language and reading: Reconciling a beautiful hypothesis with some ugly facts'. In H.W. Catts & A.G. Kamhi (eds), *The connections between language and reading disabilities* (pp. 3–24). Mahwah, NJ: LEA.

Stanovich, K.E. (1986). 'Matthew effects in reading: Some consequences of individual differences in the acquisition of literacy'. *Reading Research Quarterly, 21*(4), 360–406.

—— (1993). 'Does reading make you smarter? Literacy and the development of verbal intelligence'. In H. Reese (ed.), *Advances in child development and behavior, Vol. 24* (pp. 133–180). San Diego, CA: Academic Press.

Stein, N.L., & Glenn, C.G. (1982) 'Children's concept of time: the development of story schema'. In W Friedman, J. (ed.), *The Developmental Psychology of Time* (pp. 255–282), New York: Academic Press.

Stothard, S.E., & Hulme, C. (1992). 'Reading comprehension difficulties in children: The role of language comprehension and working memory skills'. *Reading and Writing, 4,* 245–256.

Yuill, N., & Joscelyne, T. (1988). 'Effect of organisational cues and strategies on good and poor comprehenders' story understanding'. *Journal of Educational Psychology, 80,* 152–158.

Yuill, N., & Oakhill, J. (1988). 'Understanding of anaphoric relations in skilled and less skilled comprehenders'. *British Journal of Psychology, 79,* 173–186.

Yuill, N.M., & Oakhill, J.V. (1991). *Children's problems in text comprehension: An experimental investigation.* Cambridge: Cambridge University Press.

Yuill, N.M., Oakhill, J.V., & Parkin, A.J. (1989). 'Working memory, comprehension skill and the resolution of text anomaly'. *British Journal of Psychology, 80,* 351–361.

Zwaan, R.A., & Radvansky, G.A. (1998). 'Situation models in language comprehension and memory. *Psychological Bulletin, 123,* 162–185.

Chapter 5

The acquisition of spelling patterns

Early, late or never?

Nenagh Kemp

hi dr. kemp i no this is prob not ur area but if u could give me someones email who is that would be nice. their is a little conjecture as to if the essay plan and intro are on just the bio prespective or comparison of bio and cog prespectives? cheers sarah.

In order to become fully literate, an individual must learn not only to read, but to write and spell: to represent spoken language as a series of printed symbols, in a conventional order. In English, this involves learning patterns that go beyond phonology. Computerised spell-checkers have made it easier to achieve many correct spellings, but can remain unhelpful for such distinctions as *passed* or *past*; *you're* or *your*. The advent of text-messaging might lead to a generation of writers who find that such distinctions are often not even relevant: the whole *you're/your* dilemma is precluded if one can simply write *ur*. The email above was written by an undergraduate who apparently had little concern as to the conventionality of her spelling, and to the impression that it might make. Nevertheless, many people would still agree that the ability to spell remains essential for making oneself understood, for appearing intelligent and literate (Gerber & Hall, 1987), and for keeping sufficient cognitive resources available to decide what to write next (Bereiter, 1980).

This chapter briefly considers the nature of the English spelling system, and some of the models that have described its typical course of acquisition. Many orthographic and morphological spelling conventions do seem to require several years of writing instruction to achieve, and are thus acquired relatively 'late'. However, other evidence suggests that children may represent some simple conventions from when they first begin to write, and thus relatively 'early'. This chapter discusses how the patterns studied, and the methodology chosen, can lead to rather different conclusions about the timing of the acquisition of many spelling patterns. Further, it presents evidence that some apparently simple English spelling conventions may take much longer to acquire than is commonly assumed, and in some cases, may be achieved not just 'late', but 'never'.

The English spelling system

The English spelling system is basically alphabetic: the letter, or grapheme *b*, for example, corresponds to the sound, or phoneme /b/. However, the spelling of many words cannot be predicted entirely on the basis of such grapheme-phoneme correspondences. Several plausible sound-based spellings may exist (e.g. *sight, cite, site*), or a letter sequence may not fully reflect a sound sequence (e.g. *yacht, laugh*). In these cases, the correct spelling must simply be memorised. Some sound-based spellings are overridden by orthographic conventions, which can vary with word position. For example, the sound /ɔɪ/ is written *oi* in the middle of words (e.g. *boil*), but *oy* at the end (e.g. *boy*), and some letters may be doubled in the middle of words (e.g. *mm*) but not at the beginning or end.

English orthography sometimes represents the morphological structure of words, at the expense of reflecting their particular phonetic form. This structure determines the spelling of inflectional endings such as past-tense *–ed* and plural *–s*. For example, despite variations in pronunciation, the ending *–ed* is maintained across regular past verbs, as in *walked, warned, waited*. Similarly, because regular plurals end in *–s*, plurals with a final /ks/ sound require the spelling *cks* (e.g. *tracks*), whereas non-plurals with this final sound require *x* (e.g. *tax*). Words can also be derived from related words (e.g. *darkness* from *dark*; *forgetful* from *forget*), and another morphological influence on English spelling is that the spelling of many 'base' words is maintained in their inflected and derived forms, despite changes in pronunciation (e.g. *deal/dealt, define/definite*). Writers must learn such conventions to be able to write the many words whose spelling cannot be achieved on the basis of sound alone.

Models of English spelling development

Various models have described the development of English spelling, from the pre-schooler's first scribbles to the adolescent's representation of complex letter patterns (e.g. Bear & Templeton, 1998; Ehri, 1992; Frith, 1985; Gentry, 1982; Henderson, 1985, 1992). Some describe an initial stage of a preliterate jumble of letters and symbols, followed by the more conventional use of letter sounds/names (e.g. *et* for *eat*). The next major stage involves writing words on the basis of letter–sound correspondences. However, this phonetic approach is not enough. Children soon need to learn to represent the orthographic and morphological patterns that characterise the spelling of many English words. The models generally agree that children next learn simple orthographic conventions (e.g. the 'silent *e*' of *rat/rate, kit/kite*). After two to three years of instruction, children learn more complex patterns (e.g. *–ight, –ough*), and then morphological patterns, beginning with common inflectional endings such as *–ed, –s*, and *–ing*, and then consonant doubling rules (e.g. *supper/super*). Only in the final stages are children seen to begin to represent more complex derivational patterns (e.g. *equal/equality*), and to use analogy to spell similar-sounding words (e.g. *critical/criticise*). The authors of these models recognise that learning to spell in English is a lifelong process, but do suggest that the typical child acquires the major spelling rules and patterns by the end of primary school.

However, this view of spelling development may overlook some of the complexities of children's early spelling knowledge. Research in more general cognitive development has led to the idea of children's knowledge progressing not in discrete steps, but in 'overlapping waves' (e.g. Siegler, 1994), and this idea has been extended to account for spelling development as well (e.g. Caravolas, 2004; Varnhagen *et al.*, 1997). In a longitudinal study, Rittle-Johnson and Siegler (1999) showed that children used a variety of spelling strategies from early on (including sounding-out, whole-word retrieval, analogy, and rules), and that as more efficient strategies were added, children became better at choosing the most appropriate one.

The above models, whether composed of 'steps' or of 'waves', describe the development of spelling strategies, but they do not provide an explicit explanation of how spelling skills are actually acquired. Connectionist models, in contrast, can provide a framework for explaining how children might learn some of the regularities of their writing system (e.g. Bullinaria, 1997; Houghton & Zorzi, 2003). These models are trained to associate phonological input with orthographic output, and to date they have shown some success. A connectionist approach focuses on how the output (spelling) reflects the statistical patterns in the input: for the models this input is the words' sounds, but for the beginning speller, input comes also from printed letter patterns. This approach emphasises the importance of statistical regularities in learning to represent written words. Since learning is based on the input, and since these regularities are varied, it is predicted that children learn a variety of spelling patterns simultaneously, rather than serially. Although much further work will be necessary to elaborate these models, already a number of spelling researchers have begun to interpret their findings in terms of a connectionist or statistical learning framework (e.g. Nation, 1997; Pollo *et al.*, 2007).

Spelling patterns that emerge 'early'

Phonological conventions

Most researchers would agree that phonology is the main influence on early spelling. Supporting evidence comes from a range of studies in English, both naturalistic (e.g. Chomsky, 1979; Treiman, 1993) and experimental (e.g. Beers & Beers, 1992; Varnhargen *et al.*, 1997), and from other alphabetic orthographies as well, including French (Sprenger-Charolles *et al.*, 2003), Arabic (Abu-Rabia & Taha, 2006), and Greek (Bryant *et al.*, 1999). However, other studies suggest that children at the 'phonetic' stage are not restricted to spelling according to sound alone, but may be sensitive to other conventions as well.

Orthographic conventions

As stage models of spelling development suggest, some orthographic patterns do take years to acquire, although the conclusions drawn depend on the particular patterns tested. For example, children fail to consistently double the consonant when adding an inflectional ending such as *-ed* to real words such as *pat–patted* in grade 3 (Walker & Hauerwas, 2006), and to pseudowords such as *rop–ropped* in grade 6 (Beers & Beers, 1992). Walker and Hauerwas also showed that children in grades 1 and 2 were better at dropping *e* (as in *hope–hoping*) than at doubling the consonant, and better at both when adding *-ing* than when adding *-ed* to pseudoword stems.

More subtle orthographic conventions also exist in English spelling. The spelling of word-final consonants can depend on the preceding vowel/s (Kessler & Treiman, 2001). For example, /f/ is spelled *ff* more often after a vowel spelled with one letter (e.g. *cliff*) but as *f* or *fe* after a vowel spelled with two letters (e.g. *loaf, knife*). Similarly, the spelling of some word-initial consonants is affected by their following vowels. For example, /k/ is normally spelled *c*, but before *e* and *i* it is more often spelled *k* (e.g. *keep, kiss*). Adults tend to follow such orthographic conventions when spelling pseudowords (e.g. Perry & Ziegler, 2004; Treiman *et al.*, 2002). Even children are sensitive to these orthographic conventions. The effects of word-initial consonants on the spelling of following vowels, and of preceding vowels on the spelling of word-final consonants, are evident in the pseudoword spelling of children in the first two years of school, although it seems to take several more years for these effects to become reliable for all letters/sounds tested (Hayes *et al.*, 2006; Treiman & Kessler, 2006).

Sensitivity to simple orthographic conventions may be present from when children first begin to write. Treiman (1993) observed that first-graders rarely doubled word-initial consonants illegally, and used frequently doubled consonants (e.g. *ee*, *bb*) more often than illegal ones (e.g. *hh*, *kk*). These observations were confirmed experimentally by Cassar and Treiman (1997), who asked participants to decide which member of various pseudoword pairs 'looked best'. Above-chance performance was shown as early as kindergarten for doublet position (e.g. *piff* vs. *ppif*) and by grade 1 for doublet identify (e.g. *soll* vs. *sohh*). Cassar and Treiman then allocated participants to spelling model 'stages' (Gentry, 1982; Ehri, 1992), based on their general spelling. They found that even children apparently spelling at a semi-phonetic or phonetic stage showed sensitivity to these simple orthographic conventions.

Taken together, these studies support a statistical learning view: since orthographic patterns are not always explicitly taught, both children and adults must learn them simply through repeated exposure to printed words. Further, rather than entering a stage of successful 'orthographic spelling' after some years of writing instruction, children seem to learn a variety of orthographic patterns one by one, beginning with simple consonant-doubling patterns, and gradually progressing to increasingly complex, context-dependent patterns.

Derivational morphological conventions

The spelling models' prediction, that an understanding of derivational links is not acquired until relatively late, makes intuitive sense. Derivational relations are generally more complex and less predictable than inflectional relations: the links of meaning between, for example, *sign* and *signal*, or *heal* and *healthy*, are not as transparent as those between *sign* and *signs*, or *heal* and *healed*. Further, it is clear that statistical learning alone is probably insufficient as a strategy to spell such words. However, not all derivational relationships are as opaque as the examples frequently given. It is difficult to imagine that even young children fail to notice the links of meaning between *mud* and *muddy*, or *teach* and *teacher*. The usual method of testing such understanding has been to observe whether children spell the common stem of the two words in the same way, regardless of changes in pronunciation.

Both naturalistic and experimental studies have shown that although transparently derived forms (e.g. *active*, from *act*) are generally spelled correctly by the age of 11–12 years, the representation of more opaquely derived forms (e.g. *equality*, from *equal*) is still inconsistent (Green *et al.*, 2003; Sterling, 1983), and may remain so for at least several more years (Carlisle, 1988). Evidence from these and similar studies (e.g. Templeton, 1980; Zutell, 1980) concurs that writers can abstract out the base words of derivationally related forms before the end of primary school, but there is still room for further improvement.

Testing this ability can be simplified by providing children with the spelling of part of the word, and asking them just to spell the base section. Deacon and Bryant (2006) found that children in grades 1 to 3 were significantly better at spelling base morphemes (e.g. *mess* in *messily*) than identical but non-morphemic segments (e.g. *mess* in *message*). This was taken to show early appreciation of the role of base morphemes in spelling derived forms. However, this scoring technique must be used with caution. Younger children do not yet know many derived words (Nagy *et al.*, 1989), and thus testing whether children know to spell, for example, *inflammation* on the basis of *inflame* (Zutell, 1980) might prove meaningless if participants do not know these words in the first place. In contrast, the very simplicity of more transparent derivational relations can make it impossible to tell whether these links have been noticed. If a child writes *sun* for 'sun' and *suny* for 'sunny', this spelling consistency might indicate not a recognition of the common meaning, but merely of the common sounds. Thus, if we are to draw valid conclusions about young children's understanding of transparent derivational relations, we must be careful about the words that we ask them to write.

Some studies have used a more lenient scoring system, testing whether writers maintain the spelling of a crucial section of a base word in its derived or inflected form. This 'crucial section' is typically the base word's final phoneme, to which a morphological ending is then added (e.g. *pin–pinned; noise–noisy*). Treiman *et al.* (1994) showed that American children in kindergarten to grade 4 used the correct letter, *t* or *d*, significantly more often to represent the medial 'flap' sound /ɾ/ of two-morpheme words such as *dirty* and *cloudy*, than of similar one-morpheme words such as *duty* and *sturdy*. The authors concluded that children must have used the final sound of the base words (e.g. *dirt*) to help spell the ambiguous sound of their inflected/derived forms (e.g. *dirty*). These conclusions were confirmed by Kemp (2006): British children in grades 1 to 4 used *s* and *z* correctly significantly more often to spell the medial /z/ sound of two-morpheme (e.g. *noisy, breezy*) than one-morpheme words (e.g. *daisy, dizzy*).

Overall, studies on children's representation of derivational morphology have produced a mixed range of findings, depending on both the nature of the words used, and the stringency of the scoring system. More complex derivational relationships do seem to take a long time to acquire. However, recent evidence provides a more positive assessment of young writers' early morphological knowledge. It appears that even children in kindergarten, and certainly those in their first two years of school, have at least a rudimentary ability to analyse words into their component morphemes, and to use this ability when spelling derived words.

Spelling patterns that emerge 'late'

So far the news has been relatively good. Although children do seem to take several years to acquire some spelling patterns, there is mounting evidence that stage-based spelling models may underestimate early sensitivity to some aspects of English orthography. Now for the bad news. Some of the rules and patterns which the spelling models would predict that individuals learn and use consistently by the end of primary school, do not seem to be acquired so easily after all. In some cases, even highly literate adults show only a very shaky grasp of apparently simple rules for spelling words appropriately for the context.

Plural –s

Perhaps the most striking example of an accepted 'early' convention (Gentry, 1982; Henderson, 1985) that may actually be acquired rather late is the plural ending –s. English has a clear morphological rule: regular plural nouns are spelled with a final s, whether pronounced with /s/ (as in cups) or /z/ (as in mugs). Children's spelling of this inflection has received relatively little experimental attention, but naturalistic studies suggest that children tend to use –s consistently for plurals from when they first begin to write (Read, 1986; Treiman, 1993). However, a series of studies by Kemp suggest that the apparent early use of this inflectional rule might in fact reflect the use of statistical regularities: the frequency with which certain letters tend to co-occur in certain word positions.

Most spellers of English could explain the 'plural rule' that regular plurals are spelled with –s, even if they could not also explain that singular nouns with a final /z/ can be spelled with z, zz, ze or se, but virtually never with s (the handful of exceptions includes proper names such as James, and the singular nouns lens and summons). However, subtle orthographic constraints also govern the spelling of word-final /z/. When a singular noun ends in a voiced consonant (such as /b/ or /g/), its plural form is always pronounced with a final /z/ and spelled with s (e.g. fibs, frogs). Simply through exposure, children may learn that /z/ can be represented as s or z, that final spelling sequences such as bz and gz never occur, and that word-final sounds /bz/ and /gz/ are spelled bs and gs. They would not have to use the plural rule, but rely on statistical learning. However, for words ending in a long (tense) vowel sound + /z/, only the plural rule can distinguish when to use a final s (for plurals such as trays and fleas), versus a non –s spelling, such as se or ze (for non-plurals such as phrase and freeze).

Kemp and Bryant (2003) asked British children in grades 1 to 4 to write real words and pseudowords, both plural and non-plural, ending in the sound /z/, to test the extent to which writers relied on morphological and orthographic constraints to spell their endings. Some of the words were 'overdetermined' plurals (e.g. buns, wigs): the need to use a final s was determined both by orthographic constraints (the singular form ended in a voiced consonant) and morphological constraints (the sentence context made it clear that words were plurals). Other words were 'morphologically determined' plurals (e.g. jaws, fleas): the need to use a final s could not be determined from orthographic constraints (e.g. fleeze and fleese would be orthographically plausible representations of fleas), but only from morphological constraints (the plural sentence context). In Experiment 1 (real words), children used s correctly significantly more often to spell overdetermined plurals (mean 91 per cent) than morphologically determined plurals (mean 73 per cent). Experiment 2 (pseudo-words) included morphologically determined non-plurals (e.g. preeze) as well as plurals (e.g. prees). Again, children correctly used s significantly more for over-determined plurals such as pleens (mean 74 per cent) than for morphologically determined plurals such as prees (mean 37 per cent), for which the use of –s did not differ significantly from the use of –s for morphologically determined non-plurals such as preeze (mean 32 per cent). Better spellers (mean spelling age 9.5 years) did use –s significantly more for morphologically determined plurals than non-plurals, although only to a limited extent, while the poorer spellers did not discriminate.

Table 5.1 Mean proportions of use of 's' to spell pseudoword endings, by university students

Word Type	Study					
	Kemp & Bryant (2003); Study 3, Uni students, $n = 19$		Kemp (2002), $n = 60$		Kemp (in prep), $n = 112$	
End sound	/s/	/z/	/s/	/z/	/s/	/z/
Overdetermined plurals (e.g., *pleens, prooks*)	–	0.97 (0.06)	0.95 (0.11)	0.97 (0.09)	–	–
Morphologically determined plurals (e.g., *prees, smicks*)	–	0.64 (0.35)	0.78 (0.27)	0.65 (0.29)	0.98 (0.08)	0.92 (0.15)
Morphologically determined non-plurals (e.g., *preeze, smix*)	–	0.11 (0.15)	0.43 (0.34)	0.30 (0.29)	0.32 (0.36)	0.07 (0.13)
Morphologically determined words in neutral sentences (e.g., *prees/preese/preeze, smicks/smix*)	–	–	0.67 (0.23)	0.48 (0.25)	0.74 (0.24)	0.40 (0.24)

Even if the plural rule takes longer to acquire than predicted by spelling models, it would seem reasonable to assume that it would be consistently applied by adulthood. However, Kemp and Bryant's (2003) Experiment 3 showed that this is not the case. The mean use of *s* for the same pseudowords, spelled by the 19 adult participants who had a tertiary education, is shown in Table 5.1. These adults were more often correct than the children (and than adults with a secondary education) in their use of *s* for plurals and avoidance of *s* for non-plurals, but performance was still far from perfect. A further study (Kemp, 2002) investigated this unexpected finding. Sixty British undergraduates wrote, to dictation, pseudowords embedded in sentences which made their plural or non-plural status clear. Neutral contexts (e.g. *His garden is full of* _____) were also included. Half of the pseudowords had a final /z/ sound, and half had a final /s/, which was preceded by /k/ and either a long (tense) or short (lax) vowel sound (e.g. *prooks, smicks/smix*). English words ending in /ks/ preceded by a long vowel sound (two vowel letters) are usually spelled with *k(e)s*, but not *x* (e.g. *beaks, lakes*). Thus, the spelling of words ending in long vowel + /ks/ is 'overdetermined': *ks* is usually the correct spelling, regardless of morphology. The spelling of words ending in a short vowel + /ks/, however, can only be determined by morphology; the spellings *x* and *cks* are both possible (e.g. *tax, tucks; six, socks*). As shown in Table 5.1, participants' spelling of pseudoword endings was remarkably similar to that reported in Kemp and Bryant's (2003) Experiment 3. In both studies, overdetermined plurals (e.g. *pleens, prooks*) were spelled correctly with *s* nearly all of the time. Morphologically determined plurals (e.g. *prees, smicks*) were spelled correctly with *s* much less often. Morphologically determined non-plurals (e.g. *preese/ preeze, smix*) were spelled incorrectly with *s* more often in Kemp's (2002) study than in Kemp and Bryant's (2003) study, and the use of *s* was greater for /s/ than /z/ pseudowords. Nevertheless, the incorrect use of *s* was significantly less than the use of *s* in the 'baseline', neutral condition.

The results from these studies converge on the same conclusion: when writing plurals, children and adults are influenced less by a reliable, morphology-based rule, than by sensitivity to untaught, position-dependent letter patterns. Perhaps if writers are encouraged to attend to words' morphological structure, they will be more likely to use a morphological rule. A further study (Kemp, in preparation) tested this idea, by presenting morphologically determined words which could be spelled in several ways, depending on context. For example, /faɪz/ would be spelled *fies* as a plural, but *fize* or *fise* as a non-plural. Sentence pairs were presented to 112 British undergraduates. The first sentence contained a form of the target pseudoword, either inflected or uninflected, and the second sentence contained an alternative form, for example:

- Plural to singular: *That man keeps several* fizes. *Have you ever seen a* fize?
- Singular to plural: *Could you get me a* pree? *Actually, get me three* prees.
- Neutral to neutral: *She put* droes/droze *all over the cake. I hate cake covered in* droes/droze!

Half the participants heard and wrote the second form of the target pseudoword to dictation, while the other half had to produce it themselves from the first form, as in Berko's (1958) 'Wug' test, and then write it down. This latter process was assumed to require more attention to the morphology of the pseudowords, than merely writing the target form to dictation. Within each condition, 32 pseudowords (half with a final /s/ sound, half with /z/) were presented in plural, non-plural, and neutral sentences. Unexpectedly, condition seemed to have little effect, and so the results, summarised in Table 5.1, are collapsed across the four conditions. The use of *s* in neutral sentences was broadly similar to that reported by Kemp (2002). However, focusing attention on pseudoword morphology did seem to improve spelling. The appropriate use of *s* for plurals increased, and the inappropriate use of *s* for non-plurals decreased for /z/ pseudowords. Yet, participants still used *s* inappropriately for non-plural /s/ pseudowords about one-third of the time, which suggests an incomplete understanding of the morphological basis of the plural rule.

Thus, the use of even such an apparently simple orthographic rule is not always consistent, even in highly literate adults. Even when it appears that a particular rule is being used, more careful investigation may reveal that there are other spelling strategies also at play: in this case, statistical knowledge about the likelihood with which certain word-final letter combinations occur in English words.

Plurals and possessives: using apostrophes

Morphemes that are silent in spoken language but marked in written language are especially difficult to acquire. In French, the final –*s* of plural nouns (e.g. *la lampe, les lampes*) and the final –*ent* of plural verbs (e.g. *il mange, ils mangent*) usually go unpronounced. French children take one to two years of school instruction to spell these endings consistently (Totereau *et al.*, 1997), and often go through a period of overgeneralising endings to the wrong grammatical class (e.g. Fayol, Thévenin *et al.*, 1999). In English, the apostrophe represents a spelling distinction with an entirely morphological basis. This symbol distinguishes words that are pronounced identically: the possessive (e.g. *the **baby's** cry; the **babies'** cries*), the plural (e.g. *the **babies*** *cry*), and some contractions (e.g. *the baby's crying*). It can thus provide a particularly strong test of morphological understanding.

Few studies have attempted such a test, but Bryant *et al.* (1997) taught children in grades 5, 6, and 7, over ten sessions, to include apostrophes in possessives and omit them from plurals. The grade 5 children performed similarly to control groups, with virtually no change from pre- to post-test. In contrast, grade 6 and 7 children in the training group showed a dramatic improvement in their spelling of possessives. However, at post-test they continued to misspell plurals with as many inappropriate apostrophes as before. A later cross-sectional study confirmed that children in grades 4, 5, and 6 performed poorly at including apostrophes in possessives (barely above 50 per cent correct) and omitting them from plurals (below 50 per cent correct) (Bryant *et al.*, 2000), even though school instruction in apostrophe use had begun in grade 5. Thus, the ability to recognise and represent the apparently clear semantic distinction between plurality and possession seems to present continuing difficulties, even with intensive training.

It might nevertheless seem reasonable to expect that apostrophe use would be understood by intelligent, literate adults. I asked 65 Australian undergraduates, with English as a first language, to write to dictation a short passage which included four nouns (*lady, boy, watch,* and *dish*) each appearing in plural, singular possessive, and plural possessive forms. Despite some inappropriate apostrophe intrusions (e.g. *The boy's went shopping*), the plural forms (e.g. *boys*) were spelled mainly correctly (mean 94 per cent correct, $SD = 14$). However, singular possessives (e.g. *lady's*) were spelled significantly more poorly (61 per cent, $SD = 39$), and plural possessives (e.g. *ladies'*) significantly more poorly still (39 per cent, $SD = 38$), $F(2, 128) = 64.2$, $p < .001$. Possessive errors included apostrophe omission (21 per cent occurrence for singular possessives and 44 per cent for plural possessives), apostrophes included in the wrong place, as in *boy's* for *boys'* (6 per cent singular possessives, 16 per cent plural possessives), and even apostrophes included in unconventional places, as in *ladie's* and *dish'es* (9 per cent singular possessives, 2 per cent plural possessives). Most students could not remember being formally taught the rules for apostrophe use, and claimed to use apostrophes when they 'looked right', a judgement which the data suggest to be rather unreliable.

These students' difficulty with using apostrophes correctly is perhaps not surprising given the abundance of signs and brochures, advertising, for example, *mascara's* and *Womens magazines*, or the defiant *Residents refuse to be put in bins* (seen above the waste disposal area of a housing block). It seems that many writers develop the ability to decide when to include or exclude the apostrophe not merely 'late', but often 'never'.

Orthographic patterns

As already described, adults are sensitive to subtle orthographic conventions in their spelling, but they appear to be better at learning these untaught, frequency-based patterns than the simpler rules about joining syllables and morphemes described in the spelling models. Fischer *et al.* (1985) and Burt (2006) asked good and poor spellers at university to write down suffixed pseudowords to dictation, for which the written stems were provided (e.g. *prin–prinnish, regrun–regrunnable*). In both studies, mean scores were quite low overall (about 44 per cent), with significant differences between good and poor spellers. These two studies provide evidence that even into adulthood, 'syllable junction' rules, seen by stage models to develop during the mid- to late primary school years, are not yet fully attained. Adults seem to fall back on an 'earlier' sound-based strategy when their specific orthographic strategies prove inadequate.

Derivational morphological conventions

Just as stage models of spelling development may underestimate early understanding of morphological relations, they may also overestimate adults' ability to represent derivational links. Derwing et al. (1995) asked undergraduate students to spell 50 words, some derived (e.g. acknowledge, from know), and some not, but which could potentially be seen as such (e.g. infinitesimal might be seen to come from infant). Participants' spelling was far from perfect, for both word types. University students also have difficulty in representing the links of meaning between related real words (e.g. confer–conference, addict–addiction) (Fischer et al., 1985; Kemp, 2005), and in choosing 'possible' (e.g. reblit–reblissable) versus 'impossible' (e.g. vordant–vordition) spellings for ostensibly related pseudoword pairs (Burt, 2006), with better spellers outperforming poorer ones. Together, these findings point to the important conclusion that even literate adults may have developed only a partial ability to represent links of meaning in spelling. Further, in many cases adults seem to recruit other, less adequate, strategies to spell more difficult words, often without complete success.

Some intervention studies

Intervention with children

There is ample evidence that phonology-based intervention can improve children's skills in reading, spelling, and linguistic awareness (e.g. Bradley & Bryant, 1983; Hatcher et al., 2004). Fewer studies have considered the effects of morphology-based intervention. Arnbak and Elbro (2000) gave 12 weeks of remedial training to children with dyslexia in grades 4 and 5. These children improved in reading comprehension and spelling of morphologically complex words, significantly more than children given non-morphological training. Nunes et al. (2003) gave 12 weekly intervention sessions to children in grades 3 and 4, with game-like activities focused on morphological stems, endings, and grammatical categories. The spelling of derivational suffixes (e.g. –ion, –ian) improved significantly more in groups who had learned about morphology with the support of writing than in groups who had not had the aid of writing, or who had learned about phonological distinctions instead. However, there was no effect of morphological training on the preservation of the base form of derived words (e.g. 'soam' in the pseudoword soamer). These findings suggest that it is possible to improve children's spelling of some, but by no means all, morphological patterns through a dozen training sessions. This lends support to the contention of stage-based spelling models, that the mastery of the written representation of derivational morphology takes more than a few years to achieve, even with focused intervention. From the 'overlapping waves' view of spelling development (Rittle-

Johnson & Siegler, 1999), it seems that derivation-based spelling strategies may need to be supplemented by other spelling strategies for a number of years.

Intervention with adults

Anyone who has marked a high-school or university essay may have noticed the frequent confusion of similar-sounding words, which suggests that orthographic and morphological spelling conventions are not always followed (a suggestion supported by the research evidence discussed earlier). Remembering the plural rule would help students to avoid such errors as '*Adolescence* often show this behaviour', and thinking about the role of past-tense *-ed* might reduce the number of mistakes such as '*Passed* research in this area', or 'Some participants *past* this test'. Possessive pronouns and their homophones are also frequently misspelled (e.g. *it's* for *its*, *there* for *their*), but the spelling of these simple, frequent words can also be disambiguated by the use of grammatical rules.

Inspired by Nunes *et al.*'s (2003) (partially) successful morphological intervention, I developed a similar training programme for undergraduates. I reasoned that if the spelling of these apparently simple words is indeed largely in place by the end of primary school, then a short but focused intervention should suffice to 'remind' young adults of how to write these words correctly. Perhaps optimistically, I assumed that students must, at some level, understand that regular past verbs require *-ed*, that apostrophes indicate contraction or possession, and that *whose* and *who's* are different – they simply don't always bother to represent this understanding in writing. Three weekly intervention sessions were designed to remind students of the nature and use of morphology-based spelling conventions. The results of one part of this study are summarised here, and in Kemp (2007).

Participants were 121 Australian university students, aged 19 to 64 years, with a mean age of 23 years. The 87 intervention participants were undergraduate psychology students, who recruited 34 of their same-age university friends to act as controls. General spelling ability, assessed on the spelling subtest of the Wide Range Achievement Test 4 (Wilkinson & Robertson, 2006), did not differ significantly between the intervention group (mean = 112.84, SD = 12.77) and the control group (mean = 108.63, SD = 12.62). At pre- and post-test, participants wrote, to dictation, one of two sets of counterbalanced words, embedded in a cloze passage. In each set there were 16 'content' words of relatively low frequency: 8 inflected words matched to 8 non-inflected control words, ending in the sound /s/ or /z/. The inflected words were nouns and verbs that required a final *-s* spelling (e.g. *hammocks, arrays*), and were matched to similar but non-inflected words which required an alternative spelling (e.g. *equinox, malaise*). The 15 'function' words included possessive pronouns and their homophones (e.g. *your, you're; its, it's*).

Run with groups of about 25, the intervention sessions used explicit teaching and game-like activities to focus on a variety of spelling patterns, including possessive pronouns and their homophones, and inflectional and non-inflectional word endings. Activities included looking for spelling regularities in related words, distinguishing words' grammatical category on the basis of their endings (e.g. *tax, rays* vs. *tacks, raise*), and sorting clippings from advertising brochures into 'right' and 'wrong' spelling categories. Control participants received no training.

Both groups experienced some difficulty in spelling the experimental words. When writing the endings of content words, the intervention group produced a mean of 91 per cent (SD = 11) correct spellings at both pre-test and post-test. The control group produced 84 per cent (SD = 19) at pre-test and 87 per cent (SD = 15) at post-test. For function words, the intervention group's mean percentage of correct spellings was 81 per cent (SD = 19) at pre-test, and 88 per cent (SD = 15) at post-test. The control group wrote 73 per cent correct (SD = 21) at pre-test, and 81 per cent (SD = 19) at post-test. A repeated-measures ANOVA showed a significant improvement in overall spelling of the experimental words from pre- to post-test, $F(1, 117)$ = 19.8, p < .001, but no significant effects of, or interactions with, group. Thus, although writing a similar set of words a second time may have made participants more careful about their spelling, the three weeks of intervention had no specific effect on the spelling of morphologically determined words overall.

Content words were spelled significantly better than function words, $F(1, 117)$ = 27.1, p < .001. It is interesting that this small, closed, highly frequent set of possessive pronouns and their homophones was spelled so poorly by these highly literate, educated adults, and that even specific training did not lead to specific improvement. The intervention participants still erred about 12 per cent of the time, and their control peers about 19 per cent of the time, in spelling words such as *there* and *their*. Finally, time and word type interacted significantly, $F(1, 117)$ = 9.70, p = .002. The spelling of content words did not improve from pre- to post-test, but the spelling of function words did. Again, the lack of interaction with group suggests that this improvement probably stemmed from practice, rather than intervention. Thus, some errors may reflect a lack of care, rather than a lack of understanding. It is possible that the large-group format was not sufficiently engaging for all participants, and to address this, a repeat intervention is currently underway with smaller groups. However, overall these results suggest that a short but focused intervention programme is not enough to 'remind' university students of simple spelling patterns which are conventionally assumed to be in place by the end of primary school.

Implications and conclusions

The experiments summarised in this chapter demonstrate that spellers of all levels show a variety of strengths and weaknesses, and do not fit neatly with the descriptions of conventional stage-based models of spelling development. Some spelling patterns do take several years or more to acquire. Others seem to be learned much earlier, or instead much later (if at all), than the models would predict. It is clear that children's spelling improves with time and experience. However, rather than moving step-wise through stages of strategy use, it seems that writers are able to use strategies based on phonology, orthography, and morphology at each point in development, even if at some points they tend to rely more on some strategies than others. These findings are consistent with an 'overlapping waves' view of spelling development (Rittle-Johnson & Siegler, 1999). In the future, connectionist models (e.g. Bullinaria, 1997; Houghton & Zorzi, 2003) could provide a more complete framework for understanding the way that spelling strategies might be acquired.

This chapter emphasises evidence that many skilled adult spellers may have only a shaky grasp on many spelling conventions, especially complex relations, such as those symbolised by apostrophes and in derivationally related words. But their difficulties extend still further: adults also often struggle with even relatively simple conventions, such as those concerning the doubling of consonants when adding inflections, the spelling of possessive pronouns, and even the use of –*s* to spell plural nouns. Adults may instead spell words simply as they sound, or on the basis of frequent letter co-occurrences. Although the 'waves' of spelling strategies clearly continue to 'overlap' during adulthood, it seems that many adults still find themselves quite 'at sea' when it comes to choosing the appropriate way to tackle the spelling of many words.

The findings presented here have important implications for the teaching of spelling, at all educational levels. If children are sensitive to orthographic and morphological spelling patterns from relatively early, then it would seem appropriate to point these patterns out explicitly to children struggling to learn them. Some of the spelling errors made by educated adult spellers may stem from the literary laziness that comes with the frequent use of informal communication. However, not all errors can be attributed to carelessness, as demonstrated by the brief but focused intervention programme described above. Future intervention would do well to highlight the orthographic and morphological conventions that govern the spelling of so many English words.

If its any constellation i didnt do as well as i had hopped last semester because of an overload in subjects i think!!!

Although many spelling patterns are in place relatively early, and others relatively late, there is still plenty of scope for intervention for those that seem to be acquired 'never'.

References

Abu-Rabia, S., & Taha, H. (2006). 'Phonological errors predominate in Arabic spelling across grades 1–9'. *Journal of Psycholinguistic Research, 35*, 167–188.

Arnbak, E., & Elbro, C. (2000). 'The effects of morphological awareness training on the reading and spelling skills of young dyslexics'. *Scandinavian Journal of Educational Research, 44*, 229–251.

Bear, D.R., & Templeton, S. (1998). 'Explorations in developmental spelling: Foundations for learning and teaching phonics, spelling, and vocabulary'. *The Reading Teacher, 52*, 222–242.

Beers, C.S., & Beers, J.W. (1992). 'Children's spelling of English inflectional morphology'. In S. Templeton & D.R. Bear (eds), *Development of orthographic knowledge and the foundations of literacy: A memorial Festschrift for Edmund H. Henderson* (pp. 231–252). Hillsdale, NJ: LEA.

Bereiter, C. (1980). 'Development in writing'. In L.W. Gregg & E.R. Steinberg (eds), *Cognitive processes in writing* (pp. 73–93). Hillsdale, NJ: LEA.

Berko, J. (1958). 'The child's learning of English morphology'. *Word, 14*, 150–177.

Bradley, L., & Bryant, P.E. (1983). 'Categorising sounds and learning to read – a causal connection'. *Nature, 301*, 419–421.

Bryant, P.E., Devine, M., Ledward, A., & Nunes, T. (1997). 'Spelling with apostrophes and understanding possession'. *British Journal of Educational Psychology, 67*, 91–110.

Bryant, P.E., Nunes, T., & Aidinis, A. (1999). 'Different morphemes, same spelling problems: Cross-linguistic developmental studies'. In M. Harris & G. Hatano (eds),

Learning to read and write: A cross-linguistic perspective (pp. 112–133). Cambridge: Cambridge University Press.

Bryant, P.E., Nunes, T., & Bindman, M. (2000). 'The relations between children's linguistic awareness and spelling: The case of the apostrophe'. *Reading and Writing, 12,* 253–276.

Bullinaria, J. (1997). 'Modelling reading, spelling, and past tense learning with artificial neural networks'. *Brain and Language, 59,* 236–266.

Burt, J.S. (2006). 'Spelling in adults: The combined influences of language skills and reading experience'. *Journal of Psycholinguistic Research, 35,* 447–470.

Caravolas, M. (2004). 'Spelling development in alphabetic writing systems: a crosslinguistic perspective'. *European Psychologist, 9,* 3–14.

Carlisle, J.F. (1988). 'Knowledge of derivational morphology and spelling ability in fourth, sixth and eighth graders'. *Applied Psycholinguistics, 9,* 247–266.

Cassar, M., & Treiman, R. (1997). 'The beginnings of orthographic knowledge: Children's knowledge of double letters in words'. *Journal of Educational Psychology, 89,* 631–644.

Chomsky, C. (1979). 'Approaching reading through invented spelling'. In L.B. Resnick & P.A. Weaver (eds), *Theory and practice of early reading* (Vol. 2, pp. 43–61). Hillsdale, NJ: LEA.

Deacon, S.H., & Bryant, P.E. (2006). 'Getting to the root: Young writers' sensitivity to the role of root morphemes in the spelling of inflected and derived words'. *Journal of Child Language, 33,* 401–417.

Derwing, B.L., Smith, M.L., & Wiebe, G.E. (1995). 'On the role of spelling in morpheme recognition: Experimental studies with children and adults'. In L.B. Feldman (ed.), *Morphological aspects of language processing* (pp. 3–27). Hillsdale, NJ: LEA.

Ehri, L.C. (1992). 'Review and commentary: Stages of spelling development'. In S. Templeton & D.R. Bear (eds), *Development of orthographic knowledge and the foundations of literacy: A memorial festschrift for Edmund H. Henderson* (pp. 307–332). Hillsdale, NJ: LEA.

Fayol, M., Thévenin, M.G., Jarousse, J.P., & Totereau, C. (1999). 'From teaching to learning French written morphology'. In T. Nunes (ed.), *Learning to read: An integrated view from research and practice* (pp. 43–63). Dordrecht: Kluwer.

Fischer, F.W., Shankweiler, D., & Liberman, I.Y. (1985). 'Spelling proficiency and sensitivity to word structure'. *Journal of Memory and Language, 24,* 423–441.

Frith, U. (1985). 'Beneath the surface of developmental dyslexia'. In K. Patterson, M. Coltheart., & J. Marshall (eds), *Surface dyslexia* (pp. 301–330). London: LEA.

Gentry, J.R. (1982). 'An analysis of developmental spelling in GYNS AT WRK'. *The Reading Teacher, 36,* 192–200.

Gerber, M.M., & Hall, R.J. (1987). 'Information-processing approaches to studying spelling difficulties'. *Journal of Learning Disabilities, 20,* 34–42.

Green, L., McCutchen, D., Schwiebert, C., Quinlan, T., Eva-Wood, A., & Juelis, J. (2003). 'Morphological development in children's writing'. *Journal of Educational Psychology, 95,* 752–761.

Hatcher, P.J., Hulme, C., & Snowling, M.J. (2004). 'Explicit phoneme training combined with phonic reading instruction helps young children at risk of reading failure'. *Journal of Child Psychology and Psychiatry, 45,* 338–358.

Hayes, H., Treiman, R., & Kessler, B. (2006). 'Children use vowels to help them spell consonants'. *Journal of Experimental Child Psychology, 94,* 27–42.

Henderson, E.H. (1985). *Teaching spelling.* Boston, MA: Houghton Mifflin.

—— (1992). 'The interface of lexical competence and knowledge of written words'. In S. Templeton & D.R. Bear (eds), *Development of orthographic knowledge and the foundations of literacy: A memorial festschrift for Edmund H. Henderson* (pp. 1–30). Hillsdale, NJ: LEA.

Houghton, G., & Zorzi, M. (2003). 'Normal and impaired spelling in a connectionist dual-route architecture'. *Cognitive Neuropsychology, 20*, 115–162.

Kemp, N. (2002). Adults' spelling of plural pseudowords – Not as good as you'd think. Poster presented at the IX Annual Meeting of the Society for the Scientific Study of Reading, Chicago, IL, June.

—— (2005). Discrete is to disgression … Adults' spelling of base-derived relationships. Poster presented at the XII Annual Meeting of the Society for the Scientific Study of Reading, Toronto, June.

—— (2006). 'Children's spelling of base, inflected, and derived words: Links with morphological awareness'. *Reading and Writing, 19*, 737–765.

—— (2007). Spelling roolz: Intervening to improve university students' spelling of morphological patterns. Paper presented at the XIII Annual Meeting of the Society for the Scientific Study of Reading, Prague, July.

Kemp, N. (in preparation). 'Adults' spelling of plural pseudowords'.

Kemp, N., & Bryant, P. (2003). 'Do beez buzz? Rule-based and frequency-based knowledge in learning to spell plural –*s*'. *Child Development, 74*, 63–74.

Kessler, B., & Treiman, R. (2001). 'Relationships between sounds and letters in English monosyllables'. *Journal of Memory and Language, 44*, 592–617.

Nagy, W., Anderson, R.C., Schommer, M., Scott, J.A., & Stallman, A.C. (1989). 'Morphological families in the internal lexicon'. *Reading Research Quarterly, 24*, 262–282.

Nation, K. (1997). 'Children's sensitivity to rime unit frequency when spelling words and nonwords'. *Reading and Writing, 9*, 321–338.

Nunes, T., Bryant, P., & Olsson, J. (2003). 'Learning morphological and phonological spelling rules: An intervention study'. *Scientific Studies of Reading, 7*, 289–307.

Perry, C., & Ziegler, J.C. (2004). 'Beyond the two-strategy model of skilled spelling: Effects of consistency, grain size, and orthographic redundancy'. *Quarterly Journal of Experimental Psychology A: Human Experimental Psychology, 57A*, 325–356.

Pollo, T.C., Treiman, R., & Kessler, B. (2007). 'Three perspectives on spelling development'. In E.L. Grigorenko & A.J. Naples (eds), *Single-word reading: Behavioural and biological perspectives* (pp. 175–190). New York: LEA.

Read, C. (1986). *Children's creative spelling*. London: Routledge and Kegan Paul.

Rittle-Johnson, B., & Siegler, R.S. (1999). 'Learning to spell: Variability, choice, and change in children's strategy use'. *Child Development, 70*, 332–348.

Siegler, R.S. (1994). 'Cognitive variability: A key to understanding cognitive development'. *Current Directions in Psychological Science, 3*, 1–5.

Sprenger-Charolles, L., Siegel, L., Béchennec, D., & Serniclaes, W. (2003). 'Development of phonological and orthographic processing in reading aloud, in silent reading, and in spelling: A four-year longitudinal study'. *Journal of Experimental Child Psychology, 84*, 194–217.

Sterling, C.M. (1983). 'Spelling errors in context'. *British Journal of Psychology, 74*, 353–364.

Templeton, S. (1980). 'Spelling, phonology, and the older student'. In E.H. Henderson & J.W. Beers (eds), *Developmental and cognitive aspects of learning to spell: A reflection of word knowledge* (pp. 85–96). Newark, DE: International Reading Association.

Totereau, C., Thévenin, M.G., & Fayol, M. (1997). 'The development of the understanding of number morphology in French'. In C. Perfetti, M. Rieben, & M. Fayol (eds), *Learning to spell: Research, theory and practice across languages* (pp. 97–114). Hillsdale, NJ: LEA.

Treiman, R. (1993). *Beginning to spell: A study of first-grade children*. New York: Oxford University Press.

Treiman, R., & Kessler, B. (2006). 'Spelling as statistical learning: Using consonantal context to spell vowels'. *Journal of Educational Psychology, 98*, 642–652.

Treiman, R., Cassar, M., & Zukowski, A. (1994). 'What types of linguistic information do children use in spelling? The case of flaps'. *Child Development, 65*, 1318–1337.

Treiman, R., Kessler, B., & Bick, S. (2002). 'Context sensitivity in the spelling of English vowels'. *Journal of Memory and Language, 47*, 448–468.

Varnhagen, C.K., McCallum, M., & Burstow, M. (1997). 'Is children's spelling naturally stage-like?' *Reading and Writing, 9*, 451–481.

Walker, J., & Hauerwas, L.B. (2006). 'Development of phonological, morphological, and orthographic knowledge in young spellers: The case of inflected verbs'. *Reading and Writing: An Interdisciplinary Journal, 19*, 819–843.

Wilkinson, G.S., & Robertson, G.J. (2006) *Wide Range Achievement Test – 4*. Lutz, FL: Psychological Assessment Resources.

Zutell, J. (1980). 'Children's spelling strategies and their cognitive development'. In E. Henderson & J. Beers (eds), *Developmental and cognitive aspects of learning to spell: A reflection of word knowledge* (pp. 52–73). Newark, DE: International Reading Association.

Chapter 6

Viewing spelling in a cognitive context

Underlying representations and processes

Sarah Critten and Karen J. Pine

Mastering spelling does not always come easy for children. One reason for this is that English orthography is far from straightforward. Success at spelling demands that a great deal of complex information be processed and integrated. Descriptive accounts of spelling development elucidate the skills and knowledge underlying this success (e.g. Ehri, 1998, 1999, 2002; Frith, 1985). These models, together with longitudinal studies of spelling performance, also provide insight into the approximate order in which these skills are acquired (e.g. Caravolas *et al.*, 2001; Nunes *et al.*, 1997). However, far less is known about the cognitive processes underlying spelling development, or the nature of children's spelling representations.

General cognitive models such as the Representational–Redescription (RR) model (Karmiloff-Smith, 1992) and the Overlapping Waves model (Siegler, 1996) have been used to explain cognitive processes of development in other domains. For example, language, notation, and physics (Karmiloff-Smith, 1992), understanding of balance (Pine & Messer, 1998, 1999, 2003), and understanding of basic numerical principles (Chetland & Fluck, 2007) have all been described in relation to the RR model, while processes underlying arithmetic (Cooney *et al.*, 1988; Siegler, 1987, 1988) clock reading (Siegler & McGilly, 1989), and physics (Maloney & Siegler, 1993) have been set in the context of the Overlapping Waves model.

Both models have the potential to define spelling within a cognitive context. The RR model in particular draws on cognitive processes such as implicit and explicit knowledge, and by framing spelling development within this model we can account for what children's verbal explanations reveal about their spelling understanding, going beyond traditional measures of accuracy and errors. We aim to show how, by adopting this approach, greater insight is gained into the explicitness of children's spelling representations. It reveals the extent to which a child's developing knowledge of spelling becomes consciously accessible as well as the strategies children use as they spell. Children's verbal explanations provide an empirical method for testing what children are thinking as they spell, the explicitness of the knowledge they draw upon, why certain errors are made and how representations can be conceptualised.

How is spelling development currently understood?

Traditional accounts of how children learn to spell either document the co-development of reading (e.g. Ehri, 1998, 1999, 2002; Frith, 1985; Share, 1995) or concentrate on spelling alone (e.g. Bear *et al.*, 2000; Gentry & Gillet, 1993; Nunes *et al.*, 1997; Temple *et al.*, 1988). Classic stage-like progression has more recently been usurped by more phase-like approaches (e.g. Ehri, 1998, 1999, 2002), where the type of knowledge applied may depend on experience with the words being spelt.

Joint models and single spelling models

Models of spelling, whether documenting a co-development with reading, or concentrating on spelling alone, tend to describe similar stages/phases of the type of knowledge acquired and the approximate order of occurrence. It is suggested that early lexical processing is purely logographic or visual and involves automatised processes of recognition and production of familiar words and the development of a sight word vocabulary. Accordingly, children are unable to apply phonological knowledge to decipher a word or spell it. Treiman & Broderick (1998) showed that even when young children are able to write their names they cannot always name the letters they have written. The researchers argue that the letters have been remembered for their visual shape alone.

As development progresses, children gain understanding of letter names and letter sounds. They understand connections between spellings and pronunciations: grapheme–phoneme correspondences. Treiman *et al.* (2008) explain that knowledge of letter names leads to understanding of letter sounds. Decoding ability develops gradually as children try to read and spell novel and nonsense words using their phonemic knowledge. Ehri (2005) says children detect salient consonants and vowels in a word they hear and incorporate this in their spelling attempts, e.g. br or bvr to represent *beaver*. As knowledge of grapheme–phoneme correspondence increases, so does the ability to decode and spell longer words. Finally, it is suggested that as the alphabetic principle develops, internalised orthographic representations are formed, storing and providing access to common word units or patterns without phonemic conversion, e.g. consonant doublets (e.g. the double 'l' in filled), and morphological rules (e.g. the suffixes –ed, –ing, –er, –est).

While joint models of spelling and reading refer to automatised processes of both recognition and production in early spelling, single spelling models tend to only focus on processes involved in early production, e.g. letter formation. This highlights the great complexity involved in understanding spelling development: there are two different meanings of spelling. Ehri (2000) explains that spelling can refer to writing out a word correctly: spelling production. Or it can refer to the ability to recognise whether words are spelt correctly: spelling recognition. Therefore if cognitive models can enhance understanding of spelling, they need to account for both recognition and production processes.

What is lacking from current descriptions of development?

Both joint models of spelling and reading and single models of spelling elucidate the knowledge involved in successful spelling and the approximate order in which knowledge is acquired. Recent models emphasise the need for a more flexible conceptualisation of development and a departure from stage-like progression. However these accounts fail to consider issues that general cognitive models can address.

First, there is still little known about the cognitive mechanisms underlying the development of spelling knowledge. How do children incorporate and apply these different elements of spelling information to achieve spelling competence? Furthermore, what is the nature of the underlying representations and how do they develop? Also, what strategies do children employ when spelling and how do these develop? Not only do traditional accounts under-specify how children learn to spell, they also view the learning of spelling in isolation from other cognitive domains. Spelling development, whilst resting on domain specific knowledge, may be underpinned by some domain general cognitive principles.

Second, although recent research has acknowledged the need for more flexible ways of conceptualising development – phase-like or item-based for example – it could be argued that traditional accounts have not gone far enough in simulating actual learning. The process of learning is not necessarily neat or linear. While it is clear that certain types of knowledge will predominate over others as children learn, a multi-representational and multiple-strategy theory should not be ruled out in favour of linear models.

Finally, traditional accounts of spelling development could be interpreted within a framework of knowledge explicitation. We have seen that spelling development is characterised by early, automatised processes of recognition and production followed by the incorporation and application of phonological and morphological information. It appears that early implicit knowledge forms the foundation for later phonological and morphological principles. We argue that conceptualising spelling development in this new way will provide insight into the driving force or catalyst for change as children learn.

How is spelling development typically measured in children?

The preceding section made the case for why general cognitive models could contribute to our theoretical understanding of how children learn to spell. When operationalising these theories, general cognitive models offer new ways of empirically measuring and classifying children's spelling ability.

Accuracy and error classification

Both cross-sectional and longitudinal studies of children's spelling development tend to employ standardised tests of performance, and when process is examined there is heavy concentration on accuracy and outcomes. Caravolas *et al.* (2001), for example, examined the developmental relationship between spelling and reading ability in children's first three years of schooling. A comprehensive range of tests was administered including letter names and sounds tests, phonemic knowledge tasks and single-word spelling and reading tests.

Caravolas *et al.* (2001) found that children aged 4–5.5 years could use phonological knowledge (mappings between phonemes and graphemes) in spelling before reading. This was reflected in the nature of the children's reading and spelling errors. In the first two years of the study, when spelling, children tended to employ knowledge that was largely phonological in nature. They commonly formed words by 'sounding-out' the phoneme to grapheme correspondences often producing phonologically plausible error versions, e.g. *sod* for *sold*. However, whilst reading, children rarely used a similar method and if a word was unfamiliar, made no response at all or produced an incorrect word that had the same initial letter but was not phonologically plausible, e.g. *so* or *sand* when the target word was *sun*.

Nunes *et al.* (1997) used children's spelling errors as the basis for a model of development. In a three-year longitudinal study with children aged 6–8 years, Nunes *et al.* (1997) demonstrated how typical spelling errors reveal the phonological to morphological development of spelling. Spelling tests comprising regular past tense verbs, e.g. *filled*, irregular past tense verbs, e.g. *sold*, and non-verbs, e.g. *soft*, were given to the children. As expected early stages in spelling development (e.g. stages 1 and 2) are phonological in nature. Words that can be phonetically spelt such as *sold* are produced correctly but words such as *kissed* are commonly expressed as the phonetic error *kist*; the morphological rule of –ed not yet being used.

However in stages 3 and 4 morphological knowledge of spelling is applied alongside phonological knowledge. This could result in overgeneralisation errors with the morphological rule of –ed being over-applied to irregular verbs and non-verbs as well, e.g. *solded* instead of *sold*, *colded* instead of *cold*. These previously unreported errors were of particular interest to Nunes *et al.* because they signified a u-shaped performance curve. Many 6-year-old children could correctly produce words such as *sold* and *cold* but as 7-year-olds, made overgeneralisation errors that disappeared at the age of 8. Due to the important finding of spelling overgeneralisation errors and performance trajectory, this study was later used as the basis for further research using the RR model to gain insight into what cognitive mechanisms may underlie this phenomenon (see discussion of Critten *et al.*, 2007 in section on 'Spelling representational levels').

What other methods can be used to test spelling ability?

Generally measures of spelling development have therefore been performance-based, tracking levels of accuracy and error type. While this gives researchers insight into children's spelling competence, and how ability changes as knowledge increases, it tells us little about what children *understand* about spelling and *why* they make the types of errors they do. There is little data telling us whether children recognise and spell words automatically or whether they employ more conscious processes, thinking about how to spell and decipher words. By gaining access to children's cognitive processes and strategy use we can infer the nature of underlying representations and cognitive mechanisms driving the developmental process.

One method that yields rich data involves capturing children's verbal explanations about their understanding of spelling as well as their spelling performance. Children's explanations can reveal strategy use, relevant to the Overlapping Waves model, as well as implicit or explicit knowledge, which the RR model rests upon (see following section for discussion of model frameworks). Furthermore, children's explanations or justifications of spelling errors can signify whether these errors are randomly produced or arising systematically from an underlying representation. If children's development is tracked over time, verbal explanations will also provide a further resource for examining how both children's knowledge *and* their understanding becomes more sophisticated.

What cognitive processes are involved in spelling development?

Descriptive stage and phase models have dominated the spelling literature, with researchers relying heavily on measures of performance and error type. We have argued that by applying general models of cognitive development to this domain, new methods can be applied. This approach promises to shed more light on the nature of representations and mechanisms underlying spelling development. Not only does this allow a perspective of spelling from a broader cognitive context inviting comparisons to the nature of learning in other domains, but it also presents learning as a multifaceted process rather than a linear stage or phase-like progression. If children's verbal explanations are considered alongside traditional performance measures we can explore what children understand as they spell, whether knowledge is drawn from implicit or explicit representations, and why they make the types of errors they do. This will provide insight into *how* we incorporate and apply the new information we acquire when learning and how this relates to the type of errors children produce and even where they might stall along the developmental path.

The Overlapping Waves and Representational–Redescription models of cognitive development will now be outlined in more detail.

The Overlapping Waves model

The Overlapping Waves model (Siegler, 1996) accounts for how children acquire new knowledge and describes domain specific changes in strategy use. The model proposes that children will use a variety of strategies to solve a problem. Some or all of these strategies, and the corresponding ways of thinking, may coexist in a parallel fashion over a long period of time, not in short or specific changes. The model describes learning as involving the development of multiple strategies in which frequency of strategy use changes and simple strategies lead to more advanced ones. For Siegler, most of development is characterised by this strategy variability and by 'cognitive diversity' (1996: 38).

Siegler's model has explained the variability of procedures children employ in domains such as arithmetic (Cooney et al., 1988; Siegler, 1987, 1988) and clock reading (Siegler & McGilly, 1989), physics (Maloney & Siegler, 1993). It has also been applied to children's spelling development (e.g. Kwong & Varnhagen, 2005; Rittle-Johnson & Siegler, 1999). Rittle-Johnson & Siegler (1999) reported that children deployed two main types of strategies to decode an unknown word: automatic retrieval and back-up strategies (e.g. sounding out the word, analogy, application of a morphological rule, etc.). Children's verbal explanations of how they spelt a word were also considered when characterising the strategy employed, revealing either automaticity or awareness of process. The questions children were asked, however, could be seen as leading in nature, e.g. 'Did you just know how to spell it? Sound it out? Use a rule?' (1999: 336).

Rittle-Johnson & Siegler's (1999) work made headway in both the approach adopted and in demonstrating variability of strategy use in spelling. They also took account of children's verbal explanations to gain an insight into process, revealing differences in awareness of strategy use. The notion of multiple strategy use endorses further the adoption of a multifaceted approach to understanding spelling development rather than a linear progression of knowledge.

Nonetheless, some unanswered questions remain from Rittle-Johnson & Siegler's (1999) study. The authors offer little by way of explanation for the u-shaped development, for overgeneralisation errors, or for 'why children persist in using time-consuming back-up strategies that initially do little to improve performance' (1999: 345).

The implicit/explicit distinction

When considering processing and types of learning one ubiquitous characterisation within cognitive psychology is the distinction made between implicit and explicit knowledge (see Reber, 1989). The notion of implicit or unconscious processing has been mooted in spelling for some time (e.g. Donaldson, 1978; Marcel, 1980) but has not been fully taken up. Clearly, as already discussed, the initial visual or logographic stages/phases in spelling suggested by Frith (1985) and Ehri (1998, 1999, 2002) could be construed as implicit. Studies in recognition and production (e.g. Treiman & Broderick, 1998) would support this. It has also already been suggested that the later development of phonological and morphological information could be viewed as a more explicit process, although this has not, as yet, been explored empirically.

The initial development of the alphabetic principle may also be an implicit process. Ellis (1997) argues that even though phonemic awareness tends to be measured using explicit tasks, e.g. phoneme segmentation, phoneme blending, and phoneme substitution, implicit phonological awareness is also involved in early spelling (see also Marcel, 1980). An example of this is provided by Stanovich et al. (1984), who looked at children's early experience of nursery rhymes. They discovered that there was no correlation between explicit non-rhyming tasks that required children to analyse words for explicit sound content and rhyming tasks that required perception of word sound similarity. Ellis (1997) concludes that there are two different (measurable) levels of phonemic awareness, explicit as denoted by the non-rhyming tasks and implicit as denoted by the rhyming tasks.

More recently Steffler (2001) also highlighted the importance of studying implicit spelling. She explains that we may not always be aware of the spelling conventions we are following. This, Steffler points out, is unsurprising, given the existing number: 2,000 phoneme to grapheme correspondence rules to represent a corpus of 17,000 words (Hanna et al., 1966).

In addition to this are the findings of Rittle-Johnson & Siegler (1999) that children are sometimes unaware or unable to explain how they have spelt a word. It therefore seems logical to explore this possible implicit/explicit distinction using a general model of cognitive development that can account for implicit and explicit knowledge. This will uncover the nature of possible implicit and explicit representations and the cognitive mechanisms implicated in their development.

The Representational–Redescription (RR) model

The RR model (Karmiloff-Smith, 1992) of cognitive development describes learning as a process whereby initial implicit representations (Implicit level) are redescribed to become increasingly explicit (levels E1, E2, and E3), see Table 6.1. Knowledge therefore gradually becomes consciously accessible and verbalisable until more explicit formats allow it to be generalised across and within domains of learning.

Representational development can be triggered by events in the environment but the emphasis is placed on endogenous change within a self-organising system. Cognitive development follows a linear path via these levels but importantly this model also identifies a u-shaped development in *performance*.

The RR model proposes an implicit to explicit continuum with a developmental gap between performance and understanding. Task success and knowledge can be dissociated in this model. The model also allows for domain specific change and does not propose overarching cognitive reorganisation. The model also describes a multi-representation system. When redescription occurs, the original representations remain intact and available within the cognitive system so there may be redress to earlier forms of representation when speed or automaticity is required. However, explicit representations are called upon when knowledge needs to be verbalised or general-ised to a new situation. The developmental nature of this model provides insight into how knowledge changes over time to form fully explicit representations.

The RR model has been previously applied post-hoc to account for development in language, notation, maths, and physics (Karmiloff-Smith, 1992). Pine & Messer (1999) applied the RR levels in an empirical study of children's behaviour on a balance beam task using a series of beams. Some beams were symmetrical (would

Table 6.1 Summary of levels (Implicit, E1, E2, E3) from the Representational–Redescription model (Karmiloff-Smith, 1992)

RR Level	Performance	Characteristics
Implicit	• Task success or 'behavioural mastery' • Inability to verbalise or analyze knowledge in terms of component parts	• Information is encoded in data-driven format • Responds directly to stimuli in environment • Representations stored separately so cannot be generalized to different tasks • Knowledge cannot be *consciously* accessed
Explicit Level 1 (E1)	• Can be a decrement in performance compared to the Implicit level, producing a u-shaped performance curve • Knowledge still unavailable for verbal report	• Emphasis shifts from adapted responses to the environment to internal representational change • External data can be ignored as an over-general theory or strategy is adopted that can lead to errors
Explicit Level 2 (E2)	• Performance starts to improve again compared to level E1 • Theories no longer dominating	• Balance starts to occur • The E1 representations containing overgeneralised theories become integrated with information in the environment
Explicit Level 3 (E3)	• Performance improves to match implicit level • Knowledge can now be fully analyzed and communicated verbally	• Fully explicit representations • Recognition of exceptions to rules • Flexibility in use and application of knowledge compared to E1 • Conscious access to knowledge • Knowledge applied within and between domains

balance in the middle) and some were asymmetrical. Children were then asked to justify verbally why they had been successful or unsuccessful in balancing the beams. Children at the Implicit level were able to balance both the symmetrical and asymmetrical beams but used a trial-and-error approach each time and were inconsistent in their strategy use. Lacking access to their representations, they were unable to explain how they balanced the beams. In contrast, children at the E2 and E3 levels were able to both balance the beams correctly and provide verbal explanations for how they were able to do this.

However it was the children allocated to level E1 who displayed the most interesting behaviour. They stubbornly placed all beams on the fulcrum at the centre declaring that asymmetrical beams 'could not be balanced' (a phenomenon previously noted by Karmiloff-Smith & Inhelder, 1974). This 'centre theory' led to performance errors and a u-shaped performance curve. However, despite the RR model predicting that knowledge at this level would be unavailable for verbal report, 45 per cent of those children allocated could explain their 'centre theory'. Consequently Pine & Messer (1999) suggested splitting level E1 into two forms: Abstraction non-verbal and Abstraction verbal. In applying the RR model to other domains, therefore, it could be inferred that children at level E1 may be able to verbalise or articulate the rule they are using.

The RR model and literacy development

Application of the RR model to the domain of literacy has appeared in a theory of metalinguistic development that links the RR principle to accessibility of linguistic knowledge when learning to read. Gombert (1992) suggested three phases of reading development. During acquisition of linguistic skills, children start to form implicit-type representations of written-word structure, leading to recognition success in lexical decision tasks. In the second phase, Gombert describes the acquisition of epilinguistic control, used for cognitive control of linguistic behaviour, though not yet consciously accessible. In his third phase, children gain control over phonological structures and can manipulate them in response to external factors. These phases have some correspondence with the Implicit, E1, and E3 levels in the RR model.

Gombert's (1992) model acknowledges the implicit/explicit distinction in literacy development. However these levels have not yet been empirically tested. Furthermore the nature of children's explanations and spelling performance at all the implicit and explicit levels is underspecified, as is the method that might be used to assess this. Furthermore, Pine & Messer's (1999) finding that level E1 knowledge can be verbalised merits empirical study in the literacy domain. A central tenet of Karmiloff-Smith's (1992) approach was also the notion of overgeneralisation errors at level E1. Empirical work is necessary to understand the types of theory children hold and how this leads to overgeneralisation errors (e.g. Nunes et al., 1997).

Both Gombert (1992) and Steffler (2001) recognised that the RR model could be applicable to literacy development. Steffler particularly drew attention to how children's spelling behaviour might be conceptualised at each of Karmiloff-Smith's (1992) levels. It was these predictions that formed the basis for the study by Critten et al. (2007).

Spelling representational levels

Critten *et al.* (2007) sought to test whether spelling could be understood within the framework of the RR model. The methodology and assessment process used both children's verbal explanations and performance measures to infer the accessibility of knowledge and the nature of underlying representations. Critten *et al.* also set out to account for the type of overgeneralisation error reported by Nunes *et al.* (1997) and therefore derived the words and errors from this study. In two experiments 95 children aged 5–7 years were given 15 sets (see Table 6.2) of three alternative spellings of a target word, only one of which was correct. The alternative spelling might be *sold, solded, soled* and the task for the child was to identify the target word by being asked, 'Which of these is the correct spelling of sold?' Then the children were asked to justify verbally which alternatives they believed to be correct: 'Why do you think this is spelt correctly?' and incorrect: 'Why do you think this is spelt wrong?'

Table 6.2 Alternative word sets presented in the recognition task (Critten *et al.*, 2007)

Card	Word 1	Word 2	Word 3
1	Called	Caled	Calld
2	Leftd	Left	Lefted
3	Opened	Opend	Opened
4	Nexed	Next	Nexted
5	Sold	Soled	Solded
6	Herrd	Hearded	Heard
7	Coled	Cold	Coldt
8	Losted	Losed	Lost
9	Dressd	Dressd	Dressed
10	Laughed	Laughd	Larfed
11	Golled	Goled	Gold
12	Fild	Filled	Filed
13	Slept	Slepted	Sleped
14	Ground	Grouned	Groned
15	Softed	Sofed	Soft

Nature of the spelling representations

On the basis of recognition performance and coding of verbal explanations from each word set, all participants were allocated to a predominant representational level of spelling understanding (Implicit, E1A, E1B, E2, or E3) derived from the levels of the RR model. This coding method was also used by Karmiloff-Smith (1992) and Pine & Messer (1999). Inter-rater reliability tests produced a concordance rating of 73 per cent.

Children at the *Implicit* spelling level demonstrated task success by consistently (= > 70 per cent) identifying the correct spelling alternative of the word. However their knowledge was deemed to be implicit because they failed to justify verbally why their choice was correct or why alternative spellings were incorrect, due to an inability consciously to access knowledge. For example, when asked to explain why they believed a word to be spelt correctly, typical responses might include:

'I don't know'
'It looks right' — *would that a appropriate response*
'I just know it'.

If participants did try to justify a choice it was apparent from the content of the explanation that they were simply trying to make any response rather than accessing any explicit spelling knowledge. For example when asked why the alternative spelling for filled: filld, was incorrectly spelt, a child at the I-level might reply: 'because it has i'. Of course the correct spelling of filled has 'i' as well.

Critten *et al.* (2007) also found support for the explicit levels in children's understanding of spelling. Following Pine & Messer (1999) modification of level E1 was also required. Two distinct types emerged: labelled *E1A* and *E1B*. Children at *level E1A* were beyond implicit, as they could verbally justify answers and also made recognition errors. Instead phonological information had been abstracted. This was sometimes over-applied leading to phonetic recognition errors, e.g. choosing filld instead of, filled. Verbal justifications provided at this level were also phonologically based, for example:

'Filld is correct because it has two l's'.

The morphological rule of –ed was not recognised as important and was not referred to. In fact children remained at this level even if they made a correct recognition if they failed to mention –ed as a unit in any of their explanations, for example when justifying why solded is an incorrect spelling:

'It has two d's'. ?

Children at *level E1B* had abstracted morphological information about the –ed rule but over-applied it to irregular past tense verbs and to non-verbs. Thus they produced morphological recognition errors, e.g. choosing solded instead of sold. Verbal justifications again focused on the presence or absence of –ed:

'Solded is right because it has –ed'
'Sold is wrong because it is missing –ed'.

Children remained at this level even if they made correct recognitions and could explain why spellings were incorrect (making reference to the –ed unit) if they continued to fail to explain why they believed a spelling to be correct.

Children at *level E2* displayed better recognition performance than those in level E1 and a growing integration and correct application of phonological and morphological knowledge. However performance was a little inconsistent and verbal explanations as to why words were correct were sometimes lacking:

'Filled is correct as it has two l's and –ed'

when compared to a level E3 answer:

'Filled has the word "fill" and an –ed to make it past (tense)'.

The latter answer indicates that those participants allocated to *level E3* have a more fully explicit understanding of phonological and morphological aspects of spelling, applying them appropriately without overgeneralisation errors and verbalising knowledge thoroughly.

There are potential difficulties associated with relying on children's verbal self-reports. However, steps were taken within Critten *et al.*'s study to minimise this possibility as the spelling recognition task examined performance in *conjunction* with children's verbal reports. Therefore correct/incorrect recognition in combination with responses to the remaining spelling alternatives, and the explanations produced, led to characterisation of the underlying representations. This multifaceted approach to assessment combined with inter-rater reliability measures increases the likelihood that a valid model has been produced. This can be demonstrated when examining how incorrect recognition is assessed: an error would suggest either E1A or E1B representations. If there is a phonological error accompanied by some basic phonological knowledge in the verbal explanation then level E1A is likely. However if it is a morphological recognition error and the verbal explanation refers to the aspect of morphology then level E1B is likely. This balance between assessment of performance and verbal explanations increases the likelihood of exposing the actual content and nature of children's representations.

Indeed, in a recent microgenetic study of children's orthographic knowledge, Sharp *et al.* (2008) also used children's verbal explanations. Furthermore, they cited Critten *et al.*'s research as evidence for the advantages this type of data provides and the growing support for the method.

Patterns of children's spelling knowledge

As mentioned earlier, Critten *et al.* conducted two studies, the second with slightly younger children (5–6 years) compared to the first (6–7 years), which produced slightly different patterns of allocations to levels (see Table 6.3).

Table 6.3 Number (%) of children at each spelling representational level (Implicit, E1A, E1B, E2, E3) in Experiments 1 and 2

Representational Level	Experiment 1	Experiment 2
Implicit	0 (0)	3 (7)
E1A	18 (35)	29 (66)
E1B	21 (41)	8 (18)
E2	8 (17)	4 (8)
E3	4 (8)	0

Note: Experiment 1 N = 51, Experiment 2 N = 44

Table 6.3 indicates that most of the younger children in Experiment 2 had predominantly level E1A representations, χ^2 (3, N = 44) = 45.46, p = .03. They had abstracted and were applying basic phonological knowledge, sometimes producing phonological recognition errors, e.g. filld, together with basic verbal explanations of why words were correctly or incorrectly spelt. Most of the slightly older children in Experiment 1 were similarly at level E1 although many of them were level E1B, χ^2 (3, N = 51) = 15.27, p = .04. They displayed a rudimentary knowledge of the morphological rule of –ed, sometimes producing overgeneralisation recognition errors, e.g. solded, and accompanying verbal explanations. As would be expected, children with predominantly implicit representations were found in the younger age group. Children showing more advanced explicit representations and verbal explanations were more frequent within the older age group.

Using the RR model has also helped to address those questions left unanswered by Rittle-Johnson & Siegler (1999). Critten *et al.* (2007) demonstrated that level E1 spelling representations are characterised by stubborn application of particular theories of phonology and morphology; a behaviour that often leads to errors. Therefore the children in the Rittle-Johnson & Siegler study who persistently applied ineffective strategies may have held level E1 representations. A similar explanation can be proffered for the overgeneralisation errors reported by Nunes *et al.* (1997). Continual overgeneralisation errors are an inherent part of the process of explicitation according to the RR model. They demonstrate that children have to consolidate their knowledge and begin to build theories about when it is appropriate to apply rules and when it is not. Furthermore, the explicitation account allows for a developmental gap to exist between performance and understanding in spelling, in common with other domains. Children with predominantly implicit representations were successful at recognition but had no insight into why spellings were correct or incorrect. In contrast children at E1 would sometimes make recognition errors but they could explain why they believed words to be correct or incorrect. This provided considerable insight into the rules they were using and what they understood about spelling. Therefore while it would be unwise to base a model of spelling development solely on children's verbal explanations, using them in conjunction with performance measures provides a powerful source of data.

In a similar fashion to Nunes *et al.* (1997), the longitudinal study by Caravolas *et al.* (2001) would have also been enhanced by children's verbal explanations as it would have been possible to see if their finding that children were able to utilise phonological knowledge in spelling before reading was supported by children's understanding of spelling versus reading. For example, would they have been able to provide simple phonological explanations for their spelling but still have to fall back on implicit representations when reading as they are unable to access phonological knowledge in relation to this process?

A further significant finding was that although all children could be characterised as one predominant representation type, evidence was found for the multi-representation system described by Karmiloff-Smith (1992). The coding process highlighted some children exhibiting behaviour of more than one level. Others seemed to be in transition between two levels (usually E1B and E2). The latter could be explained in terms of capturing representational-redescription as it occurs, whilst the former suggests evidence of variability within the cognitive system. As mentioned earlier, Karmiloff-Smith (1992) states that even though representations are redescribed, earlier versions still remain intact and available for use. Depending upon the words they were presented with, some children were accessing representations at different representational levels within the domain, resulting in variability. For example, some children correctly chose and verbally justified the use of –ed in *opened* but then failed to apply the rule correctly for *called* and chose *calld* instead.

What have the findings contributed to spelling theory?

The study by Critten *et al.* (2007) has extended our understanding of spelling development by addressing aspects of children's representations that existing theories have overlooked. This has provided new insight into the representations underlying the phonological to morphological development of spelling and the overgeneralisation errors described by Nunes *et al.* (1997). Furthermore, by applying the implicit to explicit framework of the RR model it was able to characterise spelling development as a process of explicitation suggesting the nature of underlying implicit and explicit representations. While other models (e.g. Ehri, Frith) and studies (e.g. Ellis, 1997) have long suggested implicit and explicit involvement in spelling, the principle has not been used as a possible mechanism driving the process of development in children's spelling knowledge and ability.

Furthermore instead of looking only at spelling accuracy or the lack of it, this method takes account of children's explanations to infer their understanding. By empirically testing spelling within the framework of the RR model we have derived a practical methodology that assesses performance and understanding of spelling in order to infer the nature of the underlying representations. This complements Overlapping Waves studies that used verbal explanations to infer the nature of strategy use. Verbal explanations enhanced our understanding of the Nunes *et al.* findings by showing that children were making overgeneralisation errors due to their dominant, phonological or morphological theory and were able to explain this to the experimenter, e.g. 'all words have to have –ed'.

The findings also build upon the traditional descriptive accounts by suggesting the nature of representational development and cognitive mechanisms that may underlie development. It can be inferred that initially passive and implicit/automatic representations are redescribed entering a more explicit and active phase of representational development where phonological and morphological information is abstracted, interpreted, and applied, sometimes producing overgeneralisation errors. As knowledge becomes more consciously accessible, children's understanding of spelling and the exceptions to rules becomes more sophisticated, as evidenced by their verbal explanations.

This view sheds light on the internal reorganisation and active processing required in becoming a successful speller. Learning is not purely a passive process where the learner absorbs and then reproduces input. Information gained from the environment both implicitly via words in books, information signs, on television for example and explicitly via instruction in schools has to be processed and made fully explicit to reach competence in spelling. This gives rise, for example, to children at E3 recognising the exceptions to spelling rules. The path to competence is not always linear, depending on children's experience and level of exposure. There may be greater explicit understanding of some concepts before others, e.g. understanding of magic 'e' may precede understanding of when to apply the –ed rule. This is apparent from the multi-representations reported by Critten *et al.* (2007).

This lack of uniformity within children's knowledge and understanding within the same task characterises the type of variability in strategy use reported by Rittle-Johnson & Siegler (1999). While a child may have a predominant mode of knowledge at any given time, other representational forms or strategies may also be competing for use. Returning to the example of the children who were able to apply and explain the –ed rule correctly in relation to *opened*, but not to *called*: perhaps they were able to draw upon a more sophisticated and explicit representation in that instance because the target word mapped more closely onto one used in teaching. However the children have yet to apply the rule consistently to other similar words, thus showing evidence of a multi-representational system.

While Ehri's phase-like structure and Share's item-based account do make allowances for differences in the learning process for experience and task type, they do not address the possible cognitive mechanisms underlying these exceptions. Through Critten *et al.*'s study we can understand the multifaceted nature of learning via access to multiple representations. Explicitness of these representations explains both performance differences and variability in children's access to their own understanding. Similarly the nature of the representation accessed drives the child's strategy choice. As different representations are accessed it is possible that the strategy will differ too, thus accounting for multiple strategy use reported in relation to the Overlapping Waves model.

A final point to consider is the perspective of learning as a cyclical rather than purely linear process, e.g. visual–phonological–orthographic. According to multi-representational theory it is possible to predict that children may be able to access fully explicit representations in relation to a particular set of words and spelling rules. For example the short/long vowel rule in relation to silent 'e', where the word 'hop' would be pronounced with a short vowel sound but the word hope requires a silent 'e' at the end to make the vowel sound long. However when children learn their next spelling rule, e.g. the past tense rule of –ed, they are not going to automatically have fully explicit knowledge of it in the same way. They have to go 'back to the drawing board' as it were and go through the error process (E1) to understand when to apply this rule correctly. In this way by advancing a multi-representational model we are building up a more realistic picture of how children learn to spell.

Ongoing work to validate the approach

A programme of work has arisen from the study by Critten *et al.* (2007) designed to provide further validation of use of the RR model for understanding spelling and more recently reading development. One study is exploring further the nature of implicit spelling representations using a spelling production task as well as the recognition format to consider both aspects of spelling (Ehri, 2000). The recent introduction of more explicit literacy instruction in UK schools has seen children rapidly progress beyond this type of early representational phase. Therefore younger children (aged 4–6 years) are being tested in order to capture children's early implicit representations.

A second major focus using longitudinal techniques concerns the development and identification of reading representational levels. These will be informative about the crossover between spelling and reading during development. Not only will this type of study be important for gaining insight into representational development, it will provide a necessary further test of the RR model for this domain and in others. The RR model has not been tested in a long-term non-interventionist study of development although Pine & Messer (1998, 2003) and Pine *et al.* (1999) have conducted short-term intervention studies (of a week or so) to facilitate children's explicit knowledge of the balance beam task. Critten *et al.*'s cross-sectional studies have identified children at each of the different representational levels for spelling and demonstrated that the older children were more likely to be at the later levels of explicitness. Furthermore it was in the younger age group that children at the implicit level were identified. This would suggest that the process of explicitation occurs in spelling development but the developmental trajectory needs empirical verification.

Summary

To conclude, by viewing spelling development as another cognitive domain we can build on and extend traditional descriptive accounts. Not only do we gain insight into the nature of underlying implicit and explicit representations, we can infer what children understand using their verbal explanations, the spelling strategies children employ, and the cognitive mechanisms involved in learning.

References

Bear, D., Invernizzi, M. Templeton, S., & Johnston, F. (2000). *Words their way: Word study for phonics, vocabulary, and spelling instruction.* Upper Saddle River, NJ: Prentice Hall.

Caravolas, M., Hulme, C. & Snowling, M.J. (2001) 'The foundations of spelling ability: Evidence from a 3-year longitudial study'. *Journal of Memory and Language, 45,* 751–774.

Chetland, E., & Fluck, M. (2007). 'Children's performance on the "give x" task: A microgenetic analysis of "counting" and "grabbing" behavior'. *Infant and Child Development, 16*(1), 35–51.

Cooney, J.B., Swanson, H.L., & Ladd, S.F. (1988). 'Acquisition of mental multiplication skill: Evidence for the transition between counting and retrieval strategies'. *Cognition and Instruction, 5,* 323–345.

Critten, S., Pine, K.J. & Steffler, D. (2007). 'Spelling development in young children: A case of Representational-Redescription?' *Journal of Educational Psychology, 99,* 207–220.

Donaldson, M. (1978) *Children's minds.* London: Fontana Press.

Ehri, L.C. (1998) 'Word reading by sight and by analogy in beginning readers'. In C. Hulme & M. Joshi (eds), *Reading and spelling: Development and disorders* (pp. 87–112). Mahwah, NJ: LEA.

—— (1999) 'Phases of development in learning to read words'. In J. Oakhill & R. Beard (eds), *Reading development and the teaching of reading: A psychological perspective* (pp.79–108). Oxford: Blackwell Publishers.

—— (2000). 'Learning to read and learning to spell: Two sides of a coin'. *Topics in Language Disorders, 20,* 19–36.

—— (2002) 'Phases of acquisition in learning to read words and implications for teaching'. *British Journal of Educational Psychology: Monograph Series, 1,* 7–28.

—— (2005). 'Development of sight word reading: Phases and findings'. In M. Snowling & C. Hulme (eds), *The science of reading: A handbook.* Boston, MA: Blackwell Publishing.

Ellis, N. (1997). 'Interactions in the development of reading and spelling: Stages, strategies and exchange of knowledge'. In L. Rieben, C.A. Perfetti, & M. Fayol (eds), *Learning to spell: Research, theory and practice across languages.* Mahwah, NJ: LEA.

Frith, U. (1985). 'Beneath the surface of developmental dyslexia'. In K. Patterson, M. Coltheart, & J. Marshall (eds.), *Surface dyslexia* (pp. 301–330). London: LEA.

Gentry, J.R., & Gillet, J.W. (1993). *Teaching kids to spell.* Portsmouth, NH: Heinemann.

Gombert, J.E. (1992) *Metalinguistic awareness.* Chicago, IL: University of Chicago Press.

Hanna, P.R., Hanna, J.S., Hodges, R.G., & Rudorf, E.H. (1966). *Phoneme-grapheme correspondences to spelling improvement.* (OE-32008). Washington, DC: Office of Education, United States Department of Health, Education and Welfare.

Karmiloff-Smith, A. (1992). *Beyond modularity: A developmental perspective on cognitive science.* Cambridge, MA: MIT Press.

Karmiloff-Smith, A. & Inhelder, B. (1974). 'If you want to get ahead, get a theory'. *Cognition, 3,* 195–212.

Kwong, T.E., & Varnhagen, C.K. (2005). 'Strategy development and learning to spell new words: Generalization of a process'. *Developmental Psychology, 41,* 148–159.

Maloney, D.P., & Siegler, R.S. (1993). 'Conceptual competition in physics learning'. *International Journal of Science Education, 15,* 283–295.

Marcel, A.J. (1980) 'Phonological awareness and phonological representation: Investigation of a specific spelling problem'. In U. Frith (ed.), *Cognitive processes in spelling* (p. 373–403). New York: Academic Press.

Nunes, T., Bindman, M., & Bryant, P. (1997). 'Morphological spelling strategies: Developmental stages and processes'. *Developmental Psychology. 33,* 637–649.

Pine, K.J. & Messer, D.J. (1998) 'Group collaboration effects and the explicitness of children's knowledge'. *Cognitive Development 13,* 109–126.

Pine, K.J. & Messer, D. (1999). 'What children do and what children know: Looking beyond success using Karmiloff-Smith's R-R framework'. *New Ideas in Psychology, 17,* 17–30.

Pine, K.J. & Messer, D.J. (2003). 'The development of representations as children learn about balancing'. *British Journal of Developmental Psychology, 21,* 285–301.

Pine, K.J., Messer, D.J. & Godfrey, K. (1999) 'The teachability of children with naive theories: An exploration of two teaching methods'. *British Journal of Educational Psychology, 69,* 201–211.

Reber, A.S. (1989) 'Implicit learning and tacit knowledge'. *Journal of Experimental Psychology: General, 118,* 219–235.

Rittle-Johnson, B. & Siegler, R.S. (1999) 'Learning to spell: Variability, choice and change in children's strategy use'. *Child Development, 70,* 332–348.

Share, D.L. (1995) Phonological recoding and self-teaching: Sine qua non of reading acquisition. *Cognition, 55,* 151–218.

Sharp, A.C., Sinatra, G.M. & Reynolds, R.E. (2008). 'The development of children's orthographic knowledge: A microgenetic perspective'. *Reading Research Quarterly, 43,* 206–226.

Siegler, R.S. (1987). 'Strategy choices in subtraction'. In J.A. Slobda & D. Rogers (eds), *Cognitive processes in mathematics: Keele cognition seminars* (Vol. 1, pp. 81–106). Oxford: Oxford University Press.

—— (1988). 'Strategy choice procedures and the development of multiplication skills'. *Journal of Experimental Psychology, 117,* 258–275.

—— (1996). *Emerging minds: The process of change in children's thinking.* New York: Oxford University Press.

Siegler, R.S., & McGilly, K. (1989). 'Strategy choices in time telling'. In I. Levin and D. Zakay (eds) *Time and human cognition: A life-span perspective.* Amsterdam: North Holland.

Stanovich, K.E., Cunningham, A.E., & Cramer, B.B. (1984). 'Assessing phonological awareness in kindergarten children: Issues of task comparability'. *Journal of Experimental Child Psychology, 38,* 175–190.

Steffler, D.J. (2001). 'Implicit cognition and spelling development'. *Developmental Review, 21,* 168–204.

Temple, C., Nathan, R., Burris, N., & Temple, F. (eds), (1988). *The beginnings of writing* (2nd edn). Boston, MA: Allyn & Bacon.

Treiman, R. & Broderick, V. (1998). 'What's in a name: Children's knowledge about letters in their own name'. *Journal of Experimental Child Psychology, 70,* 97–116.

Treiman, R., Pennington, B.F, Shriberg, L.D & Boada, R. (2008). 'Which children benefit from letter names in learning letter sounds?' *Cognition, 106,* 1322–38.

Chapter 7

What spelling errors have to tell about vocabulary learning

Ruth H. Bahr, Elaine R. Silliman and Virginia Berninger

Introduction: what spelling errors have to tell about vocabulary learning

For almost 100 years concern has been expressed about the quality of spelling assessment and instruction in the United States. Spelling was the topic of the earliest application of the scientific method to education. In a large-scale study that included schools throughout the United States, Rice (1913) evaluated the optimal instructional time for spelling instruction and found that children who received 15 minutes of weekly spelling instruction achieved significantly higher spelling test scores than those drilled for an hour or more a week. The benefits of 'more' may be offset by the mind's habituation, that is, the failure to continue to respond to repetitive practice. 'Less' may result in more efficient spelling learning, but the nature of the spelling instruction also matters.

In almost 100 years, minimal progress has taken place in the understanding of spelling as a language-based function. This linguistic activity serves as the representational support system for both reading and writing. For example, after students reach a certain level of proficiency in phonological awareness, they may access written spellings from memory while performing phonemic awareness tasks. That is why novel pseudowords not represented in memory are used to assess phonemic awareness.

Assessment

Spelling has long been considered a 'mechanical skill' best learned by rote. It is still not unusual to find spelling described as the 'mechanical' aspect of writing (Harris & Graham, 1996), albeit a facet that does 'influence perceptions about a child's competence' in writing (Graham & Harris, 2006: 64). This notion that spelling makes a peripheral contribution to writing parallels the older notion that the grapho-motor movements supporting handwriting were the primary influence on how to spell words accurately. However, there is some merit to the role of grapho-motor skill in spelling. Children with poor spelling at the end of second grade were lower in spelling if they also had poor handwriting than if they did not (Berninger *et al.*, 1998). Nevertheless, orthographic, phonological, and vocabulary skills uniquely predicted their spelling ability (Berninger *et al.*, 1992). Children with dyslexia are impaired in spelling as well as word reading but may or may not have handwriting problems (Berninger *et al.*, 2008a).

Studies of spelling disability in samples with reading, writing, or oral language impairment typically select samples on the basis of low achievement on norm-referenced standardized measures of spelling that only take into account level of achievement in spelling (e.g. Bishop & Clarkson, 2003; Dockrell *et al.*, 2007; Holm *et al.*, 2008; Larkin & Snowling, 2008; Puranik *et al.*, 2008). Only one study, involving students with oral language impairment, constructed a fine-grain measure (elaborated on later) in which word selection and scoring was based on phonological, orthographic, and morphological categories and features (Silliman *et al.*, 2006). However, studies that first select on the basis of low spelling achievement often do conduct additional analyses that contribute to spelling disability, such as phonological, orthographic, and morphological word form storage and processing (Berninger *et al.*, 2008c; Plaza & Cohen, 2004).

Instruction

Allal (1997) observed that 'Researchers in the area of language instruction often seem to share the attitudes of teachers and students for whom spelling is a necessary but altogether disliked component of the school curriculum' (p. 129). From a teaching perspective, spelling remains the stepchild of the curriculum (Ehri & Rosenthal, 2007). Moreover, the secondary status and negative stance may be due in large part to the failure to understand the linguistic nature of spelling (described later) and effective ways to teach it (for review see Berninger, 2008; Berninger & Fayol, 2008). Furthermore, it is unclear how many students in the United States receive systematic instruction in spelling. As a consequence of the whole language movement that began in the 1980s, many teachers believe that spelling should only be taught incidentally in 'teachable moments' and many teacher education programs do not include explicit preparation in how to teach spelling effectively.

In a review of nine textbook series on spelling, Wilde (1990) found that these textbooks accounted for four existing practices in spelling instruction, all of which appear to have deleterious effects on the writing and spelling abilities of elementary-age children from low income homes (Foorman *et al.*, 2006; Moats *et al.*, 2006). Undoubtedly, these same textbooks perpetuate teachers' negative attitudes about spelling.

First, *word lists* have long predominated in spelling instruction with the expectation that learning will transpire through memorization and practice with frequently used words. This discredited method (Allal, 1997) still remains the primary classroom approach for spelling instruction. Recent results from Fresch (2007), who conducted a representative national survey of 355 teachers in grades 1 to 5 on methods of spelling instruction, reaffirmed the memorization model.

Second, the emphasis still placed on *spelling rules* as a supposed process for generalization to similar instances, in reality, functions as reinforcement for word lists and memorization. Wilde (1990) provides an example of rule-bound learning based on her analyses of the textbook series. In instances where vowel digraphs, such as *ee* occur, the long vowel *e* 'rule' in *keep* could apply to the long vowel in *seem*. However, the long vowel *e* might create an exception for a child when *seam* is encountered despite the fact that the *ea* is still the long vowel *e*. Students are expected to learn to group long vowel *e* words and, to a great extent, engage in incidental learning of their spellings even for the exceptions. This type of implicit approach may contribute little to children's understanding that English orthography is a system that maps onto more than one kind of regularity (Fischer *et al.*, 1985). These occurrences, known as alternations, which are variable, or less predictable, correspondences (Venezky, 1999), likely account for the bewilderment that many teachers express about spelling predictability. This bewilderment is exemplified in a teacher comment that 'There aren't really any rules set in stone as to how words are spelled' (Fresch, 2007: 323).[1] We do acknowledge that these alternations may vary across English dialects, for example, those spoken in England, Canada, Australia, and the United States and even within regions of a country (e.g. New England and the Deep South).

Third, *spelling activities* are seldom contextualized, much less organized as a search for predictable patterns. Instead, activities typically consist of discrete word lists where one is to identify a particular consonant or vowel of the week, using flashcards, or filling in a word from the list to complete a sentence, and/or giving word definitions (Wilde, 1990). The persistent emphasis on disconnected, non-patterned learning may be related to a variety of sources. One is the continuing belief that learning to spell is a visual memory activity, despite compelling evidence that it is a phonological activity (Joshi *et al.*, in press), as well as an orthographic and phonological–orthographic activity (Berninger *et al.*, 1998) and an orthographic–phonological–morphological activity (e.g. Treiman & Cassar, 1997). Another contributing factor is teacher education, which has been criticized for not including content on the developmental aspects of spelling (Fresch, 2007) or assisting prospective teachers in understanding spelling as a patterned linguistic system.

Finally, Wilde found that a number of the nine spelling series contained *mistakes* and *misrepresentations*. For example, misrepresentations that could be misleading and confusing to developing spellers included the following: 'The long **e** is spelled by the letters **ee** in **freeze**. It is spelled by the letters **ea** in **please**' (Wilde, 1990: 273, emphasis in original). There is no mention of why the silent *e* at the end of the two words is also included.[2]

In sum, current spelling measures yield information about the level of spelling achievement but little insight into the linguistic nature of misspellings or their instructional implications. Furthermore, instructional practices seem to have changed little over time. In fact, it might be fair to say that as more knowledge is obtained on the linguistic underpinnings of spelling, the attempts to communicate this new knowledge to prospective or inservice teachers have been relatively nonexistent or ineffective. Little is changing in typical classroom practices, which range from no explicit, systematic instruction to instructional activities that are not grounded in language and are not evidence-based.

Spelling as a linguistic activity supporting word learning

Spelling is a language activity in which oral linguistic units are converted into written units (Perfetti, 1997). As noted previously (Fresch, 2007; Wilde, 1990), this concept is still not necessarily understood widely by classroom teachers, although research on the linguistic knowledge sources of spelling has increased.

The late model. An expansive linguistic perspective is the stage-related view (Henderson, 1990), which first emerged over 25 years ago as a descriptive account of qualitative changes in spelling development (Gentry, 1982). The stage perspective is also referred to as the late model (Pacton & Deacon, 2008) because of the presumed later acquisition of morphology (Moats, 2000), especially derivational morphology knowledge.

In one version of the stage model spelling represents three layers of information (Templeton & Morris, 2000): alphabetic, pattern, and meaning. These layers represent the direction of spelling development: (1) from reliance on phonology (the alphabetic layer where phonemes are mapped to corresponding graphemes in a left to right way, e.g. c-a-t, m-a-t), to (2) appreciating orthographic relationships (the pattern layer within and between syllables, such as when to add a final -e and when to double consonants), to (3) understanding the morphological consistency in relationships among word roots, prefixes, and suffixes regardless of changes in pronunciation (the meaning layer). This late stage supposedly dominates the 'intermediate and middle grade years' (Bear et al., 2004: 218).

In defense of a developmental stage theory, Templeton and Morris (2000) note that a metalinguistic lag exists between students' ability to spell certain features, for example the past tense -ed, irrespective of whether this inflectional marker is pronounced as /t/ (kissed), /d/ (hugged), or /əd/ (hunted). Mastery of these variant past tense pronunciations in children's everyday use of their oral language system typically occurs by the late preschool years. According to Templeton and Morris, invariant spelling of the past tense indicates metalinguistic sensitivity to the orthographic form of past tense inflectional morphology, which remains unmarked in these instances (i.e. the spelling does not change). Despite some level of appreciation on the students' part, Templeton and Morris (2000) argue that many students (and, perhaps, many adults) still explain this orthographic regularity in terms of variations in pronunciation (sound) rather than utilize an explicit morphophonemic account. Morphophonemics characterizes English orthography since 'spellings encode both morphemes and phonemes' (Deacon & Bryant, 2006: 401). The deeper awareness that spellings have constancy even though pronunciations may change provides learners with a rational basis for many English spellings that may otherwise seem illogical (Moats, 2000).

For example, presuming that the capacity exists to segment root words at their morphemic boundaries, a deeper level of morphophonemic awareness leads to the understanding that three patterns of regularity exist in the spelling of past tense (Venezky, 1999): (1) When the morphemic unit (kiss) ends in an unvoiced consonant /s/, the past tense inflection is mapped to /t/; (2) when the morphophonemic unit (hug) ends in a voiced consonant /g/, the past tense inflection is mapped to /d/; and (3) in all other situations, such as the morphemic unit (hunt) ending in a consonant cluster /nt/, the past tense inflection is /əd/. The result for the latter form is not a /t/, but a final flap, which is produced by 'a quick tap of the tongue against the top of the mouth' (Treiman & Cassar, 1997: 73). Since a flap is voiced, it is comparable to /d/ and, in the hunt example is combined with a preceding unstressed vowel. It appears that by ages of 6 to 8 years, children's spellings reflect morphemic consistency for these three inflectional markers (Deacon & Bryant, 2005), although controversy continues about the meaning of mastery (e.g. Kuo & Anderson, 2006). In addition, the processes by which children achieve mastery remain unexplained (Treiman & Cassar, 1996). These inflectional findings lead

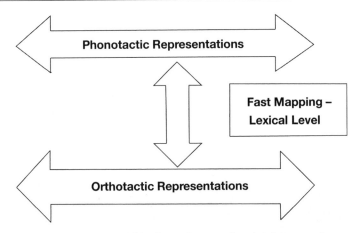

Figure 7.1 Statistical properties within the spoken word and written word

Moats (2001) to suggest that errors in past tense spelling by students struggling with reading and writing in grades 4 and above are related to inadequate morphophonemic awareness. In sum, the late model tends to examine an array of different linguistic structures that are related through the 'distinct type of knowledge' (Reece & Treiman, 2001: 140) that children are assumed to have during the particular stage.

The early model. In contrast to the late model is the early model (Pacton & Deacon, 2008), which originated with Treiman and colleagues (Treiman & Cassar, 1996, 1997). That work inspired a recent study showing that, from first to sixth grade, phonological, orthographic, *and* morphological processes discriminated good, average, and poor spellers (Garcia, 2007; Nagy *et al.*, in preparation). These results indicated that all three language processes – phonological, orthographic, and morphological – showed significant growth from first grade on and contributed jointly to spelling development from the beginning. A second linguistically grounded perspective consistent with the early model integrates a variety of empirical studies of spelling and takes into account two kinds of horizontal processing within spoken and written words and two kinds of vertical mapping, as well as vocabulary knowledge (Berninger & Fayol, 2008):

(a) *Horizontal processing* occurs within spoken words in one of two ways. Phonotactic structure is abstracted statistically about probable positions and sequences of specific sounds in spoken words (see Figure 7.1) or the spoken word is parsed into phonemes, onsets and rimes, or syllables (see Figure 7.2). Horizontal processing occurs within written words in one of two ways – orthotactic structure is abstracted statistically about probable positions and sequences of specific letters or letter sequences (see Figure 7.1) or the written word is parsed[3] into graphemes (1 or 2 letters), rimes, and syllables (see Figure 7.2). Although not depicted in Figures 7.1 or 7.2, morphotactic structure may also be abstracted and words can also be parsed into base words and affixes.

(b) *Vertical processing* involves mapping relationships between written and spoken words or spoken and written words at one of two levels – the lexical level (see Figure 7.1) and the sublexical level (Figure 7.2). Lexical-level mapping, which is word-specific, is fast mapping (i.e. the temporary storage of new meanings following a brief exposure; see Figure 7.1). Initially, the fast maps may be formed on the basis of association by looking at all the letters in the word and saying its name close in time as, for

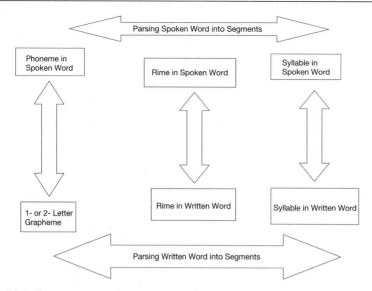

Figure 7.2 Following parsing the written word each unit is mapped onto a speech unit of corresponding size. Following parsing of the spoken word each unit is mapped onto a written unit of corresponding size

example, in acquiring a small set of 'sight' words in reading. However, with experience the bidirectional cross-word form fast mapping between spoken and written words draws increasingly on abstracted phonotactic and orthotactic statistical patterns (and also morphotactic patterns).

In contrast, sublexical vertical mapping is slow mapping that involves stages of information processing. First, the spoken or written word has to be parsed into sublexical units. Then each of those units has to find a corresponding unit in the other word form. Then each of the units has to be synthesized into a whole unit (see Figure 7.2). Abstracted phonotactic and orthotactic information that is not word-specific may also play a role in sublexical vertical mapping. Also, as is the case for the horizontal mapping, abstracted morphotactic patterns or parsed morpheme units may also play a role in the sublexical vertical mapping.

(c) Word-specific spelling has links to vocabulary knowledge, which may include a rich array of cognitive representations (Stahl & Nagy, 2006). Spelling is not a mechanical skill but rather a fundamental writing process for translating cognitive representations into written language. A recent brain imaging study provides evidence that good and poor writers may differ in the frontal regions that support this idea-to-spelling translation process (Richards *et al.*, submitted).

The findings of one study with beginning readers (Berninger, 1989) support the claim that lexical mapping is faster than sublexical mapping. In this computerized experiment completed in the second, fifth, and eighth month of first grade, children were asked to name real words with regular letter-sound correspondences, real words with irregular letter-sound correspondences, or pronounceable nonwords that were unfamiliar and had to be decoded with sublexical mapping. Children did not differ in their speed of naming regular and irregular real words (suggesting that they were relying on lexical rather than sublexical mapping for both since irregular words could not be named solely on the basis of sublexical mapping), but they were faster in naming real words than the nonwords, suggesting that the added source of semantic knowledge increased decoding speed.

Comparison of early and late models. Work using the early model tends to empha- size the *multidimensional and probabilistic nature of spelling development*. Attention is placed on: (1) how children spell particular linguistic patterns, such as the tendency of 6-year-old children who are American English speakers and of middle-class back- grounds to produce more accurate spellings of /t/ flaps when there is a root word (e.g. *dirty*). They are more likely to generate a /d/ flap when a root word is absent as in *city* (Treiman *et al.*, 1994); (2) the influence of linguistic variables on individual differences in performance, such as the effects of the phonological complexity of words (Reece & Treiman, 2001); and (3) from a theoretical perspective, language- specific experience about the probability of occurrence of phonemes, onsets and rimes, and syllables within the words of a language (referred to as phonotactic prob- abilities), as well as the patterns regulating the ordering of these elements within words in a language (also known as phonotactic regularity) (Brea-Spahn & Silliman, in press). This language–specific knowledge forms the basis for the statistical learning of spelling (Pollo *et al.*, 2007; Treiman & Kessler, 2006; Treiman *et al.*, 2002; Treiman *et al.*, 2000). These authors propose that spelling-to-sound correspondences are more predictable when phonetic context is taken into account. For vowels, this type of relationship is more common in the rime portion of a word (Treiman *et al.*, 2002). With consonants, children learn to recognize meaningful patterns among consonants and consonant–vowel sequences (a type of phonotactic regularity) and then use this knowledge to guide spellings, at least initially (Pollo *et al.*, 2007). For instance, in English, a *ck* consonant sequence is most likely to occur after a short vowel, as in *back*, while a *k* usually appears after a long vowel, as in *bake*. This reliance on phonotactic regularities does not rule out the possibility that children, employing situationally specific learning, just memorize the spellings of certain words because of their more uncommon spellings (Foorman & Ciancio, 2005).

In contrast to the fine-grained focuses of the early model, the late model tends to examine an array of different linguistic structures that are related through their 'distinct type of knowledge' (Reece & Treiman, 2001: 140) that children are believed to have during the particular stage. This knowledge is assumed to be cumulative and the stages mutually exclusive. In addition, the concept of orthographic processing is very limited in the late model. For example, the beginning alphabetic principle and decoding are not exclusively phonological but both phonological (phonemic) and orthographic (graph- emic) elements are involved in learning to map phonemes, which represent *minimal sound* units that make a *difference in meaning*, onto *letters* of the alphabet. That is, phonological, orthographic, and morphological/semantic (meaning of base words) units are built into the alphabetic principle in a morphophonemic orthography.

Stated another way, the late model does not recognize (1) this source of multiple linguistic contributions to early spelling of monosyllabic words; (2) the fact that, as children learn to spell monosyllabic words, all phonological sources (phonemes and onset-rimes as well as intonation for the whole lexical unit) map predictably onto orthographic units of varying size; and (3) that orthographic or phonological units typically have morphological representations as well. In contrast, the early model is based on a richer conceptualization of the phonological, orthographic, and morphological variables contributing to spelling early and throughout spelling development. Seymour *et al.* (2003) concluded that children learning to spell (and read) Danish, English, French, and Portuguese relied on more than the alphabetic principle and decoding. They also relied on syllabic complexity and orthographic depth.

Research evidence is accumulating that spelling acquisition does not rely exclusively on the alphabetic principle for encoding written words from spoken words. Rather, children learn considerable knowledge of spelling through implicit abstraction of orthographic regularities (e.g. Pacton *et al.*, 2001) and morphological regularities (e.g. Pacton *et al.*, 2005). Simply stated, beginning spellers are learning to abstract and apply both phonotactic and orthotactic knowledge (Apel *et al.*, 2006), as well as morphotactic knowledge (Treiman & Cassar, 1997).

Finally, early model studies found that children as young as age 6 years employed not only phonological knowledge in their spellings but also displayed budding metalinguistic sensitivity to morphological (e.g. Plaza & Cohen, 2004) and orthographic knowledge (e.g. Berninger *et al.*, 1992), as well as phonological, orthographic, and morphological knowledge (Nagy *et al.*, in preparation; Treiman & Cassar, 1997). This developing awareness of morphological constancy includes not only inflections but also derivations where the semantic relationship between the root word and derivation are transparent, as in *teach – teacher* and *nice – nicely* (Carlisle & Nomanbhoy, 1993; Deacon & Bryant, 2006; Rabin & Deacon, 2008; Treiman & Bourassa, 2000).[4] Multiple aspects of linguistic knowledge interact simultaneously within and across children to yield increasingly conventional spellings. Phonological aspects, therefore, do not act independently of the other components. This approach is consistent with what instructional research has shown are effective ways to teach spelling to beginning spellers (Berninger, 2008).

Classification of spelling errors: what errors have to tell

Misspellings occur because the linguistic complexity of words exceeds children's ability to utilize one or more linguistic components. While the late and early models provide two different perspectives of spelling development, both also provide ways to classify error patterns in children and afford opportunities for valuable information to be gathered for instructional and intervention purposes. A brief summary of the more commonly used approaches will follow.

Legality in phonetic and orthographic spelling

Phonetic errors can be analyzed using a constrained or unconstrained system (Bruck & Waters, 1988). In a constrained system, a misspelled word is considered phonetically accurate if the production of each grapheme results in a match to the target word, for example, *reche* for *reach* and *kepe* for *keep*. Although the previous examples are misspelled, the *–e* at the end of each word marks the long vowel, and the word would be pronounced like the target. The unconstrained system, on the other hand, accepts a misspelling as phonetically accurate if each sound in the word is represented by a grapheme according to English pronunciation, such as *rech* for *reach* or *necesite* for *necessity* (Bruck & Waters, 1988). Although the words are spelled incorrectly, there is a match between phonemes and graphemes making the words phonetically plausible.

Because spelling can occur through direct retrieval of the orthographic word form (Bruck & Waters, 1988), several systems have been developed that focus on the orthographic accuracy of spelling attempts. One of the earliest approaches focused on bigrams. Bigrams consider individual letters and their correct order in the misspelled word as compared to the target word. The percentage of bigrams produces a visual accuracy score, which is really an orthographic accuracy score. An example from Bruck and Waters (1988) illustrates the bigram measure. The word *nature* has five bigrams: (na+at+tu+ur+re) and six letters. If a child spelled the word as *nachure,* the child's spelling would match the target word with 3 bigrams and 5 letters for a total bigram + letter score of 8 out of a possible 11; therefore, the percent of bigrams would be .73 for visual accuracy. This form of scoring only accounts for direct matches in orthography. No consideration is given to phonetic spellings or alternate spellings to the orthographic target.

Variations of the visual accuracy approach have been proposed by Ball (1993) and Tangel and Blachman (1992, 1995). These systems utilize a 5- or 6-point scale to note how many speech sounds are correctly represented by letters or by alternative letter sequences. For instance, 'bead' could be spelled *bead*, which would receive the full number of points for a correct spelling or it could be misspelled as *beed*, which would receive a score that was one point lower because of the alternative grapheme sequence for the same vowel sound. These systems were devised to document developmental improvements in the use of orthography in early spellings.

These three orthographic approaches do not overtly account for the orthographic legality of the letter sequences (Treiman & Bourassa, 2000). For example, *mfbvg* is not orthographically legal because the sequence of consonants does not exist in English. However, *frip* for *trip* does not violate English orthography. Hence, orthographic legality was designed to assess structural and positional orthotactic knowledge. In this case, the spelling of each word is analyzed to determine if the words contain orthographically legal sequences of graphemes. The child receives credit even if the word is misspelled as long as the sequence of graphemes is legal. Therefore, the spelling error *frip* for *trip*, although misspelled, would receive full credit using the orthographic legality approach.

With its emphasis on the legality of letter sequences, this scoring method is more reminiscent of the early model of spelling development because it highlights children's knowledge of orthographic probabilities. More informative would be an analysis of the specific letters that violate orthographic legality for the source of the error. In the example above, the confusion of the /f/ and /t/ phoneme shows the problem is in the phoneme–grapheme mapping and therefore not totally related to the orthography.

Linguistically-based error classifications

While the above phonetic and visual approaches can provide a sense of how close the child's spelling is to the target, they fail to highlight the linguistic source of the spelling error and are therefore of minimal use to guide spelling instruction. Apel *et al.* (2004) recognized this shortcoming and proposed a system that analyzed children's linguistic knowledge, including phoneme–grapheme correspondence, graphemic rules, and positional constraints. Consistent with Bear *et al.* (2004) and

Ganske (2000), Apel *et al.* (2004) described orthographic development within the late model. However, their proposed system does not follow a strict developmental sequence and does recognize some overlap among levels. For example, children may learn to spell *sh* early in development but may not know the rule that sh can be written as *c(i)*, *t(i)*, or *s(i)* until they begin to spell derived morphemes with the 'shun' ending, like *physician, action* and *conclusion*.

While Apel *et al.* (2004) do acknowledge the role of phonology and morphology in the development of spelling, their emphasis is on the orthographic knowledge that these linguistic sources require, and not on the individual contributions of phonology, orthography, and morphology in the development of spelling. Nevertheless, this type of linguistically based approach has both diagnostic and instructional potential.

Another late-model approach to error analysis (Moats, 1995, 2001) also attempts to identify linguistic patterns in the misspellings of typically developing children and children with dyslexia. This system outlined linguistic feature errors within orthographic, phonological, and morphophonological categories. From these information sources, Moats defined eight different orthographic substitutions, which are described as 'speech sounds spelled according to identifiable phonetic strategies' (Moats, 2001: 53). Included in this category are: homophones, letter name spellings, sound by sound spellings, and plausible schwa misspellings, among others. The category of phonologically inaccurate spellings includes errors on nasal phonemes, vowel substitutions, deletion of schwa, and whole syllable or stressed syllable deletions, etc. Morphophonological misspellings focus on errors with *–ed* and *–s*, which occur in tense marking, contractions, and inflections.

The problem with this system is that it does not adequately differentiate between the linguistic sources of knowledge. For instance, Moats classified homophones as orthographic substitutions instead of recognizing the semantic basis for that error. Children must first analyze the semantic context of a word in order to know if *their* or *there* is the appropriate choice. In addition, inflectional endings, when added directly to the root, were classified as orthographic errors, such as *haveing/having* or *easyer/easier* (Moats, 2001: 54). This pattern seems to be governed by a more complete knowledge of inflectional morphology. In terms of phonological errors, Moats listed *werey/worry* as a phonological error with an r-controlled vowel. Given that the phonological structure of the word is preserved, it is possible that this is an orthographic error in that the child spelled the word the way it sounded and neglected to associate the phonology with the orthography of the appropriate root word. In any case, the identification of spelling errors is complex and involves interactions between the phonological, orthographic, and morphological knowledge bases of the child. A third linguistically based system that attempts to do this is the Phonological, Orthographic, and Phonological Assessment of Spelling (POMAS) as described by Silliman *et al.* (2006).

The Phonological, Orthographic, and Morphological Assessment of Spelling (POMAS)

The POMAS (Silliman *et al.*, 2006), which is motivated by the early model of spelling, allows for a qualitative assessment of errors by linguistic category. In contrast to the phonetic and visual accuracy approaches previously described, the POMAS categorizes misspellings using the linguistic categories of phonology, orthography, and morphology, and then further identifying specific features within each category. This type of analysis begins to tap into children's underlying linguistic representations and, like Apel *et al.* (2004) and Moats (2001), allows insight into the problem areas that individual children may be experiencing. The primary difference in this approach over those proposed by Apel *et al.* (2004) and Moats (2001) is that the POMAS has been empirically tested with children who are typically developing and those with language learning disabilities, as well as in written samples (both expository and narrative) taken from typically developing students in grades 1–9 (Bahr *et al.*, in preparation; Silliman *et al.*, in preparation), as described below.

Recent work with the POMAS. The POMAS system was used to code spelling errors in writing samples from students in grades 1–9 who had been studied for other purposes that did not include analysis of spelling errors (Berninger *et al.*, 1994; Berninger *et al.*, 1996; Berninger *et al.*, 1992). The original studies by Berninger and colleagues showed that orthographic coding (storing and processing written words in working memory), phonological coding (storing and processing spoken words in working memory), and vocabulary contributed uniquely to spelling accuracy in grades 1 to 6 (Berninger *et al.*, 1992). The current investigations involved an in-depth analysis of the errors produced by these students.

Students were selected from seven different schools in the Pacific Northwest. The sample consisted of 895 students (approximately 100 per grade level with roughly equal gender distribution). They represented urban, suburban, suburban/rural communities, as well as varied ethnicities and levels of mothers' education (both representative of the United States population at the time the study was conducted). Each participant provided 5-minute written responses to a narrative and expository prompt. The misspellings from these naturalistic texts were extracted for further analysis. Table 7.1 illustrates the mean number of errors produced by grade level.

These misspellings were analyzed with the POMAS. Coders first classified the error into one of the three broad areas of development and then identified the linguistic features involved. For instance, if the word *and* was misspelled as *ad*, the error would be classified as a phonological error because not all of the phonological elements of the word were represented in the child's spelling. This error would then be further classified as difficulty with a nasal (sonorant) cluster. However, if the child wrote *triped* for *tripped*, this would be coded as an orthographic error because the child was

Table 7.1 Mean number of errors produced in 5-minute written texts across grades 1–9.

Grade	Mean	SD
1	7.87	5.92
2	5.77	5.42
3	4.74	4.67
4	4.99	4.93
5	3.91	4.08
6	3.16	3.17
7	3.46	3.31
8	2.57	3.15
9	3.22	3.80

able to convey the phonological structure of what he/she wanted to say, but did not demonstrate the appropriate orthographic notation. This error would be classified as difficulty with the linguistic feature of consonant doubling. In a similar way, morphological errors were scored when the child demonstrated difficulty with inflections and derivations. The misspelling of homonyms (e.g. *there* for *their*) would also be included in the morphological code.

Patterns of misspellings. Once the scoring was completed, the total number of errors within each broad category was tabulated. Differences in the number of errors were analyzed across error type, grade, genre (narrative vs. expository), and gender. Significant differences were evident across error type. Orthographic errors occurred the most frequently in all grades. Phonological errors were the next most frequent error pattern for all students, while morphological (both inflectional and derivational) errors were more frequent in grades 5–9. The latter finding supports previous findings (Nagy *et al.*, 2006) and is most likely related to a greater use of derivations in the upper grades. However, it should be noted that morphological errors were present in the writing of children in grades 1–4 (primarily related to the use of inflections and prefixes). In addition, there continued to be phonological errors in the texts of students in grades 5–9. These findings lend further support to the early model in that there are continuous interactions among phonology, orthography, and morphology in the development of written spellings.

There were no significant effects related to genre (expository or narrative) or gender. However, a grade effect was noted for the first graders who made more errors in general than children in the other grades. The spellings of early appearing inflectional morphemes appeared to be governed by good spelling–sound translations or by specific spelling patterns, like *-ful* to mean *full* as in *cupful*. Later difficulties with phonology dealt with the representation of the appropriate feature patterns. For instance, the schwa in *cinnamon* was misspelled as *cinmin*, which is lacking the medial schwa. More detailed linguistic analyses of the spelling errors revealed the error patterns as illustrated in Table 7.2.

It is interesting to note that the complexity of errors increased with grade level. Errors in the early grades (1–4) seem to describe difficulties with representing all of the linguistic elements in the word. In the later grades, students appear to struggle with spelling multisyllabic words and with choices between possible spellings for a particular sound, like *au* and *ou* for the *aw* vowel sound. Another common error involved spelling the word as it was typically pronounced instead of the more formal way of saying it (e.g. *restraunt* for *restaurant*). This oral phenomenon is described by the phonological process of syncope or the deletion of an unstressed syllable. This rule often occurs in the colloquial productions of words like 'family' and 'interest' as *famly* and *intrest*. It is possible that the writer was not connecting the phonological production of the target word with its orthographic representation.

Another possible reason for the increase in spelling errors as word length increased would be the nature of the derivation involved in forming the target word. According to Carlisle and Nomanbhoy (1993), when attempting to formulate derivations in the earlier grades, children tend to use prefixes and suffixes that do not alter the phonological or orthographic structure of the word, like changing *teach* into *teacher*. As their vocabulary continues to expand, other types of words become available (Carlisle, 2000), which may involve more complex derivations involving orthographic

Table 7.2 The most frequently occurring linguistic error patterns across grades 1–4 and 5–9.

Grades	Phonological	Orthographic	Morphological
1–4	**Silent e** *kit* for *kite* **Sonorant Cluster** *ad* for *and* **Final Consonant Voicing** *becus* for *because*	**Letter Name** *cr* for *car* **Digraph** *sip* for *ship* **Letter Sound** *sereal* for *cereal* **Vocalic r** *sistr* for *sister*	**Inflections** *kist* for *kissed* **Homonyms** *see* for *sea* **Contractions** *weve* for *we've*
5–8	**Consonant Deletion** *favoite* for *favorite* **Syllable Reduction** *restraunts* for *restaurants* **Voicing Error** *Princible* for *Principal*	**Consonant Doubling** *untill* for *until* **Short V Digraph** *thaught* for *thought* **Vowel Error** *enamy* for *enemy*	**Inflections** *studys* for *studies* **Homonyms** *there* for *they're* **Contractions** *would'nt* for *wouldn't* **Derivation of Root** *practly* for *practically*

shifts (*stop* to *stoppable*, where a letter is doubled), phonologic shifts (*comfort* to *comfortable*, where there is a change in the stress pattern of the word when the suffix is added), and phonologic–orthographic shifts (*vegetable* to *vegetarian*, where word stress and the root word orthography are altered). The last type of shift is by far the most difficult for students to master and this difficulty is probably related to their level of metalinguistic awareness and vocabulary depth. In other words, the student's ability to spell *vegetarian* is facilitated by his/her knowledge of the spelling of the root word and his/her understanding of suffix spellings.

An increasing number of combination errors (i.e. phonological–orthographic or orthographic–morphological, etc.) were noted as students matured. One example of this would be letter reversal (*freind* for *friend*) where it is unclear if the child was trying to represent the short *e* vowel or just confused the letter order for the vowel digraph. Another case would be difficulties with silent e, as in *gon* for *gone*. In this case, it is unclear if the student did not include the final *e* because the word sounded correctly or he/she did not represent the word with the appropriate orthography.

Finally, the older students produced numerous instances of root words and suffixes that were misspelled, as in *presontor* for *presenter*. These error types suggest that the root word may not be fully established in the students' vocabulary, resulting in a loose connection between the corresponding phonological and orthographic information. The current data revealed that grade 5 students were beginning to spell these types of derivations and that by grade 9, the number of errors on these types of words had notably increased (e.g. *muscler* for *muscular*). In the latter example, the student has recognized the root word, but was not familiar with the derivation necessary to arrive at the target spelling. The interrelationships among these three linguistic categories need further study, but the sheer frequency of these types of error in the written texts of students would suggest that spelling instruction targeted to roots and their possible derivations and inflections could serve to improve overall spelling skill.

It would also be helpful to analyze these misspellings in the context of the written text to note how often a particular phonological, orthographic, or morphological pattern was spelled correctly. Finally, it would be interesting to submit students' spellings (both correct and incorrect) to the database provided by the English Lexicon Project (Balota *et al.*, 2007), which would then provide information on word frequency, spelling to sound regularity, neighborhood density, and syntactic class. This type of information could be used to examine the relative merits of the early versus late models of development, as well as to derive specific instructional targets.

Broader application of this classification system. The contributions of phonological, orthographic, and morphological processes to spelling not only begin early but also continue throughout spelling development in grades 1 to 9. Triple word form theory, which emphasizes the concurrent contributions of all three linguistic processes throughout spelling development, provides a conceptual framework that acknowledges the interrelationships among these three linguistic processes, how they are coordinated, and how they may vary across development (Berninger *et al.*, 2009; Berninger & Fayol, 2008). While this system was developed using misspellings from American English, triple word form theory should be applicable across alphabetic languages, taking into account language-specific features. These features might include accents in Romance languages, the absence of vowel length differences, and the nonexistence of letter doubling in many languages with more transparent orthographies, etc.

Current and future directions in spelling research

Stages or concurrent influences?

More research is needed on how phonological, orthographic, and morphological processes may be interconnected early in spelling development and then possibly in different ways at subsequent phases. Rather than phonology, orthography, *or* morphology *alone* characterizing specific stages of spelling development, *the ways in which they are coordinated and interrelated* may characterize specific phases or stages of spelling development, as well as individual differences among children.

These phases or stages may have developmental trajectories that are best described as overlapping cascades rather than linear trends. Which names for these specific phases or stages best captures how the three language processes – phonological, orthographic, and morphological – are synchronized and interrelated in phase- or stage-specific spelling requires clarification. (See Berninger *et al.*, 2009, for further discussion of these issues.)

Horizontal and vertical mapping of spoken and written words

More research is also needed on Berninger and Fayol's (2008) proposal that phonotactic and orthotactic knowledge may underlie the vertical lexical fast mapping process that explains much of spelling learning in typically developing students (see Figure 7.2). McGregor's (2004) concept of fast mapping, a process by which minimal exposure to a novel meaning results in at least partial storage of the meaning, accounts for the incidental learning of oral vocabulary and may also be a mechanism applied to learning to spell spoken words. The fast mapping process can explain why many children can spell words correctly that adults do not explicitly teach.

Support for the influence of fast mapping in spelling comes from the work of Treiman *et al.* (2000) which documented the role of implicit phonotactic knowledge in learning to spell, as well as the research of Pacton *et al.* (2001, 2005), which highlighted the contributions of implicit orthographic and morphological statistical regularities. The work of Apel *et al.* (2006) also showed that children began to apply phonotactic and orthotactic knowledge early in spelling development. However, additional investigations are needed on how these sources of implicit knowledge continue to contribute to fast lexical mapping throughout spelling development, especially in languages with deep orthographies, like English.

Spelling links to vocabulary

Skilled spellers have automatic access to word-specific spellings that have links to: (1) representation of all the letters in a word (whether or not the letters have phonological or morphological codes), (2) the pronunciation of the spoken word, (3) the morphological features of words, such as inflectional or derivational suffixes, and (4) semantic information (concepts and other forms of cognitive representations). Semantic relationships are the cognitive basis of vocabulary knowledge in the language system. As such, vocabulary draws on rich language–cognitive mappings, which may not be one to one, and that may provide an important source of information in learning word-specific spellings and vice versa (see Stahl & Nagy, 2006).

Moreover, Perfetti's (2007) lexical quality hypothesis, which is intended to explain the central role of vocabulary in oral and reading comprehension, may also enrich the understanding of vocabulary–spelling linkages. High quality lexical representations in reading comprehension are a combination of well-specified orthographic, phonological, and grammatical representations combined with more generalized and less context-bound meanings that are all tightly bound together as a unit. Applied to spelling, individuals with rich lexical representations may be good spellers because the fusion of phonological, orthographic, and morphological units promotes *stability* in rapid retrieval, *synchrony* between the activation of word identity constituents and their actual identification, and the *integration* of meanings for producing a broad diversity of conventional spellings.

To state the preceding point another way, it may be that children who become good spellers do so in part because their horizontal processing within word forms, such as abstracting phonotactic patterns or parsing words into segments, promotes their vertical processing across word forms so that their lexical fast mapping occurs with accuracy and ease. In contrast, children who struggle with spelling (encoding) and word reading (decoding) do so because of the lower quality lexical representations that comprise their oral or written lexicons. Because their lexical representations consist of less well-specified and less tightly bound phonotactic, orthotactic, and morphemic units, the speed and accuracy of horizontal and vertical processing will be impacted with more variable consequences for achieving a stable, coordinated, and integrated spelling system. Perfetti (2007), consistent with Nagy (2005, 2007), makes the strong case that the lexical quality of representations 'is acquired through effective experience with words' (p. 365), through oral language and literacy experiences, including spelling experiences. In effect, how, when, and where one 'knows' a word to spell is a function of the grading of lexical quality 'across words for a given individual and across individuals for a given word' (Perfetti, 2007: 380).

Effective instruction for spelling

Finally, evidence is accumulating on effective spelling instruction (for review, see Berninger, 2008; Berninger & Fayol, 2008); however, much additional research is needed on how best to teach children to coordinate and integrate phonological, orthographic, and morphological knowledge. Spelling acquisition is characterized by the awareness that the three word forms are coded and parts analyzed. Eventually, this growing metalinguistic awareness must be harmonized and integrated with high quality lexical representations (Perfetti, 2007) to develop accurate and automatic spelling (Steffler *et al.*, 1998), not only for monomorphemic words, but also complex multisyllabic words. Spellings that draw on phonological, orthographic, and morphological awareness are linked to new vocabulary acquisition (Stahl & Nagy, 2006) and the quality of written compositions in the primary and intermediate grades (Berninger *et al.*, 2008a).

Notes

1 For an alternative, based on Venezky (1999) in which the alternations are explicitly taught as options to apply strategically and in the context of word-specific learning, see Berninger and Abbott (2003), Lesson Sets 4, 5, 7, 10, 11, and 12.
2 In American English, final *e* is included when the preceding vowel is long; but there are always less predictable occurrences, such as *plead* and *reed*, as well as *give, have,* and *love*. In the last three examples, final *e* is attached even though the preceding vowel is short. Here, *–e* signals that the spelling is the voiced /v/; otherwise the final consonant would be pronounced as /f/ as in *Romanov* (see Venezky, 1999: 86 for an alternate graphemic explanation related to the late Middle English origin of *–ve*). Spellings of English origin do not end in just *v*. Research has shown that children benefit from teaching all the high frequency alternations in high frequency words, as in long e sounds (see Berninger & Abbott, 2003, with a review of the supporting literature).
3 It is recognized that parsing occurs in a variety of oral language functions; however, as used here, parsing refers to both oral and written words and varies in size of parsed segments.
4 The early model studies were originally done with French-speaking children (e.g. Deacon *et al.*, 2007; Martinet *et al.*, 2004; Pacton *et al.*, 2005; Sénéchal *et al.*, 2006) but have been recently extended to English (e.g. Berninger *et al.*, 2008a; Garcia, 2007; Nagy *et al.*, in preparation).

References

Allal, L. (1997). 'Learning to spell in the classroom'. In C.A. Perfetti, L. Rieben & M. Fayol (eds), *Learning to spell: Research, theory and practice across languages* (pp. 129–150). Mahwah, NJ: LEA.

Apel, K., Masterson, J.J., & Niessen, N.L. (2004). 'Spelling assessment frameworks'. In C.A. Stone, E.R. Silliman, B.J. Ehren & K. Apel (eds), *Handbook of language and literacy: Development and disorders* (pp. 644–660). New York: Guilford.

Apel, K., Wolter, J., & Masterson, J. (2006). 'Effects of orthotactic and phonotactic probabilities during fast mapping on 5-year-olds learning to spell'. *Developmental Neuropsychology, 29*, 21–42.

Bahr, R.H., Silliman, E. R., & Berninger, V.W. (in preparation). 'Spelling development: Grades 1–4'.

Ball, E.W. (1993). 'Assessing phoneme awareness'. *Language, Speech, & Hearing Services in Schools, 24*, 130–139.

Balota, D.A., Yap, M.J., Cortese, M.J., Hutchison, K.A., Kessler, B., Loftis, B., *et al.* (2007). 'The English lexicon project'. *Behavior Research Methods, 39*, 445–459.

Bear, D.R., Invernizzi, M.A., Templeton, S., & Johnston, F. (2004). *Words their way: Word study for phonics, vocabulary, and spelling instruction* (3rd edn). Upper Saddle River, NJ: Pearson.

Berninger, V. (1989). 'Orchestration of multiple codes in developing readers: An alternative model of lexical access'. *International Journal of Neuroscience, 48*, 85–104.

Berninger, V. (2008). 'Evidence-based written language instruction during early and middle childhood'. In R. Morris, & N. Mather (eds), *Evidence-based interventions for students with learning and behavioral challenges* (pp. 215–235). Mahwah, NJ: LEA.

Berninger, V., & Abbot, A. (2003). *PAL research-supported reading and writing lessons*. San Antonio, TX: Harcourt/PsyCorp.

Berninger, V., & Fayol, M. (2008). 'Why spelling is important and how to teach it effectively'. *Encyclopedia of language and literacy development* (pp. 1–13). London, ON: Canadian Language and Literacy Research Network. Retrieved May 6, 2008 from: http://www.literacyencyclopedia.ca/pdfs/topic.php?topld+234.

Berninger, V., Yates, C., Cartwright, A., Rutberg, J., Remy, E., & Abbott, R. (1992). 'Lower-level developmental skills in beginning writing'. *Reading and Writing, 4*, 257–280.

Berninger, V., Cartwright, A., Yates, C., Swanson, H.L., & Abbott, R. (1994). 'Developmental skills related to writing and reading acquisition in the intermediate grades: Shared and unique variance'. *Reading and Writing: An Interdisciplinary Journal, 6*, 161–196.

Berninger, V., Whitaker, D., Feng, Y., Swanson, H.L., & Abbott, R. (1996). 'Assessment of planning, translating, and revising in junior high writers'. *Journal of School Psychology, 34*, 23–52.

Berninger, V., Vaughan, K., Abbott, R., Brooks, A., Abbott, S., Reed, E., *et al.* (1998). 'Early intervention for spelling problems: Teaching spelling units of varying size within a multiple connections framework'. *Journal of Educational Psychology, 90*, 587–605.

Berninger, V.W., Nielsen, K.H., Abbott, R.D., Wijsman, E., & Raskind, W. (2008a). 'Writing problems in developmental dyslexia: Under-recognized and under-treated'. *Journal of School Psychology, 46*, 1–21.

Berninger, V.W., Nielsen, K.H., Abbott, R.D., Wijsman, E., & Raskind, W. (2008b). 'Gender differences in severity of writing and reading disabilities'. *Journal of School Psychology, 46*, 151–172.

Berninger, V., Raskind, W., Richards, T., Abbott, R., & Stock, P. (2008c). 'A multidisciplinary approach to understanding developmental dyslexia within working-memory architecture: Genotypes, phenotypes, brain, and instruction'. *Developmental Neuropsychology, 33*, 707–744.

Berninger, V., Garcia, N., & Abbott, R. (2009). 'Multiple processes that matter in writing instruction and assessment'. In G. Troia (ed.), *Instruction and assessment for struggling writers. Evidence-based practices*. New York: Guilford.

Bishop, D.V.M., & Clarkson, B. (2003). 'Written language as a window into residual language deficits: A study of children with persistent and residual speech and language impairments'. *Cortex, 39*, 215–237.

Brea-Spahn, M. R., & Silliman, E.R. (in press). 'Tuning into language-specific patterns: Nonword repetition and the big picture of bilingual vocabulary learning'. In A.Y. Durgunoglu (ed.), *Language learners: Their development and assessment in oral and written language*. New York: Guilford.

Bruck, M., & Waters, G. (1988). 'An analysis of spelling errors of children who differ in their reading and spelling skills'. *Applied Psycholinguistics, 9*, 77–92.

Carlisle, J.F. (2000). 'Awareness of the structure and meaning of morphologically complex words: Impact on reading'. *Reading and Writing, 12*, 169–190.

Carlisle, J.F., & Nomanbhoy, D.M. (1993). 'Phonological and morphological awareness in first graders'. *Applied Psycholinguistics, 14*, 177–195.

Deacon, S.H., & Bryant, P. (2005). 'What young children do and do not know about the spelling of inflections and derivations'. *Developmental Science, 8*, 583–594.

Deacon, S.H., & Bryant, P. (2006). 'Getting to the root: Young writers' sensitivity to the role of root morphemes in the spelling of inflected and derived words'. *Journal of Child Language, 33*, 401–417.

Deacon, S.H., Wade-Woolley, L., & Kirby, J. (2007). 'Crossover: The role of morphological awareness in French immersion children's reading'. *Developmental Psychology, 43*, 732–746.

Dockrell, J.E., Lindsay, G., Connelly, V., & Mackie, C. (2007). 'Constraints in the production of written text in children with specific language impairments'. *Exceptional Children, 73*, 147–164.

Ehri, L.C., & Rosenthal, J. (2007). 'Spellings of words: A neglected facilitator of vocabulary learning'. *Journal of Literacy Research, 39*, 389–409.

Fischer, F.W., Shankweiler, D., & Liberman, I.Y. (1985). 'Spelling proficiency and sensitivity to word structure'. *Journal of Memory and Language, 24*, 423–441.

Foorman, B.J., & Ciancio, D.J. (2005). 'Screening for secondary intervention: Concept and context'. *Journal of Learning Disabilities, 38*, 494–499.

Foorman, B.R., Schatschneider, C., Eakin, M.N., Fletcher, J.M., Moats, L.C., & Francis, D.J (2006). 'The impact of instructional practices in grades 1 and 2 on reading and spelling achievement in high poverty schools'. *Contemporary Educational Psychology, 31*, 1–29.

Fresch, M. (2007). 'Teachers' concerns about spelling instruction: A national survey'. *Reading Psychology, 28*, 301.

Ganske, K. (2000). *Word journeys.* New York: Guilford.

Garcia, N. (2007). Phonological, orthographic, and morphological contributions to the spelling development of good, average, and poor spellers. Unpublished PhD, University of Washington.

Gentry, J.R. (1982). 'An analysis of developmental spelling in GNYS AT WRK'. *The Reading Teacher, 36*, 192–200.

Gillis, S., & Ravid, D. (2006). 'Typological effects on spelling development: A cross-linguistic study of Hebrew and Dutch'. *Journal of Child Language, 33*, 621–659.

Graham, S., & Harris, K.R. (2006). 'Preventing writing difficulties: Providing additional handwriting and spelling instruction to at-risk children in first grade'. *Teaching Exceptional Children, 38*, 64–66.

Harris, K.R., & Graham, S. (1996). *Making the writing process work: Strategies for composition and self-regulation.* Cambridge, MA: Brookline Books.

Henderson, E.H. (1990). *Teaching spelling* (2nd edn). Boston, MA: Houghton-Mifflin.

Holm, A., Farrier, F., & Dodd, B. (2008). 'Phonological awareness, reading accuracy and spelling ability of children with inconsistent phonological disorder'. *International Journal of Language & Communication Disorders, 43,* 300–322.

Joshi, R.M., Treiman, R., Carreker, S., & Moats, L. (in press). 'Isn't spelling just memorizing words? Answers to some common questions about spelling'. *American Educator.*

Kuo, L.J., & Anderson, R.C. (2006). 'Morphological awareness and learning to read: A cross-language perspective'. *Educational Psychologist, 41,* 161.

Larkin, R.F., & Snowling, M.J. (2008). 'Comparing phonological skills and spelling abilities in children with reading and language impairment'. *International Journal of Language & Communication Disorders, 43,* 111–124.

McGregor, K. (2004). 'Developmental dependencies between lexical semantics and reading'. In C.A. Stone, E.R. Silliman, B.J. Ehren & K. Apel (eds), *Handbook of language literacy: Development and disorders* (pp. 302–317). New York: Guilford.

Martinet, C., Valdois, S., & Fayol, M. (2004). 'Lexical orthographic knowledge develops from the beginning of literacy acquisition'. *Cognition, 91,* B11–B22.

Moats, L.C. (1995). *Spelling: Development, disabilities, and instruction.* Baltimore, MD: York Press.

Moats, L.C. (2000). *Speech to print: Language essentials for teachers.* Baltimore, MD: Paul H. Brooks.

Moats, L.C. (2001). 'Spelling disability in adolescents and adults'. In A.M. Bain, L.L. Bailet & L.C. Moats (eds), *Written language disorders: Theory into practice* (2nd edn, pp. 43–75). Austin, TX: Pro-Ed.

Moats, L., Foorman, B., & Taylor, P. (2006). 'How quality of writing instruction impacts high-risk fourth graders' writing'. *Reading & Writing, 19,* 363–391.

Nagy, W. (2005). 'Why vocabulary instruction needs to be long-term and comprehensive'. In E.H. Hiebert, & M.L. Kamil (eds), *Teaching and learning vocabulary: Bringing research to practice* (pp. 27–44). Mahwah, NJ: LEA.

Nagy, W. (2007). 'Metalinguistic awareness and the vocabulary-comprehension connection'. In R.K. Wagner, A.E. Muse & K.R. Tannenbaum (eds), *Vocabulary acquisition: Implications for reading comprehension* (pp. 52–77). New York: Guilford.

Nagy, W., Berninger, V.W., & Abbott, R.D. (2006). 'Contributions of morphology beyond phonology to literacy outcomes of upper elementary and middle-school students'. *Journal of Educational Psychology, 98,* 134–147.

Nagy, W., Carlisle, J., Abbott, R., & Berninger, V. (in preparation). 'Theoretical and instructional implications for reading and writing of phonological, orthographic, and morphological growth in grades 1 to 6'.

Pacton, S., & Deacon, S.H. (2008). 'The timing and mechanisms of children's use of morphological information in spelling: A review of evidence from English and French'. *Cognitive Development, 23,* 339–359.

Pacton, S., Perruchet, P., Fayol, M., & Cleeremans, A. (2001). 'Implicit learning out of the lab: The case of orthographic regularities'. *Journal of Experimental Psychology, 130,* 401–426.

Pacton, S., Fayol, M., & Perruchet, P. (2005). 'Children's implicit learning of graphotactic and morphological regularities'. *Child Development, 76,* 324–339.

Perfetti, C.A. (1997). 'The psycholinguistics of reading and spelling'. In C.A. Perfetti, L. Rieben & M. Fayol (eds), *Learning to spell: Research, theory, and practice across languages* (pp. 21–38). Mahwah, NJ: LEA.

Perfetti, C. (2007). 'Reading ability: Lexical quality to comprehension'. *Scientific Studies of Reading, 11,* 357–383.

Plaza, M., & Cohen, H. (2004). 'Predictive influence of phonological processing, morphological/syntactic skill, and naming speed on spelling performance'. *Brain and Cognition, 55,* 368–373.

Pollo, T.C., Treiman, R., & Kessler, B. (2007). 'Three perspectives on spelling development'. In E.I. Grigorenko, & A.J. Naples (eds), *Single-word reading: Behavorial and biological perspectives*. Mahwah, NJ: LEA.

Puranik, C.S., Lombardino, L.J., & Altmann, L.J.P. (2008). 'Assessing the microstructure of written language using a retelling paradigm'. *American Journal of Speech-Language Pathology, 17*, 107–120.

Rabin, J., & Deacon, H. (2008). 'The representation of morphologically complex words in the developing lexicon'. *Journal of Child Language, 35*, 453–465.

Reece, C., & Treiman, R. (2001). 'Children's spelling of syllabic /r/ and letter-name vowels: Broadening the study of spelling development'. *Applied Psycholinguistics, 22*, 139–165.

Rice, J.M. (1913). *Scientific management in education*. New York and Philadelphia: Hinds Noble & Ridge.

Richards, T., Berninger, V., & Fayol, M. (submitted). 'BOLD activation differences between good and poor writers during fMRI spelling and orthographic coding tasks'.

Sénéchal, M., Basque, M.T., & Leclaire, T. (2006). 'Morphological knowledge as revealed in children's spelling accuracy and reports of spelling strategies'. *Journal of Experimental Child Psychology, 95*, 231–254.

Seymour, P., Aro, M., & Erskine, J. (2003). 'Foundation literacy acquisition in European orthographies'. *British Journal of Psychology, 94*, 143–174.

Silliman, E.R., Bahr, R.H., & Peters, M.L. (2006). 'Spelling patterns in preadolescents with atypical language skills: Phonological, morphological, and orthographic factors'. *Developmental Neuropsychology, 29*, 93–123.

Silliman, E.R., Bahr, R.H., & Berninger, V.W. (in preparation). 'Spelling development: Grades 5–9'.

Stahl, S.A., & Nagy, W.E. (2006). *Teaching word meanings*. Mahwah, NJ: LEA.

Steffler, D.J., Varnhagen, C.K., Friesen, C.K., & Treiman, R. (1998). 'There's more to children's spelling than the errors they make: Strategic and automatic processes for one-syllable words'. *Journal of Educational Psychology, 90*, 492–505.

Tangel, D.M., & Blachman, B.A. (1992). 'Effect of phoneme awareness instruction on kindergarten children's invented spelling'. *Journal of Reading Behavior, 24*, 233–261.

Tangel, D.M., & Blachman, B.A. (1995). 'Effect of phoneme awareness instruction on the invented spelling of first grade children: A one year follow-up'. *Journal of Reading Behavior, 27*, 153–185.

Templeton, S., & Morris, D. (2000). 'Spelling'. In M.L. Kamil, P.B. Mosenthal, P.D. Pearson & R. Barr (eds), *Handbook of reading research* (Volume III, pp. 525–543). Mahwah, NJ: LEA.

Treiman, R., & Cassar, M. (1996). 'Effects of morphology on children's spelling of final consonant clusters'. *Journal of Experimental Child Psychology, 63*, 141–170.

Treiman, R., & Cassar, M. (1997). 'Spelling acquisition in English'. In C.A. Perfetti, L. Rieben & M. Fayol (eds), *Learning to spell: Research, theory, and practice across languages* (pp. 61–80). Mahwah, NJ: LEA.

Treiman, R., & Bourassa, D.C. (2000). 'Children's written and oral spelling'. *Applied Psycholinguistics, 21*, 183–204.

Treiman, R., & Kessler, B. (2006). 'Spelling as statistical learning: Using consonantal context to spell vowels'. *Journal of Educational Psychology, 98*, 642–652.

Treiman, R., Cassar, M., & Zukowski, A. (1994). 'What types of linguistic information do children use in spelling? The case of flaps'. *Child Development, 65*, 1318–1337.

Treiman, R., Kessler, B., Knewasser, S., Tincoff, R., & Bowman, M. (2000). 'English speakers' sensitivity to phonotactic patterns'. In M.B. Broe, & J.B. Pierrehumbert (eds), *Papers in laboratory phonology V: Acquisition and the lexicon* (pp. 269–282). Cambridge: Cambridge University Press.

Treiman, R., Kessler, B., & Bick, S. (2002). 'Context sensitivity in the spelling of English vowels'. *Journal of Memory and Language, 47,* 448–468.

Venezky, R.L. (1999). *The American way of spelling: The structure and origins of American English orthography.* New York: Guilford.

Wilde, S. (1990). 'Spelling textbooks: A critical review'. *Linguistics and Education, 2,* 259-280.

Part 2

Reading and spelling across languages

Chapter 8

Reading and spelling development in transparent alphabetic orthographies

Points of convergence, divergence and arising issues

Selma Babayiğit

General introduction

Research in different writing systems has established beyond doubt that alongside many similarities, there are also important differences in the way in which reading and spelling develop across languages (Joshi & Aaron, 2006). Different languages and orthographies can make differential demands on the cognitive–linguistic systems that underlie literacy development, thereby giving rise to different patterns of relationships (Perfetti & Bolger, 2004). It is primarily for this reason that research on different writing systems is important to clarify the complex triad of relationships between language, orthography, and literacy.

Orthographic transparency, broadly defined as the level of consistency in grapheme–phoneme relationships, and its effect on literacy development has attracted much research attention. English is one of the most opaque writing systems with many inconsistent and complex grapheme–phoneme relationships. Therefore, it provides a benchmark for comparison with transparent orthographies characterised by simple and consistent grapheme–phoneme relationships, such as Finnish and Turkish.

The primary aim of this chapter is to pull together the diverse research evidence from studies conducted in English and transparent alphabetic orthographies in relation to reading and spelling development and to highlight the common as well as divergent points. The chapter also highlights a number of methodological and conceptual issues that need to be considered for a coherent evaluation of the role of phonological awareness in transparent writing systems.

Theories of reading and spelling have developed based mainly on evidence from studies in English. I begin, therefore, with an overview of the theories of reading and spelling development in English. The subsequent sections build upon this background knowledge and evaluate the research evidence from transparent orthographies.

Learning to read and spell in English: in a nutshell

It is not sufficient to learn the grapheme–phoneme associations of the alphabet in order to read and spell accurately in English. The same phoneme can be represented by different letter (s) (e.g. /k/ is written as <ck> in <back> but as <c> in <cash>) and the same grapheme can be pronounced differently in different words (e.g. < c > in <car> and <city>). The English orthography is more consistent at the level of onset-rime than at the level of grapheme and children seem to capitalise on this statistical regularity of the language, and process words at onset-rime levels as well (Goswami *et al.*, 2003). Furthermore, due to the morphophonemic nature of English orthography, the learner needs to develop an understanding of the morphology and learn the instances when morphology overrides phonology. For instance, some words that share the same base are in some cases pronounced differently (e.g. nature–natural) but not in others (e.g. care versus careless). Similarly, grammatical suffixes, such as past tense –ed can be pronounced differently, yet remain the same in writing (e.g. waited, walked, warned) (Nunes *et al.*, 1997).

Hence, learning to read and spell in English requires learning multiple rules and statistical regularities of the orthography at multiple linguistic levels, as well as idiosyncratic cases that have to be learnt by rote. This means that the development of literacy skills in English can only be accomplished by learning to apply these different rules, strategies and knowledge appropriately, flexibly, and efficiently. The next question is how children develop this wide repertoire of processes and the knowledge base that is the hallmark of skilled literacy.

Reading and spelling development in English

Ehri's phase theory of reading and spelling development provides a clear outline of the major facets of reading and spelling processes (Ehri, 1992, 2002). In the absence of any knowledge of letter-sound correspondences, word recognition is based on making arbitrary connections between the salient visual features of a word and its pronunciation. For instance, the recognition of the logo sign 'STOP', based on its colours and patterns. This is referred to as pre-alphabetic reading, which is an optional and transient reading process and seems to play little or no role for future reading attainment (Share, 1995).

As soon as children start to acquire some letter knowledge and develop phonological sensitivity, they use this knowledge to identify words. This is phonetic-cue reading, which can contribute to real word errors and confusions with similarly spelled words such as reading '<house>' as '<horse>' (Ehri, 2002: 13). As alphabet knowledge increases, it becomes possible to process serially all the graphemes of a written word and build up its pronunciation. This is called phonological recoding, which enables accurate decoding of regular words but leads to errors when reading words that do not conform to the default phoneme–grapheme correspondence rules (e.g. reading <have> as /heɪv/).

Once the connections between the letter strings and their pronunciations are consolidated, it becomes possible to recognise a word rapidly as a whole unit or larger spelling units without the need for serial processing of all the individual graphemes. At the same time, acquisition of morphosyntactic knowledge, the knowledge of higher-order letter–sound relationships, and word-specific pronunciations enables accurate decoding of irregular or complex words. This is called orthographic reading characterised by accurate, effortless and fast word recognition, which is the hallmark of skilled reading (Ehri, 1992).

Similar processes have been proposed for spelling. Initially, children understand that writing is different from drawing. Their writings may include scribbles or letter-like shapes, but lack any alphabet knowledge. As children start to learn that speech is represented by the letters of the alphabet through exposure to print and/or reading instruction, they may start to use partial alphabetic knowledge or the letter–name strategy to represent words (e.g. writing <r> to represent <are>) (Treiman, 2006). This is called semi-phonetic spelling, which lacks complete representations of the sounds. Increase in alphabet knowledge enables full alphabetic spelling, where all the sounds of the dictated words are represented in writing (Ehri, 1986). However, full alphabetic processing can lead to errors when spelling complex words (e.g. spelling of <their> as <there>). This problem is gradually resolved through the acquisition of the knowledge of higher-order grapheme-phoneme relationships, morphosyntactic or word-specific spelling knowledge (i.e. orthographic spelling).

There is now substantial support for the multi-process account of literacy development, which states that children may utilise one or more of these reading and spelling processes from the very onset of literacy development depending on their alphabet knowledge, print experience and word characteristics (e.g. Rittle-Johnson & Siegler, 1999; Share, 1995). Nonetheless, broadly, children's early reading and spelling processes tend to be phonological, and the orthographic (e.g. morphological) processing skills tend to be more rudimentary (Kemp, 2006; Treiman & Cassar, 1997). What seems to develop is the depth and breath of their phonological and orthographic knowledge and efficiency to employ different reading and spelling processes.

Questions that remain ...

Orthographic processing constitutes one of the most contentious issues in the reading literature. There is a large gap in our understanding of the nature of orthographic representations; the specific mechanism underlying the acquisition of orthographic representations and its component processes; and finally, the relationship between orthographic processing with other processing skills including phonological processing, print exposure, general language skills (e.g. vocabulary, morphosyntactic skills), visual processing, and cognitive skills (Burt, 2006; Cunningham, 2006; Hagiliassis *et al.*, 2006).

Operationalisation of orthographic processing independent of phonological processing tends to be problematic (Wagner & Barker, 1994). For instance, exception word reading is considered to be an index of orthographic reading skills but as the notion of quasi-regularity states, even parts of the so-called exception words in English such as <yacht> can be partly read phonologically, as the letter Y is regular in this instance (Plaut *et al.*, 1996). Similarly, studies often found that it is very difficult to delineate morphological processes that are considered to reflect orthographic processes, from phonological processes when children are spelling inflected or derived words (Carlisle & Stone, 2003).

There seems to be consensus that phonological recoding is central to but not sufficient for orthographic reading (Cunningham, 2006; Nation *et al.*, 2007; Share, 1995). It is not clear what the other possible component processes of orthographic processing might be. A number of processing skills have been cited including visual processes (Martens & de Jong, 2006), paired associate learning (Manis *et al.*, 1987; Windfuhr & Snowling, 2001), sensitivity to letter patterns (Share, 2004), attentional control processes (Breznitz & Berman, 2003), and semantic and grammatical knowledge (Laing & Hulme, 1999; Snowling *et al.*, 1999). It is primarily the multidimensional nature of orthographic processing that complicates the research in this area.

Finally, with the exception of a few studies (e.g. Duncan & Seymour, 2003), empirical research into the development of reading and spelling almost exclusively focused on monosyllabic words. It remains to be seen to what extent these findings can be extended to the processing of complex polysyllabic and polymorphemic words. This is particularly relevant for highly inflected or agglutinative languages, such as Turkish and Finnish where long words with a series of attached affixes are the characteristic feature of the language.

Before I turn to the question of to what extent these developmental patterns and processes observed in English also apply to transparent writing systems, it is important to highlight several points about orthographic transparency, which have implications for evaluation of the research evidence from cross-linguistic studies.

Operationalisation of orthographic transparency

Opaque orthographies not only have complex grapheme–phoneme relationships but also complex syllable structures composed of a string of consonant clusters such as CCVCCC (C: consonant; V: vowel). In contrast, the syllable structures in transparent systems tend to be simple and mainly CV-type (Seymour *et al.*, 2003). Hence, simple syllable structure is an overlapping feature of the transparent orthographies, which can facilitate the development of phonological awareness and literacy skills (Durgunoğlu & Öney, 1999; Seymour *et al.*, 2003).

It is also important to highlight that transparency is a multidimensional construct and writing systems can be more consistent at different linguistic levels (e.g. body-rime levels) and the degree of transparency can be different for reading and spelling (Ziegler *et al.*, 1996). For instance, 84 per cent of German monosyllabic words have been reported to be consistent for reading but only 47 per cent for spelling (Ziegler, 2001, cited in Wimmer & Mayringer 2002). Hence, German is asymmetrically transparent. In contrast, Turkish and Finnish are relatively symmetrically transparent.

So far, the statistical information for quantification of transparency at different linguistic segments, with representative samples of words (e.g. multisyllabic words) and for both spelling and reading is highly limited (Aro & Wimmer, 2003). In fact, this is a major issue that complicates a systematic comparison of languages and needs to be borne in mind when evaluating cross-linguistic studies.

Reading and spelling development in transparent orthographies

Reading and spelling develop faster in transparent orthographies: Why?

Studies consistently report that irrespective of variations in the age of onset of formal literacy instruction, preschool literacy activities and method of reading instruction, children learning transparent systems make faster progress in their reading and spelling development (Aro & Wimmer, 2003; Ellis & Hooper, 2001; Seymour *et al.*, 2003). Seymour and colleagues found that it took about two and a half years to achieve >90 per cent level of accuracy in English that has been achieved within the first year of formal literacy instruction in the transparent systems (e.g. Italian, Finnish,

Spanish, and Greek). Similar results came from other cross-linguistic studies comparing English with transparent orthographies, such as Albanian (Hoxhallari *et al.*, 2004), Welsh (Ellis & Hooper, 2001; Spencer & Hanley, 2003), and Turkish (Durgunoğlu & Öney, 1999).

A child learning to read in English from the very start is faced with many idiosyncratic pronunciations such as <have>. This means that the English orthography demands acquisition of phoneme–grapheme correspondence rules as well as orthographic knowledge for accurate reading right from the onset of formal reading instruction. This is clearly an extra cognitive burden, which along with the resultant inconsistent feedback from the orthography seem to slow down the acquisition of accurate and fluent reading skills (Ellis & Hooper, 2001). Whereas a child learning to read a transparent system can rely on one strategy (i.e. phonological recoding) that gives accurate results, and hence positive feedback almost all the time with the results of accurate and fast reading.

The flexible-unit hypothesis states that it is the need to develop as well as switch between different unit sizes, such as grapheme–phoneme, larger units of rimes, or whole words, that underlies the observed developmental lag of children learning English (Brown & Deavers, 1999). Indeed, in a direct test of flexible-unit hypothesis, English-speaking children showed switching cost when presented with a mixed list of nonwords that could be read either through phonological recoding or orthographic reading (i.e. reading through analogy to a real word). However, their German counterparts did not show any switching cost, further confirming that children were using only phonological recoding, hence a single strategy when reading in German (Goswami *et al.*, 2003).

The complexity of grapheme–phoneme relationships in opaque systems seems to be further compounded by the complex syllable structures and ambiguous syllable boundaries that arguably make it harder to develop fine-grained phoneme levels of lexical representations. In fact, several cross-linguistic studies have found that children learning transparent systems outperform their English-speaking peers on a range of phonological awareness measures (Caravolas & Bruck, 1993; Durgunoğlu & Öney, 1999; Spencer & Hanley, 2003). Hence, a simple orthography not only facilitates the development of reading and phonological awareness, but seems to further fuel their mutual facilitative relationship with the result of accurate and fast reading within a year of formal reading instruction.

So far, cross-linguistic research on spelling development is relatively limited. However, based on the available research evidence from several studies comparing English with German, Greek, Czech, French, and Italian, it can be concluded that despite the fact that the spelling systems of these orthographies are less transparent in comparison with reading, it was still possible to find significant advantage in spelling development (Caravolas *et al.*, 2003; Cossu, 1999; Harris & Giannouli, 1999; Wimmer & Landerl, 1997).

It is not clear whether or how asymmetrical and symmetrical transparency influence reading and spelling development (Rahbari *et al.*, 2007). Studies tend to examine reading and spelling development separately. Given that reading and spelling development are highly interactive processes (Bosman & van Orden, 1997; Perfetti, 1997), understanding of reading and spelling development as a function of orthographic transparency calls for a more integrated approach (Fletcher-Flinn *et al.*,

2004). Furthermore, with the exception of a few (e.g. Hanley *et al.*, 2004), cross-linguistic studies have focused on early stages of literacy development. Therefore, we do not know how these developmental profiles take shape during the later stages of literacy development when children need to process more complex words and sentences (Patel *et al.*, 2004).

Finally, all these findings should be evaluated with the acknowledgement that any cross-linguistic study is inherently limited due to sparse information on the statistical properties of the languages/orthographies as noted before, and the difficulty of constructing comparable, yet at the same time ecologically valid experimental measures of reading and spelling (Seymour *et al.*, 2003).

In what ways may reading and spelling development differ in transparent orthographies?

There is no convincing evidence, as yet, to suggest that at a fundamental level reading or spelling development in a transparent orthography is qualitatively different from English. The overall consensus states that the difference is quantitative and the observed divergence in the developmental profiles of children can be largely explained in terms of the faster rate of literacy development in transparent systems.

The proposed processes of reading in English (i.e. pre-alphabetic, phonetic-cue, full alphabetic, and orthographic reading) have been also observed in transparent systems albeit with some differences. For instance, studies in Greek, Spanish, German, and Dutch found little or no evidence for pre-alphabetic reading (Harris & Giannouli, 1999; Valle-Arroyo, 1989; Valtin, 1997; Wimmer & Hummer, 1990). It seems that the observed optional and highly transitory nature of pre-alphabetic reading in English is even more pronounced in transparent systems. There are, however, clear differences in children's early reading errors in transparent systems.

When children attempt to read words in English, they sometimes refuse to read or produce utterances that bear little phonological resemblance to the target word and can be random guesses such as reading 'sun' as 'doggie' and their errors also do not tend to be plausible nonwords (Caravolas *et al.*, 2001: 770). Numerous studies, however, have reported that the reading errors in transparent systems tend to be predominantly nonwords that share a salient common letter sound with the target word and there are seldom if any random guesses or refusals to read (Ellis *et al.*, 2004; Seymour *et al.*, 2003). Clearly, certain features of phonetic-cue reading are not observed to the same degree in a consistent writing system where phonological recoding seems to be the dominant reading process.

With regards to spelling development, just as in English, phonological spelling dominates the early spelling processes in transparent systems (for reviews, see Caravolas, 2006; Treiman & Kessler, 2005). However, once again as with reading, depending on the characteristics of the orthography, children's spelling errors can be different.

The vowel sounds and letters are very complex in English and children often make more vowel errors than consonant errors (Treiman, 1993). In contrast, in transparent systems with simple vowels, like Portuguese, children make more errors with consonants than vowels. In Portuguese, a vowel letter name corresponds to its sound and acts as a discrete single unit of utterance and this seems to facilitate the acquisition of accurate vowel spellings (Pollo *et al.*, 2005).

Likewise, phoneme length seems to pose a challenge for young spellers in Finnish (Lehtonen & Bryant, 2004). Phoneme length is indicated by double letters in Finnish and can change the meaning of words. The discrimination of phoneme length seems to complicate this otherwise simple spelling system, and misspellings often involve representing double letters with a single letter (Lehtonen & Bryant, 2004).

Although Turkish has a very simple spelling system, the phoneme Γ which is denoted by the letter < ğ > ('soft g') can cause ambiguity during spelling. This is a 'voiced soft palatal velar fricative' and during articulation 'the back of the tongue is raised to the velum' (Çapan, 1989: 193). Depending on its phonemic context, Γ can loose its phonemic salience and serves to lengthen the preceding vowel or can sound as weak /v/ or /j/ (Alderson & Iz, 1984; Demircan, 2001). The 'soft g', however, does not seem to cause any problem for reading. Among a group of first graders, we found the mean error rate of spelling 'soft g' to be much higher (61 per cent) than that of reading (27 per cent) (Babayiğit, 1999). These findings were further confirmed in a recent study, which has also showed that the spelling of 'soft g' is particularly difficult for young children in Turkish (Babayiğit, in preparation).

With respect to the overall developmental pattern of phonological and orthographic reading and spelling processes, the evidence from transparent systems such as French, Dutch, and Spanish also supports the multi-process accounts of reading and spelling development (Coenen et al., 1997; de Manrique & Signorini, 1998; Sprenger-Charroles et al., 2003). Depending on the demands of the task, the levels of alphabet knowledge, phonological awareness skills, and print experience, children seem to utilise both phonological and orthographic reading and spelling processes from the very early stages of literacy development.

What seems to constitute an important point of divergence in transparent systems is the relative balance between orthographic and phonological processes in reading. In comparison to English, orthographic reading tends to emerge more slowly and phonological reading seems to play a more dominant role in transparent systems. For instance, in a cross-linguistic study, Öney et al. (1997) compared reading responses of children at grades 2 and 5 to phonological priming in English and Turkish. Phonological priming was stronger in Turkish than English for both age groups suggesting that there is more reliance on phonological processing in Turkish. Seymour et al. (2003) also found that orthographic reading declined as transparency increased. These reports also link with the findings that children learning English rely more on semantic knowledge than children learning a transparent orthography during the early stages of reading development (Kang & Simpson, 1996).

Clearly, as transparency increases, reliance on phonological processing also increases ('The orthographic depth hypothesis', Frost et al., 1987). This is because phonological recoding yields accurate results in transparent systems and, during the early stages of reading development, the writing system does not make any demands to focus on the information beyond the grapheme–phoneme levels (Goswami et al., 2003).

The observed developmental lag in orthographic strategies in transparent orthographies fits well with the *dynamic systems theory*, which states that change can only proceed after the system becomes unstable (Siegler, 2007). As phonological processing provides consistent positive feedback, the system is kept at equilibrium and there is little or no push for learning higher-order graphemic patterns in transparent orthographies during the early stages of literacy acquisition. Conversely, in opaque orthographies, phonological processing elicits inconsistent feedback, which weakens the dominance of phonological processing causing instability and thereby paving the way for change in strategies and lexical representations (i.e. development of orthographic processes).

What about the role of morphosyntactic processing, which is an important dimension of orthographic processing? Even highly transparent systems require knowledge of some higher-order orthographic conventions, especially in the case of spelling. A study in Spanish found that children make use of morphosyntactic knowledge only when they are spelling the word-final <s> which is not reflected in its spoken form (i.e. 'silent s') (Titos *et al.*, 2003). The use of morphosyntactic knowledge in this study emerged after grade 3, and as in English there was a tendency for more complex morphological strategies to develop later during the course of literacy development. Similar findings came from Greek (Nunes *et al.*, 2006), French (Senechal *et al.*, 2006), and Dutch (Notenboom & Reitsma, 2007). Hence, when the phonology fails to provide information about accurate spelling, as in the case of silent morphemes, children draw upon orthographic knowledge just as in English (for a review, see Notenboom & Reitsma, 2007).

It is notable that the observed u-shaped developmental function of the spelling of silent morphemes in English (Critten *et al.*, 2007; Nunes *et al.*, 1997; Steffler, 2001) has been also reported in Dutch (Notenboom & Reitsma, 2007), and pointed Hebrew (Share, 2004). This suggests that very similar processes seem to underlie the development of orthographic representations across different orthographies and links with the developmental theories of mental representations of knowledge and language (see Karmiloff-Smith, 1992; Vihman, 1996).

At this point, two important questions arise in relation to highly transparent but agglutinative systems, such as Finnish and Turkish. (1) What is the role of morphosyntactic skills in agglutinative writing systems with perfectly transparent morphology? (2) How does orthographic processing take shape in an agglutinative system where the same word base can appear in hundreds of different forms (e.g. < ev-ler > (homes); < ev-ler-imiz > (our homes); < ev-ler-imiz-den > (from our homes)).

Arguably, in Finnish and Turkish there is no need for morphosyntactic knowledge for accurate reading or spelling during the early stages of literacy development. However, morphosyntactic knowledge is likely to become more important during the later stages of literacy development when the emphasis is on reading comprehension and children are increasingly faced with more complex words and sentence structures. Our preliminary findings provided some support for this hypothesis: the strength of the relationship of morphosyntactic skills with reading comprehension tended to increase with increasing age in Turkish (Babayiğit, 2007).

It is not clear how polymorphemic words are processed in agglutinative systems (see Dunabeitia *et al.*, 2007). It seems that in the context of agglutinated words, the differentiation between phonological, morphological, and syntactic processes becomes even more complicated, as these are tightly intertwined within the context of a single word. It is conceivable that multiple processes are involved in the processing of complex words in agglutinative systems. Hence, orthographic and phonological processing and their distinction as conceptualised mainly in the context of monosyllabic words in English, might take a different form in the context of complex polymorphemic words.

In summary, research evidence suggests that orthographic processing tends to play a more central role during the early stages of literacy development in English than in transparent orthographies. The problems of operationalising orthographic processing and understanding the development and processing of polysyllabic and polymorphemic words outlined in relation to English, naturally extends to transparent orthographies. It is essentially for this reason that the developmental theories of reading and spelling in English with a primary focus on monosyllabic words are particularly limited in explaining the literacy acquisition in highly inflected systems, such as Turkish, Finnish, and Hungarian (see Csepe, 2006).

The role of phonological awareness in transparent orthographies

The overall research evidence into the role of phonological awareness in transparent orthographies tends to be highly contradictory. This is in sharp contrast to the findings of the studies conducted in English. Longitudinal studies, training studies, and studies on children with literacy problems have consistently reported that phonological processing skills are central for literacy development in English (Brady & Shankweiler, 1991; Snowling, 2000). Delineating two important factors, the nature of the relationship (longitudinal or cross-sectional) and literacy outcome measure, is essential for a coherent evaluation of the role of phonological awareness in transparent systems.

Longitudinal versus cross-sectional relationships

The ability to analyse speech sounds facilitates reading and spelling and vice versa. Cross-sectional designs allow us to evaluate whether this mutual relationship can be detected even after controlling for other important cognitive and linguistic correlates of literacy skills, such as letter knowledge, vocabulary, and verbal short-term memory. Numerous studies based on typical populations have consistently reported reliable concurrent relationships between phonological awareness and literacy skills in transparent systems among younger as well as older children (Turkish: Babayiğit & Stainthorp, 2005; Babayiğit & Stainthorp, 2007; Czech: Caravolas et al., 2005; Finnish: Müller & Brady, 2001; Greek: Nikolopoulos et al., 2006; Dutch: Patel et al., 2004).

The most striking difference between transparent systems and English emerges in the longitudinal analysis of the data. Studies that systematically controlled for pre-existing reading skills (autoregressor) and letter knowledge in transparent systems failed to find reliable longitudinal relationships between phonological awareness and subsequent reading skills or the observed effects tended to be very small and highly volatile and confined to the very early stages of reading development (de Jong & van der Leij, 1999; Holopainen et al., 2001; Wimmer et al., 1991).

In a series of studies, we explored the concurrent and longitudinal relationships of phonological awareness with reading and spelling from preschool through to the end of primary grades in Turkish (Babayiğit, 2006).[1] First, we conducted a 2-year longitudinal study and followed 55 children from preschool (before the onset of reading instruction) (mean age = 5.6) into grade 2. Children's reading accuracy was at ceiling level by the end of grade 1. Therefore, reading speed was used as an index of reading skills. After making adjustments for nonverbal IQ, vocabulary, short-term memory, and letter knowledge, the preschool phonological awareness measures failed to explain any reliable variance in later reading speed. It is notable that in this study preschool phonological awareness emerged as the strongest and most consistent longitudinal predictor of spelling skills at both grades 1 and 2 (Babayiğit, 2006; Babayiğit & Stainthorp, 2007). We, then, conducted a cross-sectional analysis of the data. After making adjustments for vocabulary and short-term memory, phonological awareness made unique contributions to concurrent measures of both reading and spelling at each of the five primary grade levels (mean age ranged between 6.6 and 10.3 years) (Babayiğit, 2006; Babayiğit & Stainthorp, 2005).

Hence, the overall results from this study in Turkish have clearly suggested that irrespective of the level of transparency, there is a mutual facilitating relationship between phonological awareness and literacy skills; but as the findings from longitudinal analysis suggested the possible causal nature of this relationship seems to be evident only in the case of spelling and not reading in a highly transparent orthography. This brings the discussion to the role of the nature of literacy outcome measure in the observed pattern of results.

The nature of literacy outcome measures

Due to ceiling levels of performance on the reading accuracy measures, studies in transparent systems often have to rely on reading speed as an index of individual differences in reading skills. Although reading accuracy and speed are related, they also tap different component skills (Compton & Carlisle, 1994). Even in English there seems to be a tendency for phonological awareness to be more strongly related to reading accuracy than reading speed (Lovett, 1987; Savage & Frederickson, 2005). Hence, it is highly conceivable that the observed unreliable relationships between phonological awareness and reading speed in transparent systems might be further exaggerated due to this methodological artifact.

Nonetheless, clearly the facilitating effect of a simple orthography seems to override the role of phonological awareness skills in reading. In fact, it is possible to find good readers with very poor phonological awareness skills in transparent systems, such as Finnish, Spanish, and German (Carrillo, 1994; Holopainen et al., 2001; Wimmer et al., 1991). At this point, it is important to underline the word *reading*, as in our study, preliterate phonological awareness emerged as a strong and consistent predictor of spelling skills in Turkish. Similar findings have been also reported in Dutch, German, and Greek (Harris & Giannouli, 1999; van Bon & van Leeuwe, 2003; Wimmer & Mayringer, 2002). For example, in a study in German, Wimmer and Mayringer (2002) found that preschool phonological awareness was the best index of spelling performance assessed three years later. In this study, children with impaired phonological awareness skills turned out to have spelling problems, but not reading problems.

Spelling is considered a more sensitive index of phonological processing skills and the quality of phonological representations (Perfetti, 1997; Treiman, 1993). These findings from the transparent orthographies further corroborate this view and suggest that irrespective of orthographic transparency phonological processing skills seem to play a more central role in spelling development.

Conclusions

In conclusion, literacy draws upon existing cognitive–linguistic processing skills (Hulme *et al.*, 2005). Viewed in this way, the underlying basic processes are necessarily the same across the writing systems. Indeed, the research evidence from the neuroimaging studies of different languages also corroborates this view (Perfetti & Liu, 2005). However, the specific features of the orthography–language complex can make different demands on these basic processing systems and shape the functional architecture of the brain (Perfetti & Bolger, 2004), hence the observed patterns of relationships. Without doubt, orthographic transparency is one of the central distinguishing features of a writing system that can have profound effects on the nature of print processing and literacy development.

Note

1 This study was conducted for my doctoral degree at the Institute of Education, University of London. My special thanks go to my research supervisor Professor Rhona Stainthorp for her support and guidance.

References

Alderson, A.D. & Iz, F. (1984). *The Oxford Turkish–English Dictionary* (3rd edn). Oxford: Clarendon Press.

Aro, M. & Wimmer, H. (2003). 'Learning to read: English in comparison to six more regular orthographies'. *Applied Psycholinguistics, 24,* 621–635.

Babayiğit, S. (1999). 'The role of syllabic and phonemic awareness in reading and spelling skills of Turkish-speaking first graders'. Unpublished Masters dissertation, Institute of Education, University of London.

—— (2006). 'The longitudinal and concurrent predictive roles of phonological awareness in literacy development: evidence from Turkish'. Unpublished PhD thesis, Institute of Education, University of London.

—— (2007). 'Understanding the correlates of reading comprehension in Turkish'. Interactive paper presented at the 14th Annual Conference of the Society of the Scientific Study of Reading, Prague, Czech Republic, July.

—— (in preparation). 'Orthographic spelling in a highly transparent spelling system: The case of soft g in Turkish'.

Babayiğit, S. & Stainthorp, R. (2005). 'The role of phonological awareness in reading and spelling skills in a highly transparent orthography'. Paper presented at the 11th Biennial Conference of the European Association for Research on Learning and Instruction, Nicosia, Cyprus, August.

Babayiğit, S. & Stainthorp, R. (2007). 'Preliterate phonological awareness and early literacy skills in Turkish'. *Journal of Research in Reading, 30*(4), 394–413.

Bosman, A.M.T. & van Orden, G.V. (1997). 'Why spelling is more difficult than reading'. In C.A. Perfetti, L. Rieben & M. Fayol (eds), *Learning to spell: Research, theory, and practice across languages* (Vol. 10, pp. 173–194). Mahwah, NJ: LEA.

Brady, S.A. & Shankweiler, D.P. (1991). *Phonological processes in literacy: A tribute to Isabelle Y. Liberman.* London: Lawrence Erlbaum.

Breznitz, Z. & Berman, L. (2003). 'The underlying factors of word reading rate'. *Educational Psychology Review, 15*(3), 247–265.

Brown, G.D.A. & Deavers, R.P. (1999). 'Units of analysis in nonword reading: Evidence from children and adults'. *Journal of Experimental Child Psychology, 73,* 208–242.

Burt, J.S. (2006). 'What is orthographic processing skill and how does it relate to word identification in reading?' *Journal of Research in Reading, 29*(4), 400–417.

Çapan, S. (1989). 'A linguistic study of reading and writing disorders in Turkish, an agglutinative language'. In P.G. Aaron & R.M. Joshi (eds), *Reading and writing disorders in different orthographic systems* (pp. 191–202). Dordrecht: Kluwer.

Caravolas, M. (2006). 'Learning to spell in different languages: How orthographic variables might affect early literacy'. In R.M. Joshi & P.G. Aaron (eds), *Handbook of orthography and literacy* (Vol. 30, pp. 497–511). London: LEA.

Caravolas, M. & Bruck, M. (1993). 'The effect of oral and written language input on children's phonological awareness: A cross-linguistic study'. *Journal of Experimental Child Psychology, 55*, 1–30.

Caravolas, M., Hulme, C., & Snowling, M. (2001). 'The foundations of spelling ability: Evidence from a 3-year longitudinal study'. *Journal of Memory and Language, 45*, 751–774.

Caravolas, M., Bruck, M., & Genesee, F. (2003). 'Similarities and differences between English- and French-speaking poor spellers'. In N. Goulandris (ed.), *Dyslexia in different languages: Cross-linguistic comparisons* (Vol. 9, pp. 157–180). London: Whurr.

Caravolas, M., Volin, J., & Hulme, C. (2005). 'Phoneme awareness is a key component of alphabetic literacy skills in consistent and inconsistent orthographies: Evidence from Czech and English children'. *Journal of Experimental Child Psychology, 92*, 107–139.

Carlisle, J.F. & Stone, C.A. (2003). 'The effect of morphological structure on children's reading of derived words in English'. In E. Assink & D. Sandra (eds), *Reading complex words: Cross-language studies* (Vol. 2, pp. 27–52). New York: Kluwer/Plenum.

Carrillo, M. (1994). 'Development of phonological awareness and reading acquisition: A study in Spanish language'. *Reading and Writing: An Interdisciplinary Journal, 6*, 279–298.

Coenen, M.J.W.L., Bon, v., W.H.J., & Schreuder, R. (1997). 'Reading and spelling in Dutch first and second graders: Do they use an orthographic strategy?' In C.K. Leong & R.M. Joshi (eds), *Cross-language studies of learning to read and spell* (pp. 249–269). Dordrecht: Kluwer.

Compton, D.L. & Carlisle, J.F. (1994). 'Speed of word recognition as a distinguishing characteristic of reading disabilities'. *Educational Psychology Review, 6*, 115–140.

Cossu, G. (1999). 'The acquisition of Italian orthography'. In M. Harris & G. Hatano (eds), *Learning to read and write: A cross-linguistic perspective* (Vol. 2, pp. 10–33). Cambridge: Cambridge University Press.

Critten, S., Pine, K., & Steffler, D. (2007). 'Spelling development in young children: A case of representational redescription?' *Journal of Educational Psychology, 99*(1), 207–220.

Csepe, V. (2006). 'Literacy acquisition and dyslexia in Hungarian'. In R.M. Joshi & P.G. Aaron (eds), *Handbook of orthography and literacy* (Vol. 15, pp. 231–247). London: LEA.

Cunningham, A.E. (2006). 'Accounting for children's orthographic learning while reading text: Do children self-teach?' *Journal of Experimental Child Psychology, 95*(1), 56–77.

de Jong, P.F. & van der Leij, A. (1999). 'Specific contributions of phonological abilities to early reading acquisition: Results from a Dutch latent variable longitudinal study'. *Journal of Educational Psychology, 91*(3), 450–476.

de Manrique, A.M. & Signorini, A. (1998). 'Emergent writing forms in Spanish'. *Reading and Writing: An Interdisciplinary Journal, 10*, 499–517.

Demircan, Ö. (2001). *Türkcenin Ses Dizimi (the Turkish Phonology)* (2nd edn). Istanbul, Türkiye: Der Yayinlari.

Dunabeitia, J.A., Perea, M., & Carreiras, M. (2007). 'Do transposed-letter similarity effects occur at morpheme level? Evidence for morpho-orthographic decomposition'. *Cognition, 105*(3), 691–703.

Duncan, L.G. & Seymour, P. (2003). 'How do children read multisyllabic words? Some preliminary observations'. *Journal of Research in Reading, 26*(2), 101–120.

Durgunoğlu, A.Y. & Öney, B. (1999). 'A cross-linguistic comparison of phonological awareness and word recognition'. *Reading and Writing: An Interdisciplinary Journal, 11*, 281–299.

Ehri, L.C. (1986). 'Sources of difficulty in learning to read and spell'. *Advances in Developmental and Behavioural Pediatrics, 7*, 121–195.

—— (1992). 'Reconceptualising the development of sight word reading and its relationship to recoding'. In P.B. Gough, L.C. Ehri & R. Treiman (eds), *Reading acquisition* (Vol. 5, pp. 107–143). London: Erlbaum.

—— (2002). 'Phases of acquisition in learning to read words, and implications for teaching'. *British Journal of Educational Psychology 1*, 7–28.

Ellis, C.N. & Hooper, A.M. (2001). 'Why learning to read is easier in Welsh than in English: Orthographic transparency effects evidenced with frequency-matched tests'. *Applied Psycholinguistics, 22*, 571–599.

Ellis, N.C., Natsume, M., Stavropoulou, K., Hoxhallari, L., van Daal, V., Polyzoe, N., *et al.* (2004). 'The effects of orthographic depth on learning to read alphabetic, syllabic, and logographic scripts'. *Reading Research Quarterly, 39*(4), 438–468.

Fletcher-Flinn, C.M., Shankweiler, D.P., & Frost, S.J. (2004). 'Coordination of reading and spelling in early literacy development: An examination of the discrepancy hypothesis'. *Reading and Writing: An Interdisciplinary Journal, 17*, 617–644.

Frost, J., Katz, L., & Bentin, S. (1987). 'Strategies for visual word recognition and orthographical depth: A multilingual comparison'. *Journal of Experimental Psychology: Human Perception and Performance, 13*, 104–115.

Goswami, U., Ziegler, J.C., Dalton, L., & Schneider, W. (2003). 'Nonword reading across orthographies: How flexible is the choice of reading units?' *Applied Psycholinguistics, 24*, 235–247.

Hagiliassis, N., Pratt, C., & Micheal, J. (2006). 'Orthographic and phonological processes in reading'. *Reading and Writing: An Interdisciplinary Journal, 19*, 235–263.

Hanley, J.R., Masterson, J., Spencer, L.H., & Evans, D. (2004). 'How long do the advantages of learning to read a transparent orthography last? An investigation of the reading skills and reading impairment of Welsh children at 10 years of age'. *Quarterly Journal of Experimental Psychology, 57A*(8), 1393–1410.

Harris, M. & Giannouli, V. (1999). 'Learning to read and spell in Greek: The importance of letter knowledge and morphological awareness'. In M. Harris & G. Hatano (eds), *Learning to read and write: A cross-linguistic perspective* (Vol. 4, pp. 51–70). Cambridge: Cambridge University Press.

Holopainen, L., Ahonen, T., & Lyytinen, H. (2001). 'Predicting delay in reading achievement in a highly transparent language'. *Journal of Learning Disabilities, 34*(5), 401–413.

Hoxhallari, L., van Daal, V., & Ellis, N.C. (2004). 'Learning to read words in Albanian: A skill easily acquired'. *Scientific Studies of Reading, 8*(2), 153–166.

Hulme, C., Snowling, M., Caravolas, M., & Carroll, J.M. (2005). 'Phonological skills are (probably) one cause of success in learning to read: A comment on Castles and Coltheart'. *Scientific Studies of Reading, 9*, 351–365.

Joshi, R.M. & Aaron, P.G. (eds), (2006). *Handbook of orthography and literacy*. London: LEA.

Kang, H. & Simpson, G.B. (1996). 'Development of semantic and phonological priming in a shallow orthography'. *Developmental Psychology, 32*, 860–866.

Karmiloff-Smith, A. (1992). *Beyond modularity: A developmental perspective on cognitive science*. Cambridge, MA: MIT Press.

Kemp, N. (2006). 'Children's spelling of base, inflected, and derived words: Links with morphological awareness'. *Reading and Writing: An Interdisciplinary Journal, 19,* 737–765.

Laing, E. & Hulme, C. (1999). 'Phonological and semantic processes influence beginning reader's ability to learn to read words'. *Journal of Experimental Child Psychology, 73,* 183–207.

Lehtonen, A. & Bryant, E.P. (2004). 'Length awareness predicts spelling in Finnish'. *Reading and Writing: An Interdisciplinary Journal, 17*(9), 875–890.

Lovett, M.C. (1987). 'A developmental approach to reading disability: Accuracy and speed criteria of normal and deficient reading skill'. *Child Development, 58,* 234–260.

Manis, F.R., Savage, P.L., Morrison, F.J., Horn, C.C., Howell, M.J., Szeszulski, P.A., *et al.* (1987). 'Paired associate learning in reading-disabled children: Evidence for a rule learning deficiency'. *Journal of Experimental Child Psychology, 43,* 25–43.

Martens, V.E.G. & de Jong, P. (2006). 'The effect of visual word features on the acquisition of orthographic knowledge'. *Journal of Experimental Child Psychology, 93,* 337–356.

Müller, K. & Brady, S.A. (2001). 'Correlates of early reading performance in a transparent orthography'. *Reading and Writing: An Interdisciplinary Journal, 14,* 757–799.

Nation, J.K., Angell, P., & Castles, A. (2007). 'Orthographic learning via self-teaching in children learning to read English: Effects of exposure, durability, and context'. *Journal of Experimental Child Psychology, 96,* 71–84.

Nikolopoulos, D., Goulandris, N., Hulme, C., & Snowling, M. (2006). 'The cognitive bases of learning to read and spell in Greek: Evidence from a longitudinal study'. *Journal of Experimental Child Psychology, 94,* 1–17.

Notenboom, A. & Reitsma, P. (2007). 'Spelling Dutch doublets: Children's learning of a phonological and morphological spelling rule'. *Scientific Studies of Reading, 11*(2), 133–150.

Nunes, T., Bryant, E.P., & Bindman, M. (1997). 'Learning to spell regular and irregular verbs'. *Reading and Writing: An Interdisciplinary Journal, 9,* 427–449.

Nunes, T., Aidinis, A., & Bryant, E.P. (2006). 'The acquisition of written morphology in Greek'. In R.M. Joshi & P.G. Aaron (eds), *Handbook of orthography and literacy* (Vol. 13, pp. 201–218). London: LEA.

Öney, B., Peter, M., & Katz, L. (1997). 'Phonological processing in printed word recognition: Effects of age and writing system'. *Scientific Studies of Reading, 1*(1), 65–83.

Patel, T.K., Snowling, M., & de Jong, P. (2004). 'A cross-linguistic comparison of children learning to read in English and Dutch'. *Journal of Educational Psychology, 96*(4), 785–797.

Perfetti, C.A. (1997). 'The psycholinguistics of spelling and reading'. In C.A. Perfetti, L. Rieben & M. Fayol (eds), *Learning to spell: Research, theory, and practice across languages* (Vol. 2, pp. 21–38). London: LEA.

Perfetti, C.A. & Bolger, D. (2004). 'The brain might read that way'. *Scientific Studies of Reading, 8*(3), 293–304.

Perfetti, C.A. & Liu, Y. (2005). 'Orthography to phonology and meaning: Comparisons across and within writing systems?' *Reading and Writing: An Interdisciplinary Journal, 18,* 193–210.

Plaut, D.C., McClelland, J.L., & Seidenberg, M.S. (1996). 'Understanding normal and impaired word reading: Computational principals in quasi-regular domains'. *Psychological Review, 103*(1), 56–115.

Pollo, T.C., Kessler, B., & Treiman, R. (2005). 'Vowels, syllables, and letter names: Differences between young children's spelling in English and Portuguese'. *Journal of Experimental Child Psychology, 92,* 161–181.

Rahbari, N., Senechal, M., & Arab-Moghaddam, N. (2007). 'The role of orthographic and phonological processing skills in the reading and spelling of monolingual Persian children'. *Reading and Writing: An Interdisciplinary Journal, 20*, 511–533.

Rittle-Johnson, B. & Siegler, R.S. (1999). 'Learning to spell: Variability, choice, and change in children's strategy use'. *Child Development, 70*(2), 332–348.

Savage, R. & Frederickson, N. (2005). 'Evidence of a highly specific relationship between rapid automatic naming of digits and text-reading speed'. *Brain and Language, 93*, 152–159.

Senechal, M., Basque, M., & Leclaire, T. (2006). 'Morphological knowledge as revealed in children's spelling accuracy and reports of spelling strategies'. *Journal of Experimental Child Psychology, 95*, 231–254.

Seymour, P.H.K., Aro, M., & Erskine, J.M. (2003). 'Foundation literacy acquisition in European orthographies'. *British Journal of Psychology, 94*, 143–174.

Share, D.L. (1995). 'Phonological recoding and self-teaching: Sine qua non of reading acquisition'. *Cognition, 55*, 151–218.

—— (2004). 'Orthographic learning at a glance: On the time course and developmental onset of self-teaching'. *Journal of Experimental Child Psychology, 87*, 267–298.

Siegler, R.S. (2007). 'Cognitive variability'. *Developmental Science, 10*(1), 104–109.

Snowling, M. (2000). *Dyslexia*. Oxford: Blackwell.

Snowling, M., Nation, J.K., & Muter, V. (1999). 'The role of semantic and phonological skills in learning to read: Implications for assessment and teaching'. In T. Nunes (ed.), *Learning to read: An integrated view from research and practice* (pp. 195–208). London: Kluwer.

Spencer, L.H. & Hanley, J.R. (2003). 'Effects of orthographic transparency on reading and phoneme awareness in children learning to read in Wales'. *British Journal of Psychology, 94*, 1–28.

Sprenger-Charroles, L., Siegel, L.S., Bechennec, D., & Serniclaes, W. (2003). 'Development of phonological and orthographic processing in reading aloud, in silent reading, and in spelling: A four-year longitudinal study'. *Journal of Experimental Child Psychology, 84*, 194–217.

Steffler, D.J. (2001). 'Implicit cognition and spelling development'. *Developmental Review, 21*, 168–204.

Titos, R., Defior, S., Alegria, J., & Martos, F.J. (2003). 'The use of morphological resources in Spanish orthography: The case of the verb'. In R.M. Joshi, C.K. Leong & B.L.J. Kaczmarek (eds), *Literacy acquisition: The role of phonology, morphology and orthography* (Vol. II, pp. 113–118). Oxford: IOS Press.

Treiman, R. (1993). *Beginning to spell: A study of first-grade children*. New York: Oxford University Press.

—— (2006). 'Knowledge about letters as a foundation for reading and spelling'. In R.M. Joshi & P.G. Aaron (eds), *Handbook of orthography and literacy* (Vol. 35, pp. 581–599). London: LEA.

Treiman, R. & Cassar, M. (1997). 'Spelling acquisition in English'. In C.A. Perfetti, L. Rieben & M. Fayol (eds), *Learning to spell*. Mahwah, NJ: LEA.

Treiman, R. & Kessler, B. (2005). 'Writing systems and spelling development'. In M. Snowling & C. Hulme (eds), *The science of reading* (Vol. 7, pp. 120–134). Oxford: Blackwell.

Valle-Arroyo, F. (1989). 'Reading errors in Spanish'. In P.G. Aaron & R.M. Joshi (eds), *Reading and writing disorders in different orthographic systems* (Vol. 9, pp. 163–175). Dordrecht: Kluwer.

Valtin, R. (1997). 'Strategies of spelling and reading of young children learning German orthography'. In C.K. Leong & R.M. Joshi (eds), *Cross-language studies of learning to read and spell* (pp. 175–193). Dordrecht: Kluwer.

van Bon, W.H.J. & van Leeuwe, J.F.J. (2003). 'Assessing phonemic awareness in kindergarten: The case for the phoneme recognition task'. *Applied Psycholinguistics, 24,* 195–219.

Vihman, M.M. (1996). *phonological development: The origins of language in the child.* Oxford: Blackwell.

Wagner, R.K. & Barker, T.A. (1994). 'The development of orthographic processing ability'. In V.W. Berninger (ed.), *The variety of orthographic knowledge 1: Theoretical and developmental issues* (pp. 243–276). Dordrecht: Kluwer.

Wimmer, H. & Hummer, P. (1990). 'How German-speaking first graders read and spell: Doubts on the importance of the logographic stage'. *Applied Psycholinguistics, 11,* 349–368.

Wimmer, H. & Landerl, K. (1997). 'How learning to spell German differs from learning to spell English'. In C.A. Perfetti, L. Rieben, & M. Fayol (eds), *Learning to spell: Research, theory and practice across languages* (pp. 81–96). Mahwah, NJ: Erlbaum.

Wimmer, H. & Mayringer, H. (2002). 'Dysfluent reading in the absence of spelling difficulties: A specific disability in regular orthography'. *Journal of Educational Psychology, 94*(2), 272–277.

Wimmer, H., Landerl, K., Linortner, R., & Hummer, P. (1991). 'The relationship of phonemic awareness to reading acquisition: More consequence than precondition but still important'. *Cognition, 40,* 219–249.

Windfuhr, K.L. & Snowling, M. (2001). 'The relationship between paired-associate learning and phonological skills in normally developing readers'. *Journal of Experimental Child Psychology, 80,* 160–173.

Ziegler, J.C., Jacobs, A.M., & Stone, B. (1996). 'Statistical analysis of the bidirectional inconsistency of spelling and sound in French'. *Behaviour Research Methods, Instruments & Computers, 28,* 504–515.

Chapter 9

How do children and adults conceptualise phoneme–letter relationships?[1]

Annukka Lehtonen

Traditionally, children's and adults' understanding of alphabetic relationships has been conceptualised in terms of phonemes. Consequently, it has been thought that the skill that beginning readers need to learn, and the skill that experienced readers have presumably developed, is understanding the correspondences between phonemes in speech and the letters used to represent them. The phoneme has acquired its central position because the English alphabet is based on the phoneme. Thus, it is not necessarily the phonological unit that is best suited for representing speech in writing. Furthermore, phoneme–letter relationships are somewhat different in other writing systems, and thus there is no optimal relationship between spoken and written language. Surprisingly, how children begin thinking about writing in terms of phonemes, or whether skilled readers continue to do so after they have become proficient in reading and spelling, has not been investigated in detail. It appears that children only gradually learn to understand the principles through which speech is represented in writing and that adults do not necessarily use phonemes in tasks that demand them to do so.

In this chapter I discuss how the structure of different writing systems may affect literacy development, and what is known about the process through which children begin to make connections between sound units in speech and letters. Present knowledge about adults' understanding of letter–sound relationships is also considered. I then discuss two experiments that look at children's developing understanding of letter–sound relationships as well as reviewing work by Lehtonen and Treiman (2007) that investigated adults' use of different units in conceptualising the relationship between sounds and letters. Finally, I discuss the findings in the light of children's and adults' conceptions of the relationship between spoken language and print.

What kind of knowledge is involved in literacy acquisition?

Research has established many important connections between children's phonological knowledge and literacy skills. For example, children's awareness of syllables and their subunits, onsets and rimes has been found to predict their later reading and spelling skills (e.g. Bradley & Bryant, 1983; Bryant *et al.*, 1990). Phoneme awareness has also emerged as a significant predictor of reading and spelling (e.g. Caravolas *et al.*, 2001; Juel, 1988). On a more detailed level, it has been demonstrated that children's phonemic awareness parallels their spelling skills in specific ways. Treiman *et al.* (1995b) found that children who failed to segment consonants as independent units in CVCC (C = consonant, V = vowel) words were more likely to omit the first consonants of final clusters in a spelling task, while children who counted all the phonemes in the CVCC words were less likely to omit consonants in the spelling task. The close connection between phonemic knowledge and spelling in English makes sense, as children need to understand the phonemic structure of the words in order to map the phonemic information they hear in the words onto the English writing system.

Although research has focused on how children's increasing phonological awareness affects their knowledge of letter–sound relationships, the influence appears to be bidirectional. For example, Morais and colleagues (Morais *et al.* 1979; Morais *et al.*, 1986) found that literate Portuguese adults were significantly better at phoneme segmentation than illiterate Portuguese adults from the same socioeconomic background. However, the effect of literacy tuition is not absolute; even the illiterate group showed some phoneme awareness, especially when dealing with real words. Wood (2004) further found that pre-literate children with no literacy skills performed no worse in phoneme awareness tasks than children who had been exposed to some degree of alphabetic tuition. Thus awareness of phonemes in the context of literacy ability is not as clear-cut as has been assumed.

Mann (1986) demonstrated that the characteristics of a writing system can influence phonological development. She suggested that the crucial factor that promotes phonemic awareness is knowledge of a writing system that is in some way based on phonemes. She found that Japanese children who had been exposed to Romanji, an alphabetic version of Japanese, were much better in phoneme segmentation tasks than children who had not yet learnt Romanji. Mann showed that American first-year children who were learning English were significantly better in the phoneme-based tasks. In contrast, Japanese children were significantly better with the syllable items. Experience of written words also guides children's performance: Ehri and Wilce (1980) showed that fourth graders were more likely to count /t/ in words where it was represented in the spelling (e.g. *pitch*) than where it was not (e.g. *rich*).

It is also worth noting that before literacy tuition begins, children seem to acquire some understanding of the ways writing works through their exposure to environmental print. Ferreiro and Teberosky (1982) conducted semi-structured interviews with pre-literate children, and found that many children who did not yet understand the phonological function of letters were nevertheless familiar with some characteristics of print; they for example knew that letters in words had to be different and words usually had to have at least three letters to be legal.

Different writing systems, different challenges

I am only going to say a few words about other writing systems, since differences between them are not the main focus of this chapter (see Babayiğit in Chapter 8 in this volume for a review). However, it is important to observe that phoneme–grapheme relationships are by no means fixed and predetermined; writing systems differ in how they represent speech, and these differences are likely to influence the process of becoming a competent reader and speller. In some writing systems a certain letter is almost always pronounced the same way. In contrast, in English a single letter or group of letters may have multiple pronunciations. Some writing systems are easy to spell, because a particular phoneme in the language is always represented by the same letter, but in English a given phoneme often has many different spellings. Furthermore, some writing systems do not represent words on the level of phonemes; the Japanese Kana is based on syllables, and some African and Indian languages are spelled with alphasyllabaries that combine characteristics of alphabets and syllabaries. Overall, there is great variety how speech is represented.

The phoneme-letter correspondences characteristic of English have often caused it to be labelled an irregular writing system. This is not necessarily so; as Kessler and Treiman (2003) observed that factors affecting the English writing system are the unadapted spelling of loan words (e.g. *quiche*) and the representation of nonphonetic information such as morphological relationships (e.g. *heal* and *health* are morphologically related, and thus spelled similarly; equally, the ending in *rolled*, *kissed* and *waited* is pronounced differently, yet spelled the same since it denotes past tense verb). Furthermore, there are spelling patterns that enable the reader to choose between different alternatives (e.g. /k/ is usually spelled *ck* after a vowel that is spelled with one letter (e.g. *duck*), and *k* after a vowel that is spelled with two letters (e.g. *book*); Kessler & Treiman, 2003). It has been demonstrated that children can use the surrounding context both when they read consonants (Hayes *et al.*, 2006) and when they read vowels (Treiman *et al.*, 2006). However, despite these regularities, the English writing system still presents a challenge for the novice reader and speller to a greater degree than more transparent writing systems do.

One way to conceptualise these learner differences between writing systems comes from Ziegler andGoswami's (2005) psycholinguistic grain size theory. They suggest that the process of phonological recoding and the development of different reading strategies are dependent on the characteristics of the writing system that is being learned. Thus, children who are learning to read consistent writing systems would be more likely to rely on phoneme-letter correspondences. In contrast, children learning to read less consistent writing systems would be sensitive not only to phoneme-letter relationships but also larger 'grain sizes', such as syllables, onsets and rimes, even whole words. It is likely that this leads the readers of consistent writing systems to conceptualise the relationships between the spoken and written language mainly in terms of phoneme-letter correspondences. The equivalent conceptualisations for readers of more inconsistent writing systems are likely to be more heterogeneous. In order to take advantage of the additional consistency given by context, they would need to process units larger than single phonemes. Readers of non-alphabetic orthographies, on the other hand, are altogether less likely to rely on phonemes, as Mann's (1986) work demonstrated. Although the psycholinguistic grain-size theory does not address some issues in reading acquisition, such as fluency (Wimmer, 2006), and although it assumes that pre-literate children have no access to the phonemic level of representation (Caravolas, 2006), the theory does nevertheless demonstrate the differences between beginning readers of different writing systems.

The beginnings of children's understanding of letter–sound relationships

As discussed above, awareness of phonemes is crucial in the process of acquiring literacy, but children also need knowledge of the principles governing how phonemes relate to the letters of the alphabet. The importance of this knowledge has been suggested by intervention studies, which are usually more successful if they combine phonological training with information about phoneme–letter relationships, instead of using phonological training alone (e.g. Bradley & Bryant, 1983; Hatcher *et al.*, 1994). But how do children get to the point where they can start working out which phonemes are represented by which letters? Several studies have now examined this in detail.

The first connections between phonemes and letters are formed on the basis of letters in the written words that young children are first exposed to, such as in their own names, and the names of letters in the alphabet. Treiman and Broderick (1998) asked children to produce letter names and the sounds made by those letters, and found that children were more likely to know the name of the letter that their own first name began with. This knowledge did not extend to knowing the sound made by that letter though. Another study (Treiman *et al.*, 2001) showed that children's intrusion errors, that is, their use of inappropriate letters, in their spellings were motivated by the spellings of their own name. Furthermore, Treiman *et al.* (1998) showed that children between the ages of 4 and 7 were more likely to know the sound that a letter made if this sound was easily derived from the name of the letter (e.g. *v*), as opposed to letters for which this was not the case (e.g. *w*). Therefore, one significant influence on the process through which young children build their understanding of letter-sound relationships is through familiar letters and letters whose correspondence to their sounds is a simple one.

It's so simple – one sound for each letter and vice versa?

Since children seem to first connect letters and phonemes through relationships between single sounds and single letters, it is likely that children initially assume that there is a one-to-one correspondence between letters and phonemes. In other words 'each unit in their conceptualization of a spoken word should be spelled with a single letter and … there should be no extra letters' (Reece & Treiman, 2001: 161). This idea was first proposed by Reece and Treiman (2001) in their longitudinal study of first-grade children's developing spellings of syllabic /r/ and final (silent) *e*. Syllabic /r/ is a phoneme that appears in American English (e.g. in words such as *sir* or *girl*) and in stressed syllables is spelled with one or two vowel letters and the letter *r*. Thus, like the final *e* spellings, syllabic /r/ is an example where a single phoneme is spelled with two or more letters. Reece and Treiman found that children initially tended to spell syllabic /r/ with a single *r*, for example producing SR for *sir* (capital letters will be used in the following to represent children's spellings), without the preceding vowel. When children subsequently started to include the vowel, they did not necessarily place the vowel correctly, but sometimes included it only after the *r*, as in SRE. Furthermore, children who spelled the syllabic /r/ without the vowel also tended to spell letter–name vowels without the final *e* (e.g. *cone* as CON). The vowel in the syllabic /r/ began to appear in parallel with the use of final *e*.

Reece and Treiman (2001) proposed that this developmental progression reflects children's gradually increasing understanding of the spelling conventions of English. However, the nature of the English writing system means that even young spellers are frequently exposed to many words in which phoneme–letter relationships are not one-to-one, and children are often sensitive to the discrepancy between the phonemes and letters before they begin to fully appreciate the phonemic function of the 'additional' letters. At this point, they may regard the 'additional' letters as just extra. When they then are taught or realise themselves that a vowel is conventionally included, they start incorporating it into their spellings, but without a clear idea of why it is there. It might merely be 'an extra letter that lacks phonological purpose, just like the *e* of *make*' (Reece & Treiman, 2001: 161).

Support for this idea of children's one-to-one theory also comes from a study by Ehri and Soffer (1999), in which they asked second, third, fifth and seventh graders to do a task where the participants were given written spellings and asked to mark as units those letters or groups of letters that corresponded to the 'smallest sounds' in words. In some words, every phoneme in the spoken word corresponded to a single letter in the spelling (e.g. *red*, *stop*), while some of the words had more complex relationships between phonemes and letters (e.g. *she*, *ball*). The younger children were likely to consider each letter to represent one sound, circling every letter in a word such as *she*; these errors were in accord with Reece and Treiman's (2001) suggestion about children's assumption of one-to-one phoneme–letter correspondences. In contrast, the most common error among the older children was to group together letters that corresponded to multiple phonemes.

These findings suggest that the process of learning phoneme–letter correspondences is more laborious and piecemeal than the traditional spelling models would lead us to assume. Phonemes are far from a self-evident unit, and understanding how they relate to letters is by no means a sudden insight. The hypothesis of one-to-one correspondences between units of sound and letters makes a lot of sense given the way in which children build up their knowledge of phoneme–letter correspondences. Thus, it is hardly surprising that children give it up only gradually as they encounter more and more examples in the writing system that do not conform to this initial hypothesis.

How do experienced readers conceptualise the relationship between phonemes and letters?

Literate adults are generally assumed to possess literacy skills and the related meta-linguistic abilities in their fully developed form; thus, adults would be expected to perform flawlessly in phoneme awareness tasks. This assumption has not been extensively tested, although several studies have contested this view. Scholes (1993) found that the mean number of sounds counted by university students in phoneme counting tasks rarely corresponded to either the number of phonemes or the number of letters in the words, but was usually fewer. Poor performance was also demonstrated by Moats (1994) and Mather *et al.* (2001) for teachers in the United States and by Serrano *et al.* (2003) for Spanish-speaking teachers. Likewise, Scarborough *et al.* (1998) found that eighth graders' errors in pseudoword phoneme counting and deletion tasks almost always consisted of removing a portion larger than a single phoneme and undercounting phonemes. In another experiment, Scarborough and colleagues examined adults' understanding of phoneme–letter relationships in a graphophonemic task like the one used by Ehri and Soffer (1999). Interestingly, adult participants often marked as a unit letters that represented two or more phonemes, while responses violating onset-rime and syllable boundaries were rare. This is in keeping with the results from older children in Ehri and Soffer's (1999) experiment.

These results suggest that adults do not always use phoneme-sized units even when asked to do so. However, it is not clear what factors influence adults' choice of units in a task that explicitly asks about phoneme–letter correspondences. Onsets and rimes seem to play a part, and it has been found that adults are sensitive to these units in tasks that require the processing of spoken language (e.g. Treiman et al., 1995a; Treiman & Danis, 1988; Treiman, 1986). Lehtonen and Treiman (2007) have suggested that sonority might play a part in adults' conceptions about phoneme–letter relationships. Sonority means the vowel-like quality of phonemes; vowels are the most sonorous phonemes, with liquids, nasals, fricatives and obstruents, in this order, decreasing in sonority. As pointed out by Lehtonen and Treiman (2007), several experiments (e.g. Treiman, 1983; Stemberger, 1983) suggest that liquids following a vowel (/r/ as in *pork* in rhotic dialects, /l/ as in *bulk*) are more closely linked with that vowel than the following consonant, while postvocalic obstruents (e.g. /s/ in *mist*, *dusk*) are more strongly connected to the consonant. Nasals are somewhere in-between liquids and obstruents. However, again, these studies concern spoken language, and it is impossible to draw a direct conclusion about phoneme–letter relationships on the basis of this work. However, it is possible that sonority is one factor that influences proficient readers and spellers' conceptualisations of phoneme–letter relationships.

Models of literacy development suggest that one of the cornerstones in the learning process is the establishment of phoneme–letter correspondences. However, there is not very much work investigating this particular issue directly. Furthermore, skilled reading and spelling is not well understood. Spelling models refer to large 'chunks', but it is not known what kinds of factors influence the use of these 'chunks', and when experienced readers and spellers are likely to use them.

I will approach the general issue of phoneme–letter relationships by first looking at the early phases of literacy acquisition. I will then discuss additional data that suggest ways in which the phonological properties of sound units affect children's judgements of phoneme–letter relationships. Finally, I will mention two experiments by Lehtonen and Treiman (2007), looking at how adults' conceptualisation of letter–sound relationships is affected by the phonological properties of the sounds in question.

The development of children's understanding of phoneme–letter relationships

The aim of the study reported here (Lehtonen & Treiman, unpublished) was to examine how children's early ideas of phoneme–letter relationships work with words where these relationships are not one to one, and how children's phonemic awareness is related to their knowledge of phoneme-letter relationships. Most work to date has considered this question indirectly by looking at children's spelling errors: children's explicit understanding of phoneme–letter relationships has only been investigated by Ehri and Soffer (1999). However, they did not systematically vary the types of words they used. Instead, they included a collection of words with simple one-to-one and more complex phoneme–letter relationships, and therefore it is difficult to know whether children's responses were influenced by the structure of the words. For example, it is not clear whether children were equally good with words that had one-to-one phoneme–letter relationships as with words that did not. Furthermore, it is not known how children's phoneme awareness affects their performance. It is possible that phoneme–letter knowledge follows directly from advanced phoneme segmentation skill. Alternatively, the two could be independently contributing to spelling skills.

In this study, first- and second-grade children were asked to complete a spelling segmentation task and a phoneme segmentation task. The spelling segmentation task was similar to that used by Ehri and Soffer (1999) and included different types of words in which phoneme–letter correspondences are not one to one: words with digraphs, doublets and syllabic /r/, as well as control words that had one-to-one phoneme–letter correspondences. Thus, it was possible to see whether children's understanding of phoneme–letter relationships was influenced by the types of phoneme–letter correspondences in a word. Children would be expected to be more accurate in the spelling segmentation task with control words rather than words with more complex phoneme–letter correspondences. It would also be expected that both phoneme awareness and spelling segmentation ability would influence spelling.

Fifty first- and second-grade children from parochial and public schools in St Louis, Missouri, took part in the study. All children had English as their first language and had no speech, hearing, or reading disabilities. Children were tested in October and again six months later in the following April to see how their spelling had developed over time.

The first task was spelling segmentation, where the items were 36 pseudo-words, divided into four conditions: (1) digraph (e.g. *shug, fush*); (2) doublet (e.g. *hoon; luff*); (3) syllabic /r/ (e.g. *nerk, mirb*); and (4) control CVC syllables (e.g. *gan, nep*). There were also six fillers (e.g. *ip, ut*). Although in Ehri and Soffer's (1999) task children were asked to circle the letters in the words, the task was changed into multiple-choice format. This way, it was possible to compare the prevalence of particular types of responses, since with a multiple-choice format children had equal opportunity to pick any of the responses. Moreover, multiple-choice was judged an easier task than free circling, and was therefore more likely to produce reliable data.

Thus, children were provided with four alternative ways to segment the words: (1) phonemic (e.g. [t h] [u] [p]); (2) letter by letter (e.g. [t] [h] [u] [p]); (3) onset-rime (e.g. [t h] [u p]); (4) one letter of the digraph as silent (e.g. [t] h [u] [p]). The silent letter of a digraph was always the second one, except for the syllabic /r/ items in which the vowel preceding /r/ was left uncircled. For the control items that only had three letters, the phonemic and onset-rime responses were used in addition to the silent response (i.e. the medial vowel uncircled, e.g. [g] a [n]) and a fourth option in which the first two letters were grouped together and the last one on its own (e.g. [ga] [n]).

The letter-by-letter response was included because of the high prevalence of this type of response in Ehri and Soffer's (1999) results, and the silent option was used because children often miss out letters in their early spellings, and thus this choice reflected a spelling typical for young children. There were two versions of the response sheet where the items were in different random orders, and the four choices were also presented in different random orders.

At the beginning of the task, the researcher explained what she meant by 'little bits of sound', saying that /u/ was one sound, in /ɪk/ there were two, while /næd/ and

/dʌp/ had three each. Usually, she let the child segment the third and fourth words him/herself. The researcher then introduced a toy cat and explained that the cat wanted to know how the little bits of sound in words go together with the letters that are used to spell the words. The researcher had a sheet of paper on which were written six practice words, with spaces between the letters: *ep, nad, ack, feen, psen, ribt*, and she then showed that for the words *ep* and *nad*, one should circle each letter separately since each of them makes a sound in the word, while the *ck* in *ack* and *ee* in *feen* should be circled as one as they together make a sound in the word. Finally, the *p* and *psen* /sen/ and *b* in *ribt* /rɪt/ do not make a sound, so they should not be circled at all. Children were asked to explain what to do with *feen* and *ribt* on their own, and they received corrective feedback in case they made an error. The experimenter did not provide feedback for the experimental items.

The phoneme segmentation task used the same experimental items as the spelling segmentation task. In addition to the 36 experimental items, the phoneme segmentation task included 14 fillers that each consisted of one or two phonemes: /eɪ/, /i/, /æp/, /æg/, /ɑm/, /ɪd/, /ʌt/, /ʌb/, /ʌr/, /ɪp/, /ow/, /ɪm/, /æb/, and /ʌg/ . The fillers added variety to the list and were easier to segment than the experimental items, due to their brevity.

At the start of the session, the researcher introduced herself and the toy cat. She also showed the child a set of four cups that were glued onto a cardboard strip, and four colourful plastic tokens. She explained that she had a list of funny words that the cat would like to hear in little bits of sound, one at a time, and asked whether the child would like to say the words to the cat this way. After the child agreed, the experimenter demonstrated what she meant by a 'little bit of sound', saying that /u/ was one sound, in /ɪk/ there were two, while /næd/ and /dʌp/ had three each. Usually, the experimenter let the child segment the third and fourth words him/ herself. The experimenter asked the child to put down a token into a cup for each little sound s/he heard in the word.

To determine the children's spelling level, children were asked to do the Test of Written Spelling (TWS-4; Larsen *et al.*, 1999). This was given in the first session after the phoneme segmentation task. The test requires children to write words that get progressively harder. The test is stopped after the child gets five consecutive items wrong. The score of the task is simply the number of items correctly spelled.

The results for the spelling segmentation task were looked at first. To score this task, the proportions of different types of responses (phonemic, letter by letter, silent, onset-rime) were calculated for the four spelling patterns. The means and standard deviations are presented in Table 9.1. The scores were inspected by separate repeated-measures ANOVAs. Time (time 1, time 2) and spelling pattern (digraph, doublet, syllabic /r/, control) were the within-subjects factors and grade (first, second) was the between-subjects factor.

An ANOVA of the letter-by-letter responses revealed the significant main effect of spelling pattern, $F(2, 96) = 19.971$, $p < .001$, and the almost significant main effect of time, $F(1, 48) = 3.955$, $p < .052$. Thus, overall there were fewer letter-by-letter responses at time 2 than at time 1. Post-hoc *t*-tests ($p < .001$) for the spelling pattern main effect showed that syllabic /r/ produced significantly more letter-by-letter responses than either digraphs or doublets, which did not differ from each other in this respect.

Table 9.1 Mean proportions and standard deviations of responses in the spelling segmentation task of Experiment 1

			Digraph	*Doublet*	*Syllabic /r/*	*Control*
Letter-by-letter	Time 1	Grade 1	.22 (.27)	.19 (.18)	.33 (.31)	n/a
		Grade 2	.12 (.20)	.08 (.12)	.26 (.32)	n/a
	Time 2	Grade 1	.13 (.22)	.10 (.13)	.26 (.31)	n/a
		Grade 2	.04 (.06)	.04 (.07)	.33 (.33)	n/a
Silent	Time 1	Grade 1	.14 (.26)	.08 (.11)	.33 (.36)	.09 (.21)
		Grade 2	.01 (.02)	.02 (.05)	.19 (.28)	.03 (.06)
	Time 2	Grade 1	.06 (.19)	.03 (.10)	.27 (.30)	.06 (.11)
		Grade 2	.02 (.07)	.03 (.10)	.13 (.23)	.01 (.05)
Onset-rime	Time 1	Grade 1	.17 (.22)	.20 (.23)	.11 (.22)	.24 (.24)
		Grade 2	.09 (.17)	.07 (.16)	.06 (.15)	.10 (.18)
	Time 2	Grade 1	.10 (.17)	.07 (.15)	.07 (.16)	.17 (.19)
		Grade 2	.08 (.17)	.06 (.13)	.04 (.10)	.10 (.18)

For the silent letter responses, there were significant main effects of spelling pattern, $F(3, 144) = 17.982$, $p < .001$, time $F(1, 48) = 5.313$, $p = .026$, and grade, $F(1, 48) = 7.443$, $p = .009$. Post-hoc tests ($p < .001$) showed that the syllabic /r/ spelling pattern produced significantly more of the silent letter responses than any other spelling pattern, which did not differ from each other. The main effects of time and grade were significant because there were significantly more silent letter responses in grade 1 than grade 2, and more silent responses at time 1 than at time 2.

For the onset-rime responses, there were significant main effects of time, $F(1, 48) = 8.073$, $p = .007$, and spelling pattern, $F(3, 144) = 7.023$, $p < .001$. The main effect of time showed that there were overall more onset-rime responses at time 1. Post-hoc tests showed that the main effect of spelling pattern emerged because syllabic /r/ items produced significantly fewer of these responses than the other spelling patterns, while control items produced the largest number. The digraph and doublet patterns were intermediate and did not significantly differ from each other. There was also a significant interaction between time and grade, $F(1, 48) = 5.051$, $p = .029$. Post-hoc tests revealed this to emerge because there was no effect of time in the responses of the second-grade children.

Next, the phoneme segmentation task was scored by counting the number of times children allocated three segments (the correct number) for the experimental words. The proportions of correct responses at time 1 were .64 and .82 for the first and second graders, respectively. At time 2, these proportions were .84 and .82, again for first and second graders, respectively. This suggests that although first graders showed considerable improvement between times 1 and 2, there is no marked further development in the same time interval for the second graders, although they do not perform at ceiling.

We were interested in the relationship between children's spelling segmentation and phoneme segmentation. Since the study had a longitudinal design, it was possible to inspect whether children's early scores in these tasks independently predicted their later spelling performance. It would be expected that children's scores in the phoneme segmentation task would be connected to both their later spelling segmentation and spelling performance. In addition, it would be expected that the phoneme responses, but no other response types in the spelling segmentation task, would be connected to children's spelling ability. The first step in inspecting the relationships between tasks was to look at the correlation coefficients between the tasks. Table 9.2 shows the correlation coefficients between time 1 phoneme segmentation and spelling segmentation tasks and time 1 and time 2 spelling performance. The coefficients are for partial correlations controlling for age, since in some tasks, but not all, there were age-related differences between scores in the different conditions. The phoneme segmentation scores are the proportion of experimental items that children segmented correctly. There were four different spelling segmentation scores: the total proportion of responses in each four response categories (phonemic, letter by letter, silent, onset-rime). The spelling scores are the standardised TWS spelling scores at times 1 and 2.

Table 9.2 shows that the phoneme segmentation responses correlate significantly and positively with the phonemic responses in the spelling segmentation task as well as the later spelling scores. In contrast, the phoneme segmentation scores correlated negatively with the letter, silent and onset-rime responses, and only the correlation with letter responses reaches significance. This pattern of correlations was the same as for the spelling segmentation task scores from time 2.

The correlation coefficients also show that while the phoneme spelling segmentation responses show significant positive correlation coefficients with later spelling ability, all the other response types in the spelling segmentation task correlate negatively with later spelling skills.

The correlation analyses already showed that different aspects of the children's phonemic and phoneme–letter knowledge are associated with their spelling skills. However, it is not clear whether phoneme segmentation ability and letter–phoneme knowledge contribute independently to children's later spelling skills. To investigate this question, simultaneous regression analyses were run, where the dependent variable was spelling at time 2 as measured by the TWS-4 test, and the independent variables were age, phoneme segmentation (3-phoneme responses) and spelling segmentation (proportion of phonemic responses) at time 1.

The analysis (presented in Table 9.3) showed that 35 per cent of children's spelling at time 2 was predicted by the regression. However, the only significant predictor was the children's time 1 spelling segmentation score. Age and phoneme segmentation scores explained very little variance, as shown by the low Beta weights. When only age and phoneme segmentation are entered in the equation, phoneme segmentation does predict a modest amount of variance (10.7 per cent). This suggests that phoneme segmentation is not at ceiling (as also indicated by the means) and does make a contribution as such towards spelling ability, but not over and above spelling segmentation ability. When the predictors were age, phoneme segmentation score and spelling segmentation score at time 2, the regression only predicted 20.6 per cent of the variance, substantially less than with time 1 predictors. However, the only significant predictor was the children's spelling segmentation score. Furthermore, phoneme segmentation no longer predicted spelling ability even when spelling segmentation score is not in the regression.

In general, the findings here suggest that the silent letter and letter-by-letter responses are more common with younger children, and at time 1 rather than at time

Table 9.2 Correlation coefficients in Experiment 1

	Phoneme awareness	Phonemic	Letter-by-letter	Silent	Onset-rime	T1 Spelling	T2 Spelling
Phon. awareness	—						
Phonemic	.350*	—					
Letter-by-letter	-.420**	-.493***	—				
Silent	-.001	-.607***	-.064	—			
Onset-rime	-.170	-.716***	-.081	.314*	—		
T1 Spelling	.335*	.655***	-.467***	-.302*	-.405**	—	
T2 Spelling	.305*	.572***	-.270	-.373**	-.402**	.830***	—

Table 9.3 Regression analyses

	B	Std. Error	β
Dependent Variable: Time 2 TWR-4			
1. Time 1 Age	−1.164	3.483	−.041
2. Time 1 Phoneme Segmentation	6.178	6.647	.119
3. Time 1 Spelling Segmentation	33.119	7.995	.547***
Dependent Variable: Time 2 TWR-4			
1. Time 2 Age	−.827	3.929	−.029
2. Time 2 Phoneme Segmentation	−6.704	9.297	−.096
3. Time 2 Spelling Segmentation	35.728	10.634	.465**

2. This supports our hypothesis that these are responses indicating immature understanding of phoneme–letter relationships. This also agrees with Reece and Treiman's (2001) argument that early on in literacy acquisition children go through a period when they do not fully understand the phonemic function of letters in words for spelling patterns that deviate from the one-to-one principle.

It seems that syllabic /r/ is more likely than the other spelling patterns to produce these less mature spelling segmentation responses; children seem to have more difficulty understanding the relationship between the vowel preceding the letter *r* and the *r* itself, either considering the vowel an extra letter that does not have a phonemic function, or assuming that it makes a sound on its own. The doublet and digraph patterns do not significantly differ from control patterns in this respect, which suggests that children at this stage have already worked out that some spelling patterns are spelled with two letters and this does not present them additional difficulty. Why is there such a difference between the different two-letter spelling patterns that are used to spell single phonemes? It is possible that syllabic /r/ can lead children to think that there is a vowel and an /r/, while *th* and *sh* are fairly unlikely to make children think that there is a /t/ and a /h/. Since most syllables do contain a vowel, children's assumption that there is one in syllabic /r/ is quite a logical one (R. Treiman, personal communication, 29 October 2007).

Importantly, the regression analyses demonstrate that spelling segmentation predicts spelling ability over and above children's phoneme awareness. This suggests that the spelling segmentation task is not merely another index of phoneme awareness, but captures an independent skill that is closely related to later spelling ability – children's understanding of the relationship between phonemes and letters. Furthermore, it seems that mere awareness of phonemes as phonological units is not enough; children also need to work out how phonemes are represented by letters.

What about multi-letter spelling patterns?

As discussed already, several reading and spelling models (e.g. Ehri, 1995; Frith, 1985) propose that advanced literacy skills are characterised by the use of multi-letter spelling patterns in addition to individual letters. It can be argued that these are more efficient when it comes to processing capacity and speed, as well as memory. Given that spelling-to-sound correspondences are often conditioned by surrounding letters (Kessler & Treiman, 2001; Kessler & Treiman, 2003) in English, using multi-letter

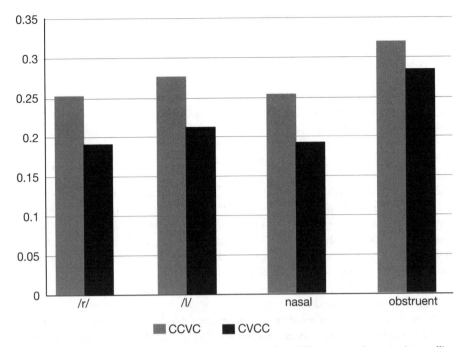

Figure 9.1 The proportions of cluster responses for different word types in spelling segmentation task of Experiment 2

spelling patterns would also make sense. Furthermore, Ziegler & Goswami's grain size theory (Ziegler & Goswami, 2005) also supports the argument for larger processing units, since they propose that readers and spellers of more inconsistent orthographies use a greater variety of processing units of different grain sizes. This might also be a general characteristic of developed reading skills, as suggested by Paulesu (2006) in his critique of the psycholinguistic grain size theory. He points out that skilled readers of consistent reading systems, such as Italian and Spanish, are faster at reading real words than nonwords (Paulesu *et al.*, 2000), and also show neighbourhood effects in reading nonwords (Arduino & Burani, 2004). Finally, research on more experienced readers and adults suggested that they do sometimes use responses that group together several phonemes or letters. However, there has been little work investigating factors that might govern more advanced readers' and spellers' use of different processing units in tasks that require phonemic and orthographic knowledge.

Lehtonen and Treiman (unpublished) investigated whether young children's understanding of phoneme–letter relationships is influenced by sonority, and at which point this influence might start taking effect if it indeed does emerge. The participants were 93 children from grades 1, 2 and 4, who were asked to do the spelling segmentation task. This consisted of CCVC (e.g. *drum, sled, snug, skip*) and CVCC words (e.g. *fork, salt, sand, dust*), in which the consonants in consonant clusters preceding or following vowels varied in sonority (/r/, /l/, nasal or obstruent). The children also did the TWS-4 spelling test.

The mean proportions for different types of responses (cluster, consonant + vowel) and for stimuli containing target consonants of different degrees of sonority are presented in Figure 9.1. The children were divided into poorer, intermediate and better spellers according to their TWS-4 scores.

The results showed that in the cluster responses (e.g. grouping together *s* and *k* in *mask*), obstruent consonants were significantly more often grouped with the preceding or following consonant than consonants of any other type. The responses combining vowels and consonants (e.g. grouping together *i* and *l* in *silk*) are presented in Figure 9.2 and demonstrated that sonority had an effect on the responses of the better and intermediate spellers, but did not influence the performance of the poorest spellers. The better spellers grouped the most sonorant target consonants (/r/) significantly more often with a vowel than any other consonants. Overall, sonority did not affect children's responses for the CCVC words, but /r/ in CVCC words was significantly more often grouped with the vowel than other consonants were. Finally, onset–rime responses showed that children were more likely to use onset–rime responses for CCVC words than CVCC words. In addition, the poorer spellers were significantly more likely to choose onset–rime responses than better spellers were, while the intermediate spellers did not significantly differ from either of the poorer or better groups in this regard.

The results of this experiment provide tentative evidence that as children's spelling skills mature, they become sensitive to the sonority of the phonemes they are dealing with and use units larger than single phonemes, based on sonority, when conceptualising the relationship between letters and phonological units. This was only a

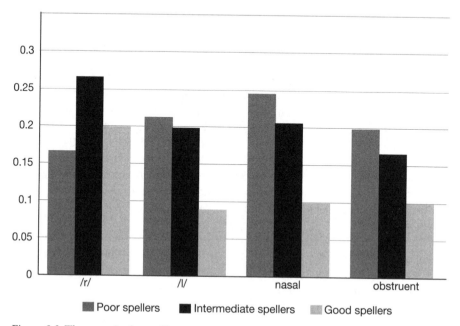

Figure 9.2 The sonority by spelling group interaction for vowel + consonant responses in Experiment 2

trend in the responses concerning consonant clusters, but was a clear and significant effect for the responses that combined vowels and consonants in the different types of words. Furthermore, use of large units based on onsets and rimes appears to decrease with increasing spelling ability, as was the case in the previous experiment, too.

Adults' conceptualisations about the relationships between phonemes and letters

The results discussed above suggest that from relatively early on, after only a few years of reading and spelling instruction, children start showing signs of sensitivity to phoneme sonority and this affects their choice of units even when encouraged to use phonemes by the instructions. Thus, responses in tasks that in theory require phonemic responses could be based on phonological principles, even if these are not exclusively phonemic ones. However, although the results just discussed suggest that children at some points of their literacy development give such responses, this could be either a passing developmental phase or, alternatively, the end point of the developmental progression. Work with adults reviewed earlier in this chapter would suggest that this is not just an intermediate phase; instead, large-unit responses are part of adults' response repertoire just as they are a part of children's. Furthermore, Lehtonen and Treiman (2007) recently investigated this issue in detail, testing undergraduates in a similar spelling segmentation task as presented above.

Participants for the first experiment were 78 undergraduates, who did a spelling segmentation task investigating sonority as described above. The main question was whether the sonority of the postvocalic (and in the case of CCVC words, prevocalic) consonants would influence the way in which adults grouped the letters of the words to correspond to what they considered to be the smallest units of sound in the spoken words.

The findings suggested that while sonority had no effect on adults' initial cluster responses, consonants that followed the vowel in CVCC words were significantly more often grouped with the final consonant if they were obstruents than if they were liquids (/r/ or /l/). Nasals were significantly more often grouped with the final consonant than liquids were. Likewise, sonority did not affect C+V responses in CCVC words. However, the first consonants of final clusters in CVCC words were significantly more often grouped with the vowel if these consonants were liquids or nasals than if they were obstruents. The onset–rime responses only revealed that words with initial consonant clusters prompted more onset–rime responses.

This suggests that indeed, sonority appears to be one of the factors that influences adults' responses in a task that explicitly requires identifying the precise relationships between phonemes and letters. Although adults are generally considered to possess well-developed phonemic awareness, they do not always seem to use phonemes as processing units even when specifically asked to do so. However, adults are sensitive to the phonological properties of the phonemes in question and these influence their choice of units. Thus, Lehtonen and Treiman's (2007) results are in agreement with the findings from the equivalent experiment with children discussed above, which suggest that this is not just a passing developmental phase.

It could be considered somewhat surprising that adults and children proficient in literacy skills so commonly use units larger than single phonemes, even when explicitly asked about the smallest units of sound. However, this is unexpected only if adults' use of these units is considered fixed, that is, if it is assumed that they always rely on these large units. One would not expect this for example on the basis of Ziegler and Goswami's (2005) psycholinguistic grain size theory, which posits that readers of inconsistent writing systems are flexible in their use of different units, not that they are stuck with using units of a particular size. This might also be the case for readers of consistent writing systems (Paulesu, 2006).

Furthermore, there is evidence that adults' responses can be influenced by instruction. Connelly (2002) asked university students to do the graphophonemic task used by Scarborough *et al.* (1998) and then provided half of the participants with ten minutes of training on phoneme–grapheme correspondences before the graphophonemic awareness task was administered again. The other half of the participants identified authors before they did the graphophonemic awareness task the second time. In the post-intervention graphophonemic awareness task, the experimental group made significantly more phonemic responses than the control group. Interestingly, neither group was close to ceiling in their performance. In general, therefore, it seems that adults' tendency to use units larger than single phonemes when considering phoneme–letter relationships might be merely a preference, not a fixed response pattern.

This was supported by Lehtonen and Treiman (2007), who asked half of their participants to do the spelling segmentation task after a counting task that required participants to count phonemes in words. The other half of the participants did a task requiring counting of words in sentences. After the counting task, both groups did the spelling segmentation task. Phonemic responses turned out to be significantly more common for participants who had been counting phonemes than for participants who had been counting words: 71 per cent as compared to 48 per cent. In contrast, onset–rime responses were significantly more frequent following word counting than phoneme counting: 16 per cent vs. 6 per cent.

Thus, it seems that adults – like the experienced child spellers – often use units larger than single phonemes in phonemic tasks, and that these units are at least to a degree, if not always, influenced by sonority of the phonemes involved. As Lehtonen and Treiman (2007) have argued, it also seems that adults' use of different phonemic units is flexible.

Conclusion

Overall, it seems that the task of representing phonemes with letters is more elusive than one might think, and it also does not appear to be the obvious end point of literacy acquisition. Phonemic awareness is important during developing literacy, but this does not mean that alternative strategies would not be useful. Returning to Ziegler and Goswami's (2005) theory, it would make sense that skilled readers would use the processing units that are most efficient from the point of view of the task at hand.

Interesting though the results presented here are, it is important to note that further work is needed in order to understand more comprehensively how children conceptualise the relationship between letters and phonemes, how this develops across time, and how it is related to their phonemic awareness and reading/spelling skills. There are also other factors that could affect how young children and more advanced readers alike use different phonological units when determining phoneme–letter relationships. Letter names are one example of this, and Lehtonen and Treiman (2007) did find some evidence of letter name effects for adults, although this finding was not replicated. Given the strong effects of letter names on children's performance in different literacy- and language-related tasks, it could reasonably be expected that children demonstrate letter name effects in their responses. Work investigating this possibility is currently underway.

Another avenue for future work is investigating this issue in other orthographies and finding out how the structure of the writing system in question affects the way in which adults and children conceptualise phoneme–letter relationships. It might be that readers and spellers of consistent orthographies would not show equally strong sensitivity to phoneme sonority or onset-rime structure as readers of English, simply because they are less likely to employ these units in their processing than readers of English are, or because phonemes are more accessible to readers of consistent writing systems due to their regular relationship to letters. Alternatively, as Paulesu (2006) suggests, readers and spellers of consistent writing systems might also process larger phonological units and be sensitive to sonority.

The work on children's and adults' understanding of the relationship between the sounds in words and the letters that are used to represent them is of both theoretical and practical interest. In theoretical terms, it shows how inexperienced and expert readers and spellers process language in different types of tasks and under different task demands. In practical terms, it is possible to use the results to work out the best ways to present letter–sound relationships to young children. Furthermore, it is possible to see where young children's errors may come from; they could be motivated by sonority, for example. The results presented here also suggest that phonemic awareness and phoneme–based processing is not necessarily the only and ideal goal of literacy instruction. It seems that in orthographies with inconsistent phoneme–letter relationships using units larger than single phonemes is more common than has been previously thought.

Note

1 This work was supported by a postdoctoral grant from the Finnish Cultural Foundation. I am grateful to Amanda Mount, Stuart Bernstein, Marie Cassar, Meral Topcu, Cody Elam, Rochelle Evans and Suzanne Schechtman for their invaluable help with data collection. My special thanks go to Rebecca Treiman for her insightful comments on an earlier version of the manuscript.

References

Arduino, L., & Burani, C. (2004). 'Neighbourhood effects on nonword visual processing in a language with a shallow orthography'. *Journal of Psycholinguistic Research, 33*, 75–95.

Bradley, L., & Bryant, P. (1983). 'Categorizing sounds and learning to read. A causal connection'. *Nature, 301*, 419–421.

Bryant, P., Maclean, M., Bradley, L., & Crossland, J. (1990). 'Rhyme and alliteration, phoneme detection, and learning to read'. *Developmental Psychology, 26*, 429–438.

Caravolas, M. (2006) 'Refining the psycholinguistic grain size theory: effects of phonotactics and word formation on the availability of phonemes to pre-literate children'. *Developmental Science, 9*, 445–447.

Caravolas, M., Hulme, C., & Snowling, M. (2001). 'The foundations of spelling ability: Evidence from a 3-year longitudinal study'. *Journal of Memory and Language, 45,* 751–774.

Connelly, V. (2002). 'Graphophonemic awareness in adults after instruction in phonic generalisations'. *Learning and Instruction, 12,* 627–649.

Ehri, L. (1995). 'Phases of development in learning to read words by sight'. *Journal of Research in Reading, 18,* 116–125.

Ehri, L., & Soffer, A. (1999). 'Graphophonemic awareness: Development in elementary students'. *Scientific Studies of Reading, 3,* 1–30.

Ehri, L., & Wilce, E. (1980). 'The influence of orthography on readers' conceptualization of the phonemic structure of words'. *Applied Psycholinguistics, 1,* 371–385.

Ferreiro, E. & Teberosky, A. (1982). *Literacy before schooling.* Portsmouth, NH: Heinemann.

Frith, U. (1985). 'Beneath the surface of developmental dyslexia'. In K. Patterson, M. Coltheart and J. Marshall (eds). *Surface dyslexia* (pp'. 301–329). London: LEA.

Hatcher, P., Hulme, C., & Ellis, A. (1994). 'Ameliorating early reading failure by integrating the teaching of reading and phonological skills: The phonological linkage hypothesis'. *Child Development, 65,* 41–57.

Hayes, H., Treiman, R., & Kessler, B. (2006). 'Children use vowels to help them spell consonants'. *Journal of Experimental Child Psychology, 94,* 27–42.

Juel, C. (1988). 'Learning to read and write: A longitudinal study of 54 children from first through fourth grades'. *Journal of Educational Psychology, 4,* 437–447.

Kessler, B., & Treiman, R. (2001). 'Relationships between sounds and letters in English monosyllables'. *Journal of Memory and Language, 44,* 592–617.

Kessler, B., & Treiman, R. (2003). 'Is English spelling chaotic? Misconceptions concerning its irregularity'. *Reading Psychology, 24,* 267–289.

Larsen, S., Hammill, D., & Moats, L. (1999). *Test of Written Spelling (TWS-4)'.* Bloomington, MN: Pearson Assessment.

Lehtonen, A., & Treiman, R. (2007). 'Adults' knowledge of phoneme-letter relationships is phonology based and flexible'. *Applied Psycholinguistics, 28,* 95–114.

Lehtonen, A., & Treiman, R. (unpublished) 'The relationship between young children's phonemic awareness and knowledge of phoneme-letter relationships'.

Mann, V. (1986). 'Phonological awareness. The role of reading experience'. *Cognition, 24,* 65–92.

Mather, N., Bos, C., & Babur, N. (2001). 'Perceptions and knowledge of preservice and inservice teachers about early literacy instruction'. *Journal of Learning Disabilities, 34,* 472–483.

Moats, L. (1994). 'The missing foundation in teacher education: Knowledge of the structure of spoken and written language'. *Annals of Dyslexia, 44,* 81–102.

Morais, J., Cary, L, Alegria, J., & Bertelson, P. (1979). 'Does awareness of speech as a sequence of phones arise spontaneously?'. *Cognition, 7,* 323–331.

Morais, J., Bertelson, P., Cary, L., & Alegria, J. (1986). 'Literacy training and speech segmentation'. *Cognition, 24,* 45–64.

Paulesu, E. (2006). 'On the advantage of "shallow" orthographies: number and grain size of the orthographic units or consistency per se?' *Developmental Science, 9,* 443–444.

Paulesu., E., McCrory, E., Fazio, F., Menoncello, L., Brunswick, M., Cappa, S. *et al.* (2000). 'A cultural effect on brain function'. *Nature Neuroscience, 3,* 91–96.

Reece, C., & Treiman, R. (2001). 'Children's spelling of syllabic /r/ and of letter-name vowels: Broadening the study of spelling development'. *Applied Psycholinguistics, 22,* 139–165.

Scarborough, H., Ehri, L., Olson, R., & Fowler, A. (1998). 'The fate of phonemic awareness beyond the elementary school years'. *Scientific Studies of Reading, 2,* 115–142.

Scholes, R. (1993). 'In search of phonemic consciousness. A follow-up on Ehri'. In R. Scholes (ed.). *Literacy and Language Analysis* (pp'. 45–53). Hillsdale, NJ: LEA.

Serrano, F., Defior, S., & Martos, F. (2003). 'To be or not to be phonologically aware. A reflection about metalinguistic skills in teacher trainees'. In R. Joshi, C.K. Leong, & B. Kaczmarek (eds), *Literacy acquisition* (pp. 209–215). Amsterdam: IOS Press.

Stemberger, J. (1983). *Speech errors and theoretical phonology: A review*. Bloomington: Indiana University Linguistics Club.

Treiman, R. (1983). 'The structure of spoken syllables: Evidence from novel word games'. *Cognition, 15*, 49–74.

—— (1986). 'The division between onsets and rimes in English syllables'. *Journal of Memory and Language, 25*, 476–491.

Treiman, R., & Danis, C. (1988). 'Short-term memory errors for spoken syllables are affected by the linguistic structure of the syllables'. *Journal of Experimental Psychology: Learning, Memory, and Cognition, 14*, 145–152.

Treiman, R., & Broderick, V. (1998). 'What's in a name: Children's knowledge about the letters in their own names'. *Journal of Experimental Child Psychology, 70*, 97–116.

Treiman, R., Fowler, C., Gross, J., Berch, D., & Weatherston, S. (1995a). 'Syllable structure or word structure? Evidence for onset and rime units with disyllabic and trisyllabic stimuli'. *Journal of Memory and Language, 34*, 132–155.

Treiman, R., Zukowski, A., & Richmond-Welty, E. (1995b). 'What happened to the "n" of sink? Children's spellings of final consonant clusters'. *Cognition, 55*, 1–38.

Treiman, R., Tincoff, R., Rodriguez, K., Mouzaki, A., & Francis, D. J. (1998). 'The foundations of literacy: Learning the sounds of letters'. *Child Development, 69*, 1524–1540.

Treiman, R., Kessler, B., & Bourassa, D. (2001). 'Children's own names influence their spelling'. *Applied Psycholinguistics, 22*, 555–570.

Treiman, R., Kessler, B., Zevin, J., Bick, S., & Davis, M. (2006). 'Influence of consonantal context on the reading of vowels: Evidence from children'. *Journal of Experimental Child Psychology, 93*, 1–24.

Wimmer, H. (2006). 'Don't neglect reading fluency!' *Developmental Science, 9*, 447–448.

Wood, C. (2004). 'Do levels of pre-school alphabetic tuition affect the development of phonological awareness and early literacy?' *Educational Psychology, 24*, 3–11.

Ziegler, J., & Goswami, U. (2005). 'Reading acquisition, developmental dyslexia and skilled reading across languages: A psycholinguistic grain size theory'. *Psychological Bulletin, 31*, 3–29.

Chapter 10

Do bilingual beginning readers activate the grapheme–phoneme correspondences of their two languages when reading in one language?

Vincent Goetry, Régine Kolinsky and Philippe Mousty

Introduction

Examining whether bilinguals can selectively activate the linguistic knowledge of their two languages when processing spoken or written words in one is a central issue of psycholinguistic research. However, although numerous studies have examined reading-related processes in bilingual adults, there is to our knowledge no published study examining these questions in bilingual beginning readers. This is surprising given that classrooms worldwide continue to become more linguistically diverse, resulting in a growing number of children who learn to read and spell in a second language (L2), before (or without) being formally instructed in their native language (L1).

Moreover, phonological processing is a sine qua non of successful literacy development (see e.g. Share, 1995; NICHHD, 2000). Therefore, it is important to examine whether bilingual children activate the grapheme–phoneme correspondences (GPCs) of their two languages when reading in one, as well as to determine the factors that influence the relative activation of the two languages. These questions have major educational implications for the teaching of reading to second-language learners, as efficient phonological processing requires the inhibition of the phonological and orthographic representations of the irrelevant language; and lack of such inhibition may lead to inadequate and non-fluent reading.

Until the beginning of the 1990s, the dominant conception was that bilinguals had their knowledge of the two languages separated, and could access one language selectively in line with the task being performed (e.g. de Groot, 1992, 1993; de Groot & Kroll, 1997; Kroll, 1993; Paradis, 1997). Although several early studies were compatible with the *selective access hypothesis* for phonological and orthographic information (e.g. Durgunoglu & Roediger, 1987; Gerard & Scarborough, 1989; Soares & Grosjean, 1984; Scarborough *et al.*, 1984), recent studies show that bilinguals cannot totally inhibit the language irrelevant to the task, even when its activation is detrimental to performance (e.g. Wang *et al.*, 2003; see Brysbaert, 1998; Brysbaert & Dijkstra, 2006).

For example, based on studies showing that rare words take longer to identify when preceded by visually similar frequent words (e.g. *blur* preceded by *blue*) than when preceded by visually dissimilar words (Segui & Grainger, 1990), Bijeljac-Babic *et al.* (1997) asked French–English bilinguals and French monolinguals to perform a lexical decision task on French words (e.g. *amont*). The targets were preceded by masked primes of which some were visually similar and frequent words from French (e.g. *amant*) or from English (e.g. *among*). The results show that the bilinguals with high levels of proficiencies in English, but not the ones with lower levels of proficiencies, displayed an effect of inhibition of the same magnitude for targets preceded by English words as for targets preceded by French words; whereas the monolinguals only showed an effect of inhibition for the targets preceded by visually similar French words.

Relying on the observation that words with many orthographic neighbours (words of the same length differing by one letter) are identified faster than words with few neighbours (see Andrews, 1997, for a review), van Heuven *et al.* (1998) further showed that Dutch–English bilinguals were influenced by the items' density of orthographic neighbourhood in the other language in progressive demasking and general lexical decision tasks (see also Grainger & Dijkstra, 1992). According to the authors, only models that consider lexical access to be non-selective, but allow some control of the relative level of activation of the two languages, can account for these results.

Further studies examining the processing of homographic words (words sharing the same spelling but different pronunciations and meanings across languages) in lexical decision tasks also showed interference from the other language when such items were presented in mixed lists which contained also non-homographic words of the other language (de Groot *et al.*, 2000; Dijkstra *et al.*, 2000; Dijkstra *et al.*, 1998a). These studies also show that the size of the interference was correlated with the written frequency of the homographs in the other language, even when it was lower than its frequency in the target language.

Another study by de Bruijn *et al.* (2001), which combined the measure of reaction times and of evoked potentials, further suggests that the linguistic context in which a homographic word is presented does not inhibit the activation of the words' meaning in the other language. In this study, Dutch–English bilinguals performed a general lexical decision task on triplets of items (saying 'no' if any item was a pseudo-word in both languages), of which the first item was a non-homographic word from English (e.g. *house*) or from Dutch (e.g. *zaak*). This item was followed sometimes by a homographic word whose meaning was associated with the third item (e.g. *angel-heaven*; *angel* meaning *dart* in Dutch) or not (e.g. *angel-brush*). The main issue was to examine whether a Dutch first item would inhibit the English meaning of the (second) homographic word, thus affecting the effect of semantic priming on the third item. Significant priming effects were observed both on reaction times and on evoked potentials (on the N400, which would reflect semantic integration) when the third item was semantically related to the second, but the effect was not modulated by the linguistic context provided by the language of the first item. Thus, semantic priming effects were similar for *house-angel-heaven* and for *zaak-angel-heaven*. These results are compatible with a strong non-selective access view of bilingualism.

In the domain of phonological activation, several studies also support the non-selective access hypothesis. For example, Nas (1983) showed that in an English lexical decision task, Dutch–English bilinguals produced more errors and responded slower when rejecting pseudo-words of the target language which were homophonous to words of their other language (e.g. *snay*, which is pronounced like the Dutch word *snee* -*cut*-) than when rejecting non-homophonous pseudo-words (e.g. *rolm*). Such effects were reproduced by Dijkstra *et al.* (1999) on homophonic (but not homographic) Dutch–English words (e.g. *leaf*, homophonous of the Dutch word *lief* -*gentle*-).

Phonological activation has also been observed between languages that do not share the same script. Hence, Gollan *et al.* (1997) examined Hebrew–English and English–Hebrew bilinguals in a lexical decision task in their L2 or, in another experiment, in their L1. The targets were preceded by primes (presented for 50 msec) of which some were translations of the targets in the other language. The results show a robust effect of priming by translation, but this effect was bigger for the semantically and phonologically close pairs (cognates) than for the ones that were only semantically close (non-cognates). As Hebrew and English words never look alike orthographically, the authors suggest that the advantage observed for the cognate words results from inter-language phonological similarity. Moreover, an advantage for cognate words was observed only when the primes were presented in the participants' dominant language, and the targets in their non-dominant language.

In a bilingual adaptation of the Stroop paradigm, Tzelgov *et al.* (1996) asked Hebrew–English bilinguals to name the colour of visual words either in Hebrew or (in another experiment) in English. Some stimuli were pseudo-words of the language not required in the experiment but were homophonous of colour names of the target language. The results show that the Stroop effect was as important for the English pseudo-words homophonous to colour names in Hebrew (e.g. *kahol*, which is homophonous of the Hebrew word for blue) as for the colour names written in Hebrew, although the Stroop effect induced by the Hebrew pseudo-words homophonous to colour names in English was less strong and statistically less robust. The results from these two last studies seem to indicate that phonological coding within one script automatically activates phonological representations of words in another script, even when the two scripts are visually dissimilar.

The next issue concerns whether bilinguals who know two languages that share the same script automatically activate their grapho-phonological knowledge of both languages when processing one language. Doctor and Klein (1992) report results compatible with this hypothesis of multiple phonological coding. The authors observed that in a general lexical decision task, English–Afrikaans bilinguals produced more errors and took longer to accept homophonous heterographic words (e.g. *lake-lyk*) than to accept homographic heterophonous words (e.g. *kind*, meaning *child* in Afrikaans) or control words specific to either language. The authors account for these results by assuming that the presentation of a written word induces a search in parallel in both orthographic lexicon as well as a non-selective phonological coding using the GCPs of both languages. Homophonous heterographic words would activate a single phonological representation but two distinct orthographic representations, which would induce a process of (visual) verification, slow reaction times. This hypothesis is supported by post-hoc analyses showing that for the homophonous words, response latencies were faster for visually dissimilar pairs (e.g. *eye-aai*) than for visually similar pairs (e.g. *brick-briek*).

The studies by Brysbaert and colleagues (Brysbaert *et al.*, 1999; Van Wijnendaele & Brysbaert, 2002) provide more direct evidence for automatic activation of the GCPs of both languages in bilinguals. Using the masked priming paradigm, Brysbaert *et al.* (1999) presented Dutch–French bilinguals and French monolinguals with French targets preceded by masked primes (both primes and targets were presented for 57 msec), of which some were either pseudo-words homophonous with the targets if read with the French GPCs (e.g. *fain-faim*), or Dutch words homophonous with the targets if read with the Dutch GCPs (e.g. *koel-coule*). These two conditions were compared with control primes sharing the same degree of orthographic overlap with the targets as the homophonous primes (e.g. *faic-faim* and *doel-coule*, respectively).

The results show that for the *fain-faim* pairs, the phonological priming effect (advantage for the targets preceded by homophonous primes over targets preceded by non-homophonous primes) was of the same magnitude for the bilinguals and for the monolinguals. Conversely, for the *koel-coule* pairs, only the bilinguals showed a phonological priming effect, and this effect was of the same magnitude as the one observed for the French primes. From these results the authors conclude that the reading of words in the L2 seems to automatically activate the GCPs of the L1 as well. Moreover, these results were replicated with French–Dutch bilinguals (Van Wijnendaele & Brysbaert, 2002), which suggests that the reading of words in the L1 also automatically activates the GCPs of the L2. Thus, the processing of visual words would activate all the GCPs compatible with the stimuli, irrespective of language and linguistic dominance. Brysbaert *et al.* (1999) note that these results do not exclude the intervention of inhibition processes, which would allow avoiding confusions between languages (see de Bruijn *et al.*, 2001; Dijkstra & van Heuven, 2002). However, such processes would occur only after an initial phase of non-selective activation of all the GCPs compatible with the stimuli.

The hypothesis of non-selective access to the GCPs of both languages would lead one to predict that inconsistent GCPs between languages should induce similar effects as the consistency effects observed in monolinguals with intra-language inconsistent GCPs, i.e. the fact that sequences with many 'enemies' (e.g. –*ead*, pronounced differently in *bead* and *head*) induce slower reaction times than sequences with few 'enemies' (see e.g. Jared, 1997; Peereman & Content, 1997).

To examine whether consistency effects generalize across languages in bilinguals, Jared and Kroll (2001) asked English–French and French–English bilinguals to read words with rimes either specific to English and consistent (e.g. *bump*, which has no enemy), specific to English but inconsistent (e.g. *bead*, which has enemies like *head*), or homographic between English and French and inconsistent across languages (e.g. *bait*, which has no enemy in English but enemies in French like *fait*). In all experiments, the procedure consisted in presenting a first block of English words with all three types of items, followed by a block of French, followed by a second block of English words (different from those of the first block) containing all types of items.

The results show that for the first block of English words, the French–English bilinguals, but not the English–French bilinguals, produced more errors (but not longer reaction times) to the words with enemies in French than for the words with no enemies. Conversely, both groups produced more errors and longer reaction times for the words with enemies in English than for the words with no enemies. According to Jared and Kroll (2001), these results show that the GCPs of English are activated to a greater extent than the French GCPs in all groups, even though the French GCPs are also activated for the group for which it is the dominant language.

For the second block of English words, the English–French bilinguals with high levels of proficiency in French took longer to read the words with French enemies than to read the words with no enemies. For the French–English bilinguals, the participants schooled in a francophone university, but not those schooled in an English-speaking one, produced longer reaction times and slightly more errors for the words with French enemies than for the words with no enemies. To account for these results, the authors suggest that only the French–English bilinguals schooled in an English-speaking university would be able to inhibit their knowledge of the French GCPs when reading in English. The English–French bilinguals would not have adopted such a strategy because they would not be aware of the impact of their knowledge of French on their English reading.

Jared and Szucs (2002) further observed that French–English bilinguals, but not English–French bilinguals, took longer and made more errors on homographic het-erophonous non cognate words of English and French (e.g. *coin*, meaning *corner* in French) than on English-specific words. On the basis of the results of these two last studies, Jared and Szucs (2002) suggest that the GCPs of the language irrelevant for the task are too weakly activated to induce noticeable interferences on participants' performance, except when this language is their dominant language and when the inconsistencies across language regard entire words (homographs).

This conclusion seems contradictory with the strong hypothesis of non-selective access proposed by Doctor and Klein (1992) as well as by Brysbaert and colleagues (Brysbaert *et al.*, 1999; Van Wijnendaele & Brysbaert, 2002). One factor that could account for this apparent discrepancy lies in the different materials exploited in the two sets of studies. Indeed, Jared and colleagues used homographic sequences (rimes or whole words), although Brysbaert and colleagues used heterographic sequences with graphemes specific to the language irrelevant for the task to be performed (see p. 180 for a more detailed description of these materials). Other studies have indeed showed that the make-up of the stimuli influences the relative degree of activation of the two languages in bilinguals. Hence, Grainger and Beauvillain (1987) showed that, in a general lexical decision task, French–English bilinguals produced longer reaction times for the second member of 'mixed' pairs displaying one word of each language (e.g. *rule* after *pont*) than for 'pure' pairs displaying only English words (e. g. *rule* after *sand*), except when the second item displayed specific orthographic cues to that language (e.g. *white* after *pont*, where *wh-* never occurs in French but is fre-quent in English). Such influence of orthographic specificity was also observed by Beauvillain (1989, 1992) when the specific and non-specific words of the two lan-guages were matched for frequency distributions. She indeed showed that the nega-tive regression slopes between word frequencies and reaction times were stronger for the non-specific than for the specific words. This pattern of results is compatible with the notion that non-specific words are selected within a cohort of words from both languages, whereas specific words are selected from a cohort from one language (see also Grainger, 1993, for a more detailed discussion and a reinterpretation of previous results based on the notion of specificity).

The dominant model proposed to account for written word identification in adult bilinguals is the Bilingual Interactive Activation model (BIA, see Dijkstra *et al.*, 1998b). The BIA is an adaptation of the Interactive Activation model of McClelland and Rumelhart (1981) to the bilingual situation. Several layers of units represent visual features, letters and words. In bilinguals, both lexicons are integrated into a unitary system, so that bottom-up activation induces the activation of words in the two languages. The original model also comprised a supra-lexical layer with 'language nodes', which would collect the activation of all words from that language and inhibit word activation in the other language via top-down connections. In the more recent version of the model, the 'language nodes' have been replaced by decisional and strategic processes occurring outside the recognition system (BIA+, Dijkstra & van Heuven, 2002), which could account for activation and inhibition processes driven by words' orthographic cues to language (specific/typical graphemes). However, as stated by Dijkstra & van Heuven (2002), 'we still ignore how these activation and inhibition processes which intervene in adults develop in children'.

The present study aimed at examining whether bilingual children activate the GPCs of their non-dominant reading language (in the present study, their L1) when naming words in their dominant reading language (L2), and explored whether such activation is influenced by the orthographic characteristics of the presented items. Hence, we compared these children's performances to those of monolinguals in a reading task which involved items with inconsistent GCPs across languages (e.g. *'an'*, which is routinely pronounced /ã/ in French but /an/ in Dutch).

To examine these questions, French-native children schooled in Dutch and Dutch-native children schooled in French were compared to Dutch and French mono-linguals, respectively. These four groups of children were asked to perform a naming task that included three types of items displaying inconsistent GCPs across languages: (1) non-cognate heterographic homographs (words that are spelled identically but have different pronunciations and meanings in the two languages) with cross-linguistically inconsistent GPCs (e.g. *vent*, which is pronounced /vã/ and means *wind* in French, but is pronounced /vEnt/ and means *boy* in Dutch); (2) matched words specific to French with inconsistent GPCs (e.g. *dent*, which is pronounced /dã/ and means *tooth* in French, but corresponds to the pseudo-word /dEnt/ in Dutch); (3) matched Dutch-specific words with inconsistent GPCs (*went*, which is pronounced /wEnt/ and means *(you) get used* in Dutch, but corresponds to the pseudo-word /wã/ in French). The materials also contained matched (control) pseudo-words with consistent GPCs across languages (*mele*, corresponding to the pseudo-word /mel(ə)/ in both French and Dutch).

The strong hypothesis of non-selective access would lead one to predict that the bilinguals should produce more errors and longer reaction times than the mono-linguals for the three types of items with inconsistent GCPs, but not for the pseudo-words with consistent GCPs. Conversely, under the hypothesis of selective access, bilinguals should not activate the GCPs of their irrelevant language to a sufficient extent to produce noticeable interference on their reading performance in the target language.

In post-hoc analyses examining the factors that could account for the observed pattern of results, the additional factor of typicality was considered since half of the presented Dutch-specific words contained graphemes typical in Dutch but exceptional in French ('z', 'w', 'k'), whereas none of the French-specific words contained graphemes typical to French.

Method

Forty-five participants (19 Dutch-native bilinguals schooled in French, henceforth DfB, and 26 French-native bilinguals schooled in Dutch, henceforth, FdB) were considered in the study. It is worth highlighting that these bilinguals were exclusively schooled in their L2 and had never been formally exposed to written language in their L1. Informal questionnaires presented to these children showed that some had acquired reading knowledge in their L1 at home with parents or siblings. Therefore, all bilinguals were presented with a reading pre-test in their L1, which contained isolated graphemes specific to that language (e.g. *eau* or *ain* in French, *ij* or *ei* in Dutch) or inconsistent graphemes between languages (e.g. *ui*, pronounced /wi/ in French but /æy/ in Dutch), as well as 22 words containing such graphemes. The French words were selected from NOVLEX (Lambert & Chesnet, 2001) and the Dutch words from *Wenselijke woordenschat en feitelijke frequenties* (Krom, 1990).

The results on these tests show great individual differences, with bi-modal distribution of the scores, both for the individual graphemes and for the words, which were highly correlated, for the DfB, $r = .88$; for the FdB, $r = .85$ (see Figure 10.1 for the distributions of children according to their word readings).

These results show that some bilinguals were not familiar with the graphemes and words of their native language (7 DfB, 11 FdB), while others were (12 DfB, 15 FdB). Only the results of these two last subgroups were considered in further analyses. However, the results of 4 of the FdB could not be considered because they were not presented with the homographs and related items in their L1 due to absenteeism or lack of time. Therefore, only the results of 12 DfB and 11 FdB were considered in further analyses. Their average percentage of correct responses for the specific graphemes of their L1 were 68 and 70 per cent, and 90 and 88 per cent for the related words, respectively.

The 11 FdB were compared to 28 Dutch monolinguals (henceforth, DM), and the 12 DfB were compared to 30 French monolinguals (henceforth, FM). The age and vocabulary levels of the four groups are displayed in Table 10.1. Analyses conducted on vocabulary scores in both languages, taking groups into account (monolinguals, bilinguals), did not reveal any significant difference between groups.

The four groups of children were asked to perform a naming task that included four types of items: (1) non-cognate heterographic homographs (words that are spelled identically but have different pronunciations and meanings in the two languages) with cross-linguistically inconsistent GCPs (e.g. *vent*, see p.168 for the pronunciation of the examples in both languages); (2) matched words specific to French with inconsistent GPCs (e.g. *dent*); (3) matched Dutch-specific words with

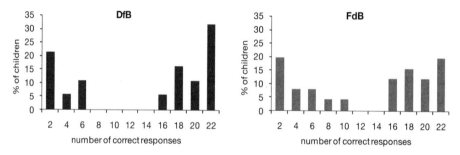

Figure 10.1 Distribution of children according to the number of correctly read words in the L1

Table 10.1 Age and vocabulary scores (standard deviations) of the children considered in the present study.

	FM	DfB	DM	FdB
Mean age	7,7	7,8	7,11	7,9
Minimum	7,5	7,5	7,3	7,3
Maximum	8,5	8,1	8,2	8,5
Vocabulary: CR (%)				
French	91,2 (3,9)	84,3 (6,8)	–	89,1 (4,6)
Dutch	–	84,2 (10,5)	95,4 (2,5)	84,3 (9,4)

inconsistent GPCs (e.g. *went*); (4) matched (control) pseudo-words with consistent GPCs across languages (e.g. *mele*). The pseudo-words were carefully selected not to look more familiar in one language than in the other, i.e. half of them ended in a consonant (typical to Dutch) and the other half ended in a vowel (typical to French).

Given the difficulty of finding homographic items in French and Dutch, we were not able to manipulate the frequency of the presented homographs in the two languages. However, the bilinguals were presented in their L1 with those items, as well as with the words specific to the L1 and the pseudo-words, which allowed us to discard a posteriori the homographs which did not elicit enough correct identification in this language.

Each child was tested individually in several sessions of approximately 30 minutes each, which were separated by at least one day. The tests reported in this chapter formed part of a larger battery that included other tests. Both the bilinguals and the monolinguals were instructed that they would have to read words in their instruction language as well as non-lexical items ('Chinese words') as fast as possible and without mistakes.

The items were presented in the middle of the screen of a computer (Macintosh Powerbook 180, font Helvetica size 48). Each item was preceded by a visual prompt (a cross in the middle of the screen, font Helvetica size 96) and by an auditory signal ('beep'). The item then appeared in the middle of the screen, activating the timing device, which stopped as soon as the child pronounced the word into a head-microphone (Shure WH20XLR). The item disappeared when the child started to answer. The experimenter then pressed a button to elicit the next item.

The pre-tests delivered to the bilinguals, as well as the reading of the homographs and related items in the L1, were presented at least one week after the reading of the homographs and related items in the L2. After asking a few question on the knowledge and use of reading materials in the L1, the experimenter presented the pre-tests and (when appropriate) the homographs and related items in the L1.

Results and discussion

Analyses of variance (ANOVAs) were performed on participants and items. Although all significant effects will be reported in the analyses, only the consistent effects by participants and by items will be further considered and discussed, given the small sample sizes and number of items considered in the present study.

Comparison of reading in the L1 and L2

Given the limited and informal contact of the bilinguals with reading materials in their L1, it is not surprising that homographs induced less correct responses (on average, 74 per cent), and longer reaction times (on average, 1293 msec) in this language than in their L2 (on average, 83 per cent and 962 msec). These differences are confirmed in the analyses of variance (henceforth, ANOVAs) performed by subjects and by items, which considered the factors language of reading (L1, L2) and groups (DfB, FdB), and show a significant effect of reading language for correct responses, $F1(1, 21) = 5.69$, $p < .05$; $F2(1, 11) = 4.19$, $p = .065$, for latencies, $F1(1, 18) = 9.48$, $p < .01$; $F2(1, 11) = 9.77$, $p < .01$. The analyses on correct responses also show a significant effect of group, $F1(1, 21) = 4.91$, $p < .05$; $F2(1, 11) = 6.25$, $p < .05$, because the DfB provided less correct answers (74 per cent) than the FdB (83 per cent). The language by group interaction is not significant, $F1$ and $F2 > 1$ in both cases.

To make sure that the homographs presented in the L2 would be susceptible to activate the corresponding phonological representations in the L1, we discarded the items that induced less than 75 per cent of correct responses in the L1. This resulted in the discarding of four homographs for the DfB (*geler, indien, lente, vent*), and of four homographs for the FdB (*geler, lange, lente, vent*). The corresponding language–specific words, as well as the matched pseudo-words, were also discarded.

The ANOVAs conducted on the remaining items, considering language (L1, L2) and groups (DfB, FdB), show that reading language is no longer significant, $F1$ and $F2 \leq 1$. However, the homographs are still read faster in the L2 (945 msec) than in the L1 (1244 msec), $F1(1, 18) = 8.16$, $p = .01$; $F2(1, 7) = 7.32$, $p < .05$. This corroborates the fact that the bilinguals have greater experience with reading in their L2, which is formally taught at school, than in their L1, which is informally acquired at home.

Reading in the L2: French

Correct responses and reaction times are presented in Figure 10.2, separately for the DfB and for the FM. As can be seen, the bilinguals seem to produce less correct responses for all the items susceptible to activate competing GPCs in the two languages, namely the homographs, the French words, and the Dutch words, but not for the pseudo-words.

Analysis of correct responses. The ANOVAs on correct responses, considering the type of items (homographs, L1 words, L2 words, pseudo-words) and the groups (DfB, FM), confirm this pattern of results, by showing a significant effect of item type, $F1(3, 120) = 54.04$, $p < .0001$; $F2(3, 28) = 10.73$, $p < .0001$, of groups, $F1(1, 40) = 5.06$, $p < .05$; $F2(1, 28) = 14.16$, $p < .001$, as well as an interaction between the two factors, $F1(3, 120) = 2.94$, $p < .05$; $F2(3, 28) = 2.3$, $p < .08$.

Further analysis of this interaction shows that the effect of group is significant for the three types of items susceptible to activate competing GPCs in the two languages, namely the Dutch words, $F1(1, 40) = 4.69$, $p < .05$; $F2(1, 7) = 7.76$, $p < .05$, the French words, $F1(1, 40) = 3.62$, $p = .064$; $F2(1, 7) = 19.4$, $p < .005$; and the homographs, although the effect is only significant by participants, $F1(1, 40) = 5.88$, $p < .025$; $F2(1, 7) = 2.84$, $p \approx .1$. Conversely, no group effect is observed for the pseudo-words, $F1$ and $F2 < 1$.

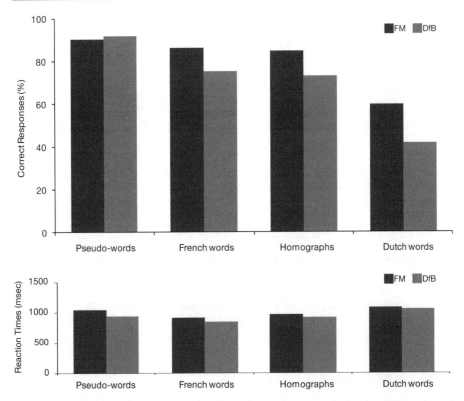

Figure 10.2 Percentages of correct responses and reaction times for the bilinguals and monolinguals schooled in French

Reaction time analysis. The effect of item type is significant in the analysis by participants, $F1(3, 114) = 8.27$, $p < .0001$; $F2 > 1$. As can be seen on Figure 10.2, this results from the fact that French lexical items (French words and homographs) are read faster than non-lexical items (Dutch words and pseudo-words) $F1(1, 114) = 17.26$; $p < .0001$. The effect of group is significant by items, $F1 < 1$; $F2(1, 28) = 6.41$, $p < .025$. The interaction is not significant $F1 < 1$; $F2(3, 28) = 2.09$, $p > .1$.

Error analysis. To examine whether the DfB were using the Dutch GPCs when reading in French, we examined whether these children were using French GPCs (e.g. /bã/ for *dans*), Dutch GCPs (e.g. /bans/ for *dans*), or 'mixed' GCPs (e.g. /bãs/ for *dans*) when misreading the Dutch words and the homographs. The distributions presented in Figure 10.3 show that the bilinguals used much more often the Dutch GPCs for these two types of items than the FM. This is confirmed by analyses showing that the distributions of errors observed among the monolinguals and the bilinguals differ significantly, both for the homographs, $\chi^2(2, N = 59) = 11.42$, $p < .005$ and for the Dutch words $\chi^2(2, N = 149) = 12.23$, $p < .005$. The fact that the FM also produced errors witnessing the use of 'Dutch GCPs' can be explained by the fact that all errors consisting in reading the final consonant of the concerned items (namely the homographs *dit, pas* and *mes,* and the related items) were classified as errors witnessing the use of 'Dutch GCPs'.

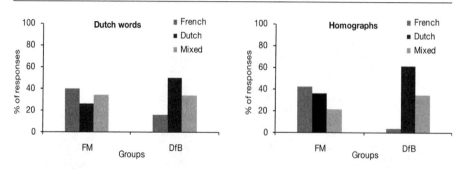

Figure 10.3 Distributions of errors according to the nature of the GCPs for monolinguals and bilinguals schooled in French

In summary, the results observed for French suggest that the Dutch-native bilinguals schooled in French (DfB) activated the GPC of Dutch when reading in French. Indeed, these children produced more errors than the French monolinguals (FM) for all the items susceptible to activate GPC of the two languages, namely the Dutch words, the French words and to a lesser extent the homographs; but not for the pseudo-words containing neutral GPCs. This interpretation is validated by the qualitative analysis showing that the bilinguals activated the GPCs of Dutch when reading in French, at least for the homographs and for the Dutch words.

Reading in the L2: Dutch

As can be seen in Figure 10.4, both the monolinguals and the bilinguals produced similar rates of correct responses and latencies for all types of items.

Analysis of correct responses. The analyses considering item type (homographs, Dutch words, French words, pseudo-words) and groups (DfB, Dm) show an inconsistent effect of item type, $F1(3, 108) = 5.65$, $p < .0025$, $F2 < 1$. The effect of group is not significant $F1$ and $F2 < 1$, but interacts significantly with the type of items by participants, $F1(3, 108) = 2.93$, $p < .05$; $F2 \cong 1$. This interaction resulted from higher rates of correct responses in the DM than in the FdB for the Dutch words $F1(1, 36) = 6.34$, $p < .025$, but not for the other item types (for the homographs, $F1(1, 36) = 2.21$, $p > .1$; for the pseudo-words, $F1 \cong 1$).

Reaction time analysis. The effect of item type is significant by participants, $F1(3, 108) = 5.65$, $p < .005$; $F2 > .05$, because the pseudo-words induce longer latencies than the three other types of items. Neither the effect of group nor the interaction between groups and item types is significant, $F1$ and $F2 > .05$; $F1$ and $F2 \cong 1$, respectively.

Error analysis. The qualitative analyses could not be conducted because the number of produced errors was too small. Indeed, for the homographs, the bilinguals produced 9 errors (among which one consisted in reading the word in French and 4 saw the use of both the French and the Dutch GCPs) and the monolinguals produced 13 errors. For the Dutch words, the bilinguals produced 8 errors (which all saw the use of the Dutch GCPs and consisted of naming a word visually similar to the target word), and the monolinguals produced 3 errors. Finally, for the French words, the bilinguals produced 12 errors (including four participants reading the word in French), and the monolinguals produced 26 errors.

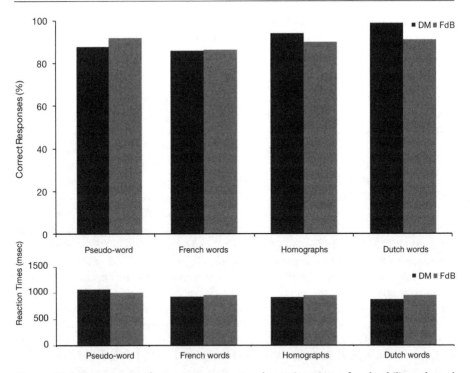

Figure 10.4 Percentages of correct responses and reaction times for the bilinguals and monolinguals schooled in Dutch

To summarize, the results of the French-native bilinguals schooled in Dutch (FdB) suggest that these children do not seem to activate the French GCPs to a sufficient extent to induce noticeable interference when reading in Dutch (except for the marginal effect observed for the Dutch words), even when they are presented with French. Thus, in contrast to the DfB, the FdB seem to read words from their L1 as pseudo-words in their L2 (e.g. /sans/ instead of /sã/ for *sans*, meaning *without*), although they know the French pronunciation of these words (cf. pre-tests in the L1, and reading of the items with inconsistent GCPs in the L1).

Several factors could account for the observed difference between the two groups of bilinguals. First, it is possible that the French words presented in the present study were less frequent and/or contained less frequent GCPs than the Dutch words. This hypothesis can be examined further since both groups of bilinguals read all items with inconsistent GCPs across languages in their two languages. The results do not corroborate the hypothesis that the French words were less frequent than the Dutch words, since the FdB produced virtually as many correct responses when they were reading the French words as such in their native language (86 per cent) as when they were reading these words as pseudo-words in Dutch (85 per cent), whereas the DfB produced more correct responses for the Dutch words when reading these words as such in Dutch (74 per cent) than when reading them as pseudo-words in French (42 per cent).

Another factor that could account for the contrasting pattern of results observed in the two groups of bilinguals is the graphemic make-up of the Dutch words. Half of these items contained graphemes that occur frequently in Dutch but not in French, namely 'k', 'z' and 'w'; whereas none of the French words contained graphemes specific and/or typical to that language. If the graphemes typical to Dutch induced the bilinguals schooled in French to activate the Dutch GPCs when reading in French, we could expect that the Dutch words with such graphemes (namely *zout, went, kans, beker, inzien, kende*) led to fewer correct responses and slower latencies than the words that did not contain such graphemes (namely *pit, glas, bange, bes, das, bent*). We examined this hypothesis by comparing the response rates and latencies for these two subgroups of items in the DfB and in the FM (see Figure 10.5).

As can be seen, the bilinguals do not produce more errors for the words containing graphemes typical to Dutch than for the other words. However, even though both groups produce slower latencies for the words containing typical graphemes than for the other words, the difference is more marked in the bilinguals than in the monolinguals. The reliability of this difference was examined in ANOVAs considering the factors typicality (typical, others) and groups (FM, DfB), which showed a significant effect of typicality $F1(1, 28) = 19.55$, $p < .0001$; $F2(1, 10) = 9.44$, $p < .025$, as well as, by participants only, a significant interaction $F1(1, 28) = 7,51$, $p < .01$; $F2(1, 10) = 1.5$, $p > .1$. Further decomposition of this interaction showed that the effect of group was marginally significant for the words containing typical graphemes, $F1(1, 28) = 3.79$, $p = .06$, but not for the other words $F < 1$. The statistical weakness of these results are probably related to the limited number of considered observations (the results of 7 monolinguals and of 5 bilinguals were discarded because they comprised an empty cell, such that the statistical analyses considered the results of 23 FM and only 7 DfB).

In any case, these results are consistent with the hypothesis that in the bilinguals words containing typical graphemes activated the knowledge of the Dutch GCPs to a greater extent than the words with no typical graphemes. Such knowledge would subsequently need to be inhibited such that the reading can be performed using the knowledge of the French GPCs, hence the longer latencies for the words with typical graphemes than for the other words.

Discussion

This study aimed at examining whether bilinguals schooled in their second language activate their knowledge of the GPCs of both languages when reading in their dominant reading language (in the present study, their L2).

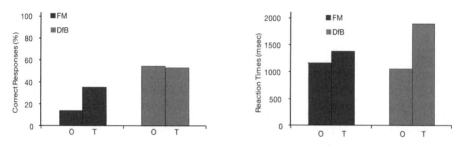

Figure 10.5 Percentages of errors consisting in reading the Dutch words for the monolinguals and bilinguals schooled in French

The two groups of bilinguals examined in this study showed discrepant results: although the Dutch-native bilinguals schooled in French (DfB) seemed to activate their knowledge of Dutch when reading in French, the French-native bilinguals schooled in Dutch (FdB) showed no sign of French activation when reading in Dutch.

To account for this difference, we hypothesized that the typical graphemes displayed by some of the Dutch words ('k', 'z', 'w') presented to both groups induced interference from Dutch in the DfB, but adequate inhibition (of French) in the FdB. As such, these results are consistent with those of other studies showing that the composition of the materials presented to the participants influences the relative levels of activation of the two languages (e.g. Beauvillain & Grainger, 1987; Dijkstra et al., 1999, 2000; van Heuven et al., 1998). Our results further suggest that, in the children examined in the present study, the influence of graphemic typicality is greater than that of lexicality, as the Dutch words displaying typical graphemes seem to have led the DfB to activate their knowledge of the Dutch GCPs, whereas the FdB did not seem to activate strongly their knowledge of the French GCPs despite the presence of words from that language in the presented material. Further studies manipulating typicality and lexicality orthogonally should be conducted to examine this issue more closely.

It is interesting to observe that in studies using homographs for examining lexico-semantic knowledge in adult bilinguals, homography does not induce noticeable effects on performance (e.g. Gerard & Scarborough, 1989; Dijkstra et al., 1998; de Groot et al., 2000) unless non-homograhic words of the other language are presented (Dijkstra et al., 1998; de Groot et al., 2000; but see De Moor, 1998; Van Heste, 1999; de Bruijn et al., 2001) or unless the participants are explicitly told that words from the two languages will be presented (Beauvillain & Grainger, 1987). Although non-homographic words of the competing language are susceptible to display specific and/or typical graphemes, homographs, by definition, never contain specific graphemic sequences, and probably do not display typical sequences either.

A similar contrast seems to characterize the few studies examining the organization of grapho-phonological knowledge in bilingual adults. Indeed, the study by Jared & Kroll (2001) used heterophonic homographic sequences (inconsistent between languages). In contrast, the studies conducted by Brysbaert and collaborators (Brysbaert et al., 1999; Van Wijnendaele & Brysbaert, 2002), which suggest that bilinguals activate all the GCPs compatible with the presented stimuli irrespective of the language they belong to, used heterographic homophonous sequences which displayed numerous graphemic sequences specific or typical to Dutch. Indeed, it can be noted that in these studies, about one-third of the primes displayed an orthographically doubled vowel (such doubling never occurs in French), and another third displayed the grapheme 'oe', which is exceptional in French. If we also consider that 'k', 'z' and 'w' are typical to Dutch, only 20 per cent of the primes displayed neither specific nor typical Dutch graphemes. Although it is not likely that such characteristics have induced reading strategies consisting in reading the primes in Dutch and the targets in French (since the primes were presented only for 57 msec and were not recognized), it is possible that such graphemic make-up of the primes have induced some (progressive) activation of the GPCs of Dutch.

The task presented to our bilingual children displayed both homographs and words with graphemic sequences typical to Dutch. Like the English–French bilinguals examined by Jared and Kroll (2001) who did not show interferences between languages before having read French words (and having been invited to read these words as such), the French–Dutch bilinguals examined in the present study, who were not presented with graphemic sequences typical to French (like 'eau') and susceptible to activate their knowledge of the French GCPs, did not show noticeable inference from French when reading in Dutch. Conversely, like the English–French bilinguals examined by Jared and Kroll (2001) after they had read French words, and like the Dutch–French bilinguals examined by Brysbaert et al. (1999), who were presented with primes displaying graphemes specific or typical to Dutch, the Dutch–French bilinguals examined in the present study, who were presented with graphemes typical to Dutch, showed interference from Dutch for these words as well as for homographic words when asked to read them in French.

In daily life, bilinguals rarely switch from one language to the other when reading. The specificity of some GCPs, and the typicality of others, may activate the language unit which corresponds to the language of the written words (cf. the BIA and BIA+ models of word recognition in bilinguals, Dijkstra & van Heuven, 2002). This unit would then inhibit the knowledge of the GCPs (as well as lexical knowledge) of the irrelevant language, which would allow the system to avoid activating the GCPs of the other language.

Conclusion

This study suggests that bilingual beginning readers are able to inhibit their knowledge of the GCPs of their non-dominant reading language when asked to read in their dominant reading language, unless the items display graphemic sequences typical to the non-dominant language. In this respect, the factor of graphemic typicality seems to play a more important role than lexicality in the activation of the GCPs of the competing language. One may speculate that developing bilingual readers quickly develop some sensitivity to the typical and specific graphemes of their two languages, such that language interferences are limited, and later on perhaps cancelled (cf. Beauvillain & Grainger, 1987), by inhibition processes. If it is the case that sensitivity to graphemic typicality/specificity is the central mechanism that prevents language interference in bilingual readers, we would expect to observe greater sensitivity to such graphemes in faster/better bilingual readers than in slower/poorer ones. Although our limited sample size did not allow us to examine subgroup performances, studies manipulating reading speeds/levels and graphemic typicality/specificity orthogonally should be conducted to further examine this hypothesis.

References

Andrews, S. (1997). 'The role of orthographic similarity in lexical retrieval: Resolving neighborhood conflicts'. *Psychonomic Bulletin & Review, 4,* 439–461.

Beauvillain, C. (1989). 'Traitement lexical et bilinguisme'. *Le Lexique, 8,* 51–64.

—— (1992). 'Orthographic and lexical constraints in bilingual word recognition'. In R.J. Harris (ed.), *Cognitive processing in bilinguals* (pp. 221–235). Amsterdam: Elsevier.

Beauvillain, C. & Grainger, J. (1987). 'Accessing interlingual homographs: Some limitations of a language-selective access'. *Journal of Memory and Language, 26,* 658–672.

Bijeljac-Babic, R., Biardeau, A., & Grainger, J. (1997). 'Masked orthographic priming in bilingual word recognition'. *Memory & Cognition, 25,* 447–457.

Brysbaert, M. (1998). 'Word recognition in bilinguals: Evidence against the existence of two separate lexicons'. *Psychologica Belgica, 38,* 163–175.

Brysbaert, M. & Dijkstra, T. (2006). 'Changing views on word recognition in bilinguals'. In J. Morais & G. d'Ydewalle (eds), *Bilingualism and second language acquisition.* Brussels: KVAB.

Brysbaert, M., Van Dijck, G., & Van de Poel, M. (1999). 'Visual word recognition in bilinguals: Evidence from masked phonological priming'. *Journal of Experimental Psychology-Human Perception and Performance, 25,* 137–148.

De Bruijn, E., Dijkstra, T., Chwilla, D., & Schriefers, H. (2001). 'Language context effects on interlingual homograph recognition: Evidence from event-related potentials and response times in semantic priming'. *Bilingualism: Language and Cognition, 4,* 155–168.

De Groot, A. (1992). 'Bilingual lexical representation: A closer look at conceptual representations'. In R. Frost & L. Katz (eds), *Orthography, phonology, morphology, and meaning* (pp. 389–412). Amsterdam: North Holland.

—— (1993). 'Word-type effects in bilingual processing tasks. Support for a mixed-representational system'. In R. Schreuder & B. Weltens (eds), *The bilingual lexicon* (pp. 27–52). Amsterdam/Philadelphia: John Benjamins.

De Groot, A., & Kroll, J.F. (1997). *Tutorials in bilingualism: Psycholinguistic perspectives.* Mahwah, NJ: LEA.

De Groot, A.M.B., Delmaar, P., & Lupker, S.J. (2000). 'The processing of interlexical homographs in translation recognition and lexical decision: Support for non-selective access to bilingual memory'. *Quarterly Journal of Experimental Psychology Section a-Human Experimental Psychology, 53,* 397–428.

De Moor, W. (1998). *Visual word recognition in bilinguals.* Unpublished Master's thesis, University of Ghent, Belgium.

Dijkstra, T., & van Heuven, W. (2002). 'The architecture of the bilingual word recognition system: From indentification to decision'. *Bilingualism: Language and Cognition, 5,* 175–197.

Dijkstra, T., van Heuven, W.J.B., & Grainger, J. (1998a). 'Simulating cross-language competition with the bilingual interactive activation model'. *Psychologica Belgica, 38,* 177–196.

Dijkstra, T., van Jaarsveld, H., & Ter Brinke, S. (1998b). 'Interlingual homograph recognition: Effects of tasks demands and language intermixing'. *Bilingualism: Language and Cognition, 1,* 51–66.

Dijkstra, T., Grainger, J., & van Heuven, W. (1999). 'Recognition of cognates and interlingual homographs: The neglected role of phonology'. *Journal of Memory and Language, 41,* 496–518.

Dijkstra, T., Timmermans, M., & Schriefers, H. (2000). 'On being blinded by your other language: Effects of task demands on interlingual homograph recognition'. *Journal of Memory and Language, 42,* 445–464.

Doctor, E.A., & Klein, D. (1992). 'Phonological processing in bilingual word recognition'. In R.J. Harris (ed.), *Cognitive processing in bilinguals* (pp. 237–252). Amsterdam: Elsevier.

Durgunoglu, A.Y., & Roediger III, H.L. (1987). 'Test differences in accessing bilingual memory'. *Journal of Memory and Language, 26,* 377–391.

Gerard, L.D., & Scarborough, D.L. (1989). 'Language-specific lexical access of homographs by bilinguals'. *Journal of Experimental Psychology-Learning Memory and Cognition, 15,* 305–315.

Gollan, T.H., Forster, K.I., & Frost, R. (1997). 'Translation priming with different scripts: Masked priming with cognates and noncognates in Hebrew–English bilinguals'. *Journal of Experimental Psychology-Learning Memory and Cognition, 23*, 1122–1139.

Grainger, J. (1993). 'Visual word recognition in bilinguals'. In R. Schreuder & B. Weltens (eds), *The bilingual lexicon* (pp. 11–26). Amsterdam/Philadelphia: Benjamins.

Grainger, J., & Beauvillain, C. (1987). 'Language blocking and lexical access in bilinguals'. *Quarterly Journal of Experimental Psychology Section a-Human Experimental Psychology, 39*, 295–319.

Grainger, J., & Dijkstra, A. (1992). 'On the representation and use of language information in bilinguals'. In R.J. Harris (ed.), *Cognitive processing in bilinguals* (pp. 207–220). Amsterdam: Elsevier.

Jared, D. (1997). 'Evidence that strategy effects in word naming reflect changes in output timing rather than changes in processing route'. *Journal of Experimental Psychology: Learning, Memory, and Cognition, 23*, 1424–1438.

Jared, D., & Kroll, J.F. (2001). 'Do bilinguals activate phonological representations in one or both of their languages when naming words?' *Journal of Memory and Language, 44*, 2–31.

Jared, D., & Szucs, C. (2002). 'Phonological activation in bilinguals: Evidence from interlingual homograph naming'. *Bilingualism: Language and Cognition, 5*, 225–239.

Kroll, J.F. (1993). 'Accessing conceptual representations for words in a second language'. In R. Schreuder & B. Weltens (eds), *The bilingual lexicon. Studies in bilingualism, Vol. 6.* (pp. 53–81). Amsterdam: John Benjamins.

Krom, R.S.H. (1990). *Wenselijke woordenschat en feitelijke frequenties'. De nieuwe streeflijst woordenschat getrancheerd naar verwervingsleeftijd en voorzien van frequentiegegevens.* Arnhem: Cito.

Lambert, E., & Chesnet, D. (2001). 'NOVLEX: une base de données lexicales pour les élèves de primaire'. *L'Année Psychologique, 101*, 277–288.

McClelland, J.L., & Rumelhart, D.E. (1981). 'An interactive activation model of context effects in letter perception: Part I. An account of basic findings'. *Psychological Review, 88*, 375–407.

Nas, G. (1983). 'Visual word recognition in bilinguals: Evidence for a cooperation between visual and sound based codes during access to a common lexical store'. *Journal of Verbal Learning and Verbal Behavior, 22*, 526–534.

National Institute of Child Health and Human Development (NICHHD). (2000). 'Report of the National Reading Panel (NRP)'. Teaching children to read: An evidence-based assessment of the scientific research literature on reading and its implications for reading instruction: Reports of the subgroups' (NIH Publication No. 00–4754). Washington, DC: US Government Printing Office.

Paradis, M. (1997). 'The cognitive neuropsychology of bilingualism'. In A.M.B. de Groot & J.F. Kroll (eds), *Tutorials in bilingualism: Psycholinguistic perspectives.* (pp. 331–354). Mahwah, NJ: LEA.

Peereman, R., & Content, A. (1997). 'Orthographic and phonological neighborhoods in naming: Not all neighbors are equally influencial in orthographic space'. *Journal of Memory and Language, 37*, 382–421.

Scarborough, D.L., Gerard, L., & Cortese, C. (1984). 'Independance of lexical access in bilingual word recognition'. *Journal of Verbal Learning and Verbal Behavior, 23*, 84–99.

Segui, J., & Grainger, J. (1990). 'Priming word recognition with orthographic neighbors: Effects of relative prime-target frequency'. *Journal of Experimental Psychology: Human Perception and Performance, 16*, 65–76.

Share, D.L. (1995). 'Phonological recoding and self-teaching: *Sine qua non* of reading acquisition'. *Cognition, 24*, 139–168.

Soares, C., & Grosjean, F. (1984). 'Bilinguals in a monolingual and a bilingual speech mode: The effect on lexical access'. *Memory & Cognition, 12*, 380–386.

Tzelgov, J., Henik, A., Sneg, R., & Baruch, O. (1996). 'Unintentional word reading via the phonological route: The stroop effect with cross-script homophones'. *Journal of Experimental Psychology-Learning Memory and Cognition, 22*, 336–349.

Van Heste, D. (1999). *Cross-language priming effects in bilinguals.* Unpublished Master's thesis, University of Ghent, Belgium.

Van Heuven, W.J.B., Dijkstra, T., & Grainger, J. (1998). 'Orthographic neighborhood effects in bilingual word recognition'. *Journal of Memory and Language, 39*, 458–483.

Van Wijnendaele, I., & Brysbaert, M. (2002). 'Visual word recognition in bilinguals: Phonological priming from the second to the first language'. *Journal of Experimental Psychology: Human Perception and Performance, 28*, 616–627.

Wang, M., Koda, K., & Pefetti, C.A. (2003). 'Alphabetic and non-alphabetic L1 effects in English word identification: A comparison of Korean and Chinese English L2 learners'. *Cognition, 87*, 129–149.

Chapter 11

Using spelling knowledge in a word game

Morag MacLean

Few studies take a qualitative look at children's understanding of spelling rules. Data drawn from a cross-linguistic study (Correa *et al.*, 2007) allow for some insights into qualitative differences in children's orthographic knowledge and their ability to develop and test hypotheses about an unknown word, using the well-known word game of 'Hangman'.

Background

Tests of children's spelling abilities have traditionally been the source of evidence of children's implicit understanding about the nature of their orthography. Researchers generally make inferences about children's understanding of spelling rules by studying spelling errors or by using carefully devised tasks which allow inferences to be made about the use of analogies (Nation & Hulme, 1998), morphological understanding (Nunes *et al.*, 1997; Landerl & Reitsma, 2005; Sénéchal *et al.*, 2006) or knowledge of legal letter combinations (Cassar & Treiman, 1997). While these approaches have yielded valuable insights into the development of children's spelling, they do not tell us much about children's spontaneous use of spelling knowledge. For this we have to look at more qualitative work such as that of Read (1986) on children's invented spelling, Downing *et al.* (1984) on children's judgements of correct spelling, Caravolas *et al.* (2005) on the strategies children report using in response to a spelling task, or the work of Critten and Pine (Chapter 6 in this volume) on explicit knowledge. However, the data gathered from more qualitative studies may also contribute to our understanding of the nature of spelling development.

The traditional game of 'Hangman', while not a pure spelling task, has built into its word-identification structure a number of possible approaches to solving the task, some of which are clearly related to spelling. The child has to identify an unknown word given only minimal information about it; knowing only the number of letters it has. This rather ghoulish game is traditional and still popular, and has the benefit of using a spelling-related approach to encourage children to make explicit their knowledge of spelling rules. The first spelling-related approach the children can take is the assembly of the word from its constituent letters, based on phoneme–grapheme correspondences. This is sometimes referred to as a non-lexical strategy (Barry, 1992). While children can use purely lexically based *guessing* when there are no letter cues, even at this early stage children can draw on their knowledge of letter frequency and letter combinations, both of which are related to spelling knowledge. This approach could be described as an orthographic one, in which there is as yet no idea of a whole word in mind. A third approach is a word-specific one in which the child retrieves a whole word to fit into the 'Hangman' template (at any stage of its completion). The child suggests a possible solution word using this lexical strategy and drawing the word from their vocabulary. Differentiating between these latter two strategies is difficult given the need to be able to identify the presence of a hypothesised word underlying the children's guessing, and a broader classification of the approaches into a broadly lexical and grapheme–phoneme correspondence has some support in the existing literature on children's spelling. Weekes (1994) and Castles *et al.* (1997) describe children's spelling styles in terms of the extent to which the children are lexically reliant or non-lexically reliant. Their definitions were based on the degree to which children made regularisation or lexicalisation errors in their spellings. Regularisation errors occurred when a misspelled word could be pronounced to sound like the target word. If the children misspelled a word by writing another word in its place, it was classified as a lexicalisation error. Their data showed that lexically reliant readers tend to be lexically reliant spellers while non-lexically reliant readers tend to be non-lexically reliant spellers. They suggest both strategies are available to typically developing spellers. The fact that the groups of lexical and non-lexical spellers did not differ in chronological age or reading age suggested that these were indeed styles and strategies and not patterns of development. As such one would expect to find both strategies being used by individual children in the context of 'Hangman'.

It is now entirely non-contentious to state that reading and spelling in an opaque orthography such as English (containing many irregular words) requires both an assembled spelling strategy and a lexical strategy (Frith, 1980; Goswami & Bryant, 1990). The main debate on reading and spelling strategies is not now on the use of lexical or non-lexical strategies, but on the degree to which transparent orthographies (with few irregularly spelled words) may also demand a lexical strategy. Barry (1992) addressed this question, using a priming methodology to contrast nonword spelling in English, Welsh and Italian. He found that while English produced significant lexical priming effects (required to cope with the irregularities), lexical priming was also found for Italian and Welsh. Two major implications can be drawn from these results. First, although the orthographic regularity of certain languages allows an efficient use of assembled spelling, this does not imply that the non-lexical strategy is the sole strategy required. The second implication concerns the functional independence of the word-specific and the assembled spelling procedures in the development of children's orthographic abilities. Lexical and non-lexical strategies might interact and are both needed in opaque and in transparent orthographies.

To compare a transparent and an opaque orthography (Brazilian Portuguese and English) and to find out what impact the orthography has on children's explicit understanding of their language, we (Correa *et al.*, 2007) used the 'Hangman' game. The game is not a spelling task per se, but successful completion draws on the child's understanding of spelling rules and on understanding the orthography in general. It is played by suggesting possible letters (to fill in the template) or words (to match the template). Children playing the game generally propose letters, filling in the spaces until they are able to infer the correct word or confirm their hypotheses. How do children select letters to propose? It is possible that they do so on the basis of explicit knowledge of the rules of spelling by using a non-lexical strategy, and that this might become clear in the justifications given for their choices of letters. This knowledge could also be implicit, as children may not always be aware of the spelling rules they are using to prompt their letter choices. However, verbal justifications are often taken as evidence of explicit knowledge in cognitive tasks and this is congruent with the Representational–Redescription model proposed by Karmiloff-Smith (1992) and the approach taken by Critten *et al.* (2007). An alternative strategy for children would be to select letters on the grounds that they knew a word of the appropriate length containing the letter. This is clearly an explicit knowledge strategy and depends on easy access to the lexicon, easy generation of vocabulary, and few limits to the choice of words except the word length. Asking children to justify their choices of letters during the game, as well as counting the trials they take to complete it allow us to investigate children's spontaneously used knowledge of their language and to look at some of the factors which might influence children's performance.

The impact of schooling on children's performance needs to be considered. With more years of schooling and increasing literacy, children's written and spoken vocabulary increases. Across a span of three school years, improvements in performance are likely to be attributable both to education effects and to the impact of explicit teaching about spelling rules. However, differences in performance on the game and justifications of letter choices are likely to be influenced by growing awareness of how to use existing knowledge. There should also be signs of increased understanding of how to deploy strategies specifically tailored to achieving success in the game. In addition to education effects it is also possible to use the game to look for the impact of orthographic-specific expectations. The expectations a reader, speller or in this case a 'Hangman' player has about the target word are likely to be determined by the individual's age and education (as these are not separable), and also by their knowledge of their orthography.

Orthographies vary considerably in terms of the salient features of words. In English, word length is associated with numbers of syllables, with longer words more likely to be of over one syllable in length, but the relationship is a complex one. It is also the case that words varying in length from one to more than seven letters may all be monosyllables, e.g. 'a', 'be', 'sea', 'deep', 'flail', 'glitch' and 'thought'. Other more transparent orthographies have tighter constraints on the relationship between letters and syllables, and Brazilian Portuguese is an example. A word with seven letters could never be a monosyllabic word in Brazilian Portuguese. As a result, children are likely to make predictions about the word to be identified on the basis of its length, by virtue of the relationship between the word length and syllabic patterns.

Teaching methods are intimately connected with the orthographic structure of the language. Spelling instruction in English schools includes an explicitly phonological approach using letter–sound correspondences for single letters as well as blends and the teaching of spelling conventions and a sight vocabulary. The difference between four- and five-letter words in English tells us little about the syllabic patterns of the words. We reasoned that the game of 'Hangman' in English would provoke use of spelling rules as well as non-lexical strategies.

English children's orthographic knowledge in the context of 'Hangman'

Ninety-five children from primary schools in Oxfordshire, England, took part in this study: 32 in Year 4 (mean age = 8 years, 11 months), 31 in Year 5 (mean age = 9 years, 11 months) and 32 in Year 6 (mean age = 10 years, 11 months), with mean Schonell raw spelling scores of 11.08 (SD = 1.11), 11.30 (SD = 1.27) and 12.44 (SD = 1.05) respectively for each year group.

The children were presented with a template comprising a set of blanks (representing the letters making up a word) and asked to justify their selection and positioning of letters. After each letter selection the children were given feedback about the correctness of the choice. If they selected a 'correct' letter but placed it incorrectly, they were told that 'Yes, there is a (letter selected) in this word but it is (correct location)'. Children entered the correct letters, crossed off letters they had selected already and drew in the details of the 'hanged man' on a whiteboard.

Children were presented with either three or four words from a list of 17 concrete words. Pre-testing established that the words presented were within the children's written vocabulary. All words were of either four or five letters. All four-letter words were monosyllabic, following the common CVCC, CVCV or CCVC patterns (e.g. band, hand, lock, sock, flag, cake). The five-letter words were either monosyllabic (CVCCV, CCVVC, CCVCC, e.g. drink, steam, frost, brain, dream, sweat) or disyllabic (CCVCC, CVCVC, e.g. hotel, table, robin, salad, gravy). All children were pre-tested and presented with at least one four-letter word and at least one five-letter word from within their written vocabulary. The consonant-vowel patterns in the words were highly frequent in four- and five-letter words that are high on concreteness and imagery ratings according to the MRC Psycholinguistic Database (Coltheart, 1981).

Table 11.1 shows the mean number of trials taken by children of different levels of schooling to complete the game for monosyllabic four- and five-letter words as well as disyllabic five-letter words. This performance measure reflects the difficulty of the task. As particular words were presented only to small numbers of children, analysis was carried out on word length. There was relatively little variation in the difficulty of identifying categories of words.

To examine differences due to schooling or to the syllabic pattern of the word presented or both, three separate Analyses of Variance were run for the four-letter words and the two types of five-letter words (monosyllabic and disyllabic). No significant differences were found between the school grades for four-letter words, $F(2,$

Table 11.1 Mean number of trials used by English children to succeed in the game

	4 letter words	5 letter words	
	One syllable	One syllable	Two syllable
Year 4	12.14	11.71	12.82
	(3.37)	(3.14)	(5.53)
Year 5	10.87	12.08	11.28
	(3.37)	(3.16)	(4.21)
Year 6	11.00	10.38	11.28
	(3.46)	(4.08)	(3.51)

92) = 1.35, p = .264, five-letter monosyllabic words, $F(2, 76)$ = 1.62, p = .205, or five-letter disyllabic words $F(2, 61)$ = 0.80, p = .453. The results show neither significant differences between the word types nor any schooling effect on the task, despite significant differences in pre-test spelling scores. The lack of effect of schooling is puzzling as one might expect children's performance to improve with age or spelling experience. However, given the range of CV patterns permissible in four- and five-letter words, even identifying one letter, for example finding a vowel early in the game, does not limit choice to any very great degree. Even the identification of a vowel and a letter for a short English word still leaves many possibilities. It is not surprising therefore that the average number of trials to completion is only just below half of the alphabet length.

The strategies used to complete the game were examined for explanations for the lack of schooling effect. Children's letter choices were categorised as indicating a lexical or non-lexical strategy to see if there was any sign of differential patterns of strategy use in the game.

Coding strategy use

Children's choices of letters were coded as a lexical strategy if they referred to a possible solution word phonologically appropriate or visually similar to the target word (e.g. "*b*", *it might be "beat"*). All other letter choices were coded as non-lexical as they were not word-based choices (e.g. '*it might have an "a" in it*').

Opening, development and end-game

Children begin the game with minimal information (only the number of letters in the target word). After a few letter choices they have some clues. These might include knowing about letters that are and are not in the target word. For letters that are in the target word, the position of those letters with the consequent constraints on future letter choices also act as clues. By the 'end-game', children are in a position to propose possible solutions. Consequently, different parts of the game might lend themselves naturally to differential strategy use. The first two choices can be seen as the 'opening', with the final two choices as the 'end-game'. The 'development' varies in length depending upon the performance of each child, and comprises the section of the game between opening and end-game. For each school year, the percentage of all choices that could be classified as lexical was calculated separately for each phase of the game.

The children's choices were coded as lexical or non-lexical. Table 11.2 shows the percentage of lexical choices made in each year group for each phase of the game. For each school year the pattern of strategy use was largely similar; children were more likely to use lexical strategies for four- than for five-letter words. However, very few lexical choices are made in the opening and development phases of the game (never making up more than 26 per cent of the choices), while the end-game is dominated by lexical choices with over 58 per cent of all choices being lexical across all three school years. Where there are differences between the school years they lie in the marginally greater readiness of Year 4 children to make lexical choices in the opening compared with children in Years 5 and 6. Averaged across the entire game, there were no significant differences between the school years.

Table 11.2 Percentage of lexical strategies used by English children

		Phases of the game					
		Opening		Development		End game	
		4 letters	5 letters	4 letters	5 letters	4 letters	5 letters
Year 4	Lexical	26	12	19	9	70	61
Year 5	Lexical	13	9	23	12	61	59
Year 6	Lexical	15	10	18	9	65	59

These results are of interest in that they do not follow the pattern usually expected in spelling tasks in English where a considerable proportion of lexical strategy use has been found. One reason for this may lie in the nature of the game. The 'Hangman' game for English speakers gives little distinguishing information to children in the early stages. A four- or five-letter word might be of one or two syllables, and might conform to several high frequency CV patterns. Until several letters are in place, the demands a lexical strategy places on the child's vocabulary may simply be too heavy for this to be feasible. It is easier to draw on the alphabet – which after all has only 26 letters as opposed to the 20,000-strong traditional vocabulary of Shakespeare's English. If the game-player is not in danger of being 'hanged' too soon, then a non-lexical, assembly-by-letter process may indeed be the best strategy. However, by the end-game the range of potential words has narrowed, and it is possible to use the lexicon to propose potential solution words to the point of success.

Qualitative analysis of the protocols of the English children illustrate their rationales. Lexical strategies were rare, but a few children used this strategy almost to the exclusion of all other strategies. Protocol A illustrates this. Early choices of letters include a vowel and later suggestions are variations on a theme, using rhymes (MITE and KITE) and half-rhymes (BATE and CAKE), indicating phonological skills minimally used.

Protocol A: lexical strategy

Pattern	Guess	Justification
N _ _ _	N	Might be nope
T _ _ _	T	Might be that
D _ _ _	D	Might be date
M _ _ _	M	Might be mite
E _ _ _	E	Might be eel
F _ _ e	F	Might be fate
S _ _ e	S	Might be shoe
B _ _ e	B	Might be bate
K _ _ e	K	Might be kite
C _ _ e	C	Might be cake

Note: Upper case letters in the protocols indicate the letter choice for the turn, lower case letters indicate letters identified in previous turns.

Non-lexical strategies vary from the apparently random to the highly organised. The apparently random approach is exemplified in Protocol B from Year 4, where letters are selected almost by lexical means – thinking of a word that begins with a specific letter. It is far from clear whether the letter or the word came first, but in this case it appears that the letter came first with the justification being a creative and imaginative summoning of salient personal information triggered by the letter. In this example it is interesting to see an alliterative justification for the 'N' ('next-door' 'neighbour' and 'nuts').

Protocol B: letters with personal justifications for each choice

Pattern	Guess	Justification
_ _a_ _J_ _	J	My name starts with J
_ _a_ _S_ _	S	Dad's name starts with S
_C_ _a_ _ _	C	My favourite food is chocolate
_ _a_ _N_ _	N	My next door neighbour is allergic to nuts
_ _a_ _n_ E	E	Mum's favourite food is egg on toast

Most words end with 'e' like time

The non-lexical, assembled-letter strategy is most frequently used by all year groups. Children call on their knowledge of successful strategy, identifying vowels first, then high frequency letters, often calling on their knowledge of plausible posi-tions for letter combinations as in Protocol C. This can range from knowing that an 'S' denotes a plural at the end of words, to knowing about specific word endings such as 'ED' or the vowel combination of 'EA'. One justification addressed vowel combinations explicitly when the child chose an 'E' after choosing an 'A', saying *They go together to make an "ee" sound*. Larger units can also be identified and these include identifying the silent 'e' when an 'R' is selected after an 'A' blank 'E' has been selected. The child went on to justify the choice of an 'R' by saying *To make an "are" sound at the end of the word*.

Protocol C: letter combinations and reference to letter position

Pattern	Guess	Justification
_D_ _ _ _ _	D	There are lots of words like 'dea' in the beginning
_ _E_ _ _ _	E	It's a popular letter. Lots of words have 'ea'
_ _A_ _ _ _	A	Lots of words have 'a'
_ _ _T_ _ _	T	I guessed
_ _ _ _L_ _	L	Lots of words have L and E as their spelling
_ _ _ _ _S_	S	Often at the end for more than one [i.e. plural]

The strategies English readers and spellers use to play the game result in fairly even performance across Years 4, 5 and 6, suggesting relatively slow development of understanding that spelling rules can be used in this context, although the school years differed in spelling skills. The task taps not spelling but explicit use of knowl-edge. The dominant strategy is a non-lexical strategy of assembly by letter until the word possibilities are so limited that a lexical strategy is feasible. In the case of Eng-lish the lexical strategy does not generally occur in these age groups until the end of the game when almost all letters have already been identified. The letter-by-letter approach may be more or less informed by their knowledge of spelling rules and is likely to be the strategy of choice where there are no indications of the constraints on the word's spelling or syllabic construction. Such information is inherent in the word length in the transparent orthography of Brazilian Portuguese.

Comparing a transparent and an opaque orthography

Much literacy instruction in Brazilian Portuguese focuses on orthographic analysis of words with an emphasis on syllables, and the teaching method is highly structured. Children are taught to read by a method that focuses on the correspondence between spoken and written language in which the syllable is the main unit of phonological analysis. The teacher chooses some disyllables or trisyllables to start with (e.g. bola, boneca). These are all regular words in which each syllable has a consonant-vowel (CV) pattern. The CV pattern is the most simple syllable pattern in Brazilian Portuguese orthography. The words are selected to be familiar to the children and are usually taken from their storybooks or spoken vocabulary. Initially the children are taught to read and write the selected words, and once this has been achieved the words are segmented into their constituent syllables (e.g. bo-la, bo-ne-ca). The children are then asked to discover which words can be formed by the re-combination of the constituent syllables (e.g. bobo, boboca, boca, cabo, caneca, canela). Syllabic families are generated for each of the syllables worked with. Children are encouraged to discover words that can be written combining the different syllabic families. Once all the linguistic knowledge and activities that can be derived from these key words are fully explored, new words are chosen until all the main aspects of the Brazilian Portuguese orthography have been introduced.

As a consequence of both the orthography, with its characteristic relatively simple syllabic structure, and the teaching methods, Brazilian Portuguese speakers, unlike children in English schools, are likely to make inferences about the syllabic structure of a word from its length, even when word length varies between only four and five letters. Four-letter words generally have a disyllabic pattern. A four-letter word could fit the expectation of being a CVCV pattern, which is the simplest regular disyllabic pattern in Brazilian Portuguese. Adding a letter to make the target a five-letter word results in the simplest syllabic pattern (made up of a pair of CV syllables) no longer being possible. As a result one might predict no differences in performance on five-letter words in the game, but clear differences for four-letter words due to their deviation from the simple CVCV pattern. Brazilian children's responses to the game of 'Hangman' were therefore expected to show differences in performance and strategies by word length and between school years.

Brazilian children's orthographic knowledge in the context of 'Hangman'

Eighty-one children from a primary school in Rio de Janeiro played the 'Hangman' game, 32 in Grade 2, 25 in Grade 3 and 24 in Grade 4 (mean ages = 9 years, 4 months, 10 years, 9 months and 11 years, 3 months, respectively).

The procedure was identical to the one used with the English children already described. For Brazilian Portuguese children we used 4 four-letter words and 3 five-letter target words, all disyllabic. Only one word 'cola' (glue) followed the CVCV pattern. Two other words 'saia' (skirt) and 'noiva' (bride) contained diphthongs. The words 'obra' (construction) and 'fruta' (fruit) had respectively two-consonant final and initial clusters, and 'unha' (nail) and 'rolha' (cork) had digraphs in the last syllable.

All choices to correct guessing (or until all the blank spaces were filled with a letter) were recorded. Table 11.3 shows the mean number of trials by level of schooling to finish the game. The results show less variability in the five-letter words than the four-letter words, while the mean number of trials to success varied considerably for the four-letter words, indicating a different level of difficulty for these words.

To assess the effect of letter length and the possibility of inferring syllabic structure on performance two separate Analysis of Variance were run for the four- and five-letter words respectively. This was done to examine differences in children's scores due to schooling or to the syllabic pattern of the word presented or both. There was no significant difference in children's scores for the types of five-letter words presented, $F(2, 156) = 1.48$, $p = .23$. However children's performance was affected by the type of four-letter words chosen as a target, $F(3, 234) = 27.23$, $p < .01$. The words 'cola' and 'obra' were the easiest, followed by 'saia'. 'Unha' was considered the most difficult word.

The differences between words of different lengths can be explained in terms of the extent to which the syllabic orthographic pattern of the words differed from a regular CVCV pattern. Five-letter words frustrate expectations of finding a regular CVCV word to be the answer. This frustrated expectation complicates matters regardless of the actual syllabic pattern of the words to be discovered.

For four-letter words the regular CVCV pattern is a salient and possible choice for the children. When the syllabic pattern of the word is very different from the regular CVCV pattern it becomes more difficult. For example, although 'obra' does not follow the CVCV pattern, it has high frequency letters and a regular grapheme–phoneme correspondence. 'Saia' caused more difficulty because of the presence of a semivowel instead of the consonant expected if the word was obeying a simple CVCV pattern. Discovering the second and fourth letter of the target word appeared to confirm the expectation of a CVCV pattern, making it difficult to look for alternative syllabic patterns. The most difficult word, 'unha' neither follows a CVCV pattern, nor is it regular (containing a digraph 'nh'). Digraphs lead to mismatches between the numbers of elements in the phonological and the orthographic syllabic patterns.

Table 11.3 Mean number of trials used by Brazilian children to succeed in the game

| | 4 letter words | | | | 5 letter words | | |
	cola	obra	saia	unha	fruta	noiva	rolha
Grade							
2	9.34	10.47	12.84	14.06	13.22	14.66	14.19
	(4.33)	(5.56)	(4.28)	(5.32)	(3.58)	(4.11)	(3.92)
3	8.92	9.16	11.96	13.84	11.00	12.24	13.32
	(3.29)	(4.05)	(4.41)	(4.22)	(3.38)	(3.70)	(4.77)
4	6.88	7.63	9.13	13.75	12.08	11.96	12.04
	(3.00)	(3.19)	(2.69)	(4.02)	(3.98)	(4.29)	(5.17)

In the Brazilian data there were clear schooling effects. For four-letter words Grade 4 took fewer trials to finish the game than Grades 3 or 2, $F(2, 78) = 9.23$, $p < .01$. For the five-letter words differences existed between Grade 2 and 3 but not between Grades 3 and 4, $F(2, 78) = 6.80$, $p < .01$. The decrease in the mean number of trials between Grades 2 and 3 as compared with Grade 4 for the four-letter words (regardless of word pattern) indicates a significant improvement in children's spelling ability at the end of their primary school years. This might be due to their reading ability, or to increases in their rule-based knowledge of the orthography of the language, or to both of these factors.

The differences observed for the effect of schooling on children's performance in the five-letter trials implies that the strategies children use for the four-letter words cannot be applied in the same way to five-letter words. The children's performance supports this possibility. Letter choices show children trying to solve the four-letter word tasks by relying on a lexical strategy, by drawing on their reading and spelling vocabulary and proposing possible words to fit the 'Hangman' pattern. An increase in the number of letters in the word (e.g. from four to five letters) or recognition (in the case of four-letter words) that the word does not follow the CVCV pattern makes the use of a lexical strategy difficult. A switch to a non-lexically based strategy is then required. Children's letter choices were categorised as indicating a lexical or non-lexical strategy to see if the difference between performance on five- and four-letter words across the three school years might be due to differential patterns of strategy use. The coding and analysis of strategies was the same as for the English data, with letter choices deemed a lexical strategy if they referred to a possible solution word phonologically appropriate or visually similar to the target (e.g. *"b"*, *it might be "bola"*). All other letter choices were coded as non-lexical.

Table 11.4 shows the percentage of letter choices for four- and five-letter words which were based on a lexical strategy for each of the three Brazilian school grades in each of the three phases of the 'Hangman' game. Children in Grade 2 used the lexical strategy more frequently for the four- than for the five-letter target words. The lexical strategy is also the children's primary strategy for the opening when the target is a word of four letters. However in the development (the mid-section of the game), there is a relative decrease in the use of a lexical strategy, possibly due to the constraints imposed by the children's previous letter choices and the limitations of their vocabulary. Spontaneous production of plausible words to fit a partially completed 'Hangman' template is difficult and provoked a shift in the strategy used, i.e. towards an increase in non-lexical strategy. Table 11.4 shows that it is at the development stage that a non-lexical strategy was dominant for the four-letter word tasks. In

Table 11.4 Percentage of lexical strategies used by Brazilian children

		Phases of the game					
		Opening		*Development*		*End game*	
		4 letters	*5 letters*	*4 letters*	*5 letters*	*4 letters*	*5 letters*
2nd grade	Lexical	57	46	33	23	50	43
3rd grade	Lexical	51	42	51	27	48	52
4th grade	Lexical	59	47	50	36	54	50

contrast, the use of lexical strategy never became dominant over the use of a non-lexical strategy for five-letter words. It seems that the more the syllabic pattern deviates from a regular CVCV pattern, the more difficult it is for the children to retrieve a word from their vocabulary to help them to solve the task.

For Grade 3 there is a slightly different pattern. Unlike Grade 2, lexical strategy use does not reduce during the development stage of the game for four-letter words. This might be due to a relative improvement in children's vocabulary by Grade 3. Children can still retrieve a list of possible words from the lexicon despite the constraints arising from their previous choices. That they can do this is also shown by the increase in the frequency of lexical strategies used in the 'end-game' for five-letter words as compared with Grade 2. Increased vocabulary allows them to take advantage of the existing clues to narrow the range of plausible words. The most noticeable difference between Grades 3 and 4 was related to the increase in lexical strategy use in the opening, possibly due to an improvement in children's vocabulary over the school years. A lexical strategy must be based on children's reading, spelling and spoken vocabulary, but it is not always possible for the children to deploy it, especially when the target word deviates from the regular CVCV pattern. This poses the question of what the use of a non-lexical strategy tells us about the children's reasoning.

The analysis suggests that the children are approaching the target word by means of letter-by-letter assembly of the word. However it does not tell us the extent to which the children's choices are based on their understanding of orthographic rules. The protocols throw some light on the nature of the children's choices. Examination of the children's use of the non-lexical strategy showed them making choices on the basis of orthographic rules, but not reliably. Children's knowledge of the orthographic pattern of words appears mainly related to the requirement for vowels and the constraints of some letter sequences.

Protocol D shows that children acknowledge the importance of vowels as the centre of the syllable, generally beginning the game with a vowel because 'all words have a vowel'. The vowels themselves were not randomly selected, but chosen for their frequency in the language. Children started with 'a', followed by 'o' or 'e', then 'i', with 'u' as their last choice. Generally children stop choosing vowels when they get two of them right.

Protocol D: focusing on vowels

Pattern	Guess	Justification
_ _ _ _A	A	Almost all the words have the letter A
C a _ a	C	I think it is 'casa'
P a _ a	P	It can be 'para'
_ a M a	M	because it can be 'cama'. Oops, I forgot the word does not have a C
S a _ a	S	It is 'sala'
s a L a	L	It is 'sala'!
s a I a	I	I was thinking of the vowels which I did not put because I could not find any consonant which fitted there, making a word that I knew

Once the children have some clues, combinations of letters can be suggested either because of specific positions in the word or because of the presence of other letters. Protocol E illustrates this in the case of 'unha'.

Protocol E: using letter combinations/positions

Pattern   *Guess Justification*

<u>u</u> <u>N</u> <u>h</u> <u>a</u>   N   Because I thought of those letters that can go with H. I thought of an L, but it wasn't it. It was not the C either. Then it could only be the N. That is: unha.

The importance of considering position and frequency of the letters for an appropriate choice was explicitly stated by some children:

> 'Every time I play this game, I start with the vowels. There are always vowels in words. It is easier. Almost in all the words the second [letter] is a vowel.'

Children cannot always explain their reasoning or show a clear rationale for their choices. However this does not mean that those choices are random. The appearance of random guessing is associated with having made many attempts, and with exasperation at the possibility of losing the game, as in Protocol F.

Protocol F: using alphabetical order

Pattern   *Guess Justification*

<u>_ o I _ a</u>   I   Because an I is a very well-known letter, like an A and an E

<u>D o i D a</u>   D   I thought of doida

<u>_ o i G a</u>   G   I am going in alphabetical order

<u>_ o i J a</u>   J   I am going in alphabetical order

<u>_ o i L a</u>   L   I am going in alphabetical order

<u>M o i _ a</u>   M   I've picked the end so many times that now I'm going to pick the beginning. I am going in alphabetical order

<u>N o i _ a</u>   N   Ah, now I can see the word, it is noiva

The use of alphabetical order is not necessarily irrational. It can be an organised way of getting to the correct word:

> 'It is cola. [How do you know that?] Because of the letters. I went through the alphabet, skipping some letters because they could not make it sound right.'

In the case of five-letter words and the difficulty they impose by virtue of not fitting the simple CVCV pattern, some children felt a need to mention this in their explanation for their choices. They showed sensitivity to the fact that they would come across consonant clusters, diphthongs or digraphs:

> 'Generally when there are five [letters] there might be loads of consonants. Then I keep putting vowels at the end because it makes it easy … [pause] … well, sometimes there are lots of vowels in the middle as well.'

Observing children solving a task such as 'Hangman' gives us valuable insights into reasoning about spelling in the transparent Brazilian Portuguese orthography. Two main strategies play a role in success on the task. A lexical strategy allows children to retrieve a range of plausible solution words based on available information. This strategy depends mainly on children's vocabulary. Its effectiveness relies on increasing vocabulary and ease of access to that vocabulary. A non-lexical strategy is used selectively by children when the word appears unlikely to follow the simple CVCV pattern. However, use of a non-lexical strategy does not always mean that children are explicitly aware of the basis of their letter choices. For example a child might not produce any justification of their choice but still select high frequency letters indicating some knowledge of the constraints imposed within the game. Explicitly rule-based choices were indicated by children showing awareness of the constraints of the partial solution or word length, or by their sensitivity to letter-string frequencies or other orthography-specific knowledge.

Discussion

The two studies described are an example of a task with apparently identical cognitive demands being presented to children developing their literacy skills in two contrasting orthographic contexts. An identical game resulted in a revealing pattern of differences and similarities in children's explicit understanding of their orthography.

Children in both orthographic communities completed the tasks in a similar number of trials. However, for the English children there was little sign of differentiation between word lengths or individual words, whereas for the Brazilian children the four-letter words were completed in fewer trials than the five-letter words, with the notable exception of the case of a word deviating markedly from the simplest CVCV pattern. In other words, there was greater heterogeneity in the transparent orthography and a less sophisticated pattern of results in response to four- and five-letter words, with relatively little lexical strategy use in the opaque orthography.

The assumption that children's performance would be influenced by their age or schooling did not hold for both orthographies. For the Brazilian children schooling effects can be seen in the higher level of performance of the older children, although the nature of the effect depends on word length. In contrast, no such schooling effect was found for the English children, despite the fact that the older children in the English sample had higher spelling scores than the younger children. The explanation for differential schooling effects most likely lies in two factors: the constraints of the orthography and the demands of the 'Hangman' game.

Babayiğit (Chapter 8 in this volume) observes that English orthography makes high cognitive demands on the beginning reader and speller, requiring deployment of orthographic knowledge and grapheme–phoneme correspondence rules from the earliest stage. It does this whilst providing little other support that could be deployed in the task described here. It is therefore not surprising that there is no schooling effect for English children, as it makes greater demands on them than it does on Brazilian Portuguese children. The game requires the children to do more than simply spell a word, they have to either generate clues to the identity of the word by proposing letters, or they have to test specific hypotheses which might relate to either a word or a combination of letters. The opening of the game gives English children very little information but provides Brazilian Portuguese speakers with both the number of syllables in the word and clues to the intrasyllabic pattern. It is not surprising that Brazilian children are progressively able to take advantage of this information with increased schooling. No such advantage is conferred on the English children for whom the word length carries no useful information about the CV pattern of a word. Subsequent letter choices are also of limited usefulness in hypothesis testing as the presence of many irregularly spelled words in English means that there are relatively few constraints on their choices. For English children there are no clues for segmenting the word, which could be split into letter clusters at any point (Treiman, 1992).

Radebaugh (1985) found that English-speaking children's reports of how they spelled a word included strategies such as segmenting words. However, the nature of the 'Hangman' task makes it very difficult to know where to start the segmentation process until the game is nearly over. English children are therefore disadvantaged in deploying what knowledge they possess about spelling rules. For Brazilian children, in contrast, there is a starting point to the segmentation process based on their knowledge of the syllabic structure, which can be deployed more effectively with increased schooling.

From the qualitative analysis of the children's protocols, it is clear that letter choices seem to be guided by sensitivity to the orthography. By its very nature the game is limited in how well it reflects children's spelling knowledge. But while the use of justification data does not guarantee that the reasoning offered is not a *post hoc* one, in combination with letter choices, justifications appear to show explicit awareness of some orthographic constraint. Choices without proffered rationales may also show some understanding of orthographic constraints. In following the children's choices throughout the course of a game, it is clear that both Brazilian and English children are sensitive to certain orthographic features. First among these is the requirement for words to contain vowels, but the relative frequency of consonants is also featured. Many children propose high frequency letters as soon as they have established the identity of the vowels in the words, indicating some explicit knowledge of the constraints on spelling in their orthography. Additionally, the protocols show that children are often also sensitive to the frequency of language-specific letter combinations.

Both lexical and non-lexical strategies were deployed by Brazilian and English children, both groups making more use of lexical strategies for four- than five-letter words. However the pattern of use was markedly different. English children made little use of lexical strategies except in the end-game, and this did not change with increased schooling. In contrast the Brazilian children made more use of lexical strategies in the opening and development phases of the game, and showed a pattern which changed with schooling.

The use of a lexical or non-lexical strategy is not only related to the nature of the orthography but also to the cognitive demands of the task in different phases of the game. This finding suggests that the notion that English orthography's irregularities provoke a lexical response to spelling may be appropriate in the case of spelling tasks, but not for all tasks using spelling knowledge. The counterpoint of this is that a lexical strategy was deployed in a transparent orthography such as Brazilian Portuguese. The analysis of strategies suggests that children were able to perform at more than one level of representation, within the game, driven by game structure and their own knowledge. This is congruent with Critten and Pine's findings reported in Chapter 6 in this volume. While the 'Hangman' game is not a true test of spelling or spelling knowledge, merely an indicator of children's use of their knowledge in a spelling-related task, it does reveal commonalities as well as differences between orthographies.

Justification data from this essentially qualitative approach provide support for Barry's (1992) suggestion that lexical and non-lexical strategies were not independent pathways to spelling. They are also in accord with the analysis provided by Babayiğit (Chapter 8 in this volume) who argues that the underlying processes of spelling single words are shared in both transparent and opaque orthographies, while the timing of their deployment and the balance between them varies. Lexical and non-lexical strategies thus interact in both transparent and opaque orthographies. The results reported here and in more detail in Correa *et al.* (2007) certainly show that both strategies are used by children of varied ages and stages of their schooling, and at various points of the 'Hangman' game.

Most published spelling-related comparisons of orthographies have used explicit spelling tasks to illuminate the impact of the orthography on children's spelling awareness. The approach reported here is rather different. A game-like task has been used to gain some insights into the spontaneous use of spelling-related understanding. It has confirmed, using a novel method, the impact of the orthography on children's spelling-related abilities.

References

Barry, C. (1992) 'Interactions between lexical and assembled spelling'. In C. Sterling and C. Robson (eds) *Psychology, spelling and education.* (pp. 71–86) Clevedon, UK: Multilingual Matters.

Caravolas, M., Kessler, B., Hulme, C. & Snowling, M. (2005) 'Effects of orthographic consistency, frequency, and letter knowledge on children's vowel spelling development'. *Journal of Experimental Child Psychology, 92,* 307–321.

Cassar, M. & Treiman, R. (1997) 'The beginnings of orthographic knowledge: Children's knowledge of double letters in words'. *Journal of Educational Psychology, 89,* 631–644.

Castles, A., Holmes, V.M. & Wong, M. (1997) 'Variations in spelling style among lexical and sublexical readers'. *Journal of Experimental Child Psychology, 64,* 98–118.

Coltheart, M. (1981) 'The MRC Psycholinguistic Database'. *Quarterly Journal of Experimental Psychology, 33A,* 497–508.

Correa, J., MacLean, M., Meireles, E., Lopes, T. & Glockling, D. (2007) 'Using spelling skills in Brazilian Portuguese and English'. *Journal of Portuguese Linguistics, 6,* 61–82.

Critten, S., Pine, K.J. & Steffler, D. (2007) 'Spelling development in young children: A case of Representational-Redescription?' *Journal of Educational Psychology, 99,* 207-220.

Downing, J., DeStephano, J., Rich, G. & Bell, A. (1984) 'Children's views of spelling'. *Elementary School Journal, 85,* 185–198.

Frith, U. (1980) 'Unexpected spelling problems'. In U.Frith (ed.), *Cognitive processes in spelling.* London: Academic Press.

Goswami, U. & Bryant, P. (1990) *Phonological skills and learning to read.* London: LEA.

Karmiloff-Smith, A. (1992) *Beyond modularity: A developmental perspective on cognitive science.* Cambridge, MA: MIT Press.

Landerl, K. & Reitsma, P. (2005) 'Phonological and morphological consistency in the acquisition of vowel duration spelling in Dutch and German'. *Journal of Experimental Child Psychology, 92,* 322–344.

Nation, K. & Hulme, C. (1998) 'The role of analogy in early spelling development'. In C. Hulme & R.M. Joshi (eds), *Reading and spelling: Development and disorders* (pp. 433–445). Mahwah, NJ: LEA.

Nunes, T., Bryant, P. & Bindman, M. (1997) 'Spelling and grammar: The necsed move'. In C.A. Perfetti & L. Rieben (eds), *Learning to spell: Research, theory, and practice across languages* (pp. 151–170). Mahwah, NJ: LEA.

Radebaugh, M.R. (1985) 'Children's perceptions of their spelling strategies'. *The Reading Teacher 38*, 532–536.

Read, C. (1986) *Children's creative spelling*. London: Routledge & Kegan Paul.

Sénéchal, M., Basque, M.T. & Leclaire, T. (2006) 'Morphological knowledge as revealed in children's spelling accuracy and reports of strategies'. *Journal of Experimental Child Psychology, 95*, 231–254.

Treiman, R. (1992) 'The role of intrasyllabic units in learning to read and to spell'. In P.B.Gough, L. Ehri & R. Treiman (eds), *Reading acquisition* (pp. 65–106). Hillsdale, NJ: LEA.

Weekes, B.S. (1994) 'Spelling skills of lexical readers'. *British Journal of Psychology, 85*, 245–257.

Chapter 12

Metalinguistic and subcharacter skills in Chinese literacy acquisition

Xiuli Tong, Phil D. Liu and Catherine McBride-Chang

Chinese children's literacy development is an important issue for developmental and educational psychology for at least two reasons. First, both reading and spelling form the foundation of children's learning (e.g. Adams, 1990). Given that approximately 20 per cent of the world's population is Chinese and that the booming Chinese economy has increased interest in learning Chinese around the world, how individuals, particularly children, go about mastering this unique orthography and whether difficulties in its mastery can be ameliorated using research findings are timely questions. Second, Chinese has its own unique orthographic, phonological, and morphological systems, and the complexity of these systems contrasts strongly with English and other alphabetic languages, about which is more currently known in the literature. The linguistic and cognitive skills underpinning the Chinese language system, particularly in relation to the availability of phonological and morphological units, may be somewhat different from that of English and other alphabetic languages due to its logographic nature. This chapter focuses on the process of Chinese children's reading and spelling acquisition to highlight some of the controversies and challenges in learning Chinese.

A developmental approach to literacy acquisition in Chinese is helpful in a number of ways. First, an investigation of the developmental routes of Chinese word reading and spelling might shed light on the issue of universals and specifics of language acquisition and development in relation to Chinese orthography. Second, different cognitive correlates of Chinese that do not conform to alphabetic reading can pinpoint how roles of different linguistic or metalinguistic skills are determined by the way in which spoken language is encoded in a given orthography. Third, this developmental approach to Chinese might provide some new ideas on educational intervention and practice.

In the first section of this chapter, the uniqueness of the Chinese orthography is briefly described. As Shu and Anderson (1999) argued, learning to read and write 'requires becoming aware of the basic units of spoken language, the basic units of the writing system, and the mapping between the two' (p. 1). This metalinguistic awareness, involving both reflection upon and manipulation of structural features of language (Nagy, 2007), will therefore be the focus of the second section. In particular, we will highlight phonological and morphological awareness in relation to early Chinese reading acquisition. Finally, we will consider current educational findings and controversies in the study of Chinese word reading and spelling.

Chinese orthography

Chinese has a relatively complex orthography. The Chinese character is the basic writing unit of Chinese and it converges in form, sound, and meaning. The character consists of different strokes forming a square-shaped structure, which differs from the linear pattern of English writing. Unlike English, the association of a specific sound to a meaning in a given writing unit (Weekes & Chen, 2002) is relatively arbitrary. For example, the Chinese characters 干 /gan1/ (do), 士 /shi4/ (soldier), 土 /tu3/ (earth) 上 /shang4/(up), and 工 /gong1/(work) have quite similar visual orthographic patterns but represent diverse meanings with different sounds in Mandarin. There are no semantic or phonetic connections between them. Perhaps correspondingly, then, the most often used strategy for young children learning to read is rote memorization.

It is particularly effective for Chinese children to distinguish these characters in terms of meaning or visual-orthographic patterns rather than sound associations since a great number of homophones abound in Chinese. In Mandarin, on average, one spoken syllable maps onto more than five different characters (Li et al., 2002), whereas in Cantonese, there are approximately three characters representing different morphemes that map onto one tonal syllable (Chow et al., 2008). Unlike the case of English, in which sounds and written forms of words are associated, in Chinese, the written form is more closely tied to meaning than sound. Thus, in Chinese, the processing route from orthography to semantics is somewhat rapid relative to the mapping of orthography to phonology (Yang et al., 2006), whereas it is the reverse in English (Harm & Seidenberg, 1999).

There are two types of written Chinese: traditional and simplified characters. The simplified characters were derived from traditional characters by reducing certain strokes or radicals, which are the basic orthographic patterns underlying Chinese characters. Simplified Chinese characters are widely used in Mainland China and Singapore, whereas traditional characters are predominant in Hong Kong and Taiwan. Both systems are meaning-based.

Chinese societies also sometimes use different languages. For example, Cantonese, which has between 6 and 12 tones, is used in Hong Kong, whereas Mandarin, which has only four tones, is used in Singapore and in much of Mainland China and Taiwan. The grammar and vocabulary of Cantonese and Mandarin can also differ, particularly in oral language contexts, but sometimes also even in written language (e.g. Chow et al., 2008). These differences, along with differences in script types taught in school, might conceivably be related to certain differences in literacy development across societies. For example, perhaps a difference in number and quality of tonal information conveyed across languages may make the role of phonological awareness different across different Chinese societies. However, relevant research in this area is sparse (Cheung & Ng, 2003).

Noteworthy is the fact that, across all Chinese writing systems and languages, the notion of a 'word' is difficult to conceptualize in Chinese. Each Chinese character corresponds to a single morpheme and syllable, and the layout of Chinese text is character-based. Often, the Chinese character can function as an independent unit in sentences, but sometimes it must be paired with another character or more to form a word. Even Chinese adults differ somewhat on their judgments of how to divide amongst characters into word levels. Most words consist of two or more characters, and more than 80 per cent make use of lexical compounding of morphemes (Packard, 2000).

Chinese phonological structure: syllable and tone

In contrast to English and some other alphabetic languages, Chinese has a relatively simple phonological structure at the level of the syllable. The most commonly used types are vowels, consonant-vowels, and consonant–vowel–consonants among 1,200 tonal syllables in Mandarin (Taylor, 2002). Consonant clusters, relatively typical in English and some other languages, do not exist in Chinese. Subsyllabic units, such as the phoneme and rime, have no direct correspondence with the written form of Chinese, although they can be conceptually segmented.

Indeed, Pinyin, a phonetic script used to aid young children learning to read Chinese characters, is phoneme-based, making use of most letters and letter combinations from the Roman alphabet. Pinyin is used to transcribe Mandarin speech, with the letters of the Roman alphabet each designated with specific sounds conforming to Mandarin, and it usually appears together with newly introduced Chinese characters in textbooks for young children (Cheung & Ng, 2003; Siok & Fletcher, 2001). In Taiwan, a similar system that is relatively onset–rime-based, Zhuyin-Fuhao, is used to teach children to read Chinese. Hong Kong is interesting in its lack of use of a phonetic system for any teaching of Chinese, however. Across Chinese societies, Hong Kong is the only one that uses Cantonese, rather than Mandarin, as its first official language. There was less of a systematic effort to create a standardized phonological coding system to represent this language as compared to Mandarin, and this lack of phonological coding system is unique and a somewhat interesting 'natural experiment' for thinking about Chinese children's literacy development.

Apart from a focus on syllables, onsets, and rhymes, in Chinese, tone is a particularly salient component of Chinese phonology. Tone can be conceptualized as the way in which pitch varies across phonologically identical syllables that represent different meanings. For example, one monosyllable /shi/ in Mandarin can represent four different meanings by changing the pitch to /shi1/ 狮 (lion), /shi2/ 石 (stone), /shi3/ 矢 (arrow), and /shi4/ 室 (room). Thus, in Mandarin, lexical tone can segment into high, low, rising and falling four tones. In contrast, in Cantonese, there are at least high-level, mid-level, low-level, high-rising, low-rising, and low falling tones, i.e. a minimum of six (Chao, 1947; Hashimoto-Yue, 1972; Zee, 1999). Unlike intonation and stress in English, the specific tone for a given syllable is fairly constant across words or syntactic contexts though words can have different boundary tones (e.g. Sanhi rules). Thus, a change in tone marks a change in meaning. Hence, tone cannot be crudely categorized as a subsyllabic or suprasegmental feature of Chinese. The existence of tone in Chinese makes it possible to use limited numbers of spoken syllables to represent a great number of meanings marked by unique Chinese characters. In addition, tone cannot exist independently of the syllable it marks.

Association of phonological awareness with Chinese word reading

According to psycholinguistic grain-size theory, the primacy of different phonological units for word recognition in a given script is influenced by the way in which speech is represented in that script (Ziegler & Goswami, 2005). The syllable is an important phonological unit in Chinese because each syllable represents a single character. Moreover, the morphosyllabic nature of Chinese makes children particularly sensitive to the syllable unit, rather than to other subsyllabic units. In addition, as noted above, tone is a requisite of the syllable representing lexical contrast. The unique morphosyllabic nature and tonal features may make Chinese children especially sensitive to syllable and tone. For example, we (McBride-Chang *et al.*, 2008b) examined three Chinese native language phonological awareness tasks, i.e. syllable deletion, tone detection, and phoneme-onset deletion, in relation to word reading in Chinese and English. Results demonstrated that syllable deletion and tone detection were uniquely associated with Chinese word reading, whereas phoneme-onset deletion was not. Interestingly, phoneme-onset and syllable awareness, but not tone awareness, explained English word reading in the same study. Thus, awareness of syllable and tone, but not phoneme onset, may be particularly salient in young Chinese children. Moreover, syllable deletion and Chinese word reading are bidirectionally associated with one another (Chow *et al.*, 2005), in line with the general relationship between phonological awareness and English word reading (Perfetti *et al.*, 1987). Another study on kindergartners in Beijing further confirmed that both syllable and tone awareness are uniquely associated with word reading in young Chinese children (Shu *et al.*, 2008). Collectively, these studies support the notion that, because the basic unit of writing in Chinese, the character, represents both syllable and tone information by its very nature, the importance of syllable and tone is salient in Chinese, whereas the importance of subsyllabic units such as phoneme onsets may be diminished in this orthography. The salience of syllables, marked by tone information, is also inextricably linked to morphemes in Chinese.

Chinese morphological aspects: morpheme and structure

Indeed, as a meaning-based system, Chinese is viewed as an important language in which to study morphology due to its special morphological system. It has been suggested that the role of morphological awareness in children's literacy development in Chinese may be comparable in importance to the role of phonological awareness in English (Nagy *et al.*, 2002). In Chinese, morphology can be understood in relation to two specific aspects: morpheme and structure.

The morpheme is essential to understanding Chinese morphology. To begin with, a large number of homophones abound in Chinese given the deviation of the mapping between spoken syllable and regularly used words. The ability to distinguish among these homophones and understand the meaning of each within a word or phrase context is essential for adequate reading. In addition to its many homophones, Chinese also has many instances in which one morpheme and character can represent different meanings in different word contexts. For example, one single character 星 represents a heavenly body in 火星 (Mars) but it indicates the meaning of star in 明星 (a star). The sound and form are exactly the same across word contexts but the meanings represented differ. An English example would be the fact that the *light* used in the English phrase *the light of a candle* as compared to *a light rain* represents distinct meanings.

Chinese also has a somewhat unique morphological structure in terms of analytical features and semantic transparency. Lexical compounding is the most often used mode to form new words in Chinese (Packard, 2000). These compound words contain relational knowledge and structural properties. A single Chinese morpheme often has strong combinability to form a new word or concept by being placed together with other morphemes. Often, these compound words share the same semantic base or connection with the individual morphemes. Of these, one of the morphemes functions as a salient semantic marker in representing the concept. For example, the meaning-opaque English word *restaurant* is comprised of two single morphemes 飯 (meal) 店 (shop), which are relatively semantic transparent, in Chinese. The two single morphemes mutually contribute to the meaning of the whole compound word. Of these, the morpheme 店 (shop) in Chinese usually indicates a shop, e.g. 書店 (bookshop), 藥店 (a chemist's shop), 百貨店 (a department store).

The uniqueness of the morphemic structure in Chinese also lies in the way in which morphemes are formed into multimorphemic words. There are at least five different types of compounding structures, as illustrated in Table 12.1. A coordinative compound refers to a structure in which the morphemes are structurally parallel and almost equally cue the meaning of the compound word. For example, a coordinative compounding word 觀看 (watch) is equally represented by the two single morphemes 觀 (observe) and 看 (look) with a parallel structure. In contrast, a modified compound is composed of a meaning-central noun, and the other morpheme comprising it describes or limits the meaning of the noun, as in the word 熱線 (hotline). The meaning of this type of compound is usually derived from the noun. A verb-object compound consists of a verb and its object, e.g. 讀書 (reading book). In contrast, one morpheme functions as the subject and the other as the predicate in a subject–predicate compound, e.g. 家教 (home teaching). Finally, the verb/adjective complement compound consists of a single verb or adjective with an accompanying adverb or adjective; in this case, the adverb or adjective serves to describe the extent of or the consequence of the action evoked by the verb, e.g. 穿透 (pass through). The latter three types of compounding structure mainly assume that the word constituents carry the same identity as the surface syntactic constituents (Packard, 2000). Across types, the single morpheme contributes to or cues the meaning of the whole compound. Moreover, the relative importance of the single morpheme in different types of compounds is different and this differentiation across structure makes it much easier to identify or capture the meanings of newly formed compounds by getting clues from the prime single morpheme in terms of the structure because of the relationship between the prime morpheme

Table 12.1 Different intra morphemic structure in compound words

Types of structure	Single Morpheme		The New formed word	Intra relationship
	Morpheme 1	Morpheme 2		
Coordinative	觀 (observe)	看 (look)	觀看 (watch)	structurally parallel
Modificatory	熱 (hot)	線 (line)	熱線 (hotline)	modifier-modified
Verb-object	讀 (read)	書 (book)	讀書 (reading book)	action-receiver
Subject-predicate	家 (home)	教 (training)	家教 (home teaching)	operator-operation
Verb/adjective complement	穿 (pass)	透 (through)	穿透 (pass through)	mutually complement

and the compound word. In addition, given that compounding is a predominant word formation process (Packard, 2000), children may show early awareness of different types of compounds, flexibly manipulate different types of compound structures, and apply rules to form a new morphologically complex word based on known words. This might be one way in which children's vocabulary size strikingly increases in a short time. In this sense, the extent to which children are aware of or manipulate different types of compounding structure might influence how children perceive and understand the meaning of morphologically complex words in Chinese.

Relationship of morphological awareness to Chinese word reading

Given the predominance of morphological awareness in Chinese, children's ability to be aware of morphemic structure and manipulate that structure, referred to as morphological awareness (Carlisle, 1995), might be uniquely important for understanding the process of learning to read Chinese (e.g. Kuo & Anderson, 2006). An emerging consensus in Chinese word reading is that morphological awareness is a crucial skill required for learning to read Chinese beyond phonological awareness (McBride-Chang et al., 2003; Shu et al., 2006). Moreover, morphological awareness is an important construct to use to diagnose the children who are at risk for Chinese word reading (McBride-Chang et al., 2008a; Shu et al., 2006). An illustration of the association of morphological awareness to Chinese word reading comes from McBride-Chang et al. (2003), who sought to measure morphological awareness using oral tasks only. They operationalized morphological awareness as the performance on morpheme identification, a measure of homophone sensitivity, and morphological construction, a measure of lexical compounding, and results suggested that both morpheme identification and morphological construction accounted for unique variance in Chinese word reading, especially in kindergarten, beyond phonological awareness and other reading-related skills. The findings on homophone awareness have been demonstrated in other studies of concurrent reading in older children as well (Li et al., 2002; McBride-Chang et al., 2003; Shu et al., 2006). In addition, we have sought to examine the relative strength of phonological awareness, morphological awareness, and orthographic awareness in Chinese word reading, spelling, and reading comprehension in a recent study. We have found that both morphological awareness and orthographic knowledge appear to explain unique variance across word reading, spelling, and reading comprehension. However, phonological awareness does not uniquely explain any of these literacy skills. An analysis of children's spelling errors has further revealed that most of the spelling mistakes young Hong Kong Chinese children make are morpho-lexically or orthographically based; very few are phonological errors (Tong et al., submitted). Similarly, a study investigating the role of phonological awareness, morphological awareness, and orthographic skills in Chinese–English biscriptal reading among advanced Chinese readers has shown that both morphological awareness and visual-orthographic skills explain unique variance of Chinese word reading. In contrast, phonological awareness is associated with English word reading only (Tong & McBride-Chang, submitted). These findings from studies of morphological awareness in Chinese word reading underscore the fact that morphological awareness is a central construct of Chinese word reading and spelling beyond phonological awareness.

Subcharacter or sublexical structure: phonetic and semantic radicals

Apart from phonology and morphology, the Chinese orthography has other unique characteristics at the character level. There are two types of Chinese characters: simple characters and complex characters (Li, 1993). Of these, the simple character makes up approximately 5 per cent of all characters, while the complex character comprises around 95 per cent of characters (Yin & Rohsenow, 1994). Moreover, most of these complex characters are semantic–phonetic compounds, which consist of a semantic radical and a phonetic radical. The phonetic radical is typically found on the right side of a given character, and it cues the sound of the syllable to an extent. In contrast, the semantic radical is usually located on the left of the character, and it gives some clue as to meaning categorization. For example, a phonetic–semantic compound 橋 /kiu4/ (bridge) can be decomposed into the semantic radical 木 /muk6/ (wood) and the phonetic radical 喬 /kiu4/.

The system of sublexical or subcharacter units is fairly complex. For example, the extent to which phonetic or semantic radicals provide sound or semantic information varies across characters. In terms of phonetic regularity, semantic-phonetic compounds can be categorized into regular, semi-regular, and irregular – three main types (Shu et al., 2003). Of these, regular characters are those in which the phonetic-semantic compound sounds the same as the phonetic radical, such as 抬 /toi4/ (carry) in Cantonese sharing the same sound as the phonetic radical 台 /toi4/ (stage). The semi-regular character indicates that the semantic–phonetic compound shares either the same onset or rime as the phonetic radical, but the tone can be different. For example, 殆 /doi6/ (danger) has the same rime as its phonetic radical 台 /toi4/(stage) in Cantonese. However, the sound of given irregular characters is irrelevant to the sound of their corresponding phonetic radicals, such as the sound 怡 /ji4/ (happy) and its phonetic radical 台 /toi4/(stage) in Cantonese. Similarly, the semantic relationship between semantic radicals and phonetic-semantic compounds can be briefly summarized as transparent, semi-transparent, or in varying degrees of semantic transparency. As estimated, approximately 92 per cent of phonetic–semantic compounds comprise simple Chinese characters which are the convergence of sound, form, and meanings. There also exists experimental evidence suggesting that the processing of phonetic radicals in compound words activates semantic meanings (Zhou & Marslen-Wilson, 1999; N. Wu et al., 1999). Thus, phonetic and semantic radicals are the functional units in forming morphologically complex words. Most of them are also independent units conveying meaning and sound. However, like the prefixes and suffixes in English such as *un–*, *pre–* and *–ly*, they cannot stand alone to represent meaning and sound. Thus, sublexical units in Chinese form a complex system with unique structural and functional properties.

Contribution of sublexical or subcharacter information to Chinese word reading

Given that most phonetic and semantic radicals are simple single Chinese characters learned at early stages by young Chinese children, it might be possible that children can make use of known information of one part of the character to infer the sound or meaning of the phonetic–semantic compound. For example, several regular phonetic-semantic compounds in Mandarin such as 钟 /zung1/ (clock), 忠 /zung1/ (loyal) and 衷 /zung1/ (heartfelt) consist of a common phonetic radical 中 /zung1/ (middle) and it might be easy for children to get the sound of these phonetic–semantic compounds on the basis of phonological information from the known single character 中 /zung1/. Similar to phonetic radicals, children might crudely access the meanings of the phonetic-semantic compounds 跑 (run), 跳 (jump), 跨 (stride), 蹦 (hop) by relying on the functional information of the semantic radical 足 (foot).

Indeed, there are at least three studies that have investigated the role of phonetic radicals in naming unfamiliar Chinese phonetic compounds. Ho and Bryant (1997) required Hong Kong second-graders to pronounce compound characters, two-character words, and pseudocharacters. Results showed that naming pseudocharacters is highly correlated with reading of compound character and two-character words. Given that pseudocharacters are novel combinations of phonetic radicals and semantic radicals that conform to constraints within the Chinese writing system, this finding might suggest that phonetic radical awareness is helpful to children's reading performance. Anderson *et al.* (2003) extended this research to examine whether second- and fourth-grade Mandarin speakers with diverse home languages could readily use tone-different and onset-different phonetic information to sound out unknown compound characters. In their study, children were given regular characters, tone-different characters, onset-different characters, and unfamiliar phonetic compounds. Of these, children more readily accessed the tone-different characters than the onset-different characters, although they could use both types of partial information to pronounce novel phonetic compounds. Another study sought to examine whether children were aware of the functional information of phonetic radicals and could use this to read unknown phonetic–semantic compound characters in second- and fourth-grade Mandarin speakers. Results again demonstrated that Chinese children can use different types of information cued by phonetic radicals (tone or onset different, bound-phonetic character, and independent-phonetic character) to sound out unfamiliar compound characters (He *et al.*, 2005). Another study by Cheung *et al.* (2007) demonstrated that types of phonetic radicals contributed to variance in character naming, whereas types of semantic radicals were associated with character comprehension rather than naming. These findings might support the idea that phonetic radical and semantic radicals cue only sound and meaning, respectively, rather than both.

Teaching of reading to Chinese children

Given the accumulated information about phonological and morphological awareness as well as phonetic and semantic radicals in relation to Chinese children's literacy development, the issues of how Chinese word recognition is currently taught and of what more and less effective ways of teaching might be are important to consider. In most Chinese societies, a phonological system (such as Pinyin in Mainland China, and Zhuyin in Taiwan) is explicitly taught at the beginning of first grade (if not in late kindergarten) to help children to recognize Chinese characters labeled using this system in textbooks. These phonological systems could be treated as a set of explicit phonological tactics, which can effectively help children to learn new words, and, thus, to learn to read (Shu *et al.*, 1993; Shu & Liu, 1994; Wu *et al.*, 2002). It should be noted, however, that although these systems are consistently paired with Chinese words in textbooks, the ultimate goal is for children to learn to recognize the characters themselves; the phonological systems are merely used as a tool for easy recognition. In Hong Kong, in contrast, word recognition is taught only using a 'look and say' method, without any phonologically auxiliary codes. In Hong Kong, children are asked simply to focus on memorizing the configurations of the characters. Not surprisingly, compared with students from Mainland China or Taiwan, Hong Kong students tend to score lowest on tasks of phonological awareness (Holm & Dodd, 1996; Huang & Hanley, 1995), presumably because they are not forced to focus on phoneme-level units of sound as is the case in other Chinese societies through the use of phonological coding systems.

Furthermore, in all mainstream Chinese educational systems, Chinese word recognition is taught mostly through an emphasis on rote copying and memorizing. Repetition in writing of characters is thought to strengthen recognition of the characters and is encouraged both in school and at home (e.g. X. Wu *et al.*, 1999). There is little attention to analysis of Chinese characters, and metalinguistic knowledge, including commonalities of phonetic radicals or semantic radicals, may be learned only incidentally in children's learning (e.g. X. Wu *et al.*, 1999), though more of a focus on structural characteristics across characters has been advocated by educators (e.g. Tse *et al.*, 1995).

There is evidence that this focus on structural elements of Chinese characters is correlated with better reading in children. For example, when asked to learn new Chinese characters, children tend to capitalize on previously learned associations of phonetic and semantic radicals to sound and meaning, respectively (e.g. Chan & Wang, 2003; Ko & Wu, 2003). Those who can read more also tend to be more skilled in making use of these radicals than are less able readers (e.g. Blote *et al.*, 2003). In another study, it was found that Hong Kong Chinese children's visual chunking skill was highly correlated with their reading abilities (Pak *et al.*, 2005). Correspondingly, the children who could not chunk strokes into larger components, i.e. semantic and phonetic radicals, also showed more difficulties in reading.

There are additional studies of educational interventions that similarly demonstrate that a more analytic approach to teaching reading can facilitate children's reading development. For example, some research has found that explicit training of either phonological or orthographic strategies significantly improves children's reading skills (Ho & Ma, 1999; Ho *et al.*, 1999a). A study targeted on morphological knowledge, Nagy *et al.* (2002) further showed that educational interventions focused on children's morphological awareness significantly improved children's acquisition of morphological knowledge, and, most important, had a significant effect on both reading and writing. In another study (Fu & Huang, 2000), phonological sensitivity training, tone awareness training, and morpheme awareness training programs were administered to second-graders from Taiwan. This metalinguistic training improved both children's metalinguistic awareness and their character recognition abilities. Collectively, this research demonstrates that analytic and metalinguistic knowledge training can facilitate children's literacy development.

Children's reading development is not only the work of teachers in schools but also involves parents. Children's language-related abilities are well developed before formal education begins, and parents' early encouragement of reading and instruction in literacy activities can effectively help children to develop these and other literacy-related abilities. For example, in a cross-cultural study on parental influences on Chinese literacy development, it was found that home literacy education significantly contributed to the prediction of Chinese literacy attainment in Beijing, Hong Kong, and Singapore in preschoolers. In that study, parents who positively engaged in literacy teaching, consciously built up a literacy environment at home, and had a positive attitude toward language learning could effectively help their children to develop literacy skills (Li & Rao, 2000). In another study of Chinese kindergartners in Hong Kong, the roles of both parent–child shared book reading and morphology training on children's literacy improvement were explored (Chow *et al.*, 2008). This research demonstrated that parents' dialogical reading, in which children are encouraged to talk a lot about the book they are reading together with their parents, is particularly effective in improving children's vocabulary knowledge and enjoyment of reading. Furthermore, parents' morphological emphasis with their children (i.e. morphological awareness training) significantly improved children's character recognition. Parents' literacy interactions with children can also be extended to writing (Lin *et al.*, in press). In the Lin *et al.* (in press) study, mothers who emphasized orthographic and morphological relations across characters, e.g. by pointing out the similarities across characters in orthography or meaning, or by focusing on the semantic radical of the character and how its meaning related to the meaning of the word, tended to have children who were better readers. In contrast, children whose mothers emphasized rote memorization and copying of Chinese characters tended to have children who were relatively poorer in word recognition (Lin *et al.*, in press).

Taken together, these studies emphasize the importance of analytic approaches to Chinese children's literacy skills for reading and writing both at home and in school. Both correlational data and intervention studies demonstrate that teachers and parents who point out explicit commonalities across Chinese characters at the sublexical level or across words at the character or morpheme level tend to facilitate children's reading and writing skills. More research on the best practices in education for young Chinese children's most efficient literacy learning will be helpful in future studies.

Some challenges for understanding Chinese word reading and spelling

Despite the basic and applied research on Chinese children's literacy development and training, there are still at least three issues that need to be resolved specifically in the area of research on Chinese word reading. The first is how to categorize lexical tone in the field of psycholinguistics. The second is the extent to which morphological awareness represents one or many aspects in Chinese. Along this same line, the third is how to conceptualize sublexical units, as part of morphological awareness or as something unique to it. Each of these questions is considered below.

Is lexical tone an independent psycholinguistic unit? According to psycholinguistic grain-size theory (Ziegler & Goswami, 2005), syllables, onsets/rimes, and phonemes are the three fundamental units of phonological awareness from relatively large to small. Moreover, children's phonological awareness progresses from large phonological units to small phonological units with development. Given the intrasyllabic division of rime and onset, a controversial issue is whether lexical tone, a necessary constituent of the syllable in Chinese, can be considered an additional psycholinguistic unit or a suprasegmental feature. Lexical tone is a unique unit with several special properties. First, tone has several segmental features, such as frequency and contour. It could also involve the same articulatory gestures as intonation or stress in English (Duanmu, 2004). Second, tone is more than a phonological unit because it conveys semantic contrasts across identical syllable structures. Third, although tone is conceptualized as the variation of pitch of a syllable, pitch alone cannot represent lexical meaning (Duanmu, 2004). That is, tone can convey lexical contrast only when it exists within a syllable. From the perspective of psycholinguistic grain-size theory (Ziegler & Goswami, 2005), it is therefore difficult to categorize tone as an independent psycholinguistic unit on the one hand or as an additional feature of the syllable on the other. If it is perceived as an independent unit, it should convey some information in isolation. However, it is a unique feature of the syllable, conveying meaning in a unique way. Tone perception also develops relatively early. Previous findings from the studies of alphabetic reading have shown that children as young as 3 to 4 years old can acquire syllable awareness, while onset–rime awareness occurs around the ages of 4 to 5 years (Ziegler & Goswami, 2005). In contrast, studies from tone perception and production have demonstrated that Chinese children (Cantonese and Mandarin) acquire tone by the age of 2 years (Tse, 1978; SoLydia & Dodd, 1995; Li & Thompson, 1977). In addition, in correlational studies, lexical tone can contribute unique variance in Chinese word reading after controlling for syllable awareness, phoneme awareness, and other reading-related skills (McBride-Chang et al., 2008a; Shu et al., 2008). A new line of research on Chinese phonological awareness could be broadened to examine whether tone awareness can be separately measured from the syllable and its independent role in Chinese word reading from these preliminary findings. Moreover, it might be theoretically interesting to investigate how tonal language speakers perceive English stress and intonation in relation to lexical tone, as well as the cross-language transfer effect of tone. In addition, a new theory incorporating lexical tone into the psycholinguistic unit system might conceptualize psycholinguistic units as different layers rather than different sizes since lexical tone cannot clearly be categorized into large vs. small units.

Another recent issue in the developmental literature on Chinese reading is whether morphological awareness is unitary or divisible. Some researchers have argued that Chinese is an important language in which to study morphology because of its unique features (Packard, 2000). In some studies (McBride-Chang et al., 2003; Shu et al., 2006), morphological awareness is defined as access to the morpheme and structure manipulation in two perspectives. Meaning access to the morpheme is measured in tasks of morpheme judgment, such as whether the meanings of the same character/syllable 生 across words 生陌 (new things) and 生字 (new character) are the same morpheme in terms of meaning (Shu et al., 2006) or by asking children to produce homophones with different meanings or morphemes with the same meanings across different words consisting of two or more morphemes.

Levels of morphological awareness might involve targeting a single morpheme, e.g. a given homophone, as compared to morphological structure, which could involve multiple-morpheme words. In addition, as some researchers point out (e.g. Kuo & Anderson, 2006), most studies focus on the development of relationship knowledge and compounding at a basic level rather than the awareness of structures of different types of compound words such as coordinative compounds, subordinate compounds, subject-predicate compounds, etc. It is possible that compounding differs across these categories because the specific roles of morphemes in formed compounds are strikingly different in different compounding words, in addition to a great variation of interrelationships of morphemes in these compound words. Given that lexical compounding is a productive mode of forming new words of all different categories in Chinese (Kuo & Anderson, 2006), it is potentially important to understand the process of structure awareness in relation to word reading

Are sublexical units a part of morphological awareness or a part of some other system, such as the orthographic system? The third issue on Chinese word reading is whether sublexical units (both phonetic radicals and semantic radicals) can be perceived as one part of morphological awareness. As discussed above, most phonetic radicals and semantic radicals can stand alone as simple Chinese characters with their own sounds and meanings. Moreover, there exists experimental evidence that the processing of sublexical units (phonetic radicals and semantic radicals) is the same as processing of whole complex characters in which both sound and meaning are activated, among both adults (Zhou & Marslen-Wilson, 1999) and children (N. Wu *et al.*, 1999). In this sense, sublexical units including phonetic radicals and semantic radicals might be perceived as independent units beyond phonological or morphological units.

However, from the perspective of the contribution of sublexical units to word reading, sublexical units are not distinct from phonological awareness or morphological awareness. Specifically, phonetic radicals and semantic radicals respectively function as cueing the sound and semantic categorization of the complex character, although their individual sounds and meanings are activated unconsciously. Moreover, previous research on sublexical or subcharacter processing has demonstrated that phonetic radicals contribute to Chinese character naming rather than comprehension. In contrast, semantic radicals are uniquely associated with character comprehension only (Cheung *et al.*, 2007). In this sense, phonetic radicals and semantic radicals can be crudely categorized according to phonology and morphology in terms of the function. However, phonetic radicals usually provide partial information to sound, e.g. in Cantonese, 青 /cing1/in 精 /zing1/. Similarly, semantic radicals cue meanings of the phonetic-semantic compound partially, e.g. 日 (sun) in 晴 (clear). Moreover, phonetic radicals and semantic radical are not the same as the phonological or morphological unit. In other words, phonetic radicals or semantic radicals fall somewhere in between phonological awareness or morphological awareness and complex character recognition. This issue is a clear challenge for understanding reading development across orthographies because these units are unique to Chinese, and this issue demands further attention in future studies on Chinese word reading.

Conclusion

The evidence on reading acquisition and development in Chinese reviewed in this chapter supports the importance of metalinguistic skills, both phonological awareness and morphological awareness, as crucial components involved in cognitive-linguistic processing of Chinese word reading. Some unique features not found in most alphabetic languages, such as lexical tone and subcharacter information (i.e. phonetic and semantic radicals) make children's specific competences uniquely important for acquiring Chinese literacy skills. In addition, reading instruction can crucially shape the course of reading development and may differ across Chinese societies and families. All of these findings underscore the complex interactions involved in learning the Chinese orthography, highlighting both language-specific and language-general elements. The special properties of the Chinese orthography, particularly the importance of lexical tone and phonetic and semantic radicals, might offer new opportunities to test specific cross-linguistic theories, such as psycholinguistic grain-size theory focused on phonological processing, as well as to probe interrelations between morphological awareness and subcharacter processing at different levels (lexical, sublexical, and nonlexical). These and other remaining research questions call for more studies on Chinese literacy acquisition. Clearly, studies conducted so far particularly highlight the importance of developing metalinguistic skill and subcharacter competencies for facilitating early word recognition in Chinese.

References

Adams, M.J. (1990). *Beginning to read: Thinking and learning about print*. Cambridge, MA: MIT Press.

Anderson, R.C., Li, W., Ku, Y.-M., Shu, H., & Wu, N. (2003). 'Children's use of partial information in learning to read Chinese'. *Journal of Educational Psychology, 95*, 52–57.

Blote, A., Chen, P., Overmasrs, E., & Van de Heijden, A. (2003). 'Combining phonological and semantic cues in reading pseudocharacters: A comparative study'. In C. McBride-Chang & H.-C. Chen (eds), *Reading Development in Chinese children* (pp.127–140). London: Praeger.

Carlisle, J.F. (1995). 'Morphological awareness and early reading achievement'. In L.B. Feldman (ed.), *Morphological aspects of language processing* (pp. 189–209). Hillsdale, NJ: LEA.

Chan, L., & Wang, L. (2003). 'Linguistic awareness in learning to read Chinese: A comparative study of Beijing and Hong Kong children'. In C. McBride-Chang & H.-C. Chen (eds), *Reading Development in Chinese children* (pp. 91–106). London: Praeger.

Chao, Y.R. (1947). *Cantonese Primer*, Cambridge, Mass: Harvard University Press.

Cheung, H., & Ng, K.H. (2003). 'Chinese reading development in some major Chinese societies: An introduction'. In C. McBride-Chang & H.-C. Chen (eds), *Reading development in Chinese children* (pp. 3–17). London: Praeger.

Cheung, H., Chan, M., & Chong, K. (2007). 'Use of orthographic knowledge in reading by Chinese–English bi-scriptal children'. *Language Learning, 57*, 469–505.

Chow, B.W.-Y., McBride-Chang, C., & Burgess, S. (2005). 'Phonological processing skills and early reading abilities in Hong Kong Chinese kindergartners learning to read English as a second language'. *Journal of Educational Psychology, 99*, 81–87.

Chow, B.W.-Y., McBride-Chang, C., Cheung, H., & Chow, C.S.-L. (2008). 'Dialogic reading and morphology training in Chinese children: Effects on language and literacy'. *Developmental Psychology, 44*, 233–244.

Duanmu, S. (2004). 'Tone and non-tone language: An alternative to language typology and parameters'. *Language and Linguistics, 4*, 891–923.

Fu, C.-L., & Huang, H.-S. (2000). 'The effects of metalinguistic awareness training of the low-achievers at elementary schools'. *Chinese Journal of Psychology, 42*, 87–100.

Harm, M.W., & Seidenberg, M.S. (1999). 'Phonology, reading acquisition, and dylexia: Insights from connectionist models'. *Psychological Review, 106*, 491–528.

Hashimoto-Yue, O.-K. (1972). *Phonology of Cantonese*. Cambridge: Cambridge Univeristy Press.

He, Y.-Q., Wang, Q.-Y., & Anderson, R.C. (2005). 'Chinese children's use of subcharacter information about pronunciation'. *Journal of Educational Psychology, 97*, 572–579.

Ho, C.S.-H. & Bryant, P. (1997). 'Phonological skills are important in learning to read Chinese'. *Developmental Psychology, 33*, 946–951.

Ho, C.S.-H., & Ma, R.N.L. (1999a). 'Training in phonological strategies improves Chinese dyslexic children's character reading skills'. *Journal of Research in Reading, 22*, 131–142.

Ho, C.S.-H., Wong, W.L., & Chan, W.S. (1999b). 'The use of orthographic analogies in learning to read Chinese'. *Journal of Child Psychology and Psychiatry, 40*, 393–403.

Holm, A., & Dodd, B. (1996). 'The effect of first written language on the acquisition of English literacy'. *Cognition, 59*, 119–147.

Huang, H.-S., & Hanley, J.R. (1995). 'Phonological awareness and visual skills in learning to read Chinese and English'. *Cognition, 54*, 73–98.

Ko, H., & Wu, C. (2003). 'The role of character component in reading Chinese'. In C. McBride-Chang & H.-C. Chen (eds), *Reading development in Chinese children* (pp. 91–106). London: Praeger.

Kuo, L.-J. & Anderson, R.C. (2006). 'Morphological awareness and learning to read: A cross-language perspective'. *Educational Psychologist, 41*, 161–180.

Li, C.N. & Thompson, S.A. (1977). 'The acquisition of tones in Mandarin-speaking children'. *Journal of Child Language, 4*, 185–199.

Li, D. (1993). *A study of Chinese characters*. Beijing: Peking University Press.

Li, H., & Rao, N. (2000). 'Parental influences on Chinese literacy development: A comparison of preschoolers in Beijing, Hong Kong and Singapore'. *International Journal of Behavioral Development, 24*, 82–90.

Li, W., Anderson, R.C. Nagy, W., & Zhang, H. (2002). 'Facets of metalinguistic awareness that contribute to Chinese literacy'. In W. Li, J.S. Gaffney, & J.L. Packard (eds), *Chinese children's reading acquisition: Theoretical and pedagogical issues* (pp. 87–106). Boston, MA: Kluwer.

Lin, D., McBride-Chang, C., Aram, D., Levin, I., Cheung, R.Y.M., Chow, Y.Y.Y., & Tolchinsky, L. (in press). 'Maternal mediation of writing in Chinese children'. *Language and Cognitive Processes.*

McBride-Chang, C., Shu, H., Zhou, A.B., Wat, C.P., Wagner, R.K. (2003). 'Morphological awareness uniquely predicts young children's Chinese character recognition'. *Journal of Educational Psychology, 95*, 743–751.

McBride-Chang, C., Lam, F., Lam, C., Doo, S., Wong, S., & Chow, Y. (2008a). 'Word recognition and cognitive profiles of Chinese pre-school children at risk for dyslexia through language delay or familial history of dyslexia'. *Journal of Child Psychology and Psychiatry, 49*, 211–218.

McBride-Chang, C., Tong, X.L., Shu, H., Wong, A.M.-Y., Leung, K.-W., & Tardif, T. (2008b). 'Syllable, phoneme, and tone: Psycholinguistic units in early Chinese and English word reading'. *Scientific Studies of Reading, 12*, 1–24.

Nagy, W. (2007). 'Metalinguistic awareness and the vocabulary-comprehension connection'. In R.K. Wagner, A.E. Muse, & K.R. Tannenbaum (eds), *Vocabulary acquisition: Implications for reading comprehension* (pp. 52–77). New York: Guilford.

Nagy, W., Kuo-Kealoha, A., Wu, X., Li, W., Anderson, R.C., & Chen, X. (2002). 'The role of morphological awareness in learning to read Chinese'. In W. Li, J.S. Gaffney, &

J.L. Packard (eds), *Chinese language acquisition: Theoretical and pedagogical issues* (pp. 59–86). Norwell, MA: Kluwer.

Packard, J.L. (2000). *The morphology of Chinese: A linguistic and cognitive approach.* New York: Cambridge University Press.

Pak, A.K.H., Cheng-Lai, A., Tso, I.F., Shu, H., Li, W., & Anderson, R.C. (2005). 'Visual chunking skills of Hong Kong children'. *Reading and Writing, 18,* 437–454.

Perfetti, C.A., Beck, I., Bell, L., & Hughes, C. (1987). 'Phonemic knowledge and learning to read are reciprocal: A longitudinal study of first grade children'. *Merrill-Palmer Quarterly, 33,* 283–319.

Shu, H., & Liu, B. (1994). 'The role of pinyin on young primary school children's early reading'. *Psychological Development and Education (Chinese), 3,* 11–15.

Shu, H., & Anderson, R.C. (1999). 'Learning to read Chinese: The development of metalinguistic awareness'. In J. Wang, A.W. Inhoff, & H.-C. Chen (eds), *Reading Chinese script: A cognitive analysis* (pp. 1–18). Mahwah, NJ: LEA.

Shu, H., Chen, X., Anderson, R.C., Wu, N., & Xuan, Y. (2003). 'Properties of school Chinese: Implications for learning to read'. *Child Development, 74,* 27–47.

Shu, H., Zeng, H., & Cheng, Z. (1993). 'An experimental study on young primary school children's new-word learning with pinyin'. *Psychological Development and Education (Chinese), 1,* 18–22.

Shu, H., McBride-Chang, C., Wu, S., & Liu, H. (2006). 'Understanding Chinese developmental dyslexia: Morphological awareness as a core cognitive construct'. *Journal of Educational Psychology, 98,* 122–133.

Shu, H., Peng, H., & McBride-Chang, C. (2008). 'Phonological awareness in young Chinese children'. *Developmental Science, 11,* 171–181.

Siok, W.T., & Fletcher, P. (2001). 'The role of phonological awareness and visual-orthographic skills in Chinese reading acquisition'. *Developmental Psychology. 37,* 886–899.

SoLydia, K.H., & Dodd, B.J. (1995). 'The acquisition of phonology by Cantonese-speaking children'. *Journal of Child Language, 22,* 473–495.

Taylor, S. (2002). 'Phonological awareness in Chinese reading'. In W. Li, J.S. Gaffney, & J.L. Packard (eds), *Chinese language acquisition: Theoretical and pedagogical issues* (pp. 59–86). Norwell, MA: Kluwer.

Tong, X., & McBride-Chang, C. (submitted). 'Chinese–English biscriptal reading: Cognitive component skills across orthographies'.

Tong, X., McBride-Chang, C., Shu, H., & Wong, A.M.-Y. (submitted). 'Morphological awareness and orthographic knowledge: Keys to understanding word reading, spelling acquisition and errors, and reading comprehension in Hong Kong Chinese children'.

Tse, J.K.P. (1978). 'Tone acquisition in Cantonese: A longitudinal study'. *Journal of Child Language, 22,* 473–495.

Tse, S.K., Chan, W.S., Ho, W.K., Law, N., Lee, T., Shek, C. *et al.* (1995). *Chinese language education for the 21st century: A Hong Kong perspective.* Faculty of Education, University of Hong Kong.

Weekes, B.S., & Chen, M.J. (2002). 'Picture-word interference effects on naming in Chinese'. In H.R. Kao, D.G. Gao, & C.K. Leong (eds), *Cognitive and neuroscience studies of Chinese language* (pp. 101–127). Hong Kong: University of Hong Kong Press.

Wu, N.N., Zhou, X., & Shu, H. (1999). 'Sublexical processing in reading Chinese: A development study'. *Language and Cognitive Process, 14,* 503–524.

Wu, X., Li, W., & Anderson, R.C. (1999). 'Reading instruction in China'. *Journal of Curriculum Studies, 31,* 571–586.

Wu, X., Li, H., Shu, H., Anderson, R.C., & Li, W. (2002). 'The role of pinyin in Chinese children's shared book reading'. *Psychological Science (China), 25,* 548–639.

Yang, J.F., Zevin, J.D., Shu, H., McCandliss, B.D., & Li, P. (2006). 'A "Triangle Model" of Chinese reading'. Poster presented at the Cognitive Science Conference.

Yin, B., & Rohsenow, J.S. (1994). *Modern Chinese characters*. Beijing: Sinolingua.

Zee, E. (1999). 'Change and variation in the syllable-initial and syllable-final consonants in Hong Kong Cantonese'. *Journal of Chinese Linguistics, 27*,120–167.

Zhou, X., & Marslen-Wilson, W. (1999). 'The nature of sublexical processing in reading Chinese characters'. *Journal of Experimental Psychology: Learning, Memory, and Cognition, 25,* 1–19.

Ziegler, J.C., & Goswami, U. (2005). 'Reading acquisition, developmental dyslexia, and skilled reading across languages: A psycholinguistic grain size theory'. *Psychological Bulletin, 131,* 3–29.

Part 3

Written language difficulties and approaches to teaching

Enhancing word reading, spelling and reading comprehension skills with synthetic phonics teaching

Studies in Scotland and England

Rhona S. Johnston, Joyce E. Watson and Sarah Logan

Phonics is a method of teaching reading whereby children learn that letter sounds can be used to decode unfamiliar words. While not encompassing all of the skills children need when reading, it does support the development of the basic building block of reading, that is, word recognition skill. Although phonics has historically been taught in English-speaking countries for many years, it has not generally taken the form of teaching children, at the start of reading tuition, to sound and blend the letters, or graphemes, in printed words, e.g. /k/ /a/ /t/ - > 'cat'. This approach, called synthetic phonics, is commonly used in languages that have a straightforward connection between spelling and pronunciation. For example, German has regular grapheme-to-phoneme correspondences, and in countries such as Austria (Feitelson, 1988) children are taught to read using the synthetic phonics approach soon after starting school. It is also used in many other European countries, such as the Netherlands and Sweden.

There has been considerable resistance, however, to using synthetic phonics in the UK, in part due to the belief that the English spelling system is not sufficiently alphabetic for it to work. This is because some words contain only a limited guide to pronunciation, e.g. 'yacht', 'aisle'. The suggestion, therefore, that children should learn to read English by using grapheme-to-phoneme conversion right at the start of reading tuition is an anathema in some quarters. In 1994, Goswami argued that a teaching method where children are initially taught to read at the grapheme-to-phoneme conversion level poses unnecessary difficulties for them, proposing that children should be taught to read by making analogies between known sight words and unfamiliar words, with a focus on common rimes and onsets, e.g. /k/ /at/ - > 'cat' (Goswami, 1994). Although this view has been very influential with teachers in the UK, Goswami (2008) has recently acknowledged that children learning to read need to learn grapheme-to-phoneme conversion skills. However, she still argues that they also need to be taught rhyme-analogy skills, making no comment on the order in which these approaches should be taught. Dombey (2006) has also written about the challenges that English orthography presents to learner readers. She argues that 'it is never going to be enough to teach children the phoneme–grapheme correspondences of words such as "dog" and "cat" ... We need to help them become aware of other patterns. Rhyme is particularly useful here ... the rime is a stable spelling that represents a stable pronunciation, and so provides a better clue to word identification than does a grapheme-by-grapheme analysis.'

Another strongly held view is that it is beneficial for children to be trained in phonological awareness skills prior to learning to read (Maclean *et al.*, 1987; Fraser, 1997; Goswami, 1999). Although there is a well-established association between preschool phonological awareness skill and later reading ability (e.g. Bradley & Bryant, 1983), there are only a few studies showing that training this skill without print exposure is beneficial for reading and spelling (Cunningham, 1990; Lie, 1991; Lundberg *et al.*, 1988). Indeed, other studies find that children only benefit from phonological awareness training if they are shown how the sounds in words are represented by letters of the alphabet (Ball & Blachman, 1991; Bradley & Bryant, 1983; Byrne & Fielding-Barnsley, 1989, 1991; Fox & Routh, 1984; Hatcher *et al.*, 1994; Williams, 1980).

Our studies have been designed therefore to examine whether children can learn to read using synthetic phonics at the start of reading tuition, whether phonological awareness training without letters is of any benefit, and to examine the long-term effects of synthetic phonics teaching on reading and spelling skills.

Studies of phonics teaching

Study 1: Longitudinal observational study of analytic phonics teaching

Until recently the predominant approach used in the UK has been analytic phonics. For her PhD, Joyce Watson began a study in 12 schools in Scotland in 1992, examining how analytic phonics was taught to children just starting school (Watson, 1998). At this time, Watson, a college of education lecturer, was a supporter of the psycholinguistic guessing method advocated by Smith (1978), where children were encouraged to work out what an unfamiliar word was by inferring its meaning from context. All 12 schools were following the regional guidelines for phonics teaching. By observing the teachers implementing the phonics programme, Watson found that for the first two terms at school, letter sounds were taught at the pace of one a week, in the initial position of words. At the start of the third term, the children learnt about letters in the final position of words, and then in the middle position. At this point, the children were taught to sound and blend simple consonant–vowel–consonant (CVC) words, e.g. c-a-t - > 'cat'. In the second year of school, the children learnt about consonant digraphs, consonant blends and vowel digraphs. The children were shown word families with similar spelling patterns, that is, consonant digraphs, e.g. '*ch*in', '*ch*op, '*ch*ill'; initial consonant blends, e.g. '*st*ing', '*st*and', '*st*op'; final consonant blends, e.g. 'ma*st*', 'lo*st*', 'fi*st*'; vowel digraphs, e.g. 'c*oa*t', 'b*oa*t', 'fl*oa*t'. Split vowel digraphs, e.g. 'c*a*k*e*', 'b*a*k*e*', 'm*a*k*e*' were taught in the third year of school. This approach was common in Scotland at the time of our study, and a similar approach was recommended in the English government scheme *Progression in Phonics* (DfEE, 1999).

At the end of the second term at school, before the children had learnt to sound and blend, the children's reading and spelling skills were tested. What Watson found was that the children had very little independent reading skill. However, when tested only two months later, after they had been taught how to sound and blend, she found that the children's reading ability had risen by around six months. The deduction that this was due to being taught to sound and blend was supported by the observation that in one class where sounding and blending had been introduced earlier, in the second term of school, these children were reading ahead of the children in the other classes. Both Frith (1985) and Ehri (2005) have outlined a stage in reading development where children use letter–sound correspondences all through the word; this is the second stage in Frith's model and the third in Ehri's. Joyce Watson's (1998) study suggested that children can attain this stage very early on through direct teaching of sounding and blending.

Study 2: The effectiveness of analytic versus synthetic phonics teaching

The question arose as to whether children would make better progress in reading and spelling if they learnt how to sound and blend right at the start of their schooling, that is, by a synthetic phonics approach. We examined this in an experimental intervention (Johnston & Watson, 2004, Experiment 2). Using a sample of 92 children who had just started school, we randomly allocated the children into three groups (taken equally from four classrooms). These children were seen in small groups for extra teaching, in addition to the classroom analytic phonics programme, where they were learning about letter sounds in the initial position of words; all four teachers were following the region's guidelines on how to teach phonics. The extra teaching sessions used the same new printed word vocabulary in all three conditions. In one condition (the no-letter training group), the children were told how these words were pronounced, but they learnt no new letter sounds, and their attention was not drawn to the letter sounds in the words. In the second condition (the accelerated analytic phonics group), the children learnt letter sounds at the rate of two a week, and their attention was drawn to the letters in the initial position of words. The third group was also taught letter sounds at the rate of two a week (the synthetic phonics group), learning to sound and blend the letters all through the words, in order to find out how they were pronounced; they also segmented spoken words for spelling. There were two 15-minute training sessions a week, for a period of 10 weeks, a total of 19 sessions. Post-testing was carried out at the end of the intervention, and then three and nine months later.

In Table 13.1, we show the children's pre-and first post-test scores on the British Picture Vocabulary Scale (Dunn & Dunn, 1982), the British Ability Scales Word Reading Test (Elliott et al., 1977), the Yopp–Singer phoneme segmentation task (Yopp, 1988), and a test of letter knowledge.

No differences were found between the groups at pre-test on these measures, and the children did not score on the reading test. When post-tested at the end of the intervention, the groups differed in single word reading ability, $F(2, 89) = 7.4$, $p < .001$. Newman Keuls tests showed that the synthetic phonics group performed better than the accelerated analytic phonics and no-letter groups, who did not differ from each other. The groups also differed in letter knowledge, $F(2, 89) = 7.7$, $p < .001$. Newman Keuls tests showed that the synthetic phonics group knew more letter sounds than the accelerated analytic phonics and no-letter groups, who did not differ from each other. On the phoneme segmentation test, the difference between groups was not quite significant, $F(2, 89) = 3.0$, $p = .055$.

The data from the final post-test, nine months after the end of the intervention, at the start of the second year at school, are of particular interest (see Table 13.2). At

Table 13.1 Mean chronological age, vocabulary knowledge (BPVS), mean reading age (British Ability Scales), letter sound knowledge, and phoneme segmentation (Yopp–Singer Test), (standard deviations in brackets), Study 2.

Research Condition	Age	BPVS	Reading Age	Letter Knowledge	Phonemic Segmentation
Pre-test	Years	Standardised Scores	Years	%	%
No-letter controls, n=29	5.0 (0.3)	94.3 (12.5)	–	8.0 (18.6)	2.7 (11.4)
Accelerated Analytic Phonics n=33	5.0 (0.3)	94.6 (15.2)	–	5.8 (16.9)	1.8 (10.3)
Synthetic Phonics n=30	5.0 (0.3)	95.5 (14.4)	–	8.6 (21.2)	1.7 (9.1)
First post-test					
No-letter controls, n=29	5.2 (0.3)	–	5.0 (0.5)	30.4 (24.0)	9.7 (21.6)
Accelerated Analytic Phonics n=33	5.2 (0.3)	–	5.0 (0.3)	37.1 (26.8)	9.0 (19.7)
Synthetic Phonics n=30	5.3 (0.3)	–	5.4 (0.3)	51.8 (21.7)	21.2 (26.5)

Table 13.2 Mean chronological age, vocabulary knowledge (BPVS), reading age (British Ability Scales), spelling age (Schonell spelling test), letter sound knowledge, phoneme segmentation (Yopp–Singer Test), and nonword reading (standard deviations in brackets), Study 2.

Research Condition	Age	BPVS	Reading Age	Spelling Age	Letter Knowledge	Phonemic Segmentation
Final post-test	Years	Standardised Score	Years	Years	%	%
No-letter controls, n=29	6.0 (0.3)	–	5.6 (0.9)	5.6 (0.8)	68.1 (22.6)	26.8 (36.2)
Accelerated Analytic Phonics n=33	6.0 (0.3)	–	5.5 (0.8)	5.4 (0.7)	68.1 (24.9)	25.8 (36.7)
Synthetic Phonics n=30	6.0 (0.3)	–	6.3 (1.3)	6.3 (0.8)	82.0 (20.1)	69.3 (36.1)

this stage, the children in all of the groups had learnt to sound and blend in the classroom phonics programme. At this point we included a test of spelling (Schonell & Schonell, 1952), and a test of nonword reading, consisting of simple CVC items such as 'hig' and 'gok'.

The groups differed in single word reading ability, $F(2, 83)$ = 5.8, p < .004. Newman Keuls tests showed that the synthetic phonics group performed better than the no-letter and accelerated analytic phonics groups. The groups also differed in letter sound knowledge, $F(2, 83)$ = 3.6, p < .05; Newman Keuls tests showed that the synthetic phonics group had better letter-sound knowledge than the other two groups, who did not differ from each other. For nonword reading, a main effect of groups was found, $F(2, 83)$ = 16.5, p < .001; Newman Keuls tests showed the synthetic phonics group read more nonwords correctly than the accelerated analytic phonics and no-letter groups, who did not differ from each other. On the spelling test, there was a main effect of groups, $F(2, 83)$ = 11.1, p < .001; Newman Keuls tests showed that the synthetic phonics group spelt more words correctly than the accelerated analytic phonics and no-letter groups, who did not differ from each other. On the phoneme segmentation task, the groups also differed, $F(2, 83)$ = 13.3, p < .001; Newman Keuls tests showed that the synthetic phonics group performed better than the accelerated analytic phonics and no-letter groups, who did not differ from each other.

It was very clear from this study that the children read best when they learnt early on by a synthetic phonics approach. The results do not support the view that children cannot learn to read at the grapheme–to–phoneme conversion level at the start of schooling (Goswami, 1994; Dombey, 2006). Teaching children about the onsets of words, as in the accelerated analytic phonics condition, was much less effective. Even when the children subsequently learnt to sound and blend in their classroom phonics programmes, those taught in the accelerated analytic phonics and the no-letter learning conditions did not catch up with the children taught this way from the start. It was also of interest that although the accelerated analytic phonics group learnt letter sounds at the same speed as the synthetic phonics group, the latter group learnt the letter sounds much better. We also found that the synthetic phonics group had significantly better awareness of phonemes in spoken words.

Since publishing this work, a meta-analysis, funded by the Department for Education and Skills in England, has claimed that when comparing randomised controlled trial studies there is no clear outcome favouring either synthetic or analytic phonics. There are few randomised controlled trial studies making this sort of comparison; the authors of the meta-analysis found three, including our Study 2 (Johnston & Watson, 2004, Experiment 2). One of the other two studies is an unpublished one (Skailand, 1971), having an invalid implementation of the synthetic phonics method (kindergarten children were taught to sound and blend complex words such as 'tube' rather than simple CVC words such as 'cat'). Torgerson et al. (2006) argue that unpublished studies like this should be included as negative results are not published; however, the Skailand (1971) study actually reported a significant difference between conditions on the trained items. Unfortunately, performance on these trained items, rather than the untrained ones, was used in the meta-analysis, contravening the procedure used by the National Reading Panel. The second study Torgerson et al. (2006) included, examined the effectiveness of synthetic phonics teaching for children at risk of reading failure, compared with an embedded phonics condition (Torgesen et al., 1999), a very long intervention lasting 2.5 years. However, Torgerson et al. (2006) chose to compare the effectiveness of the two methods after only half a year of teaching, when the children in the synthetic phonics condition had spent much of their time learning to hear the sounds in spoken words (i.e.

phonological awareness training), and the children in the embedded phonics condition had done a lot of sight word reading. At this point, the children in the embedded phonics condition scored more highly on a test of word recognition ability. However, by the end of the intervention, the children in the synthetic phonics condition were significantly ahead of those in the embedded phonics condition, and Torgesen *et al.* (1999) concluded that synthetic phonics was the most effective method for boosting word recognition, a conclusion diametrically opposed to that of Torgerson *et al.* (2006). Leaving aside Skailand's (1971) unpublished study, with its invalid implementation of synthetic phonics, we have recalculated the pooled effect sizes from the end of the two remaining interventions. We pooled the effect size from the end of Torgesen *et al.*'s (1999) intervention with the effect size from the end of our study. This calculation produced a large effect size favouring synthetic phonics (Johnston & Watson, in press). It can be concluded that synthetic phonics works well for both normal school entrants and those at risk of reading failure.

Study 3: Longitudinal phonological awareness training, with and without letters (Clackmannanshire Study)

Despite a contradictory literature on whether training phonological awareness skills without using letters and print is beneficial for children's reading and spelling, in educational circles it is generally believed to be necessary to teach children oral sounding and blending before they start to learn to read (see, for example, the new official government programme in England *Letters and Sounds*, DfES, 2007, Phase 1, Aspect 7).

This controversy led us to carry out a new study in Clackmannanshire in Scotland (Johnston & Watson, 2004, Experiment 1). We had already found (Study 2) that synthetic phonics teaching led to very high levels of phonemic awareness ability, so the question arose as to whether a phonological awareness training programme taught separately from an analytic phonics programme would similarly boost phoneme awareness ability.

In this new study, the phonics interventions replaced the normal phonics classroom programmes, and were carried out by the class teachers. The other aspects of the language curriculum remained unchanged. Study 2 found that synthetic phonics teaching led to significantly better word reading skills than analytic phonics teaching when we controlled for speed of letter learning, indicating that it was the method that led to the gains, not the accelerated teaching of letter sounds. Therefore, in this study the analytic phonics conditions had the typical speed of implementation of letter-sound learning, of one letter sound a week. This allowed us to implement a thorough phoneme awareness training programme with an analytic phonics group, whereby they had daily sessions in which they learnt to blend and segment phonemes in all positions of words, as in the synthetic phonics condition, but without letters. In their separate phonics sessions they learnt about letter sounds, but only in the initial position of words. Thus half of the 20-minute programme was devoted to analytic phonics teaching, learning letter sounds in the initial position of words, and the other half was devoted to learning how to orally segment and blend the sounds in spoken words (analytic phonics plus phonological awareness condition). The phonological awareness training element was modelled on Cunningham's (1990) programme, it being one of the few studies finding that phoneme awareness training without letters benefited reading ability. In the second condition, the children had a daily 20-minute analytic phonics programme, learning about letter sounds in the initial position of words at the rate of one letter a week (analytic phonics condition). In the third condition, the blending and segmenting of phonemes in all positions of words was carried out using letters and print (the synthetic phonics condition); of necessity, letter sounds were taught at an accelerated pace, six letters being taught every eight days. The children were pre-tested two weeks after starting school; the phonics training programmes began four weeks after starting school, and lasted for 16 weeks. The children started to use reading scheme books six weeks after the programme started.

The same tests were used as in Experiment 1. At pre-test (see Table 13.3), it was found that the groups were matched on chronological age, $F(2, 301) < 1$, verbal ability, $F(2, 301) = 2.6$, $p > .05$, word reading, $F(2, 301) = 1.4$, $p > .05$, spelling, $F(2, 301) < 1$, phoneme segmentation ability, $F(2, 301) < 1$, and nonword reading, $F(2, 301) = 2.4$, $p > .05$. A significant difference, however, was found in knowledge of letter sounds, $F(2, 301) = 3.3$, $p < .04$; the analytic–phonics-only group knew more letter sounds than the other two groups.

The first post-test was carried out on completion of the 16-week intervention. The following analyses used class as the random variable, but where the results diverged from the analyses by subjects we have also reported the latter. It was found that the groups differed in word reading ability, $F(2, 13) = 18.1$, $p < .001$; Newman Keuls tests showed that the synthetic phonics group had significantly higher reading ages than the other two groups, who did not differ from each other. There was a group difference in nonword reading, $F(2, 13) = 45.6$, $p < .001$; Newman Keuls tests showed that nonword reading was better in the synthetic phonics group than the other two groups, and the other two groups did not differ from each other. There was also a group difference in the ability to spell words, $F(2, 13) = 38.8$, $p < .001$; Newman Keuls tests showed that the synthetic phonics group had higher spelling ages than the other two groups, who did not differ from each other. Knowledge of letter sounds also differed, $F(2, 13) = 30.0$, $p < .001$; Newman Keuls tests showed that the synthetic phonics group were ahead of the other two groups, although at the pre-test they had been behind the analytic phonics group. There was also a group difference in phoneme segmentation skill, $F(2, 13) = 23.6$, $p < .001$; Newman Keuls tests showed that the synthetic phonics group performed better than the other two groups, who did not differ from each other. We also measured irregular word reading (see Table 13.4), and the groups were found to differ, $F(2, 13) = 5.1$, $p < .03$. Newman Keuls tests showed that the synthetic phonics children only read these items better than the analytic phonics + phonological awareness group, but when subjects were the random variable, $F(2, 289) = 10.3$, $p < .001$, the synthetic phonics group outperformed both of the other groups.

These findings confirm those of Study 2, showing that the synthetic phonics approach is more effective in developing reading and spelling ability than analytic phonics, even when the latter programme includes phoneme awareness training. It also shows that phonemic awareness is best learnt in the context of teaching children to blend and segment words using letters, that is in a synthetic phonics programme.

We also assessed the children's ability to read by analogy. The children were asked to read a list of 40 words, and then read 5 clue words that would assist them when

Table 13.3 Mean chronological age, vocabulary knowledge(BPVS), reading age (British Ability Scales Word Reading test), spelling age (Schonell spelling test), letter sound knowledge, phoneme segmentation (Yopp–Singer Test), and nonword reading (standard deviations in brackets), Study 3

Research Group	Age	BPVS	Reading Age	Spelling Age	Letter Knowledge	Phonemic Segmentation	Nonwords
	Years	Standardised Score	Years	Years	%	%	%
Pretest							
Analytic phonics controls n=109	5.0 (0.3)	92.5 (15.1)	4.9 (0.1)	5.0 (0.1)	9.0 (15.4)	4.5 (18.3)	0.3 (1.8)
Analytic phonics and phonological awareness n=78	5.0 (0.3)	90.2 (14.0)	4.9 (0.4)	5.0 (0.1)	3.9 (8.8)	2.7 (9.9)	0.6 (4.6)
Synthetic Phonics n=117	5.0 (0.5)	95.2 (16.8)	4.9 (0.1)	5.0 (0.0)	6.7 (14.3)	4.1 (14.5)	0.0 (0.0)
First Post-Test							
Analytic phonics controls n=104	5.4 (0.3)	–	5.4 (0.6)	5.2 (0.4)	58.1 (24.7)	17.2 (27.4)	8.8 (22.4)
Analytic phonics and phonological awareness n=75	5.4 (0.3)	–	5.4 (0.7)	5.3 (0.5)	59.9 (24.8)	34.7 (44.6)	15.8 (29.3)
Synthetic phonics n=113	5.5 (0.3)	–	6.04 (0.8)	6.0 (0.7)	90.1 (14.5)	64.8 (37.9)	53.3 (41.2)

Table 13.4 Mean % correct on analogy reading task and irregular word reading at end of training programme (first post-test), Study 3

Research group	Pre-test scores	Clue word reading scores	Post-test scores	Irregular words
Analytic phonics controls, n=104	2.9 (12.0)	6.3 (18.3)	2.6 (9.3)	21.4 (19.5)
Analytic phonics + phonological awareness, n= 75	4.9 (15.8)	11.4 (27.3)	5.5 (16.2)	15.3 (23.1)

rereading the 40 words. For example, the word 'king' would be shown in the list of 40 words, then the children would see the clue word 'ring' (read to the child if they did not know it). The list of words was shown again, including 'king', to see if their reading of the word had benefited from exposure to 'ring'. We found an interaction between groups on pre- versus post-test performance, $F(2, 10) = 10.0$, $p < .004$ (see Table 13.4). Newman Keuls tests showed that the synthetic phonics taught children were the only group to show a significant increase in reading skill between pre- and post-test on the list of 40 words, being the only group that could read by analogy.

These results do not support Goswami's (2008) most recent view that, when learning to read in English, children need to be taught to read at more than one grain size to attain competence in word reading. The synthetic phonics group in Study 3 was taught to read via all-through-the-word grapheme-to-phoneme conversion, but the children rapidly developed the ability to read by analogy without direct tuition. Thus Goswami's argument that the Rose Review (Rose, 2006) is problematical because it does not advocate teaching reading by analogy, thus failing to take into account the children's pre-existing language development (where onset–rime awareness is said to precede phoneme awareness), is unfounded.

Study 3: Long-term effectiveness of synthetic phonics teaching, from Primary 2 to Primary 7

The children in the two analytic phonics conditions carried out the synthetic phonics programme after the first post-test, completing it by the end of Primary 1. We were able to follow up the Clackmannanshire study children right through to the end of their primary schooling, by which time they had been at school for seven years. The effects of most reading interventions tend to wash out after a few years (NICHD, 2000), so it was very important to examine whether synthetic phonics teaching had a long-term effect. In our analyses we split the data according to sex, being particularly interested in the progress made by boys. In many international studies (e.g. Mullis *et al.*, 2003), it has been found that boys read less well than girls. We have examined the same children through to the end of primary schooling for each literacy skill, so that the data are strictly comparable across the years. Children who had left, or who were unavailable for testing at any point, were excluded from the following analyses.

Word reading. We used the British Ability Scales Word Reading test (Elliott *et al.*, 1977) until the children were in their fifth year of school (Primary 5). This test has an upper reading level of 14 years and 5 months and by the time the children were in Primary 6 (aged 10–11), one-third of the children achieved the highest score on this test, so we had no measure of just how well they could recognise words. Therefore, for Primaries 6 and 7 we adopted the WRAT reading test (Wilkinson, 1993).

In this analysis of word reading from Primary 2 to Primary 7, there were 105 boys and 97 girls. See Table 13.5 for means and standard deviations. There was a main effect of sex, $F(1, 200) = 5.8$, $p < .02$, a main effect of time, $F(5, 1000) = 1911.81$, $p < .001$, and a main effect of word reading advantage, $F(1, 1000) = 229.20$, $p < .001$, with reading age exceeding chronological age. There were also interactions between word reading advantage and sex, $F(1, 1000) = 4.0$, $p < .05$, and word reading advantage and time, $F(5, 1000) = 68.1$, $p < .001$, subsumed by a three-way interaction between word reading advantage, time, and sex, $F(5, 1000) = 2.56$, $p < .03$.

Table 13.5 Mean word reading ages, chronological ages and word reading advantage (extent to which word reading exceeds chronological age) in years for boys (B) and girls (G), Primary 2 to Primary 7 (standard deviations in brackets), Study 3.

	Primary 2		Primary 3		Primary 4		Primary 5		Primary 6		Primary 7	
	B	G	B	G	B	G	B	G	B	G	B	G
Word reading age	7.7 (1.1)	7.5 (1.1)	9.5 (1.9)	8.9 (1.9)	10.6 (1.9)	10.1 (1.9)	11.9 (2.1)	11.5 (2.1)	13.4 (3.0)	12.4 (3.0)	15.6 (3.2)	14.7 (3.2)
Chronological age	6.7 (0.3)	6.6 (0.3)	7.8 (0.3)	7.7 (0.3)	8.8 (0.3)	8.7 (0.3)	9.7 (0.3)	9.6 (0.3)	10.8 (0.3)	10.7 (0.3)	11.7 (0.4)	11.6 (0.4)
Word reading advantage	1.0	0.9	1.7	1.2	1.8	1.4	2.2	1.9	2.6	1.7	3.9	3.1

Newman Keuls tests showed that word reading was ahead of chronological age at all ages. It was also found that the boys and girls performed the same in word reading at Primary 2, but thereafter, very surprisingly, the boys read better than the girls. Scheffe tests showed that for both boys and girls, the advantage for reading age over chronological age was greater at Primary 7 than all previous years, showing that the gain in reading skill over chronological age was still increasing six years after the programme had ended. As the reading test had been changed in Primary 6, it was evident that the spurt in word recognition ability in Primary 7 was not due to the change of reading test. By the end of the study, overall the children were reading 3.5 years ahead of chronological age, with the boys reading around 11 months ahead of the girls.

Spelling. We found that in Primary 6 the children were moving towards ceiling on the Schonell spelling test, so for Primary 7 we adopted the WRAT spelling test (Wilkinson, 1993). In this analysis of spelling from Primary 2 to Primary 7, there were 95 boys and 84 girls. See Table 13.6 for means and standard deviations. There was no main effect of sex, $F(1, 177) = 1.85$, N.S. There was a main effect of spelling advantage, $F(1, 885) = 84.43$, $p < .001$, with spelling age exceeding chronological age, and of time, $F(5, 885) = 1,94720.59$, $p < .001$. However, spelling

Table 13.6 Mean word spelling ages, chronological ages and spelling advantage (extent to which spelling exceeds chronological age) in years for boys (B) and girls (G), Primary 2 to Primary 7 (standard deviations in brackets), Study 3.

	Primary 2		Primary 3		Primary 4		Primary 5		Primary 6		Primary 7	
	B	G	B	G	B	G	B	G	B	G	B	G
Spelling age	7.6 (0.8)	7.7 (0.8)	8.6 (1.0)	8.5 (1.0)	9.7 (1.2)	9.4 (1.2)	10.5 (1.4)	10.3 (1.4)	11.4 (1.4)	11.2 (1.4)	13.7 (3.2)	13.0 (3.2)
Chronological age	6.7 (0.3)	6.6 (0.3)	7.8 (0.3)	7.7 (0.3)	8.8 (0.3)	8.7 (0.3)	9.7 (0.3)	9.6 (0.3)	10.8 (0.3)	10.7 (0.3)	11.7 (0.4)	11.6 (0.4)
Spelling advantage	0.9	1.1	0.8	0.8	0.9	0.7	0.8	0.7	0.6	0.5	2.0	1.4

Table 13.7 Mean reading comprehension ages, chronological ages and reading comprehension advantage (extent to which word reading exceeds chronological age)
in years for boys (B) and girls (G), Primary 2 to Primary 7 (standard deviations
in brackets), Study 3.

	Primary 2		Primary 3		Primary 4		Primary 5		Primary 6		Primary 7	
	B	G	B	G	B	G	B	G	B	G	B	G
Reading	7.3	7.2	8.2	8.0	9.3	9.1	10.0	10.0	11.2	10.8	12.00	11.9
Comprehension	(1.1)	(1.1)	(1.1)	(1.1)	(1.4)	(1.4)	(1.3)	(1.3)	(2.0)	(2.0)	(2.0)	(2.0)
age												
Chronological	6.7	6.6	7.8	7.7	8.8	8.7	9.7	9.6	10.8	10.7	11.7	11.6
age	(0.3)	(0.3)	(0.3)	(0.3)	(0.3)	(0.3)	(0.3)	(0.3)	(0.3)	(0.3)	(0.4)	(0.4)
Reading	0.6	0.6	0.4	0.3	0.5	0.4	0.3	0.4	0.4	0.1	0.3	0.3
Comprehension												
advantage												

advantage and time interacted, $F(5, 885) = 22.7$, $p < .001$. Newman Keuls tests
showed that spelling was ahead of chronological age at all ages. Scheffe post hoc tests
were carried out to compare the advantage in spelling age over chronological age
across time. These analyses showed that the advantage at Primary 7 was greater than
it had been in all previous years. At the end of the study, the children spelt 20
months ahead of chronological age. Boys were spelling 8 months ahead of girls, but a
separate analysis on the Primary 7 data did not find this difference to be significant, F
$(1, 177) = 1.7$, N.S.

Reading comprehension. In this analysis of reading comprehension from Primary 2
to Primary 7, there were 89 boys and 88 girls. See Table 13.7 for means and standard deviations. There was no main effect of sex, $F(1, 175) = 1.47$, N.S. There was a
main effect of reading comprehension advantage, $F(1, 875) = 16.65$, $p < .001$, with
reading comprehension age exceeding chronological age, and of time $F(5, 875) =$
22874.00, $p < .001$. However, these factors also interacted, $F(5, 875) = 195.01$, $p <$
$.001$. Newman Keuls tests showed that reading comprehension was ahead of chronological age at all age levels. Scheffe tests indicated that the reading comprehension
advantage was greater at Primary 2 than at Primary 7, showing that the advantage for
reading comprehension age over chronological age had decreased over time,
although it was still significant. The children in Primary 7 comprehended what they
read 3.5 months above what would be expected for their chronological age.

Levels of underachievement. We have also found that there were very low levels of
underachievement in the Clackmannanshire sample. For example, at the end of the
third year at school, only 0.8 per cent of the children were more than two years
behind chronological age in word reading, 0.4 per cent being behind in spelling and
1.2 per cent being behind in reading comprehension. By the end of the seventh year
at school, this had increased to 5.6 per cent behind in word reading, 10.1 per cent
behind in spelling and 14.0 per cent behind in reading comprehension. This is a low
incidence of reading problems, given that just over half the children came from
schools in areas of moderate to severe deprivation (Johnston & Watson, 2005). In
this context, it is noteworthy that no child was a nonreader.

Study 4: Comparison of a sample in England learning to read by an analytic phonics approach, with children from the Clackmannanshire Study learning by a synthetic phonics approach

As stated before, we no longer had an analytic phonics control group from the end of the first year at school. However, the English National Literacy Strategy's programme *Progression in Phonics* (DfEE, 1999) has many of the characteristics of an analytic phonics programme. In this approach, children learn letter sounds at the beginning of words for much of the first year at school. Sounding and blending is generally taught in the last term of school for the higher achievers, with most of the children learning to sound and blend at the start of the second year at school. This is a little later than in the schools we observed in our longitudinal study of analytic phonics (Study 1), but this timescale is not uncommon in Scotland. The only divergence from the analytic phonics approach generally used in Scotland was that the children learnt to segment spoken words for spelling towards the end of the first year at school, largely as a means of developing phoneme awareness skills. Practices for teaching reading for meaning were also very similar, except that in *Progression in Phonics* children were encouraged to guess unknown words from context.

We have studied classes of 10-year-old children in England, matching them on socio-economic status (SES) with classes from the Clackmannanshire study. In England, 47 per cent of the sample came from schools in areas of severe to very severe deprivation, and 53 per cent came from schools in areas that were moderately advantaged. In the Clackmannanshire subsample, 51 per cent of the children came from schools in areas of severe to very severe deprivation, and 49 per cent came from schools in moderately advantaged areas. Thus, there were more children from advantaged areas in the sample in England. In Scotland, the children were tested in April of their sixth year at school. In England, 47 per cent of the sample were tested in June of their sixth year at school and 53 per cent were tested in October to November of their seventh year at school. The later test dates for the English children give a control for time at school; some of these children attended school for between one and three terms at school in their first year (Reception year), whereas all children in Scotland had three terms of teaching in their first year (Primary 1). As is clear from Table 13.8, the English pupils were also 3.5 months younger, due to different practices in Scotland and England for determining the age of starting school. To control for the difference in ages, we have reported age standardised scores, where the mean is 100, and the standard deviation is 15.

Table 13.8 Mean age, vocabulary knowledge, word reading, reading comprehension, spelling and attitudes to reading (standard deviations in brackets), sample in England learning by *Progression in Phonics* compared with Clackmannanshire sample, Study 4.

	Chronological age	Vocabulary knowledge	Word reading	Reading comprehension	Spelling	Attitudes
England (N=110)	10.4 (0.3)	87.6 (11.2)	97.7 (15.3)	92.5 (13.5)	94.9 (16.3)	58.2 (13.5)
Clackmannanshire (N=103)	10.7 (0.3)	90.1 (11.9)	108.0 (14.1)	99.8 (11.6)	104.4 (12.7)	55.6 (14.1)

Table 13.8 shows the children's age, vocabulary knowledge, word reading, reading comprehension, spelling skills and attitudes to reading. Vocabulary knowledge was tested using the English Picture Vocabulary Test (Brimer & Dunn, 1962), word reading was measured by the WRAT reading test (Wilkinson, 1993), reading comprehension by the Group Reading Test (Macmillan Test Unit, 2000), and spelling by the Schonell spelling test (Schonell & Schonell, 1952). Attitudes to reading were measured using the ATR2 questionnaire, devised by Ewing and Johnstone in 1981 at the former Dundee College of Education (see Appendix 13.A).

It was found that the two groups (105 children in England and 100 in Clackmannanshire) did not differ in vocabulary knowledge, $F(1, 203) = 2.4, p > .05$. The Clackmannanshire sample read a significant 10.3 points ahead of the English sample, $F(1, 211) = 25.6, p < .001$. There was also a significant difference in reading comprehension of 7.3 points favouring the Clackmannanshire sample, $F(1, 211) = 18.1, p < .001$. For spelling, the Clackmannanshire sample was 9.5 points ahead of the English sample, $F(1, 211) = 22.5, p < .001$. In terms of attitudes to reading, where a higher score indicates a more positive attitude to reading, the two samples did not differ, $F(1, 211) = 1.8, p > .05$.

Levels of underachievement. It is also of interest to examine the proportion of underachievers in the two samples. Taking the children scoring 85 or below on each test, we found on the word reading test that 19 per cent of the English sample fell into this category, and only 5.8 per cent of the Clackmannanshire sample. For spelling, 30.9 per cent of the English sample fell into this category, and only 4.8 per cent of the Clackmannanshire sample. Finally, for reading comprehension, we found that 32.7 per cent of the English sample fell into this category, and only 10.6 per cent of the Clackmannanshire sample.

We can conclude that at the age of 10, in comparison with children taught by a largely analytic phonics approach, the synthetic phonics taught children were significantly ahead in word reading, spelling and reading comprehension, and that there were far fewer underachievers. Furthermore, contrary to the idea that children taught by a synthetic phonics approach will have a less positive attitude to reading (Dombey, Newsnight, 2005, cited in Lefstein, 2008), the children in the Clackmannanshire sample had as positive an attitude to reading as the sample in England but higher word reading scores.

Consequences of the Clackmannanshire study. After reviewing the findings from our Clackmannanshire study, a UK House of Commons Parliamentary Select Committee (House of Commons Education and Skills Committee, 2005) recommended that a similar study be carried out in England. Instead, a review was carried out for the DfES (Rose, 2006). This concluded that all children should learn to read by the synthetic phonics approach by the age of 5. The DfES (now the DCSF) has now produced a synthetic phonics programme called *Letters and Sounds* (DfES, 2007), which is recommended for use in all primary schools in England.

Conclusion

We have found in our studies that children can learn to read using a synthetic phonics approach right from the start of their reading tuition, and that it is more beneficial than an analytic phonics approach even when it is supplemented by phonological awareness training. The synthetic phonics approach has both immediate and long-term benefits for children's reading and spelling, and produces a very small percentage of underachievers compared with an analytic phonics programme. Furthermore, the method has proved to be very popular with teachers (Johnston & Watson, 2007).

References

Ball, E., & Blachman, B. (1991). 'Does phoneme awareness training in kindergarten make a difference in early word recognition and developmental spelling?' *Reading Research Quarterly, 26*, 46–66.

Bradley, L., & Bryant, P.E. (1983). 'Categorizing sounds and learning to read: A causal connection'. *Nature, 301*, 419–421.

Brimer, M., & Dunn, L.M. (1962). *English picture vocabulary tests*. Bristol, England.

Byrne, B., & Fielding-Barnsley, R. (1989). 'Phonemic awareness and letter knowledge in the child's acquisition of the alphabetic principle'. *Journal of Educational Psychology, 81*, 313–321.

Byrne, B., & Fielding-Barnsley, R. (1991). 'Evaluation of a program to teach phonemic awareness to young children'. *Journal of Educational Psychology, 83*, 451–455.

Cunningham, A.E. (1990). 'Explicit versus implicit instruction in phoneme awareness'. *Journal of Experimental Child Psychology, 50*, 429–444.

DfEE (1999). *Progression in phonics*. London: DfEE. www.standards.dfes.gov.uk/primary/publications/literacy/63309/

DfES (2007). *Letters and sounds*. London:DfES. http://www.standards.dfes.gov.uk/local/clld/las.html

Dombey, H. (2006). 'Phonics and English orthography'. In M. Lewis & S. Ellis (eds), *Phonics: practice, research, policy*. London: Paul Chapman.

Dunn, L.M., & Dunn, L.M. (1982). *British picture vocabulary scales*. Windsor: NFER-Nelson.

Ehri, L.C. (2005). 'Development of sight word reading: phases and findings'. In M.J. Snowling & C. Hulme (eds), *The science of reading: A handbook* (pp. 135–154). Oxford: Blackwell.

Elliott, C.D., Murray, D.J., & Pearson, L.S. (1977). *The British ability scales*. Windsor: NFER–Nelson.

Feitelson, D. (1988). *Facts and fads in beginning reading. A cross-language perspective*. Norwood, NJ: Ablex.

Fox, B., & Routh, D.K. (1984). 'Phonemic analysis and synthesis as word attack skills: Revisited'. *Journal of Educational Psychology, 76*, 1059–1064.

Fraser, H. (1997). *Early intervention: A literature review*. Edinburgh: Moray House Institute of Education.

Frith, U. (1985). 'Beneath the surface of developmental dyslexia'. In K. Patterson, J. Marshall, & M. Coltheart. (eds), *Surface dyslexia*. London: LEA.

Goswami, U. (1994). 'Phonological skills, analogies and reading development'. *Reading, 28*, 32–37.

—— (1999). 'Causal connections in beginning reading: The importance of rhyme'. *Journal of Research in Reading, 22*, 217–240.

—— (2008). 'Reading, complexity and the brain'. *Literacy, 42*, 67–74.

Hatcher, P.J., Hulme, C., & Ellis, A.W. (1994). 'Ameliorating early reading failure by integrating the teaching of reading and phonological skills: The phonological linkage hypothesis'. *Child Development, 65*, 41–57.

House of Commons Education and Skills Committee (2005). *Teaching children to read.* Eighth Report of Session 2004–05. London: The Stationery Office. Available online at: http://image.guardian.co.uk/sys-files/Education/documents/2005/04/06/reading.pdf

Johnston, R.S., & Watson, J. (2004). 'Accelerating the development of reading, spelling and phonemic awareness'. *Reading and Writing, 17,* 327–357.

Johnston, R.S., & Watson, J. (2005). 'The effects of synthetic phonics teaching on reading and spelling attainment, a seven year longitudinal study'. Published by the Scottish Executive Education Department'. http://www.scotland.gov.uk/library5/education/sptrs-00.asp

Johnston, R.S., & Watson, J.E. (2007). 'Teaching synthetic phonics'. *Learning Matters.* Exeter.

Johnston, R.S., & Watson, J.E. (in press). 'The trials and tribulations of changing how reading is taught in schools: synthetic phonics and the educational backlash'. In K. Durkin & R. Shaeffer (eds), *Handbook of developmental psychology in action: opportunities and obstacles in giving developmental psychology away.* Oxford: Blackwell.

Lefstein, A. (2008). 'Literacy makeover: Educational research and the public interest on prime time'. *Teachers College Record, 110,* 3.

Lie, A. (1991). 'Effects of a training programme for stimulating skills in word analysis in first grade'. *Reading Research Quarterly, 26,* 234–249.

Lundberg, I., Frost, J., & Petersen, O.-P. (1988). 'Effects of an intensive programme for stimulating phonological awareness in preschool children'. *Reading Research Quarterly, 23,* 263-284.

Maclean, M., Bryant, P., & Bradley, L. (1987). 'Rhymes, nursery rhymes and reading in early childhood'. *Merrill-Palmer Quarterly Journal of Developmental Psychology, 33,* 255–281.

Macmillan Test Unit (2000). *The Group Reading Test II.* Windsor: NFER–Nelson.

Mullis, I.V.S., Martin, M.O., Gonzalez, E.J., & Kennedy, A.M. (2003). *PIRLS 2001 International Report: IEA's study of reading literacy achievement in primary schools.* Chestnut Hill, MA: Boston College.

NICHD (2000). 'Report of the National Reading Panel: Teaching children to read'. Washington, DC: National Institute of Child Health and Human Development.

Rose, J. (2006). *Independent review of the early teaching of reading.* http//www.standards.dfes.goc.uk/rosereview/report.pdf

Schonell, F.J., & Schonell, F.E. (1952). *Diagnostic and attainment testing* (2nd edn)'. Edinburgh: Oliver & Boyd.

Skailand, D.B. (1971). 'A year comparison of four language units in teaching beginning reading'. Paper presented at annual meeting of the American Educational Research Association, New York, February.

Smith, F. (1978). *Understanding reading: A psycholinguistic analysis of reading and learning to read* (2nd edn). Austin, TX: Holt Rinehart & Winston.

Torgerson, C.J., Brooks, G., & Hall, J. (2006). *A systematic review of the research literature and use of phonics in the teaching of reading and spelling.* DfES, research reports RR711. http://www.dfes.gov.uk/research/data/uploadfiles/RR711_.pdf

Torgesen, J.K., Wagner, R.K., Rose, E., Lindamood, P., Conway, T., & Garvan, C. (1999). 'Preventing reading failure in children with phonological processing disabilities: Group and individual responses to instruction'. *Journal of Educational Psychology, 91,* 579–593.

Watson, J.E. (1998). 'An investigation of the effects of phonics teaching on children's progress in reading and spelling'. PhD thesis, University of St Andrews.

Williams, J.P. (1980). 'Teaching decoding with an emphasis on phoneme analysis and phoneme blending'. *Journal of Educational Psychology, 72,* 1–15.

Wilkinson, G. 1993 *Wide Range Achievement Test, 3rd Edition (WRAT-3)*. Wilmington, DE: Wide Range.

Yopp, H.K. (1988). 'The validity and reliability of phonemic awareness tests'. *Reading Research Quarterly, 23,* 159–177.

Appendix 13.A: Attitudes to reading

SECTION I

Name _____

These questions are about reading. There are no right or wrong answers. We just want to know what you feel about different kinds of reading. Please write your name in the space provided above.

Before you start on this, here are a few questions about yourself to answer.

Attitudes to reading

There are 18 sentences listed below. Read each sentence carefully, and when you have read it show us how much you agree or disagree with that sentence by putting a tick in the box which is right for you.

For office use only

	1	2	3	4	5	
	definitely disagree	probably disagree	not sure	probably agree	definitely agree	
1. I wish we had more television programmes at school instead of books.						21
2. Most books are too long for me.						22
3. I like talking to my friends about books I've been reading.						23
4. I would be disappointed if I got a book or a book token as a present.						24
5. I can understand things better when they are written down.						25
6. If I got the chance I would spend a lot of my spare time reading.						26
7. I am glad I learned to read.						27
8. Reading is something I only do at school.						28

(continued)

	1 definitely disagree	2 probably disagree	3 not sure	4 probably agree	5 definitely agree	
9. It is difficult when you have a lot to read for your school work.						29
10. There are lots of books that I feel I would like to read.						30
11. The more pictures a book has, the better it is.						31
12. I like to get books out of the library (class or school or public).						32
13. I would like to have more time at school set aside for reading.						33
14. People who spend a lot of their spare time reading miss a lot of fun.						34
15. There is too much reading to do in school.						35
16. Reading is boring unless you want to find out something.						36
17. Reading books is the best way to learn things.						37
18. I would like to have a bigger selection of books to read for school work.						38

Does the type of reading instruction have an influence on how readers process print?

Vincent Connelly, G. Brian Thompson,
Claire M. Fletcher-Flinn and Michael F. McKay

Most theories of the development of reading, for alphabetic orthographies, attempt to provide an account of processes children use to acquire reading skill. The theories that have had wide influence, however, have not included consideration of whether normally developing children can reach equivalent levels of reading attainment by taking somewhat different learning routes, involving different uses of cognitive processes. Moreover, the theories have not considered whether different types of reading instruction lead to children taking different learning routes although they arrive at equivalent levels of skill. Nonetheless, the importance of this matter has been raised from time to time. For example, Ramus (2004, p. 817) has criticised the influential developmental theory of Frith (1985) on the grounds that 'it assumes a particular class of teaching methods based on explicit phonics instruction.' Thompson and Johnston (1993) had earlier pointed out the importance of examining the influence of different types of instruction to test theories of how children learn to read. To do otherwise would run the risk of accepting a theory as a valid account of children's learning, when in fact it was not for some types of reading instruction. Recently, there have been speculations (Harm & Seidenberg, 2004, pp. 713–14; Treiman, Kessler, & Bick, 2003, p.70; Zevin & Seidenberg, 2006, p. 148) that the type of reading instruction experienced in childhood should be a factor incorporated in theoretical models of processes of the skilled word reading of adults. This would make sense only if there were long-term developmental continuity for instructional influences on the ways of processing words in reading.

The research reviewed in this chapter addresses issues of this kind. There has been little research directly relevant to these issues. This is in contrast to the large volume of research that compares different types of reading instruction to determine which yields larger gains in children's word reading accuracy. The most frequently studied comparison has been of instruction that includes systematic phonics against other types of instruction without such phonics, or with less phonics. Until we have begun to tackle the issue of how reading instruction might interact with reading development we will not be truly sure why instruction such as systematic phonics can lead to accelerated gains in word reading accuracy (National Reading Panel, 2000; Ehri, Nunes, Stahl and Willows, 2001). Here we report on a set of studies that investigated differences in reading behaviours and learning processes between those who received beginning reading instruction that included systematic phonics and those who received text-centred teaching without such phonics.

Children taught in a programme with systematic phonics may have an initial advantage in the rate at which they acquire word reading accuracy but this does not mean that children without phonics instruction fail to learn to read. In fact, the vast majority of such children do successfully learn to read. It may take a little longer but there is a large overlap between the distributions of word reading accuracy among children with systematic phonics instruction and those without (See National Reading Panel, 2000, which reviewed many studies, mainly from the USA). Given the large proportion of children who are therefore equivalent in reading skill across programmes with and without phonics there are then many theoretically interesting questions to be posed. For example, do children with similar reading levels show differences in reading behaviours and processes that can be linked to how they have been taught to read? Do children who do not receive systematic phonics differ in their learning or performance in some compensatory way from those receiving systematic phonics? And do children, and adults, who have received systematic phonics instruction use their previously taught skills to the exclusion of other possible learning processes in reading words? We hope to provide some evidence about these questions in this chapter and demonstrate that the type of reading instruction is a factor that is important to consider in the ways in which children learn to read; not just in how rapidly they learn to read, important though that is.

Our approach to the research

In the majority of the evidence presented here our primary method has been to compare samples of participants who are matched on accuracy of real-word reading but have received different types of reading instruction. In order to minimise confounding or irrelevant effects we also matched on chronological age, aural vocabulary level, and time at school. Social and other educational variables were also included in the matching (See Connelly, Johnston, & Thompson, 1999, 2001, and Thompson, McKay, Fletcher-Flinn, Connelly, Kaa, & Ewing, 2008, for detailed descriptions of this comparative approach). Using this approach we can be confident, with careful design of tasks and comparisons, that differences found in reading behaviours and associated learning processes can be attributed primarily to instructional differences.

The research has mainly involved comparisons between readers from systematic phonics teaching in Scotland and readers from 'book experience,' a text-centred approach in New Zealand that did not include this phonics. Systematic phonics teaching has been current in many Scottish schools for many decades (See Connelly et al, 2001, for a more detailed history). For example, Elder (1971) in his study comparing the effects of types of reading instruction described systematic phonics teaching in Scotland when his data were collected in 1962. In New Zealand there has been an emphasis on text-centred teaching of reading for 40 years (New Zealand Department of Education, 1985; Thompson, 1993). From the 1960s onwards there was a shift from emphasis on the word as a focus of teaching to an emphasis on the story and text of the book. Systematic phonics was not a feature of the teaching in any of the schools in our samples from that country. (It is noted that since the 1990s some schools in New Zealand have made some modification of their practices for beginning reading to give more attention to teaching letter-sound relationships. The schools in our samples had not made such modifications.)

Our more recent studies have also included samples of children receiving phonics teaching and text-centred teaching in Australia (Thompson, et al., 2008). Whilst the studies reported can be classed as cross-national, both Scotland and New Zealand (with Australia) have been defined by their close cultural links to each other and the educational systems are also closely linked in history and shared educational culture. It is noted that in the recent international comparison of reading comprehension attainments of 10-year-olds (Mullis, Martin, Gonzalez, & Kennedy, 2003) New Zealand and Scotland had equal mean scores (Australia was not included in these comparisons).

Our data included classroom observations of lessons to describe the teaching and the children's responses to it in the classroom. Systematic phonics instruction was deliberate teaching of explicit ('sounding out') knowledge of individual letter-sound correspondences and of the use of sequences of such correspondences to read new or unfamiliar words. For example, to attempt the unfamiliar word *cot*, the child would sound out the letters as 'ki'-'o'-'ti', and hereby attempt to infer the word sound 'cot.' This teaching was a primary component of the reading programme with phonics but other components included the children's reading of story texts. In text-centred teaching, on the other hand, story texts were the basis of nearly all the reading instruction. Many book titles were provided for each finally-graded, individualised, reading level. To achieve a match between the book level and the child's reading level the teacher made ongoing individual recordings of each child's accuracy of oral reading of the books. The instruction included teacher guidance on meaning of the text and story, and on a variety of cue information obtainable from the print for word recognition: sentence context cues, letters of words (mainly initial letter or letter cluster), spelling patterns and analogies to other words. Most of this teacher guidance arose out of the children's text reading. At the early levels there was some guidance to the children on *listening* for sounds that correspond to letters and multi-letter units of selected words in the text. At no level was there sounding out of successive letters as in the systematic explicit phonics (Connelly et al., 2001; Thompson et al., 2008).

Phonological recoding using taught explicit phonics procedures

In the widely influential and extensively documented theory of Share (1995) the main processing component available to the beginning reader for attempting to read unfamiliar words is 'phonological recoding' of the explicit kind. This is a process of translating a grapheme (letter(s), e.g., *k, th, ea,* that correspond to a single phoneme) into the corresponding phoneme of the word. (The phoneme is the smallest sound unit that enables the listener to distinguish words, e.g., to distinguish 'dog' from 'bog'. In reading, pronunciation is not necessary, only activation of the brain codes that represent the phoneme.) In Share's theory, for effective learning the process of phonological recoding is said to be explicit in beginning readers, in that it has to be consciously applied by the child when attempting to read unfamiliar words (pp. 160, 197). Such phonological recoding is said to be the essential means by which the beginner reader acquires reading vocabulary.

There is evidence that children without phonics are less accurate than children taught with phonics in oral reading of new words, especially *nonwords* (also called *pseudowords*). These are made-up, pronounceable, words (e.g., *lom, yaik*) that cannot be in the child's reading or listening vocabularies. Not only does the child have to read them for the first time but also pronounce them for the first time. It is noted that the nonwords are typically presented to the participant as a sequence of isolated items, not in any form of text. At the age of 7 years, a sample of New Zealand children without explicit phonics instruction were significantly less accurate in oral reading of nonwords than a sample of Scottish children taught with phonics (Thompson & Johnston, 2000). The important point to emphasise here is that these are children matched on their accuracy in oral reading of real words, unfamiliar as well as familiar (all presented as isolated items). The children taught systematic explicit phonics demonstrated what they have learned from their phonics lessons to successfully tackle new words through explicit phonological recoding. Among the children without the phonics teaching this did not take place and hence was not necessary for the level of real-word reading they attained, which matched that of the children with phonics. Similar patterns of results were obtained for the same kind of instructional comparisons for beginning 5-and 6-year-old children (Connelly et al. 2001) and in a more recent study with four samples of 6-and 7-year-olds across three countries (Thompson et al., 2008). By the age of eight, most Scottish children taught with phonics were approaching ceiling levels on nonword pronunciation tasks while New Zealand children were only getting just over half correct in comparison.

Moreover, children taught using systematic explicit phonics could not help using explicit phonological recoding even when it was not appropriate for the set task. Johnston and Thompson (1989) and Johnston, Thompson, Fletcher-Flinn and Holligan (1995) studied 8-year-olds in Scotland, who received instruction with explicit phonics, and compared them with children in New Zealand who were matched on real-word reading level but were taught by the text-centred approach without the phonics. The children were tested on a pseudohomophone lexical decision task. This involved deciding whether each presented item (e.g., *well, wosp, help, mosh, –*) was a correctly spelt real word or a made-up word. Some (e.g., *wosp*) were pseudohomophones, that is, homophonic misspellings of real words (e.g., *wasp*). The children with explicit phonics were particularly prone to accept these as correctly spelt real words. They apparently could not avoid focusing conscious attention on the word sound obtained from their processing of explicit letter-sound correspondences. The children without this phonics teaching did not have these explicit sound associations to interfere with their conscious decisions about the pseudohomophones.

Another way to read new words?

There is more evidence (Thompson et al., 2008) about the reading of new words in a study of 6-and 7-year-old children, in their second year at school, who were making slower than average progress in learning to read (but within the normal range). These studies were conducted across the three countries of Scotland, Australia, and New Zealand, and comprised four samples of children who were matched on reading accuracy of real words (both familiar and unfamiliar). The samples received teaching of explicit phonics that ranged from high, to moderate, to nil levels. A nonword reading task was administered with items such as *jaf, jat, teeg, teep*. The nature of each child's response to the nonwords was recorded and classified. From their responses that were *without* any observed explicit phonological recoding, all samples achieved 30% to 40% mean accuracy for all items presented. Whether or not they received phonics instruction, the children were able to successfully read this percentage of the nonwords using some means other than explicit phonological recoding. Nonetheless, with responses that comprised accurate explicit sounding of any grapheme(s) beyond the initial one of the word, the sample with the high level of explicit phonics instruction added a further 20 percentage points to their accuracy on the nonwords (63% in total); the sample with a moderate level of such instruction a further 10 percentage points (53% in total); and the two with nil levels of phonics a mere 2 to 3 percentage points (35% in total in each sample). The overall pattern of these results requires explanation. It seems clear that the phonics taught children were showing success in applying systematic phonics procedures to the identification of words in their reading of text. Therefore, we have direct evidence that how a child is taught to read will have a direct effect on their reading behaviours. Furthermore, in the samples with explicit phonics teaching, some of the nonword reading that was correct without observed explicit recoding could have been achieved by internalisation of the explicit phonological recoding, and hence was no longer observable. However, this does not explain the accuracy achieved by the two samples without explicit phonics teaching, as they had virtually no successful explicit recoding to internalise.

Ziegler and Goswami (2005) in their Psycholinguistic Grain Size theory have considered children's use of different sized units in learning to read, proposing that there can be a supplementary role for units larger than the grapheme. Did the children without explicit phonics instruction compensate when attempting to read nonwords (e.g., *teep*) by making more supplementary use of larger units, such as lexical *body units* (e.g., *eep*)? These units were lexical in so far as they were shared with words of the beginner's reading vocabulary (e.g., *keep, sleep, sheep*). Nonwords with these lexical body units were compared with matched nonwords (e.g., *teeg*) having *nonlexical* body units (e.g., *eeg*) that were not shared with words of the child's reading vocabulary. McKay & Thompson (2009) have reported on normal developmental trends in the advantages children gain from lexical versus nonlexical bodies in nonword reading. Similar to their results for an equivalent reading level, our study (Thompson et al., 2008) showed a small but significant advantage to the reading of nonwords with lexical bodies over those with nonlexical bodies. Whether or not the children received explicit phonics did not significantly affect the extent of this advantage. This result does not support the hypothesis that children without explicit phonics were compensating by supplementary use of these larger units. The result is interesting, nevertheless, as it shows that children receiving explicit phonics do not limit their processing of nonwords to the taught explicit phonological recoding procedures, which are based on grapheme units (and correspondences with phonemes). All children made some use of information about word body units; information that was from words familiar to them and in their reading vocabularies.

Considering Share's (1995) account of learning to read, one would ask how the children without phonics, who do not use explicit phonological recoding of words, have managed to achieve the same level of real-word reading as the children taught systematic phonics? How do they tackle unknown words or learn to read new words without explicit phonological recoding? Do all children with or without phonics instruction, just after they start learning to read, have available to them another source of knowledge to tackle the reading of unknown words and so enable them to progress in word reading skill? Could this be a process that depends on information from the few words they have learnt to read? But if so, instead of being supplementary, as in our results for word body units, could it be more basic, encompassing grapheme units as well as any units of larger size? Children who have received phonics instruction would then have explicit phonological recoding as an *additional* mechanism, which we have seen provides them with an advantage for reading entirely new words, especially nonwords.

Implicit lexicalised phonological recoding

In the Knowledge Sources theory of reading acquisition (Fletcher-Flinn & Thompson, 2004; Thompson & Fletcher-Flinn, 1993, 2006) there are several sources of knowledge for learning to read words but two are particularly relevant here. These are the two sources of knowledge for phonological recoding that can be used to read new or unfamiliar words. One source of knowledge comes from the skills taught in systematic phonics, if this teaching is available, and so enables the children's explicit phonological recoding. The second source requires little explicit teaching. According to the theory, all children normally acquire this source of knowledge as they learn to read, irrespective of the type of instruction they receive. It is an implicit lexicalised letter-sound source of knowledge derived from children's experience with, and induction from, words in their reading vocabularies and associated phonological knowledge. It is *lexicalised*, in so far as it is derived from experiences of words. It is *implicit*, in so far as it is learnt without conscious awareness that learning is taking place.

To learn skills, the human brain is very proficient at rapidly and implicitly picking up inherent statistical patterns of information (See Sun, Slusarz, & Terry, 2005). According to the Knowledge Sources theory, after a few successful experiences of reading words, children can implicitly induce patterns of letter-sound correspondences that are common across subsets of words they have learnt to read. For example, through these processes of the brain, beginning readers who have successfully read *see, so,* and *said,* would induce a common grapheme-phoneme relationship for initial letter *s* of words; while from successful reading experience of *cat, got, a*nd *went,* they would induce a grapheme-phoneme relationship for final letter *t* of words. They can then identify these induced sublexical relations (ISRs) when they occur in new words and, most importantly, use this information to read new words. (Thompson & Fletcher-Flinn, 2006). This use is called *lexicalised* phonological recoding. In our example, the ISRs are specific to either initial or final position within the word. Other ISRs can be formed that generalise over word position. On the other hand, as reading vocabulary expands, ISRs can be acquired which have a pattern conditional on the presence of other graphemes. For example, in English orthography, the phoneme corresponding to the letter *i* usually changes when *i* is followed by *nd* or *ld* (e.g., as in *find, kind; child, mild,* versus *fin, hill*); when *o* is followed by *ld* (e.g., *old, cold,* versus *on, got*); and when *oo* is followed by *k* (e.g., *look, took,* versus *zoo, moon*).

According to the theory, as new words become familiar, they become part of the child's reading vocabulary, which in turn implicitly provides updated ISRs, from patterns of letter-sound relationships common to subsets of those words. These ISRs in turn facilitate learning of new reading vocabulary, and the new vocabulary facilitates the learning of new ISRs. This is a recursive relationship between the ISRs and the reading vocabulary. In contrast, the teaching of explicit phonological recoding does not provide this recursive function. It can only facilitate, and is not facilitated by, gains in reading vocabulary. In the theory, ISRs are a source of knowledge gained by all children as they learn to read, both children taught explicit phonics and those not. The theory provides an explanation of the results described in the study (Thompson et al., 2008) cited above, in which only some of the accuracy achieved by all children in nonword reading was attributable to explicit phonological recoding.

In a set of experiments (Thompson and Fletcher-Flinn, 1993; and Thompson, Cottrell, and Fletcher-Flinn, 1996) beginner level 5-and 6-year-olds, who were receiving text-centred teaching were given experience of new words that they were at first unable to read. These words (e.g., *cab*, *rob*) had a particular letter-phoneme relationship (e.g., for *b* in final position) that they had not encountered in their reading books. Each child was given experience reading these words in sentences, without explicit attention directed to the letter-sound relationships in the words. When these words became familiar and entered the child's reading vocabulary the knowledge gained transferred to the acquisition of a new letter-phoneme relationship (e.g., for *b* in final position). This was demonstrated by the child's gain (relative to a control condition) in ability to read unfamiliar pseudowords requiring this relationship (e.g., *ab*, *ub*, *ob*). From the information about the new words in the child's reading vocabulary and the associated phonological knowledge, the child implicitly induced a new context-sensitive letter-phoneme relationship. This ISR enabled the child to then respond to the unfamiliar pseudowords by *lexicalized* phonological recoding. Alternative explanations of the results, such as the child's use of analogies were examined but were not consistent with the results. Furthermore, there is evidence (Thompson, Fletcher-Flinn, & Cottrell, 1999) that at the beginning level entirely new letter-phoneme correspondences can be acquired as ISRs. The children were also able to show this knowledge in their responses to letters isolated from words. These studies provide specific and fairly direct evidence that lexicalised phonological recoding is available very early in learning to read. The results are contrary to Share's theory. This includes a form of lexicalised phonological recoding but only following a major developmental shift in the cognitive processes for reading, which is said to take place beyond the beginning levels (Share, 1995).

Implicit lexicalised phonological recoding in the beginning levels of learning would also explain results (Treiman, Kessler, Zevin, Bick, & Davis, 2006) from average progress children in USA first-grade classes (age 6 years), who had received some phonics instruction. These children were able to use grapheme-phoneme correspondences that are conditional on the child's experience of the relation between the correspondences and other graphemes of the word (e.g., *prook*, with *oo* pronounced as in 'look', rather than 'zoo' as taught in beginner phonics; *jold* with *o* pronounced as in 'old', rather than 'got' as in phonics). Distinct from the simple context-free correspondences, which are those initially taught in explicit phonics instruction, these are context-dependent grapheme-phoneme correspondences. As correspondences of this type were not taught in the children's phonics instruction, experience of them would be obtained from their reading of familiar words. The implicit lexicalised form of recoding would also explain results in which 6-year-olds gave the correct pronunciations of vowel digraphs, that is, two-letter graphemes (e.g., *ee, ea*) that had not been taught (Stuart, Masterson, Dixon, & Quinlan, 1999). Neither of these studies included a comparison between samples of children with and without phonics instruction. This comparison, involving USA and NZ samples of 6-year-olds was available in a study by Fletcher-Flinn, Shankweiler, & Frost (2004). For example, the USA sample with phonics instruction had not at that point been taught the sound for the digraph *th* and neither had the New Zealand sample without phonics. Both showed significant accuracy for reading *th* in nonwords.

If the distinction between implicit lexicalised phonological recoding and explicit recoding is valid, and the phonics instruction influences mainly the child's use of context-free grapheme-phoneme correspondences, then some specific predictions are warranted about the ways in which readers will respond to a nonword (e.g., *nalk*) that offers opportunity for either the taught context-free response (e.g., with the vowel of *nalk* pronounced as in 'nap') or the context-dependent pronunciation (e.g., with the vowel pronounced as in 'talk'), which is the pronunciation experienced in real words (e.g., *talk, walk, stalk*). The prediction would be that readers who have learnt to read with explicit phonics instruction, although making some use of lexicalised recoding, would have a bias to respond to these 'heterophonic' nonwords with the context-free response. This bias would not be present in readers who have learnt to read with little or no explicit phonics instruction. Results consistent with these predictions were obtained by Deavers, Solity, & Kerfoot (2000) for a United Kingdom sample of 6-year-old children in their second year at school. However, would the effects of explicit phonics instruction for beginning readers be powerful enough to continue in this way through to the skilled reading of adulthood? Or, would continuity to adulthood would not be expected, as in the theory of Share (1995) in which there is a major shift in the cognitive processes of reading beyond the beginning levels? This is the next question we will examine.

Continuity to adulthood in the influence of phonics instruction

As yet, there is only one published study on this question of long-term continuity. Thompson, Connelly, Fletcher-Flinn and Hodson (2009) investigated the reading of two samples of adult readers, one from a university in Scotland and one in New Zealand. The first sample had been taught reading with explicit phonics in their initial years of schooling in Scotland, on average 19 years previously. The other sample, without childhood phonics, had been taught in New Zealand using the text-centred approach described earlier in this chapter. All participants were matched on a measure of reading vocabulary as well as on chronological age.

The aim of the study was to investigate whether pronunciations of nonwords by skilled adult readers were influenced by the type of instruction they received in the initial years of childhood schooling. Oral reading responses were compared for sets of heterophonic nonwords of the kind already described. The *overall* levels of acceptable responses to the nonwords did not differ significantly between the two samples of adults. However, the adults with childhood instruction in explicit phonics were strongly biased toward context-free pronunciations of the kind taught in explicit phonics (e.g., pronouncing *thild* with the vowel as in 'is'). In place of the greater use of these responses, the adults without phonics tended to use context-dependent pronunciations that had been experienced in real words (e.g., pronouncing *thild* with the vowel as in 'child'). The bias to context-free pronunciations also extended to low frequency real words (not very familiar to the reader), which had meanings with few sensori-motor aspects (e.g., *truce, scarce*). It was also found that the sample of adults with childhood phonics, compared to that without, had greater awareness of phonemes of heard words, and greater overall accuracy for pronouncing the phonics sounds of individual letters. The adults without phonics showed a pattern of errors for phonics sounds that demonstrated they had acquired their letter-sound knowledge implicitly. Their attempts to pronounce phonics sounds for letters depended on inferences from their knowledge of letter names (e.g., from the initial phoneme of the names of *b, d, j, k, p*). The performance of these adults on sounds for letters (e.g., *f, h, w, e, a*) which did not have sounds similar to the initial phoneme of the corresponding letter names was inferior, compared to the performance of the adults with childhood phonics, and especially so for the vowel letters.

Taken together, it is improbable that the total pattern of differences between the two samples can be explained by some irrelevant or confounding factor. The results are contrary to what would be expected from a major shift in cognitive processes of reading described in the theory of Share (1995). The evidence shows that explicit phonics routines taught to 5-and 6-year-olds had an effect over almost two decades. In reading both nonwords and unfamiliar real words, skilled adult readers with childhood phonics instruction showed this long-lasting effect by their strong bias toward responses that were emphasised in that instruction, when alternative responses based on information from their reading vocabularies were more appropriate. The result is also consistent with the use of implicit lexicalised phonological recoding and its long-term developmental continuity. This process is apparently available to some extent for all readers, irrespective of the type of instruction received. Here, however, it was used more by those adults who had received text-centred instruction without explicit phonics.

Reading familiar words: lexical storage

To this point we have considered how readers respond to unfamiliar words, and in particular to nonwords, the most unfamiliar. We will now consider how children learn to process words that have become familiar to them in their experience of reading. Does the type of instruction they receive influence the way in which they store information about familiar words? In the developmental theories of both Frith (1985) and Ehri (1999) it is claimed that children make their first attempt at storing information about familiar print words by logographic processes, using picture-like features of words rather than storing information about the identity and sequence of the component letters. In a study of 5-year-old children who had received 9 months of reading instruction (Thompson & Johnston, 2007), it was found they were storing information about the identity of component letters, and that this orthographic lexical storage was not significantly influenced by whether or not they received some explicit phonics instruction. However, in the processes used at this early level the identities of letters of stored words were to some extent specific to the lower-case letter forms, in which the children had received most experience of the words. For example, the lower-case word form (e.g., and) was frequently recognized but the form (e.g., AND) much less frequently. At this early reading level, letters of the word were apparently not always stored as abstract letter units (ALUs), which are 'equivalence categories' for the variant visual forms of letters (e.g., *a*, A).

Further evidence on how beginner readers store information about familiar words was obtained in the second study of the previously cited research by Thompson et al. (2008), in which there was a comparison of four samples of children with 6-year-old reading levels but wide differences in the extent of explicit phonics instruction received. In this training study, the initial learning of the reading of new words was examined over the duration of several days. The words were presented in lower case but cross-case transfer to upper-case forms of the words was tested. Instruction in explicit phonics had no significant influence on the gains in learning the lower-case forms of the words, or on the extent of cross-case transfer of this learning to the upper-case forms. This transfer was significant but not complete. Hence, irrespective of whether children received explicit phonics instruction, they made only partial use of ALUs for their orthographic storage of words. Further information about theories and evidence on how children acquire ALUs for reading words is reviewed in a paper by Thompson (in press).

So far, in the limited range of studies available, there is no indication that the inclusion of explicit phonics instruction changes the way in which lexical ortho-graphic storage is acquired, for children who have reached equal levels of word reading achievement. This initial conclusion is very different to that from the research we have reviewed on the influence of explicit phonics instruction on the ways in which both children and skilled adult readers respond to new or unfamiliar words.

Reading text: Accuracy and speed

We have now considered at length the influences of type of instruction on the accu-racy of reading of words that are isolated from text. In view of the importance of reading text as a goal of instruction, it is relevant to also examine word reading accuracy in text reading. Are the children without phonics compensating in some way in order to reach a level of word accuracy in text reading equal to that of those with phonics teaching? Do the children without phonics manage to achieve the equivalent level of skill by trading off another aspect of text reading performance? In Stanovich's (1980) interactive-compensatory model of reading, children who have low profi-ciency in phonological recoding are said to compensate to some extent by making more use of cues for word identification from the context of the text. However, in order to use text context to facilitate the reading of unfamiliar words the child would use a lot of attentional capacity and in young children this is very limited. The con-sequence is that less attention is then available for the processes of comprehending the text. Connelly et al. (2001) reported that 6-year-olds with phonics instruction had a small but statistically significant advantage for comprehension of text over those without phonics, when the two samples were equal in word accuracy for oral reading of text. However, no such comprehension advantage was found in the more recent study of Thompson et al. (2008), which used larger samples of text for assessing comprehension and word accuracy. Hence, it seems unlikely that the children without phonics have traded off their attention for comprehension in order to compensate for lower proficiency in explicit phonological recoding.

Furthermore, in view of the importance of text reading, it is surprising that there is sparse evidence on the effects of systematic phonics instruction on speed, as well as accuracy, in reading text. In the review of the effects of providing systematic phonics instruction conducted by the National Reading Panel (2000, chap. 2, pt. 2) no evidence on speed of reading was presented. It might be expected that beginners without phonics could manage to acquire accuracy in reading words by trading off reading speed. They may read words in text with the same accuracy as children with phonics instruction but only at reduced speed and hence limited fluency. Speed of oral reading of text, as well as accuracy, were examined by Elder (1971) for 7- and 8-year-olds, and by Connelly et al. (2001) for 6-year-olds. Both found that children without explicit phonics, who read text at the same word accuracy level, were in fact reading it significantly faster than the children with phonics.

Thompson et al. (2008) found that in comparisons of four samples of 6- and 7-year-olds who were equal on mean word accuracy (80%) in oral reading of text, the two samples without explicit phonics were reading faster. They read on average 34 words per minute, which were 46% more words per unit of time than the high phonics sample and 20% more than the moderate phonics sample. These seem surprising results. Are there any plausible explanations for effects in this direction? As explicit sounding of words would be more frequent for children with phonics, would the time taken for this procedure explain their significantly slower speed of reading? However, again surprisingly, a covariance analysis that took into account the extent of each child's total sounding out indicated it did not contribute to the difference between the samples in text reading speed.

Another explanation for these surprising results could be the allocation of time during which the children were focussed on text reading rather than explicit phonics. According to the results of Martin-Chang & Levy (2005), young children's speed of oral reading of text increases as a result of practice with the syntactic and semantic relations among the words of text, as well as with practice in reading the component words. Furthermore, there would be a multiplier effect of practice time on reading speed. With more practice time, the speed of text reading (words read per unit of time) increases and in consequence of this, for the same unit of time in their reading, more exposures and practice of words become available to the child.

Also, the more practiced the child is at reading a word the more likely the child's processing of letters of the word would be in parallel across the word, rather than in the sequential order of the letters. Such parallel processing would enable faster responses. Connelly (1994) obtained reading response times for (isolated) words of some familiarity for the children and, consistent with parallel processing of words, found there was no effect of word length on the response times of the New Zealand 5-and 6-year-olds without phonics instruction. But there was a word-length effect on the response times for the Scottish children with phonics, who were matched on word reading accuracy. The words with more letters had longer response times than those with fewer letters. This is consistent with the hypothesis of some sequential processing of words. Overall reading response times for the words were faster for the children without phonics.

Reading instruction times were charted in the Thompson et al. (2008) study and showed that the teaching programmes that included systematic phonics did not provide as much text reading time as those which were text-centred and without the phonics instruction. The moderate phonics programmes, with the same total instruction time as the two samples without explicit phonics, had some explicit phonics instruction separate from text reading. This reduced their time available for text reading instruction, relative to the samples without phonics. Their reduced time for text reading was associated with slower text reading speed. The high phonics sample received more explicit phonics instruction time separate from text reading than all other samples and so less text reading instruction time than all others (as their total reading instruction time was significantly less). Their overall instruction was not very effective for speed of reading text. It was effective, however, for word accuracy in reading text, a result consistent with the National Reading Panel (2000, chap. 2, pt. 2) evidence on the relative effectiveness of systematic teaching of explicit phonics. It was also effective for their reading comprehension. On the other hand, the children in our samples without explicit phonics had extra exposures and practice of words in text reading that enabled them, by a different learning route, to reach the same level of accuracy of text reading (and comprehension) as those receiving instruction in explicit phonics.

Conclusions

The evidence we have considered shows that there is not one universal route for learning to read an alphabetic orthography such as English. Typically developing children who receive different kinds of reading instruction can arrive at the same level of word reading accuracy by different learning routes. The theory and research about the processes of learning to read in different instructional environments has contrasted those that included systematic explicit phonics and those that were text-centred without such phonics. It is important to keep in mind the descriptions of the observed teaching practices outlined earlier in this chapter. In those, it will be noted that the text-centred instruction did include some teacher guidance in which the children were shown how to listen for sounds that corresponded to selected words of their story texts. The text-centred instruction did not completely ignore teacher demonstration of letter-sound relationships within the context of words. It is also important to keep in mind, as explained in the introductory sections of this chapter, that our research with children is not about the rate at which beginners acquire word reading accuracy during the first few years at school. It is about how the large proportion of children from these contrasted instructional environments have arrived at the same levels of word reading accuracy.

Our consideration of the effects of these contrasting instructional environments has led us to recognise two distinct types of phonological recoding that can be used by children at the beginner level: (a) Explicit phonological recoding that can be used if taught to the child, and (b) Implicit lexicalised phonological recoding, which does not usually require explicit teaching, and depends on implicit learning from patterns of information inherent in the learner's stored experiences of the orthographic and phonological forms of familiar words. This is likely to be used to some extent by all normally developing children, whatever the type of instruction received. It provides a means to increase reading vocabulary but also has a recursive function by which information from the vocabulary, in turn, facilitates the learning of further new words. Explicit phonological recoding provides a means to increase reading vocabulary but we have no evidence yet that it has the recursive function of lexicalised phonological recoding. Further work will be required to investigate this.

Instruction in the use of explicit phonological recoding has influences that continue into adulthood which affect the way skilled readers respond to new and unfamiliar words. Skilled adults receiving explicit phonics in childhood had a strong bias toward the type of context-free pronunciations that are emphasised in this instruction. Those adults receiving text-centred childhood instruction without the phonics were more likely to respond with the context-dependent pronunciations experienced in the words of their reading vocabularies. The results show that it does make sense to include information on childhood exposure to different types of instruction as a variable in theoretical models of adult word reading processes.

In contrast to the influences on phonological recoding, there is no research evidence of an influence of explicit phonics instruction on the ways in which children store information on familiar words. However, there is only a very limited range of research evidence as yet available.

In our cross-national study, beginner readers with text-centred teaching experienced more text reading than those with lessons on explicit phonics. The consequence was some difference in the children's learning routes. Those with the systematic explicit phonics made use of it to reach their level of word reading accuracy and gained an advantage in greater success at reading nonwords separate from text, but a disadvantage in speed of reading text. Those with text-centred teaching and no explicit phonics used their extended experience of reading text to arrive at the same level of word reading accuracy but in so doing gained an advantage in their speed of reading, but a disadvantage in reading unknown words.

The research considered here has involved only the English orthography and language. As Share (2008) points out, this is poorly representative of other alphabetic orthographies. A review of similar research on other languages and their orthographies should be in prospect as such accumulates. Of particular interest is research (e.g., Landerl, 2006) which examines the influence of type of reading instruction in each orthography as a potential confounding factor in comparisons of the processes used in reading different orthographies. We look forward to a synthesis of research charting the influence of reading instruction within and between orthographies.

References

Connelly, V. (1994). *The influence of instructional approach on the reading strategies of beginning readers.* Unpublished thesis. University of St. Andrews.

Connelly, V., Johnston, R. S., & Thompson, G. B. (1999). 'The influence of instructional approaches on reading procedures', In: G.B. Thompson & T. Nicholson (Eds.), *Learning to read: Beyond phonics and whole language* (pp. 103–23). New York: Teachers College Press.

Connelly, V., Johnston, R., & Thompson, G. B. (2001). 'The effect of phonics instruction on the reading comprehension of beginning readers', *Reading and Writing*, 14, 423–57.

Deavers, R., Solity, J., & Kerfoot, S. (2000). 'The effect of instruction on early nonword reading strategies', *Journal of Research in Reading*, 23, 267–86.

Ehri, L. C. (1999). 'Phases of development in learning to read words', In J. Oakhill & R. Beard (Eds.), *Reading development and the teaching of reading* (pp. 79–108). Oxford, England: Blackwell.

Ehri, L. C., Nunes, S. R., Stahl, S. A., & Willows, D. M. (2001). 'Systematic phonics instruction helps students learn to read: Evidence from the National Reading Panel's meta-analysis', *Review of Educational Research*, 71, 393–447.

Elder, R. D. (1971). 'Oral reading achievement of Scottish and American children', *Elementary School Journal*, 71, 216–30.

Fletcher-Flinn, C. M., Shankweiler, D., & Frost, S. J. (2004). 'Coordination of reading and spelling in early literacy development: An examination of the discrepancy hypothesis', *Reading and Writing*, 17, 617–44.

Fletcher-Flinn, C. M., & Thompson, G. B. (2004). 'A mechanism of implicit lexicalized phonological recoding used concurrently with underdeveloped explicit letter-sound skills in both precocious and normal reading development', *Cognition*, 90, 303–35.

Frith, U. (1985). 'Beneath the surface of developmental dyslexia', In K. E. Patterson, J. C. Marshall, & M. Coltheart (Eds.), *Surface dyslexia: Neuropsychological and cognitive studies of phonological reading* (pp. 301–30). London: Erlbaum.

Harm, M. W., & Seidenberg, M. S. (2004). 'Computing the meanings of words in reading: Cooperative division of labor between visual and phonological processes', *Psychological Review*, 111, 662–720.

Johnston, R. S., & Thompson, G. B. (1989). 'Is dependence on phonological information in children's reading a product of instructional approach?', *Journal of Experimental Child Psychology*, 48, 131–45.

Johnston, R. S., Thompson, G. B., Fletcher-Flinn, C. M. & Holligan, C. (1995). 'The functions of phonology in the acquisition of reading: Lexical and sentence processing', *Memory and Cognition* 23, 749–66.

Landerl, K. (2006). 'Reading acquisition in different orthographies: Evidence from direct comparisons', In R. M. Joshi & P. G. Aaron (Eds.), *Handbook of orthography and literacy* (pp. 513–30). Mahwah, NJ: Erlbaum.

Martin-Chang, S. L., & Levy, B. A. (2005). 'Fluency transfer: Differential gains in reading speed and accuracy following isolated word and context training', *Reading and Writing*, 18, 343–76.

McKay, M. F., & Thompson, G. B. (2009). 'Reading vocabulary influences in phonological recoding during the development of reading skill: a re-examination of theory and practice'. *Reading and Writing*, 22, 167–84

Mullis, I. V. S., Martin, M. O., Gonzalez, E. J., & Kennedy, A. M. (2003). *PIRLS 2001 international report*. Chestnut Hill, MA: PIRLS International Study Center.

National Reading Panel (2000). *Teaching children to read. Reports of the subgroups.* Washington, DC: National Institute of Child Health and Human Development.

New Zealand Department of Education (1985). *Reading in junior classes (with guidelines to the Revised Ready to Read series)*. Wellington, New Zealand: Government Printer.

Ramus, F. (2004). 'The neural basis of reading acquisition', In M. S. Gazzaniga (Ed.), *The cognitive neurosciences* (3rd. edit., pp. 815–24). Cambridge, Mass.: MIT Press.

Share, D. L. (1995). 'Phonological recoding and self-teaching: *sine qua non* of reading acquisition', *Cognition*, 55, 151–218.

——(2008). 'On the Anglocentricities of current reading research and practice: The perils of overreliance on an "outlier" orthography', *Psychological Bulletin*, 134, 584–615.

Stanovich, K. E. (1980). 'Toward an interactive-compensatory model of individual differences in the development of reading fluency', *Reading Research Quarterly*, 16, 32–71.

Stuart, M., Masterson, J., Dixon, M., & Quinlan, P. (1999). 'Inferring Sublexical correspondences from sight vocabulary: Evidence from 6-and 7-year-olds', *The Quarterly Journal of Experimental Psychology*, 52A(2), 353–66.

Sun, R., Slusarz, P., & Terry, C. (2005). 'The interaction of the explicit and implicit in skill learning: A dual process approach', *Psychological Review*, 112, 159–92.

Thompson, G. B. (1993). 'Reading instruction for the initial years in New Zealand schools', In G. B. Thompson, W. E. Tunmer, & T. Nicholson (Eds.), *Reading acquisition processes* (pp.148–54). Clevedon, UK: Multilingual Matters.

——(in press). 'The long learning route to abstract letter units', *Cognitive Neuropsychology*.

Thompson, G. B., Connelly, V., Fletcher-Flinn, C. M., & Hodson, S. J. (2009). 'The nature of skilled adult reading varies with type of instruction in childhood', *Memory and Cognition*, 37, 223–34.

Thompson, G. B., Cottrell, D. S., & Fletcher-Flinn, C. M. (1996). 'Sublexical orthographic-phonological relations early in the acquisition of reading: the Knowledge Sources account', *Journal of Experimental Child Psychology*, 62, 190–222.

Thompson, G. B., & Fletcher-Flinn, C. M. (1993). 'A theory of knowledge sources and procedures for reading acquisition'. In G. B. Thompson, W. E. Tunmer, & T. Nicholson (Eds.), *Reading acquisition processes* (pp. 20–73). Clevedon, UK: Multilingual Matters.

——(2006). 'Lexicalised implicit learning in reading acquisition: The Knowledge Sources theory'. In C. M. Fletcher-Flinn & G. M. Haberman (Eds.), *Cognition and language: Perspectives from New Zealand* (pp. 141–56). Bowen Hills, Queensland: Australian Academic Press.

Thompson, G. B., Fletcher-Flinn, C. M., & Cottrell, D. S. (1999). 'Learning correspondences between letters and phonemes without explicit instruction', *Applied Psycholinguistics*, 20, 21–50.

Thompson, G. B., & Johnston, R. S. (1993). 'The effects of type of instruction on processes of reading acquisition', In G. B. Thompson, W. E. Tunmer, & T. Nicholson (Eds.), *Reading acquisition processes* (pp. 74–90). Clevedon, UK: Multilingual Matters.

——(2000). 'Are nonword and other phonological deficits indicative of a failed reading process?' *Reading and Writing*, 12, 63–97.

——(2007). 'Visual and orthographic information in learning to read and the influence of phonics instruction', *Reading and Writing*, 20, 859–84.

Thompson, G. B., McKay, M. F., Fletcher-Flinn, C. M., Connelly, V., Kaa, R. T., & Ewing, J. (2008). 'Do children who acquire word reading without explicit phonics employ compensatory learning? Issues of phonological recoding, lexical orthography, and fluency', *Reading and Writing*, 21, 505–37.

Treiman, R., Kessler, B., & Bick, S. (2003). 'Influence of consonantal context on the pronunciation of vowels: A comparison of human readers and computational models', *Cognition*, 88, 49–78.

Treiman, R., Kessler, B., Zevin, J. D., Bick, S., & Davis, M. (2006). 'Influence of consonantal context on the reading of vowels: Evidence from children', *Journal of Experimental Child Psychology*, 93, 1–24.

Zevin, J. D., & Seidenberg, M. S. (2006). 'Simulating consistency effects and individual differences in nonword naming: A comparison of current models', *Journal of Memory & Language*, 54, 145–60.

Ziegler, J. C., & Goswami, U. (2005). 'Reading acquisition, developmental dyslexia, and skilled reading across languages: A psycholinguistic grain size theory', *Psychological Bulletin*, 131, 3–29.

Chapter 15

The cerebellar deficit theory of developmental dyslexia

Evidence and implications for intervention

Shahrzad Irannejad and Robert Savage

A mild deficit in the cerebellum has been proposed to underlie a wide range of cognitive and behavioural indicators of dyslexia that were formerly explained by the phonological deficit hypothesis and double-deficit models of reading disability, as well as other unexplained symptoms observed in dyslexia (Nicolson, Fawcett, & Dean, 2001). In its earliest form cerebellar deficit theory was introduced within a cognitive framework of automaticity, postulating that dyslexic children have difficulties in becoming fluent in any learned skill (Nicolson & Fawcett, 1990). The incorporation of a neurological (cerebellar) basis underlying this apparent automaticity deficit is a more recent development (Nicolson & Fawcett, 1999; Nicolson *et al.*, 2001). However, the specific role of the cerebellum in dyslexia is not strongly established as there are some inconsistencies in the existing evidence. Moreover, empirical evaluations of an intervention based on the cerebellar deficit theory do not present convincing evidence, largely due to methodological issues. Consequently we argue that this area requires further investigation.

The nature of dyslexia

In the traditional view, dyslexia is seen as a distinct anomaly inherent to the individual. From this view, the presence of a discrepancy between IQ and actual achievement is a basic criterion for identifying dyslexia (Vellutino *et al.*, 2000), and it is defined as a specific learning disorder in which 'reading achievement, as measured by individually administered standardized tests of reading accuracy or comprehension, is substantially below that expected given the person's chronological age, measured intelligence, and age appropriate education' (American Psychiatric Association, 1994: 50). Thus, children diagnosed with dyslexia are assumed to be qualitatively different from those with both low attainment and low intellectual abilities, who are sometimes referred to as 'garden-variety' poor readers and suffer from basic cognitive deficits.

Given the preliminary status of neurobiological research into dyslexia, there is still no consensus as to which diagnostic criteria may identify its neurobiological cause(s). There is also evidence that dyslexia may not be a distinct condition but rather simply the tail end of a normal distribution of reading achievement where children differ solely in their degree of reading ability (e.g. Fletcher *et al.*, 1994; Shaywitz *et al.*, 1992). Consistent with this view, findings from neuroimaging studies have suggested the existence of quantitative, as opposed to qualitative, differences between the brains of individuals who experience dyslexia and those who do not (Beaton, 2002; Bishop,

2002). Furthermore, intervention studies, familial-risk studies, and lifespan studies of dyslexia indicate that genetic vulnerabilities, especially in phonological skills, interact with other cognitive and environmental factors in order to produce an increased risk for dyslexia (see Vellutino *et al.*, 2004). There is also evidence that, with regard to response to instruction, IQ-discrepant and IQ non-discrepant poor readers cannot be adequately differentiated (Fletcher *et al.*, 1994; Vellutino *et al.*, 2004).

Finally, measures of intelligence do not seem to be related to reading abilitites such as phonological decoding or word identification (e.g. Vellutino *et al.*, 2000), nor do they predict word reading performance in typically achieving readers (Vellutino *et al.*, 1996). In fact, regardless of the intelligence of the child, it seems that phonological skills play an important role in determining a child's ability to learn to read, and can distinguish between normal and dyslexic readers (Vellutino *et al.*, 2000). In the face of such evidence, measures of intellectual functioning have been omitted from many current definitions of dyslexia. Dyslexia is thus characterized by difficulties in decoding single words that reflect a deficit in phonological processing abilities occurring irrespective of an individual intellectual functioning (Lyon, 1995; Orton Dyslexia Society, 1995).

Phonological deficit theory

The phonological deficit theory proposes that children with dyslexia have difficulty acquiring the phonological skills necessary to decode words in alphabetic languages. They are suggested to have an underdeveloped sensitivity to phoneme structures, which may lead to difficulties attending to, accessing, and isolating phonemes in words (Bowers & Newby-Clark, 2002; Liberman, 1982). Moreover, difficulties in phonological coding, storage, and retrieval are suggested to impede a child's ability to learn phoneme–grapheme correspondences. This is suggested to lead to an impaired ability to store orthographic representations and slow and inaccurate recall of phonological representations (Berninger *et al.*, 1987; Bowers & Newby-Clark, 2002; Torgesen & Wagner, 1998; Vellutino *et al.*, 2000). Ultimately, fluency in word identification may be affected, making reading a slow, inaccurate, and strenuous task (Fawcett & Lynch, 2000; Nicolson & Fawcett, 1999; Pennington *et al.*, 1990; Snowling, 1998).

Experimental studies have confirmed difficulties in phonological sensitivity and awareness in dyslexic compared to typical readers (e.g. Ackerman *et al.*, 1990; Rack, 1985) as well as in studies of identical as compared to fraternal twins (e.g. Olson *et al.*, 1989). Corresponding problems in decoding both real and nonsense words have been widely reported (e.g. Fletcher *et al.*, 1994; Hynd *et al.*, 1995; Savage *et al.*, 2005a; Siegel, 1993; Siegel & Ryan, 1989). Furthermore, phonological tasks are not only related to learning to read (e.g. Berninger *et al.*, 1987), but also predict subsequent achievement and difficulties in reading (e.g. Cossu *et al.*, 1988; Naslund & Schneider, 1996; Share *et al.*, 1984; Wesseling & Reitsma, 2001).

More importantly, intervention studies indicate improved word identification, spelling, and reading ability as a result of direct instruction in phonological awareness (Bradley & Bryant, 1983; Hatcher *et al.*, 1994; Lundberg *et al.*, 1988; Vellutino *et al.*, 2004). These findings provide further support for the notion of dyslexia being a continuous phenomenon in which both genetic and environmental factors can play a role.

Beyond the phonological deficit: automaticity in reading

Other researchers argue that the phonological deficit itself may be the result of other underlying deficits. Difficulties in rapid processing of a range of stimuli have been considered indices of underlying automaticity deficits in dyslexia (e.g. Wolf & Bowers, 1999). More specifically, deficits in naming speed are suggested to reduce the rate of word recognition in individuals with reading disability and thus interfere with fluent word reading (e.g. Bowers & Wolf, 1993; Wolf & Bowers, 1999; Wolf, Bowers, & Biddle, 2000). Studies have supported the existence of an independent contribution of naming speed to reading (e.g. Bowers *et al.*, 1988; Chiappe *et al.*, 2002; Fawcett & Nicolson, 1994), though there are a number of studies that have failed to find this pattern (e.g. Savage *et al.*, 2005b; Wagner *et al.*, 1994). Some researchers also view naming speed deficits as a second core deficit in reading disability that can exist both independently from or as a 'double deficit' in combination with phonological impairment (Bowers, 1995a; Wolf & Bowers, 1999).

The naming speed deficit is argued to indicate impairment in a whole system of general processing speed that affects lower level processes (e.g. visual, auditory, and motor processes) thereby leading to reading difficulties (Wolf & Bowers, 1999). More specifically it has been suggested that the sub-processes which underlie naming speed, such as visual scanning and identification of stimuli, lexical retrieval, attention, stimulus inhibition, or articulation skills, must all be precisely timed and rapidly integrated for a successful, automatic, and fluent performance (Badian, 1995; Bowers, 1995b; Bowers & Wolf, 1993; Wolf & Bowers, 1999; Wolf *et al.*, 2000). Slower activation of these underlying processes is therefore suggested to be associated with reading difficulties (Bowers, 1995b).

Some researchers, however, have extended the notion of automaticity to more domain general deficits in automatic processing of stimuli. These researchers have argued that naming speed and phonological processing deficits might both be the result of an underlying deficit in motor timing and automaticity (e.g. Nicolson & Fawcett, 1990; Wolff, 2002; Yap & van der Leij, 1994). According to the automaticity deficit model, naming speed and phonological skills are seen as only a few of the behavioral manifestations that exist among a larger pattern of difficulties including motor skills, and working memory. More specifically, some researchers have argued that children with dyslexia experience an automatization deficit leading to difficulties in becoming automatic in any learned skill, be it motor or cognitive (Nicolson & Fawcett, 1990).

The cerebellar deficit theory of dyslexia

In its most recent form, automatization deficits have been attributed to abnormal cerebellar/vestibular areas of the brain (Reynolds *et al.*, 2003). Abnormalities in specific brain structures are suggested to be the underlying primary cause that give rise to phonological and naming speed deficits among many other manifested symptoms (Reynolds & Nicolson, 2007). More specifically, in this view a mild deficit in the cerebellum is proposed to cause a cascading series of impairments in motor and visual skill domains, difficulties in central processing speed, and in acquisition and automatization of elementary articulatory and auditory skills, which then lead to impediments in writing, spelling, rapid naming, phonological processing, and eventually in reading (Fawcett *et al.*, 2001; Nicolson *et al.*, 2002; Nicolson & Fawcett, 1999; Nicolson *et al.*, 2001).

The cerebellum, a fist-sized structure located at the lower back of the brain just above the brainstem, is a motor area implicated in the acquisition and execution of motor skills, automatization, and adaptive learning (Nicolson & Fawcett, 1999, 2000). A mild cerebellar deficit, present at birth, is thus suggested to explain the full range of difficulties experienced by dyslexic readers.

According to Nicolson and Fawcett (1999) and Nicolson *et al.* (2001), through the set of dysfunctional distal pathways, outlined in Figure 15.1, the cerebellar deficit leads to a series of more proximal impairments including motor and balance difficulties, or deficits in handwriting, and eventually causes distal impairments in spelling, rapid naming, phonological difficulties, and subsequent reading and writing problems (Fawcett, 2002; Nicolson & Fawcett, 1999; Nicolson *et al.*, 2001). Difficulties in spelling, reading, and rapid naming are believed to arise from an articulatory-based phonological impairment, in addition to deficits in automatization. According to Nicolson and Fawcett (1999), effective spelling requires both phonological skill and motor input. A reduced ability to acquire implicit knowledge of orthographic regularities, as well as a reduced ability to automatize knowledge of spelling patterns, can thus lead to severe difficulties in spelling (Nicolson & Fawcett, 1999; Nicolson *et al.*, 2001).

Pathways leading to phonological deficits and subsequent reading problems seem to be more complex. In the most direct route, the first series of difficulties that are directly caused by a mild cerebellar dysfunction include mild motor problems during the early stages of development (such as delayed abilities in sitting up or walking). Since the cerebellum is also suggested to be a key structure in developing articulatory skill, another direct effect of a cerebellar deficit is believed to be greater difficulties in articulation, which leads to problems such as delayed babbling and talking (Fawcett, 2002; Nicolson & Fawcett, 1999; Nicolson *et al.*, 2001). Problems in articulation will eventually lead to phonological deficits.

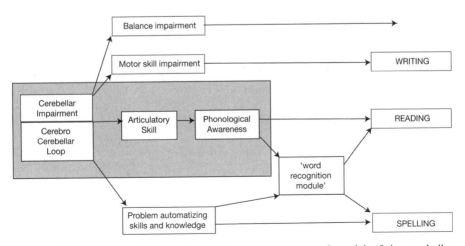

Figure 15.1 Nicolson and Fawcett's (1999) ontogenetic causal model of the cerebellar deficit hypothesis

In addition, reduced fluency and automaticity in articulation in individuals with dyslexia is proposed to result in use of more conscious resources to compensate for that difficulty (Nicolson & Fawcett, 1999). Consequently, fewer resources are left to process a sensory feedback. Less fluency in articulation is also suggested to have an indirect effect leading to reduced effectiveness of working memory, particularly the phonological loop (Nicolson *et al.*, 2001). As a result, the child may become insensitive to the phonological structure of language leading to deficits in phonological awareness.

Neurological evidence for cerebellar deficit theory

There is relatively little direct evidence linking dyslexia to the cerebellum. One recent postmortem neuroanatomical study by Finch *et al.* (2002) reported larger mean areas for cells of dyslexics as well as significant differences in the cell size distributions in some of the structures they explored (i.e. in the posterior, and anterior lobe as well as in inferior olive). They did not, however, find any significant cerebellar asymmetry. Considering the small number of brains that were examined in the study (four dyslexic and four controls) generalization to the dyslexic population should be made with caution. The study also lacked cases where a clear diagnosis of dyslexia was available.

Temple's (2002) review of recent neurobiological research into dyslexia indicated no reports of cerebellar abnormalities. In general, most findings related to dyslexia are not limited to the cerebellum and involve other areas of the brain (Ivry & Justus, 2001). Furthermore, some evidence has pointed to the involvement of the cerebellum in multiple and diverse neural circuits (e.g. Dum & Strick, 2003; Eckert *et al.*, 2003). Hence, while there may be some abnormalities in the cerebellum of dyslexic individuals, it is possible that the primary cause of the disorder is located elsewhere, exerting its effects through a modulatory influence on cerebellar processing, which may provide a more credible explanation for the subtle cerebellar signs seen in some dyslexic individuals (Zeffiro & Eden, 2001).

Behavioural evidence concerning the cerebellar deficit theory

Links between language skills and cerebellar processing

Support for the link between the cerebellum, articulation, and phonological processing has been derived from studies showing the importance of the cerebellum in deficits in naming as well as fluency of speech (e.g. Schmahmann & Sherman, 1998). Additional evidence related to a cerebellar dysfunction has also been associated with difficulties in discriminating time intervals that are equally long as acoustic speech segments as well as difficulties in categorical speech perception (Ackermann *et al.*, 1997).

The causal link between the cerebellum, articulation, and phonological or language difficulties, as outlined by the cerebellar deficit theory, is less well supported by a range of other empirical studies. For example, some findings indicate normal development of phonological, reading, and writing skills despite severe cases of speech disorders (e.g. Cossu, 2003). In other studies, cerebellar pathology has not been shown to interfere with language, speech perception, and practice effects for speech or oral movements (Fiez *et al.*, 1992; Ivry & Gopal, 1993; Schulz *et al.*, 1999). Moreover, articulation may not be directly related to reading (Neuhaus *et al.*, 2001a; Neuhaus *et al.*, 2001b; Neuhaus & Swank, 2002). The articulatory-based pathway through which a cerebellar deficit is hypothesized to lead to phonological and subsequent reading impairments is weakened by its reliance on the outdated motor theory of speech (Ramus *et al.*, 2003b). Ramus *et al.* (2003a) note, for example, that there is good evidence that some children with congenital dysarthria (a motor speech difficulty) can perform some phonological tasks well.

Evidence of automaticity deficits from dual-task studies

Initial supportive evidence for the cerebellar deficit hypothesis was derived from a series of studies that investigated automatization problems in dyslexic children. In these studies, a dual-task paradigm was used to assess the difficulty in automatizing skills in dyslexic individuals as compared to typical readers. The dual-task methodology is suggested to reveal subtle deficits in automaticity that are thought to be masked via conscious compensation in dyslexic children (Nicolson & Fawcett, 1990). The logic behind the dual-task paradigm is that due to limited cognitive resources available to complete one behaviour, this will result in a deficit for other behaviours attempted at the same time (Everatt *et al.*, 1999). The studies assessed samples of dyslexic readers aged 8, 12, 13, and 16 years, whose reading age was at least 18 months below their chronological age (Fawcett & Nicolson, 1992, 1994, 1995a, 1995b; Nicolson & Fawcett, 1990), and included balance tasks as primary tasks, such as balancing on a beam, at times blindfolded, either on both feet, one foot, or when walking up and down (Nicolson & Fawcett, 1990). While performing the primary task, a secondary task was then introduced to divert attentional resources away from the primary task. Different secondary tasks were used such as choice reaction tasks or paced backward counting from 100 in twos or threes or forward counting in twos or threes. Children experiencing dyslexia were expected to show difficulties in balance compared to non-dyslexic typical readers only when balancing was completed simultaneously with a secondary task that took up conscious processing capacity. Fawcett and Nicolson (1992) and Nicolson and Fawcett (1990) reported severe difficulties in balance and blindfold balance in children with dyslexia compared to normal controls in dual-task but not in single-task balance conditions.

The dual-task paradigm used by Nicolson and Fawcett has been criticized on methodological grounds (Savage, 2004). Drawing conclusions from findings related to dual-task methodology depends crucially on whether sufficient control has been exerted to equate speed and accuracy of the primary and secondary tasks undertaken in the single-task condition across dyslexic and control group children. As Savage (2004) notes, such control was not always obtained in the dual-task paradigm. For example, Nicolson and Fawcett (1990) reported unequal performances in the secondary task in the single-task condition amongst poor and good readers, leading to the use of 'calibration' across the groups in an attempt to obtain equivalent difficulty for both groups in the single-task condition.

The types of tasks chosen in the dual-task methodology are also crucial as they might influence interpretation of findings. As Savage (2004) has observed, the two tasks used in such studies should be independent and not tap into the same processing resources. In addition, however, both tasks should not tap into skills or processes that have been shown to be impaired in dyslexic readers, such as rapid naming or phonological processes. Consequently, choosing a task such as counting backwards in the dual-task paradigm poses a methodological problem. While counting backward might be independent from motor skills in terms of the processing resources required, it probably taps into working memory processes or skills that have often been reported as areas of specific difficulty in dyslexia. Therefore, findings related to balance difficulties in dual tasks may also be due to other more central verbal processing problems as opposed to problems in motor automaticity. Additionally, choosing verbal tasks which require articulation as secondary tasks is also problematic because the difficulties experienced in balance might be partly due to the motor requirements involved in articulation rather than solely to competing attentional demands (Dault *et al.*, 2003; Yardley *et al.*, 1999).

Finally, the purpose of dual-task methodology is to reveal subtle deficits in automaticity of motor skills that should not be seen in normal readers. However, there is older evidence indicating changes in motor skill performance, such as depression in finger tapping performance, in normal individuals as a result of engaging in simultaneous verbal tasks (e.g. Bowers *et al.*, 1978).

To avoid methodological complications and confounds involved in a dual-task paradigm, some researchers have used tasks such as implicit or motor sequence learning to investigate the quality of automatic skill learning without using dual tasks. Findings from these studies have also posed further challenge to the idea of skill automatization problems in dyslexia. For example, Kelly *et al.* (2002), explored the role of implicit processing in a choice reaction time learning task administered to dyslexic and typically reading university students. Response times to a random sequence of pictures were compared against response times to a complex but repeated spatial sequence. Results indicated that dyslexic readers could learn the complex pattern at the same pace as the average readers did.

Evidence related to motor and postural stability

One source of evidence relating cerebellar deficits to dyslexia comes from studies that investigated whether dyslexic readers displayed noticeable deficits in traditional signs of cerebellar impairment similar to those shown by patients with gross damage to their cerebellum. Fawcett and Nicolson (1999) and Fawcett *et al.* (1996) used clinical cerebellar tests to assess problems with muscle tone, posture/balance, gait or movement seen in patients with gross damage to their cerebellum. The ability to maintain posture and balance was assessed using a blindfold balance task in which children were required to stand on one or two feet with arms on their sides or outstretched in front. The children had to remain still whilst a two kilogram force was gently applied to their back without warning using a calibrated stability tester. The degree of wobble in balance was then measured. To assess muscle tone in upper limbs, tasks such as arm displacement or arm shake were used while children were in sitting or standing position. Ability to initiate and maintain a complex voluntary movement was also assessed by repeated finger to finger pointing or toe-tap speed.

Using these tasks, Fawcett *et al.* (1996) compared three groups of dyslexic readers aged 10, 14, and 18 with three groups of typical readers who were matched to the dyslexic groups on IQ and age. Based on age-matched comparisons, Fawcett and colleagues reported deficits on all cerebellar tasks in dyslexic children. Reading age matched comparisons were reported to reveal deficits for the majority of tasks (i.e. 11 out of 14 tasks). For most tasks, motor impairment was reported to be greater than reading impairment. Higher incidence rates of impairment were observed in the children with dyslexia relative to cerebellar patients, and it was therefore concluded that deficits found in dyslexic children may represent an impairment across the entire cerebellum as opposed to specific cerebellar region.

In another study, Fawcett and Nicolson (1999) attempted to replicate their findings with a larger sample that included 126 dyslexic and normal children who were divided and matched in four different age groups (8–9, 10–11, 12–13, and 14–16 years). They reported significantly worse performance in dyslexic children as compared to their chronological-age matched controls in all three tests of cerebellar function (i.e. postural stability/balance, arm shake, and toe-tapping speed). Performances were reported to be exceptionally poor in all four dyslexic groups on postural stability and limb shake. Additionally, dyslexic readers displayed more difficulties in segmentation and nonsense word repetition compared to their age-matched controls. The same pattern of results was also reported for a subgroup of dyslexic and control children that were matched for IQ (Fawcett & Nicolson, 1999).

As intriguing as these results are, researchers remain sceptical of findings related to signs of cerebellar disfunction in dyslexic individuals. Beaton (2002) pointed out that the significant differences reported between the dyslexic and control groups in cerebellar tests in Fawcett and Nicolson's (1999) study may be because the study was partly based on participants from Fawcett and Nicolson's previous research panel. Further analysis is therefore required to examine the potential contribution of practice effects to the results. Zeffiro and Eden (2001) have also argued that the overlap between clinical symptoms in patients with acquired cerebellar damage and dyslexic individuals may be too small to attribute cerebellar disorder as the underlying cause of dyslexia. They noted that symptoms in dyslexic individuals are limited to abnormalities in motor learning and automatization in movement. Zeffiro and Eden (2001) also observed cerebellar patients who did not exhibit abnormalities in reading and phonological processing.

Attempts to replicate findings related to the cerebellar deficit hypothesis, especially difficulties in balance, have yielded inconsistent results. While some researchers have observed motor difficulties in subgroups of dyslexics (Yap & van der Leij, 1994), others have not (van Daal & van der Leij, 1999). It is possible that performance on balance automaticity is more related to developmental maturation rather than to reading skills (Savage et al., 2005b). In a recent study conducted by Savage et al. (2005b), performance on phonological, rapid naming, and reading tasks as well as postural stability/balance were examined in nine 10-year-old poor readers along with nine age-matched, and nine younger reading-age-matched controls. The poor readers performed significantly worse than their chronological age-matched peers on naming speed and some of the phonological tasks. Poor readers also performed significantly worse than their reading age-matched controls in nonsense word reading. Interestingly, however, they were shown to perform significantly *better* than reading age controls on a task measuring postural stability.

Furthermore, poor balance seems to be only specific to the group of dyslexic children who also exhibited attention difficulties. For example, Wimmer et al. (1999)

compared performance on balancing tasks used by Nicolson and Fawcett (1990), as well as naming speed and phonological skills in a group of German dyslexic children and age-matched controls. To rule out the possibility that performance on motor tasks might be affected by difficulties in attention, parents were interviewed and asked to complete the Conners Attention Rating Questionnaire. Teachers were also asked to rate the children's attention skills. In the analysis attention scores were used as a covariate, and once the attention difficulties were controlled, the poor and good readers differed solely on naming speed and phonological awareness. Similar results have also been reported elsewhere (e.g. Denckla *et al.*, 1985; Raberger & Wimmer, 2003; Ramus *et al.*, 2003a).

Cerebellar difficulties distinguish IQ-discrepant and non-discrepant dyslexics?

Fawcett *et al.* (2001) have reported that cerebellar deficits can differentiate between poor readers with IQ-discrepant and IQ non-discrepant reading scores. They tested 37 children with learning difficulties (aged 7–11 years), most of whom had entered special education between ages 6 and 7 years. Children were classified into non-discrepant and discrepant poor readers based on the absence or presence of discrepancies of at least 18 months between their intellectual ability as measured by the Wechsler Intelligence Scale for Children (WISC) and reading achievement as measured by the Wechsler Objective Reading Dimension (WORD) tests of reading and spelling. Twenty-nine children were classified as the non-discrepant reading disabled group with IQ scores below 90 and were divided into two age groups (14 7–9-year-olds and 15 10–11-year-olds). Seven children were classified as the discrepant reading-disabled group with IQ scores of at least 90 and above. Due to the low number of children in this group, Fawcett *et al.* (2001) integrated nine dyslexic children (aged 8 years) from a previous study (Fawcett *et al.*, 1996) in all of their analyses except the static cerebellar tests. The analyses also included another group of 10-year-old children with dyslexia as well as the data from two groups of control children (ages 8–11) from a previous study.

Performance was measured on a range of tasks including phonological, speed, motor, and cerebellar tasks. Fawcett *et al.* (2001) reported that the non-discrepant group was at least as severely impaired as the discrepant group in phonological, speed, and motor tasks. However, performance tasks of postural stability and muscle tone distinguished between the two groups, with the non-discrepant group performing significantly better.

Fawcett *et al.*'s (2001) findings have not been replicated in a recent study by Savage (2007). This study included a group of 25 children with formal diagnosis of developmental dyslexia and another group of 18 children with formal diagnosis of intellectual disabilities (aged 11–14 years). The two groups therefore differed only on verbal and nonverbal cognitive abilities. No significant differences were found between the two groups in spelling, word reading, phonological processing, or basic verbal response speed. There was also no difference in postural stability. Rather, small non-significant advantages were observed in children with developmental dyslexia on postural stability and there were significant advantages in bead threading. Furthermore, the postural stability mean scores obtained by the two groups of children did not reveal them to be 'at risk' of dyslexia based on the Dyslexia Screening Test (Fawcett & Nicolson, 1995c).

The Dyslexia Dyspraxia Attention Deficit Treatment

One of the implications of the cerebellar deficit hypothesis, if valid, would be to guide assessment, diagnosis, and treatment. One influential treatment based on the cerebellar deficit theory is an exercise-based programme implemented in the Dyslexia Dyspraxia Attention Deficit Treatment (DDAT) clinic, now known as Dore Achievement Centres (Reynolds & Nicolson, 2007). This treatment is targeted to address the purported underlying cause of dyslexia. The purpose of the programme is therefore to retrain the cerebellum into its normal state while this structure is still in a plastic state via a series of complex oculomotor and vestibular motor task learning, such as practice at dual tasking, a range of stretching and coordination exercises, throwing and catching of bean bags. Based on children's individual needs, different groups of exercises are prescribed for a period of time and changed over time when normal vestibular/cerebellar function has been achieved. Cerebellar/vestibular function is assessed using computerized tests that measure balance, motor control, and different types of eye movements that are controlled by the cerebellum (Reynolds & Nicolson, 2007; Reynolds et al., 2003). Improving the function of cerebellar/vestibular system in this manner is then expected to lead to improvements in learning ability, and thus lead to improved acquisition of skills taught at school. Consequently, improvement in literacy is suggested to be a 'side-effect' of cerebellar improvement (Reynolds & Nicolson, 2007).

The effectiveness and long-term maintenance of the DDAT exercise programme was evaluated in two studies (Reynolds & Nicolson, 2007; Reynolds et al., 2003). In the first (Reynolds et al., 2003), 18 children with ages ranging from 7 to 10, who received the exercise treatment over a six-month period were compared to an untreated control group of 17 children with ages ranging from 8 to 10, from the same school. Of the sample, nine had a prior diagnosis of dyslexia while the others were identified as having 'Special Educational Needs' by the school. The control group was matched to the exercise group for age, reading, and motor skills as assessed by the Dyslexia Screening Test (DST; Fawcett & Nicolson, 1995a; Fawcett et al., 1993). The DST is used to screen for dyslexia in children aged between 6 and 16 years. It includes eleven subtests which are intended to cover the range of skills that are suggested to be impaired in dyslexic readers, namely motor skill and balance, literacy skills, phonological awareness, verbal memory, and memory retrieval fluency.

According to Reynolds et al. (2003), all children in the study were identified as potentially at risk of reading difficulties using the DST. All children were tested on different reading, cognitive, and cerebellar/vestibular measures both prior to and after six months of implementing the DDAT treatment programme. School reading tests including the NFER test of reading (i.e. untimed sentence completion, group reading test), as well as national standardized attainment tests (SATs) of writing, comprehension, and numeracy.

In their evaluation of the DDAT programme, Reynolds et al. (2003) reported substantial alleviation of the cerebellar/vestibular signs in the experimental group. Significant improvements in postural stability and in bead threading dexterity were reported to persist in the exercise group even after allowing for the passage of time. They also reported that benefits of the motor exercises transferred to cognitive skills that underlie literacy as well as to the reading process itself. The experimental group was reported to show improved performance on NFER reading test and SATs of writing and comprehension, and a significant acceleration of progress compared to that observed in previous years.

Reynolds and Nicolson (2007) reported follow-up data 12 and 18 months after the original intervention, based on 29 out of the 35 children who participated in the first evaluation study. The control group who had received no treatment in the first evaluation study received a six-month period of treatment during the follow-up study. Gains observed by the original evaluation study were maintained in the follow-up: based on 'age-adjusted' comparison of initial and follow-up performance, significant improvements were reported in balance, bead threading, working memory, semantic fluency, and rapid naming but not in speeded reading or spelling. However, significant improvement was reported on the test of reading comprehension. Both dyslexic and non-dyslexic low achieving children were reported to benefit from the programme (Reynolds & Nicolson, 2007).

The two evaluation studies reported above have been subjected to substantial peer criticism (McPhillips, 2003; Rack et al., 2007; Singleton & Stuart, 2003; Snowling & Hulme, 2003). Methodological problems have been identified, such as the lack of random assignment to treatment and control groups. An imbalance between the two groups in their initial reading ability was not considered statistically despite considerably higher initial performance for the control over the experimental group. The experimental group might be expected to show greater increases in their post-test scores either due to the nature of some of the subtests in the DST (Singleton & Stuart, 2003) or purely for statistical reasons such as regression to the mean effects (Richards et al., 2003). Regression to the mean refers to the tendency for individuals who score towards the extreme of a continuum on a particular measure to score closer to the mean when rested on the same or a similar measure. The subtests in the DST have also been questioned regarding their psychometric robustness and brevity (see Singleton & Stuart, 2003).

Furthermore, the sample used in the studies included participants with varying degrees of difficulties including only nine with a formal diagnosis of dyslexia and others with reading attainments above the average for their age (Richards et al., 2003; Snowling & Hulme, 2003). According to Reynolds et al. (2003), all children in the sample were considered at risk of dyslexia based on the DST. Nonetheless, the reading age of some of the children in the first evaluation study was actually above their chronological age (up to 6 and 22 months ahead in the experimental and control groups, respectively: Richards et al., 2003; Snowling & Hulme, 2003).

One further problem was the similar and significant improvements in phonological decoding skills demonstrated in both the experimental and the untreated control group in the first evaluation study (Singleton & Stuart, 2003). It has been argued that inferences about the effectiveness of the intervention were also compromised since factors such as inappropriate presentation of scores in the data (i.e. percentiles instead of raw scores) could account for the greater increase in post-test scores in the experimental as compared to the control group. The lack of a treated control group was also criticized. The presence of a placebo treatment might have ruled out some of the most obvious alternative explanations for the effectiveness of the programme such as short-term motivational gain from knowing one is in an intervention study (McPhillips, 2003; Rack *et al.*, 2007; Snowling & Hulme, 2003).

In addition to issues related to sampling and treatment, some of the variables, or lack of them, have also caused concern. These include: (a) the lack of IQ measures for both the experimental and control groups (McPhillips, 2003); (b) use of standard attainment tasks (i.e. SATs), which are generally not considered sound measures for evaluating an intervention (Richards *et al.*, 2003; Singleton & Stuart, 2003; Snowling & Hulme, 2003); (c) use of reading age which is considered inappropriate for comparing results at two different times (Turner, 1997); (d) relying on the One-Minute Reading subtest of the DST, which involves a very limited sample of reading behaviour (Singleton & Stuart, 2003; Snowling & Hulme, 2003); (e) lack of sample-based norms for some of the cerebellar/vestibular tests used in the programme, which has further compromised the evaluation of changes in reading performance (Richards *et al.*, 2003); and (f) narrow range and lack of sensitivity in measuring a range of performances on cerebellar/vestibular tasks for the normal scores that were available for some of these tests (Richards *et al.*, 2003).

Turning to the follow-up study (Reynolds & Nicolson, 2007), comparisons were made between the experimental group and the previously untreated control group. In the follow-up study, this latter group had become a delayed treatment group. Rack *et al.* (2007) argue that such comparisons are not legitimate as both groups had received treatment. Even so, the only measures that were reported to improve between the first and final follow-up test in the second evaluation study were those that were least related to literacy, such as bead threading, balance, rapid naming, semantic fluency, and working memory.

The two groups were also combined to examine the overall gains that were made over the two years of the study and follow-up. As no comparison data are available on any changes that might have happened naturally during this time had these students been left to continue their normal activities, interpretation of gains is highly problematic (Rack *et al.*, 2007). Finally, to explore maintenance of performance in those children in the group with a prior dyslexia diagnosis (i.e. 8 of 9 diagnosed cases), comparisons were made between them and the other 21 students who were identified as having 'Special Educational Needs'. These comparisons were made despite the lack of an appropriate operational definition for the latter group, thus leaving room for interpretation concerning the range of possible needs in that group. The nature and extent of the above methodological and statistical problems related to the DDAT evaluation studies have raised important questions about the conclusions that have been made regarding the effectiveness of the DDAT exercise programme.

Dyslexia and effective intervention

The research reviewed here suggests that current evidence related to the cerebellar deficit hypothesis is considered by many to be controversial and inconsistent. This pattern is evident in the behavioural findings, neuropsychological evidence, assessment practices and the DDAT intervention described above. What these findings do suggest is that cerebellar theory and treatments based upon it are at a preliminary stage.

Considering all of the wider evidence about dyslexia, the behavioural difficulties that seem to be most consistently demonstrated in children with dyslexia are deficits in phonological and rapid naming processes, pointing to a link between reading and language-based deficits. Compelling evidence indicates that improved reading skills can result from direct instruction in phonological processing. Furthermore, findings from family-risk and dyslexia lifespan studies suggest that dyslexia may be a difficulty in responding to the method of instruction, which can be modified by environmental factors (Vellutino *et al.*, 2004). Hence, the risk of developing dyslexia can decrease if external factors, such as method of instruction, enable him/her to benefit from his/her cognitive assets. On this basis then, direct instruction in specific phonological skills, decoding and reading, alongside appropriate modelling, practice, and feedback might be best practice at this time (Boudah & Weiss, 2002; Swanson & Hoskyn, 1998).

References

Ackerman, P.T., Dykman, R.A., & Gardner, M.Y. (1990). 'Counting rate, naming rate, phonological sensitivity, and memory span: Major factors in dyslexia'. *Journal of Learning Disabilities, 23*, 325–327.

Ackermann, H., Graber, S., Hertrich, I., & Daum, I. (1997). 'Categorical speech perception in cerebellar disorders'. *Brain and Language, 60*, 323–331.

American Psychiatric Association. (1994). *Diagnostic and statistical manual of mental disorders* (4th edn)'. Washington, DC: American Psychiatric Association.

Badian, N.A. (1995). 'Predicting reading ability over the long term: the changing roles of letter naming, phonological awareness and orthographic processing'. *Annals of Dyslexia, 45*, 79–96.

Beaton, A.A. (2002). 'Dyslexia and the cerebellar deficit hypothesis'. *Cortex, 38*, 479–490.

Berninger, V.W., Thalberg, S.P., DeBruyn, I., & Smith, R. (1987). 'Preventing reading disabilities by assessing and remediating phonemic skills'. *School Psychology Review, 16*, 554–565.

Bishop, D.V. (2002). 'Cerebellar abnormalities in developmental dyslexia: Cause, correlate or consequence?' *Cortex, 38*, 491–498.

Boudah, D.J., & Weiss, M.P. (2002). *Learning disabilities overview: Update 2002* (Report No'. EDO-EC-02-02). Arlington, VA: ERIC Clearinghouse on Disabilities and Gifted Education.

Bowers, D., Heilman, K.M., Satz, P., & Altman, A. (1978). 'Simultaneous performance on verbal, nonverbal and motor tasks by right-handed adults'. *Cortex, 14*, 540–556.

Bowers, P.G. (1995a). 'Implications for later reading of a naming speed deficit accompanying a phonemic awareness deficit'. Paper presented at the Annual Meeting of the Society for the Scientific Study of Reading, San Francisco, CA, April.

—— (1995b). 'Tracing symbol naming speed's unique contributions to reading disabilities over time'. *Reading and Writing, 7*, 189–216.

Bowers, P.G., & Wolf, M. (1993). 'Theoretical links among naming speed, precise timing mechanisms and orthographic skill in dyslexia'. *Reading and Writing, 5*, 69–85.

Bowers, P.G., & Newby-Clark, E. (2002). 'The role of naming speed within a model of reading acquisition'. *Reading & Writing, 15*, 109–126.

Bowers, P.G., Steffy, R., & Tate, E. (1988). 'Comparison of the effects of IQ control methods on memory and naming speed predictors of reading disability'. *Reading Research Quarterly, 23*, 304–319.

Bradley, L., & Bryant, P.E. (1983). 'Categorizing sounds and learning to read: A causal connection'. *Nature, 301*, 419–421.

Chiappe, P., Stringer, R., Siegel, L.S., & Stanovich, K.E. (2002). 'Why the timing deficit hypothesis does not explain reading disability in adults'. *Reading & Writing, 15*, 73–107.

Cossu, G. (2003). 'The role of output speech in literacy acquisition: Evidence from congenital anarthria'. *Reading & Writing, 16*, 99–122.

Cossu, G., Shankweiler, D., Liberman, I.Y., Tola, G., & Katz, L. (1988). 'Awareness of phonological segments and reading ability in Italian children'. *Applied Psycholinguistics, 9*, 1–16.

Dault, M.C., Yardley, L., & Frank, J.S. (2003). 'Does articulation contribute to modifications of postural control during dual-task paradigms?' *Cognitive Brain Research, 16*, 434–440.

Denckla, M.B., Rudel, R.G., Chapman, C., & Krieger, J. (1985). 'Motor proficiency in dyslexic children with and without attentional disorders'. *Archives of Neurology, 42*, 228–231.

Dum, R.P., & Strick, P.L. (2003). 'An unfolded map of the cerebellar dentate nucleus and its projections to the cerebral cortex'. *Journal of Neurophysiology, 89*, 634–639.

Eckert, M.A., Leonard, C.M., Richards, T.L., Aylward, E.H., Thomson, J., & Berninger, V.W. (2003). 'Anatomical correlates of dyslexia: Frontal and cerebellar findings'. *Brain, 126*, 482–494.

Everatt, J., McCorquodale, B., Smith, J., Culverwell, F., Wilks, A., Evans, D., *et al.* (1999). 'Associations between reading ability and visual processes'. In J. Everatt (ed.), *Reading and dyslexia: Visual and attentional processes.* New York: Routledge.

Fawcett, A.J. (2002). 'Dyslexia, the cerebellum and phonological skill'. In E. Witruk, A.D. Friederici, & T. Lachmann (eds.), *Basic functions of language, reading and reading disability: Neuropsychology and cognition.* (pp. 265–279). Dordrecht: Kluwer.

Fawcett, A.J., & Nicolson, R.I. (1992). 'Automatisation deficits in balance for dyslexic children'. *Perceptual & Motor Skills, 75*, 507–529.

Fawcett, A.J., & Nicolson, R.I. (1994). 'Naming speed in children with dyslexia'. *Journal of Learning Disabilities, 27*, 641–646.

Fawcett, A.J., & Nicolson, R.I. (1995a). 'Persistence of phonological awareness deficits in older children with dyslexia'. *Reading and Writing, 7*, 361–376.

Fawcett, A.J., & Nicolson, R.I. (1995b). 'Persistent deficits in motor skill of children with dyslexia'. *Journal of Motor Behavior, 27*, 235–240.

Fawcett, A.J., & Nicolson, R.I. (1995c). 'The dyslexia early screening test'. *Irish Journal of Psychology, 16*, 248–259.

Fawcett, A.J., & Nicolson, R.I. (1999). 'Performance of dyslexic children on cerebellar and cognitive tests'. *Journal of Motor Behavior, 31*, 68–78.

Fawcett, A.J., & Lynch, L. (2000). 'Systematic identification and intervention for reading difficulty: Case studies of children with EAL'. *Dyslexia, 6*, 57–71.

Fawcett, A.J., Pickering, S., & Nicolson, R.I. (1993). 'Development of the DEST test for the early screening for dyslexia'. In S.F. Wright & R. Groner (eds), *Facets of dyslexia and its remediation* (pp. 483–496). Amsterdam: North-Holland/Elsevier.

Fawcett, A J., Nicolson, R.I., & Dean, P. (1996). 'Impaired performance of children with dyslexia on a range of cerebellar tasks'. *Annals of Dyslexia, 46*, 259–283.

Fawcett, A.J., Nicolson, R.I., & Maclagan, F. (2001). 'Cerebellar tests differentiate between groups of poor readers with and without IQ discrepancy'. *Journal of Learning Disabilities, 34*, 119–135.

Fiez, J.A., Petersen, S.E., Cheney, M.K., & Raichle, M.E. (1992). 'Impaired non-motor learning and error detection associated with cerebellar damage: A single case study'. *Brain, 115*, 155–178.

Finch, A.J., Nicolson, R.I., & Fawcett, A.J. (2002). 'Evidence for a neuroanatomical difference within the olivo-cerebellar pathway of adults with dyslexia'. *Cortex, 38*, 529–539.

Fletcher, J.M., Shaywitz, S.E., Shankweiler, D.P., Katz, L., Liberman, I.Y., Stuebing, K. K., *et al.* (1994). 'Cognitive profiles of reading disability: Comparisons of discrepancy and low achievement definitions'. *Journal of Educational Psychology, 86*, 6–23.

Hatcher, P.J., Hulme, C., & Ellis, A.W. (1994). 'Ameliorating early reading failure by integrating the teaching of reading and phonological skills: The phonological linkage hypothesis'. *Child Development, 65*, 41–57.

Hynd, G.W., Morgan, A.E., Edmonds, J.E., Black, K., Riccio, C.A., & Lombardino, L. (1995). 'Reading disabilities, comorbid psychopathology, and the specificity of neuro-linguistic deficits'. *Developmental Neuropsychology, 11*, 311–322.

Ivry, R.B., & Gopal, H.S. (1993). 'Speech production and perception in patients with cerebellar lesions'. In D.E. Meyer & S. Kornblum (eds), *Attention and performance 14: Synergies in experimental psychology, artificial intelligence, and cognitive neuroscience* (pp. 771–802). Cambridge, MA: MIT Press.

Ivry, R.B., & Justus, T.C. (2001). 'A neural instantiation of the motor theory of speech perception: Comment from Richard B. Ivry and Timothy C. Justus to Nicholson *et al.*' *Trends in Neurosciences, 24*, 513–515.

Kelly, S.W., Griffiths, S., & Frith, U. (2002). 'Evidence for implicit sequence learning in dyslexia'. *Dyslexia, 8*, 43–52.

Liberman, A.M. (1982). 'On finding that speech is special'. *American Psychologist, 37*, 148–167.

Lundberg, I., Frost, J., & Petersen, O. (1988). 'Effects of an extensive program for stimulating phonological awareness in preschool children'. *Reading Research Quarterly, 23*, 263–284.

Lyon, G.R. (1995). 'Toward a definition of dyslexia'. *Annals of Dyslexia, 45*, 3–27.

McPhillips, M. (2003). 'A commentary on an article published in the February 2003 edition of "Dyslexia", "Evaluation of an exercise-based treatment for children with reading difficulties" (Reynolds, Nicolson, & Hambly)'. *Dyslexia, 9*, 161–163.

Naslund, J.C., & Schneider, W. (1996). 'Kindergarten letter knowledge, phonological skills, and memory processes: Relative effects on early literacy'. *Journal of Experimental Child Psychology, 62*, 30–59.

Neuhaus, G.F., & Swank, P.R. (2002). 'Understanding the relations between RAN letter subtest components and word reading in first-grade students'. *Journal of Learning Disabilities, 35*, 158–174.

Neuhaus, G., Foorman, B.R., Francis, D.J., & Carlson, C.D. (2001a). 'Measures of information processing in rapid automatized naming (RAN) and their relation to reading'. *Journal of Experimental Child Psychology, 78*, 359–373.

Neuhaus, G.F., Carlson, C.D., Jeng, W.M., Post, Y., & Swank, P.R. (2001b). 'The reliability and validity of Rapid Automatized Naming scoring software ratings for the determination of pause and articulation component durations'. *Educational & Psychological Measurement, 61*, 490–504.

Nicolson, R.I., & Fawcett, A.J. (1990). 'Automaticity: A new framework for dyslexia research?' *Cognition, 35*, 159–182.

Nicolson, R.I., & Fawcett, A.J. (1999). 'Developmental dyslexia: The role of the cerebellum'. *Dyslexia, 5*, 155–177.

Nicolson, R.I., & Fawcett, A.J. (2000). 'Long-term learning in dyslexic children'. *European Journal of Cognitive Psychology, 12*, 357–393.

Nicolson, R.I., Fawcett, A.J., & Dean, P. (2001). 'Developmental dyslexia: The cerebellar deficit hypothesis'. *Trends in Neurosciences, 24*, 508–511.

Nicolson, R.I., Daum, I., Schugens, M.M., Fawcett, A.J., & Schulz, A. (2002). 'Eyeblink conditioning indicates cerebellar abnormality in dyslexia'. *Experimental Brain Research, 143*, 42–50.

Olson, R., Wise, B., Conners, F., Rack, J., & Fulker, D.W. (1989). 'Specific deficits in component reading and language skills: Genetic and environmental influences'. *Journal of Learning Disabilities, 22*, 339–348.

Orton Dyslexia Society. (1995). 'Definition of dyslexia: Report from committee of members'. *Perspectives, 21*, 16–17.

Pennington, B.F., Van Orden, G.C., Smith, S.D., Green, P.A., & Haith, M.M. (1990). 'Phonological processing skills and deficits in adult dyslexics'. *Child Development, 61*, 1753–1778.

Raberger, T., & Wimmer, H. (2003). 'On the automaticity/cerebellar deficit hypothesis of dyslexia: Balancing and continuous rapid naming in dyslexic and ADHD children'. *Neuropsychologia, 41*, 1493–1497.

Rack, J.P. (1985). 'Orthographic and phonetic coding in developmental dyslexia'. *British Journal of Psychology, 76*, 325–340.

Rack, J.P., Snowling, M.J., Hulme, C., & Gibbs, S. (2007). 'No evidence that an exercise-based treatment programme (DDAT) has specific benefits for children with reading difficulties'. *Dyslexia, 13*, 97–104.

Ramus, F., Pidgeon, E., & Frith, U. (2003a). 'The relationship between motor control and phonology in dyslexic children'. *Journal of Child Psychology & Psychiatry & Allied Disciplines, 44*, 712–722.

Ramus, F., Rosen, S., Dakin, S.C., Day, B.L., Castellote, J.M., White, S., et al. (2003b). 'Theories of developmental dyslexia: Insights from a multiple case study of dyslexic adults'. *Brain, 126*, 841–865.

Reynolds, D., & Nicolson, R. I. (2007). 'Follow-up of an exercise-based treatment for children with reading difficulties'. *Dyslexia, 13*, 78–96.

Reynolds, D., Nicolson, R.I., & Hambly, H. (2003). 'Evaluation of an exercise-based treatment for children with reading difficulties'. *Dyslexia, 9*, 48–71.

Richards, I.L., Moores, E., Witton, C., Reddy, P.A., Rippon, G., Rochelle, K.S.H., et al. (2003). 'Science, sophistry and "commercial sensitivity": Comments on "Evaluation of an exercise-based treatment for children with reading difficulties", by Reynolds, Nicolson and Hambly'. *Dyslexia, 9*, 146–150.

Savage, R. (2004). 'Motor skills, automaticity and developmental dyslexia: A review of the research literature'. *Reading & Writing, 17*, 301–324.

—— (2007). 'Cerebellar tasks do not distinguish between children with developmental dyslexia and children with intellectual disabilities'. *Child Neuropsychology, 13*, 5, 389–407.

Savage, R., Frederickson, N., Goodwin, R., Patni, U., Smith, N., & Tuersley, L. (2005a). 'Relationships among rapid digit naming, phonological processing, motor automaticity, and speech perception in poor, average, and good readers and spellers'. *Journal of Learning Disabilities, 38*, 12–28.

Savage, R., Frederickson, N., Goodwin, R., Patni, U., Smith, N., & Tuersley, L. (2005b). 'Evaluating current deficit theories of poor reading: Role of phonological processing, naming speed, balance automaticity, rapid verbal perception and working memory'. *Perceptual & Motor Skills, 101*, 345–361.

Schmahmann, J.D., & Sherman, J.C. (1998). 'The cerebellar cognitive affective syndrome'. *Brain, 121*, 561–579.

Schulz, G.M., Dingwall, W.O., & Ludlow, C.L. (1999). 'Speech and oral motor learning in individuals with cerebellar atrophy'. *Journal of Speech, Language, & Hearing Research, 42*, 1157–1175.

Share, D.L., Jorm, A.F., Maclean, R., & Matthews, R. (1984). 'Sources of individual differences in reading acquisition'. *Journal of Educational Psychology, 76*, 1309–1324.

Shaywitz, B.A., Fletcher, J.M., Holahan, J.M., & Shaywitz, S.E. (1992). 'Discrepancy compared to low achievement definitions of reading disability: Results from the Connecticut Longitudinal Study'. *Journal of Learning Disabilities, 25*, 639–648.

Siegel, L.S. (1993). 'Phonological processing deficits as the basis of a reading disability'. *Developmental Review, 13*, 246–257.

Siegel, L.S., & Ryan, E.B. (1989). 'Subtypes of developmental dyslexia: The influence of definitional variables'. *Reading & Writing, 1*, 257–287.

Singleton, C., & Stuart, M. (2003). 'Measurement mischief: A critique of Reynolds, Nicolson and Hambly (2003)'. *Dyslexia, 9*, 151–160.

Snowling, M. (1998). 'Dyslexia as a phonological deficit: Evidence and implications'. *Child Psychology & Psychiatry Review, 3*, 4–11.

Snowling, M.J., & Hulme, C. (2003). 'A critique of claims from Reynolds, Nicolson & Hambly (2003) that DDAT is an effective treatment for children with reading difficulties: "Lies, damned lies and (inappropriate) statistics?"' *Dyslexia, 9*, 127–133.

Swanson, H., & Hoskyn, M. (1998). 'Experimental intervention research on students with learning disabilities: A meta-analysis of treatment outcomes'. *Review of Educational Research, 68*, 277–321.

Temple, E. (2002). 'Brain mechanisms in normal and dyslexic readers'. *Current Opinion in Neurobiology, 12*, 178–183.

Torgesen, J.K., & Wagner, R.K. (1998). 'Alternative diagnostic approaches for specific developmental reading disabilities'. *Learning Disabilities Research & Practice, 13*, 220–232.

Turner, M. (1997). *Psychological assessment of dyslexia*. London: Whurr.

van Daal, V., & van der Leij, A. (1999). 'Developmental dyslexia: Related to specific or general deficits?' *Annals of Dyslexia, 49*, 71–104.

Vellutino, F.R., Scanlon, D.M., Sipay, E.R., Pratt, A., Chen, R., & Denckla, M.B. (1996). 'Cognitive profiles of difficult-to-remediate and readily remediated poor readers: Early intervention as a vehicle for distinguishing between cognitive and experiential deficits as a basic cause of specific reading disability'. *Journal of Educational Psychology, 88*, 601–638.

Vellutino, F.R., Scanlon, D.M., & Lyon, G. (2000). 'Differentiating between difficult-to-remediate and readily remediated poor readers: More evidence against the IQ-achievement discrepancy definition of reading disability'. *Journal of Learning Disabilities, 33*, 223–238.

Vellutino, F.R., Fletcher, J.M., Snowling, M.J., & Scanlon, D.M. (2004). 'Specific reading disability (dyslexia): What have we learned in the past four decades?' *Journal of Child Psychology and Psychiatry, 45*, 2–40.

Wagner, R.K., Torgesen, J.K., & Rashotte, C.A. (1994). 'Development of reading-related phonological processing abilities: New evidence of bi-directional causality from a latent variable longitudinal study'. *Developmental Psychology, 30*, 73–87.

Wesseling, R., & Reitsma, P. (2001). 'Preschool phonological representations and development of reading skills'. *Annals of Dyslexia, 51*, 203–229.

Wimmer, H., Mayringer, H., & Raberger, T. (1999). 'Reading and dual-task balancing: Evidence against the automatization deficit explanation of developmental dyslexia'. *Journal of Learning Disabilities, 32*, 473–478.

Wolf, M., & Bowers, P.G. (1999). 'The double-deficit hypothesis for the developmental dyslexia'. *Journal of Educational Psychology, 91*, 415–438.

Wolf, M., Bowers, P.G., & Biddle, K. (2000). 'Naming-speed processes, timing, and reading: A conceptual review'. *Journal of Learning Disabilities, 33*, 387–407.

Wolff, P.H. (2002). 'Timing precision and rhythm in developmental dyslexia'. *Reading & Writing, 15*, 179–206.

Yap, R.L., & van der Leij, A. (1994). 'Testing the automatization deficit hypothesis of dyslexia via a dual-task paradigm'. *Journal of Learning Disabilities, 27*, 660–665.

Yardley, L., Gardner, M., Leadbetter, A., & Lavie, N. (1999). 'Effect of articulation and mental tasks on postural control'. *Neuroreport, 10*, 215–219.

Zeffiro, T., & Eden, G. (2001). 'The cerebellum and dyslexia: Perpetrator or innocent bystander?' *Trends in Neurosciences, 24*, 512–513.

Chapter 16

Teaching children with severe learning difficulties

Routes to word recognition using logographic symbols

Kieron Sheehy and Andrew J. Holliman

Teaching word recognition to children with severe learning difficulties (formerly referred to as 'mental retardation') is a controversial topic. Practitioners and educational researchers promote the use of pictorial and logographic symbols as part of a facilitative pedagogy for teaching word recognition. However there also exists an established body of psychological research to indicate that these approaches are no more effective than the presentation of words alone, and may hinder learning. This chapter begins by critically considering the use of symbols in this context and then discusses a new pedagogical approach based on the characteristics of logographic reading, the handle technique. This has some empirical support and is based on the local feature hypothesis of early word recognition.

Non-readers and logographic symbols

Most children learn to recognize a few single words relatively easily. Having begun to make the link between a written word and the name it represents, a variety of approaches can help to move from simple word recognition, within a small sight vocabulary, to learning the skills required to begin reading, i.e. decoding unknown words and sentences. This spans phonemic analysis (Daly *et al.*, 2004), phonological skills development (Qi & O'Connor, 2000), social learning approaches (Bennet, 1985) and computer-based multisensory programmes (Clifford & Miles, 1998). However, some children with severe learning difficulties (SLD) struggle to begin to recognize a few words, or make use of sound–letter knowledge (Sheehy & Howe, 2001). These children experience a significant and general developmental delay, often associated with a significant delay in their language development, and their ability 'to learn from instruction can remain extremely limited' (Carr & Felce, 2000: 181). A longitudinal study of 82 children found that, after five years, approximately half were able to recognize few words, if any, and only 15 pupils could recognize more than ten (Chadwick *et al.*, 2005). Similarly a study of 35 special schools concluded that relatively few such students will learn to read and write conventionally. This followed extensive use of phonics-based instruction in the children's daily literacy hour, although 'In some instances, it seemed that only a few pupils were responding to this emphasis' (Lacey *et al.*, 2007: 154). This focus is maintained even where 'teachers acknowledged that the most they could expect was that pupils would be able to recognize social signs or "a few key words"' (Lacey *et al.*, 2007: 157).

A positive correlation between phonemic awareness and learning to read is well established in English orthography (Bryant *et al.*, 1990; Atwill *et al.*, 2007). As a result, phonology has been focused on in remedial reading programmes (Byrne, 1993; Qi & O'Connor, 2000) and training in phonemic awareness has been shown to assist in the acquisition of spelling to sound links (Treiman & Hirsch-Pasek, 1985; Atwill *et al.*, 2007). But some children with SLD appear not to be developing these skills, which are consistently linked to successful reading. This suggests that for many children with SLD a phonic-based teaching approach will fail them.

Empirical studies of teaching phonological awareness to children with SLD are rare (Saunders, 2007) and inferences about appropriate pedagogy might therefore be drawn from the studies of children with less significant learning difficulties. Frith (1985) proposed a three-stage theory of reading development. In the first stage, the logographic stage, words are read as logograms; that is, as symbolic visual input. It is in the subsequent stages where phonological awareness is a key component. For learners with a range of learning difficulties significant associations have been found between phonological awareness and reading measures (Saunders & DeFulio, 2007). This evidence suggests that phonological awareness instruction might improve the reading ability of some individuals with learning difficulties. This approach seems appropriate for those with moderate or mild learning difficulties (Saunders & DeFulio, 2007) but the utility of this approach becomes questionable as the learner's degree of intellectual impairment increases (Fowler *et al.*, 1995 cited in Verucci *et al.*, 2006). Verucci *et al.* (2006) found that, in comparison to typically developing children, some individuals with Down syndrome struggled with a range of phonological awareness tests (e.g. syllable segmentation, rhyme recognition) and demonstrated particular difficulty on a word reading test which required knowledge of grapheme-phoneme correspondences. It could be that these children were more dependent on semantic cues, a characteristic of logographic reading. Although this sample had higher levels of cognitive abilities than children with SLD (O'Brien, 2004) and were presented with a regular orthography, a logographic influence was still discernible. Indeed some individuals with Down syndrome are able to recognize some words in the absence of phonological awareness skills (Cossu *et al.*, 1993). In a similar investigation, Evans (1994) found that 'some logographic reading ability had developed, while alphabetic and phonological skills were largely absent' (p. 102) and this was seen as linked to the degree of intellectual impairment present. Children with SLD may fail to recognize any words at all following years of phonic-based teaching because this approach assumes a skill-base which they do not possess. Sheehy (2002b) gives the example of 'Anthony', a 15-year-old whose educational development illustrates the need for effective pedagogy in this area.

He was able to understand simple sentences containing two key elements but his own speech was difficult to understand due to articulation difficulties. His school record describes him as being at a 'pre-reading stage' and not yet reading any whole words. Annual reviews of Anthony's progress highlighted the need for Anthony to develop a sight vocabulary. However, after many years of teaching and support from experienced professionals, Anthony had not begun to recognise words.

(Sheehy, 2002b: 48)

In contrast to the difficulties experienced with learning initial word recognition, children like Anthony learn to recognize and name logographic symbols relatively easily. These symbols are based on the rebus principle, which uses a pictorial representation of a word concept and which therefore do not require decoding into subunits or phonemes. Many of these are iconic symbols where the word concept is represented directly by a pictograph of the object. The accessibility has led to them becoming integral parts of language and communication programmes (Abbott, 2005; Jones & Cregan, 1986).

The relative advantages and disadvantages of logographic and alphabetic orthographies have been discussed (Olson, 1993). In a range of conditions and with a variety of learners that includes university students (Muter & Johns, 1985), deaf adults (Flaherty & Moran, 2004) and children with SLD (Burroughs, 1989; Rozin et al., 1971), logographic systems are learned more readily than alphabetic systems. Adults with SLD, who have never begun word recognition, are able to learn logographic symbols (House et al., 1980) and children with SLD have been helped, through the use of logographic symbol systems, to develop their language skills (Makaton Vocabulary Development Project (MVDP), 2007). Makaton symbols (Walker et al., 1985) are used in the majority of educational settings for children with SLD in the UK (Abbott, 2005) and are popular worldwide. It is now common practice for documents and materials to incorporate logographic symbols, above the words, in order to make their content and meaning accessible. When used in this way symbols are an effective means of developing print comprehension for people with learning disabilities (Jones et al., 2007).

Logographic symbols as aids to learning

As one might expect, researchers have investigated how to harness these accessible symbols to teach word recognition, as an alternative to phonic-based instruction (Carpenter 1987; Solman & Wu, 1995; Detheridge, 1993; Sheehy, 2005). Makaton symbols, derived from rebus symbols, have been used for many years in this context (Carpenter & Detheridge, 1994; MVDP, 2007). The approach requires ongoing daily practice and repetition. A picture is introduced first and the symbol is brought in next, underneath the picture, and finally the word under both. Such is the 'recognizability' of the symbols that the pictures are often removed.

Gradually the symbol can be removed, allowing the word alone to become associated with its corresponding verbal label. Some children have learned to recognize words in this way (Carpenter & Detheridge, 1994; Detheridge, 1993; Van Oosterom & Devereux, 1982) and it is a recommended teaching method (MVDP, 2007).

Sheehy and Howe (2001) note that such recommendations typically arise from case study approaches, samples without a control group or where no comparison is made with how children learn when presented with simple words alone. He highlights that when such comparisons are made a strikingly different picture emerges.

The use of symbols, placed under or inserted into the word and acting as 'extra stimulus cues' (Wu & Solman, 1993), is repeatedly found to be at best no more effective than presenting the words alone (Tabe & Jackson, 1989; Wu & Solman, 1993) or even to hamper learning (Rose & Furr 1984; Solman & Singh, 1992). Solman & Wu (1995) carried out a range of empirical research studies and concluded that there was no evidence to suggest that symbol cues can enhance word recognition. So, although various authorities have long supported this use of symbols, an equally longstanding line of experimental research indicates that symbols are not efficient when compared to word alone approaches. In one explanation of this, the symbol acts as the functional cue for eliciting the word's name and distracts attention from the orthography itself. Beginning readers are more susceptible to this type of distraction than skilled readers (Rusted & Coltheart, 1979; Solman & Wu, 1995). Analysis of the eye movement of beginning readers looking at text/picture compounds indicates that they spend most time looking at the 'major meaning carriers' (Duckett, 2003). For non-reading children with SLD this meaning is contained in the logographic symbol. Learning the new association is impeded because the 'response acquisition of a new stimulus is severely hindered when it is presented in conjunction with a previously trained effective stimulus' (Wu & Solman, 1993: 145). It is ironic that increasing the exposure to the symbol and word compound, designed to help develop word recognition, is actually counter productive. The symbol continues to act as a 'blocking element' despite altering the presentation of cues, by spacing (Saunders & Solman, 1984) or prompting and fading (McDowell, 1982) or where verbal instructions explicitly encourage the association of visual inputs (Saunders & Solman, 1984). Wu & Solman (1993) explored sources where generating an associative image between visual cues did improve associative learning (Wolf & Levin, 1972). They concluded that, theoretically, young children *should* be able to use recall aids effectively and that active paired-associate learning *should* be able to improve children's learning. To try and improve the performance of symbol cues they developed a feedback cueing method, the presentation of the uncued word *followed* by the word plus cue. This resulted in more words being learned than presenting the standard compound (word and symbol in simple juxtaposition) but remained no better than word alone presentations (Solman & Wu, 1995). Whilst the logographic approaches enable the student to 'read' an accessible logographic system, the child is blocked, by the symbol, from learning a new association between a word's name and its traditional orthographic form. Hence researchers have suggested that symbols should never be used in teaching word recognition to children with SLD (Wu & Solman, 1993; Solman & Wu, 1995) and that a more useful approach would be one which directs the reader's attention toward the 'relevant characteristics to the word itself'. The nature of what might constitute such characteristics is now considered.

In search of relevant characteristics

Two developmental models include consideration of the features used by readers in initial word recognition. The assumption is that revealing the skills which non-readers develop in attaining word recognition will thereby identify the skills which children who are not mastering word recognition need to be taught. This is an important point. The picture–symbol fading approach has developed without an explicit consideration of how children typically begin to recognize written words. Attempts to improve the performance of this approach have not considered what it is that children who *can* recognize words actually do. This has been suggested as a major omission in informing the development of a new technique (Sheehy, 1995; Sheehy & Howe, 2001).

Of the developmental models to describe the transition from non-reader to skilled reader (Frith, 1985; Seymour & MacGregor, 1984; Ehri, 2002), some suggest that children move from pre-reading to proficient reading via a series of developmental stages or phases (Seymour, 2007), although the invariate progression implied by such models has been criticized (Bastien-Toniazzo & Jullien, 2001). These models include descriptions of the performance of children when they first begin to recognize words and this is what we seek to identify. Some models describe an initial visual word recognition stage followed by a letter–sound stage(s), whilst others have these elements interwoven (Seymour, 2007).

Marsh *et al.* (1981) proposed that there are qualitative changes in how children learn to process words and that these changes define the developmental changes within their four-stage model. In the first stage, linguistic guessing and rote association is the key process, producing 'primitive pre-alphabetic visually based word recognition' (Seymour, 2007: 2). Being pre-alphabetic, children at this level demonstrate no phonemic segmentation skills and hence isolated words are inaccessible, unless they have been seen before. A second stage, 'Discrimination Net Guessing' occurs when the child has developed the ability to compare the graphemic features of unknown words with those of a known word. The 'reader', without decoding skills, uses the minimal visual features necessary for choosing between words' identities (Seymour, 2007). The third stage of the model, rote learning and the use of partial graphemic cues is reached following an increase in the store of known words and use of rules to decode new words.

A second model to consider is that of Frith (1985). She adapted Marsh *et al.*'s model, primarily by merging stages one and two and emphasizing the influence of spelling skills in the development of word reading as part of a three-stage model. It is Frith's first stage, characterized by the child's instant recognition of familiar words, which is most relevant to this discussion. Here *salient graphic features* act as important recognition cues. The child attends to random, minimal word features and does not use letter order or grapheme–phoneme correspondences as cues (Frith, 1985). This contrasts with 'sight words' which are read automatically, having previously been decoded or deciphered through analogy (Ehri, 2002). There is substantial evidence to support the existence of logographic word recognition, in contrast to the later 'decoding' of an alphabetic script (Seymour, 2007). A word is processed on the basis of its graphic elements rather than letter order or connecting graphemes to phonemes (Bowman & Treiman, 2002). Consequently visual distinctiveness and context are important for logographic readers (Byrne, 1993).

Marsh *et al.*'s (1981) and Frith's (1985) view that all children beginning to read words do so logographically has been challenged by: examples of children with precocious phonological skills who use these when beginning to look at text (Stuart & Coltheart, 1988); regular orthographies where logographic processing may not be the 'first step'; and the possible use of initial letter names as cues (Bowman & Treiman, 2002). This suggests that there may not be a series of discrete universal stages of reading and spelling through which all children pass. Goswami & Bryant (1990) argued against a stage theory account but, in reviewing the research evidence, concluded that the claims made by Marsh *et al.* and Frith that children can read logographically at first was 'entirely justified by later research' (p. 146).

Rozin *et al.* (1971) found that learners lacking phonemic awareness found reading Chinese logographs relatively easy. However, assumptions that Chinese characters are purely logographic may be ill-founded as some characters include a phonetic component (Chu & Leung, 2005) and individual differences in visual processing abilities are only predictive of initial word reading. After this period it is phonemic awareness which is predictive of reading development in Chinese (Goswami, 2007). This indicates that visual feature recognition is important for initial readers of Chinese scripts. The issue of phonemic awareness is more relevant to the alphabetic stage of word recognition rather than the very beginning of the logographic reading. There is also evidence that, for some languages, a logographic reading stage may not occur (Bastien-Toniazzo & Jullien, 2001), that not all children will pass through such a stage for a given language (Sprenger-Charolles *et al.*, 1996) and that expertise in logographic reading does not impart a significant advantage to later reading ability.

There is evidence that some children with learning difficulties may learn to read traditional English orthography in the absence of phonological awareness (Buckley, 2001; Bryden *et al.*, 1983; Cossu *et al.*, 1993) and in the terminology of developmental models of reading they are logographic readers. Laws and Gunn (2002) note that, for children with Down syndrome, this may be understandable given this group's marked delay in phonological development and mild to moderate hearing loss. These features may delay their use of phonological skills to decode words. Knowledge from teaching children with Down syndrome (who may have moderate learning difficulties) suggests that one should begin by teaching whole words followed by subsequent development of text comprehension and phonic cues (Buckley, 2001; Lacey *et al.*, 2007). This has led to the suggestion that a whole word approach of some form might be a suitable strategy for children with severe learning difficulties (Lacey *et al.*, 2007). This suggests that a logographic level is the appropriate initial level at which to teach them word recognition, although the extent to which this is a precursor to later phonemic stages has been questioned (Bastien-Toniazzo & Jullien, 2001; Seymour, 2007).

The discussion indicates that initial word recognition can be logographic. Children process words visually, via the identification of a salient feature of the word (Ehri, 2002), and phonological information (the word's name) is obtained via a semantic processor (Seymour, 2007). In addition, there is evidence, from children with learning disabilities, that word recognition can at least begin without demonstrable phonemic awareness.

The nature of salient features in logographic word recognition

Logographic readers use particular salient features to recognize words and this aspect is now considered. Word identification (Frith, 1985; Marsh *et al.*, 1981) can be seen as a psycholinguistic guessing game in which the skill involved is in selecting the fewest, most productive cues necessary to produce effective guesses. Views fall into two main areas reflecting the historical consideration of the relative importance of shape versus specific features. Prior to 1900, investigations suggested that whole words and their outline shapes were the most important features of initial word recognition (Cattel, 1886, cited in Crowder, 1982). This emerged later as the global hypothesis (Gough, 1993), in which a first word is recognized holistically as a Gestalt (Seymour & Elder, 1986). In contrast, others proposed that there is some smaller feature that the child focuses on to prompt recognition. Some suggested these were 'dominant' initial or terminal letters (Marchbanks & Levin, 1965) or that the salient graphic features were accents, or ascenders and descenders (Seymour & Elder, 1986). The idea of a single feature being used as a cue in beginning word recognition is not a new idea. As early as 1923 Gates and Boeker referred to beginning readers as 'actively studying the details until some feature, usually minute, is found by means of which the whole may be identified' (Gates & Boeker, 1923: 7). This suggests that a 'local feature' (Gough, 1993) is used in initial word recognition. Gough (1993) carried out two experiments to investigate the 'global versus local feature' issue. In the first, 'thumbprint study', children were presented with isolated words written on flashcards. Some of these words were accompanied by a salient, but irrelevant, cue in the form of a thumbprint. Gough's results showed that when a salient extraneous cue is used, the child 'will associate the spoken word with that cue, and ignore the word itself. Moreover this happens whether the words are easy or difficult to discriminate' (Gough, 1993: 184), suggesting that the whole word is not used in initial word recognition. Gough (1993) also taught children an initial vocabulary and then tested them on recognition of the left or right half of the word. The findings indicated that words were identified by a *selected local feature*. Gates & Boeker (1923) came to similar conclusions after interviewing young children. 'children said they recognized pig by means of the dot over the I ... , window because the beginning was like the end and monkey because it has a tail' (p. 470).

Other sources report similar discussions with beginning readers (Gough, 1993; Torrey, 1979; Seymour & Elder, 1986) and a focus on a salient visual feature, e.g. the 'humps' in middle of 'camel' (Bowman & Treiman, 2002). 'Objects of all types are first identified by one of their physical features, usually the most perceptually salient one' (Bastien-Toniazzo & Jullien, 2001: 122). Logographic readers name words through associating this visual feature with a semantic code, using a mnemonic link (Seymour, 2007). The orthography is directly linked to the semantic information which triggers the selection of the word's name. Seymour (2007) notes how pre-literate children treat all shapes as pictures and process them through semantics linked to non-alphabetic visual features. The distinctive nature of this 'primitive' processing can be inferred from the right hemisphere activity which occurs at this time and which changes to predominantly left hemisphere activity as the later (alphabetic) stages of reading develop (Turkentaub *et al.*, cited in Seymour, 2007). From the information reviewed so far it seems sensible to suggest that, for beginning readers, selective association using a distinctive feature is the first step in learning to recognize a word.

Developing a 'local feature' teaching approach

Hempenstall (2004) asserts that we should explicitly use what is known about the different stages of reading to construct appropriate pedagogical activities. The non-

readers with whom this chapter is concerned have yet to master the selective association needed to begin the logographic stage of reading and are therefore at a stage
before logographic word recognition. They need to be taught the skill of making a
selective association between a word's name and a salient feature of its written
equivalent. If this assumption is correct then this association will enable them to read
logographically. This chapter will now look at the relatively few studies to adopt this
perspective in developing a method for teaching word recognition. These are the first
occasions that local feature identification has been suggested as the skill which children who are unable to recognize words should be explicitly taught. It makes the
assumption that these children will learn word recognition through the same route as
other children and, rather than seeking an alternative route, should be supported
through the same developmental process as their peers, albeit at a later chronological
period.

The handle technique

The new technique, developed through initial case studies (Sheehy, 1995), uses a
mnemonic approach with a cue to represent the child's understanding of the word.
The cue is abstract (see Figure 16.1) and non-pictorial, a 'squiggle' or a line, which is
proposed as being similar to the local features children typically use in initial word
recognition. The process (Sheehy & Howe, 2001) is outlined below.

1   A word is identified from the student's spoken or signed vocabulary and written
    on a flashcard.
2   This word is then discussed with the child. The aim is to elicit their personal
    understanding of the word and select the attribute that is most personally salient.
    Table 16.1 shows examples from different children and highlights the individual
    and idiosyncratic nature of their developing word meanings.

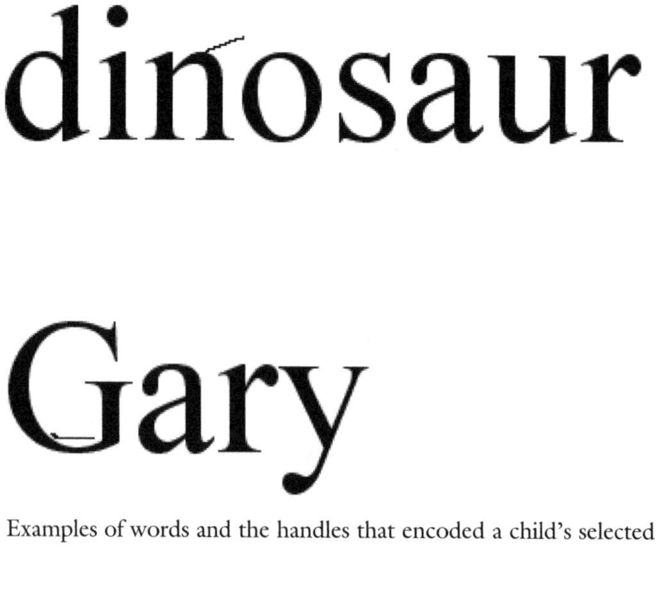

dinosaur

Gary

Figure 16.1 Examples of words and the handles that encoded a child's selected meaning

Table 16.1 Examples of idiosyncratic meanings

Word	*Meaning*
Dinosaur	"long neck ..."
Gary	"He's lazy un ... stays in bed ..."
Alice	"gives me cuddle"
Pony	"can run, walk ... nothing else"

Table 16.1 illustrates the importance of drawing out the idiosyncratic personal meaning from each participating child. It is unlikely that an adult would guess them.

The selected meaning is used mnemonically, the association of a name with a retrieval cue triggering recall (Sheehy & Howe, 2001). This feature, known as a 'handle', is intended to trigger recall of the associated image and hence the associated name from long-term memory. The handle is designed to mimic the nature of a local salient feature and have its recognition supported by its mnemonic nature, rather than through a pictorial representation. Figure 16.1 shows examples of words and the handles that encoded a child's selected meaning.

There is also correction procedure to check and readjust the association (Sheehy & Howe, 2001). It is important to emphasize that the teacher does not draw a picture, but adds a simple single line or mark representing the child's meaning. Once the child can respond correctly to the word and handle, the handle is faded out.

Is this approach more effective than using words alone?

The outcomes of a number of case studies involving children whose previous efforts to learn to read had met with complete failure, suggested that it might be effective (Sheehy, 1995). However, in the tradition of previous experimental research in the area, a direct comparison between the new technique and a word alone approach was seen as essential. This comparison also included an evaluation of a gradual fading of the handles in comparison to the feedback cueing approach (Wu & Solman, 1993). The results (Sheehy & Howe, 2001) showed that regardless of the method of fading the new 'handle' technique produced significantly more words being read (uncued) than the word alone condition. The use of an additional cue, the handle, did not reduce the effectiveness of the approach in comparison to presenting word alone and it was suggested that it might be the handle, rather than the nature of the fading process, that was the important factor. The technique was revised to use feedback cueing in preference to gradual fading, the former being more time efficient in terms of preparation. In this experiment the words were matched for each participant and taken from a predetermined vocabulary. The approach was therefore revised to include the use of words for which the child could offer a clear definition. This, albeit single, study suggested that perhaps a simple response-acquisition view of teaching word recognition with cues, as implied by the picture fading methods (MVDP, 2007; Wu & Solman, 1993) might not be applicable when abstract mnemonic cues (handles) are used.

The placement and integration of handles

Having gathered initial evidence that the 'handle technique' might have potential, two further questions were considered. First, whereabouts in a word is the optimum position for cue placement? Worrall & Singh (1983) proposed that cues placed centrally within a word would be most effective, but did not investigate this issue empirically. The second question concerns the importance of the physical integration of the handle into the word. Initially the handle was drawn as part of the word, i.e. physically integrated, to ease subsequent fading. Yet feedback cueing was found to be as effective as gradually fading (Sheehy & Howe, 2001) and this removed the original reason for integrating the handle. Therefore Sheehy (2002a) explored how the location and integration of handles influenced the ease with which children with severe learning difficulties learned to recognize words.

An established view of how symbols can be used in this context sees the spatial relationship between the word and the cue as the primary factor (Tabe & Jackson, 1989). Poor transfer from symbol to word recognition is because of the required shift of attention between the two separate items. Therefore superimposed cues will require less attentional shifting than juxtaposed cues allowing stimulus transfer to occur. This, essentially behavioural, view leads to symbol cues being placed centrally within a word, to encourage scrutiny of the traditional orthography and foster this association (Worrall & Singh, 1983). This view might explain the success of the handle technique as the result of incidental learning whilst searching within the traditional orthography for the small handle (Sheehy, 2002a). Central cues mean that more features of the overall word are noticed (Fukuda, 1992; Nazir et al., 1992), although this may not be so for skilled readers (Ellis, 2003). If the handle acts as a visual fixation point, a central location facilitates the maximum amount of visual information about the word (letter string) being noticed, whilst sites at the beginning or end of a word reduce the amount of information. The use of centrally placed cues is built on the assumption, either explicitly or implicitly, that attending to several features of the word will aid the subsequent learning of word recognition and is in keeping with an incidental learning perspective.

A conflicting perspective relates directly to what is known about logographic word reading, i.e. using a *local feature*, to prompt recall (Gough, 1993, Sheehy & Howe, 2001). Children just beginning word recognition use the first letter most frequently as a cue with the last letter being the next most frequent (Bryden et al., 1983). The least frequently used cue appears to be word shape (Bastien-Toniazzo & Jullien, 2001). This information suggests that the most frequent place for Gough's 'local features' to occur would be around the first letter or last letter (Sheehy, 2002a). Therefore cues placed at these sites would be more efficient in developing word recognition than cues placed centrally (Sheehy, 2002a). There is a small amount of support for this view as it has been previously noted that adding 'initial letter cues' is more helpful to children beginning word recognition than other sites (Crowder, 1982). Lateral cues are likely to focus attention towards the initial letter and reduce to some extent the number of other word features noticed (Fukuda, 1992, Worrall & Singh, 1983). This line of argument suggests that the 'local feature strategy' is not developed by, or perhaps does not involve, an extensive initial search of the traditional orthography. Therefore to teach someone to use a local feature approach it would be inappropriate to encourage such as search (i.e. through a small centrally placed cue). The optimum location, according to this perspective, would be where they would encourage an association which is likely to be used as a local feature (Sheehy, 2002a).

There is a conflict between these incidental learning and local feature perspectives. Consideration of logographic word recognition suggests that the optimum cue site is at the initial (or final) letter. In contrast research into the use of symbol cues promotes a central location. Sheehy (2002a) investigated this conflict and found that cues placed at the terminal positions did result in the greatest level of subsequent uncued word recognition. This gives some support to the 'logographic stage local feature' perspective. However, no significant difference was found at any point during the teaching sessions between integrated cues and non-integrated cues (Sheehy, 2002a). This goes against predictions based on pictorial symbol research (Tabe & Jackson, 1989). Non-integrated handles facilitated the transfer to traditional orthography as efficiently as integrated handles, suggesting that it is the 'nature' of the cue that is important, rather than its 'hidden' location encouraging incidental learning (Sheehy, 2002a).

This adds to the case that a simple incidental learning explanation is an inappropriate model upon which to develop a pedagogy. The effectiveness of handles at the initial and final letters implies that initial word recognition is *not* facilitated by encouraging an awareness of many features of the word.

These experiments (Sheehy & Howe, 2001; Sheehy, 2002a) were used to argue that the handles worked because of their closeness in nature to a salient local feature. However, there are several features in the technique and one of these, rather than the handle's design, could be the significant factor. Further, whilst integrated handles are no more effective than non-integrated handles, this might not be the case for integrated *picture* symbols. Lastly, the feedback cueing method, if combined with mnemonic and integrated cue features, might improve the performance of picture symbols in the teaching of word recognition (Sheehy, 2002b, 2005). There is some evidence that the superimposition of logographic rebus cues onto words improves their performance in teaching word recognition to children with severe learning difficulties. In a method known as Integrated Picture Cueing (Worrall & Singh, 1983) logographic rebuses are embedded within the word to be taught. For example in the word chair the letter 'h' might be replaced by a drawing of a chair which incorporates the letter.

Although no direct comparison with word alone approaches was made, Worrall and Singh (1983) implied that Integrated Picture Cueing might be more effective than a word alone approach. The reasoning underpinning their approach was in keeping with the incidental learning perspective described previously. If applying feedback cueing, cue integration and a mnemonic aspect could make the use of logographic symbols more effective than a word alone approach, then the nature of the handle itself would *not* be the key element in the success (Sheehy 2002a, 2002b). This would undermine the 'local feature' rationale underpinning the pedagogy. In these experiments four teaching approaches were compared: word alone, the handle technique, integrated picture cueing and integrated mnemonic cueing (Sheehy, 2002b). Integrated mnemonic cueing uses pictorial symbols which are designed to reflect the child's own understanding of the word. In this way it has the same mnemonic 'benefit' as the handle technique but retains a pictorial nature. The results of these investigations found that the handle technique remains more effective than integrated picture cueing when the variables of cue placement and teaching method (feedback cueing) are controlled (Sheehy, 2002b). Following the addition of feedback cueing to integrated picture cueing (IPC) no significant difference was found between this method and word alone (WA) approach, although a strong trend was identified (IPC > WA). The handle technique also achieved significantly higher word recognition scores than the Integrated Mnemonic Cueing approach, which was in turn consistently more effective than the word alone approach (Sheehy, 2002b). Further, the personal Integrated Mnemonic Cues were more effective in developing word recognition than pre-selected Integrated Picture Cues (Sheehy, 2002b).

Taken overall, these results (Sheehy, 2002a; 200b) suggest that the handle technique is not effective purely due to cue integration or the mnemonic element. However, these factors are influential. Applying a mnemonic element to a pictorial approach allows it to outperform a pre-selected pictorial approach and, more significantly, results in a greater number of words being recognized than the word alone approach when combined with feedback cueing (Sheehy, 2002b).

The research discussed in this chapter suggests that children with severe learning disabilities who are non-readers can be taught word recognition using symbols. There is now some, albeit small, empirical evidence to indicate that when symbols are used with particular techniques, i.e. feedback cueing and a mnemonic element, then they may be more effective that the presentation of words alone. However the handle technique has consistently proved to be the most effective approach across these studies (Sheehy & Howe, 2001; Sheehy 2002a, 2000b).

Unlike other word recognition teaching approaches the handle technique was developed through a consideration of developmental models of word recognition and the characteristics of logographic readers. Current evidence suggests that its effectiveness is due to the handles 'non-pictoriality' and it has been argued that this allows it to mimic the 'salient feature' which is used to begin logographic word recognition, and that it is this upon which its effectiveness relies.

References

Abbott, C.L.H. (2005). 'Symbol communication in special schools in England: The current position and some key issues'. *British Journal of Special Education, 32*, 196–201.

Atwill, K., Blanchard, J., Gorin, J.S., & Burstein, K. (2007). 'Receptive vocabulary and cross-language transfer of phonemic awareness in kindergarten children'. *Journal of Educational Research, 100*, 336–346.

Bastien-Toniazzo, M., & Jullien, S. (2001). 'Nature and importance of the logographic phase in learning to read'. *Reading and Writing, 14*, 119.

Bennet, J. (1985). *Learning to read with picture books*. Stroud: Thimble Press.

Bowman, M., & Treiman, R. (2002). 'Relating print and speech: The effects of letter names and word position on reading and spelling performance'. *Journal of Experimental Child Psychology, 82*(4), 305–340.

Bryant, P.E., MacLean, M., Bradley, L.L., & Crossland, J. (1990). 'Rhyme and alliteration, phoneme detection and learning to read'. *Developmental Psychology, 26*, 429–434.

Bryden, M.P., Mcsidor, A.T., Loken, M., Ingleton, M.A., Buckley, S., & Wood, E. (1983). 'The extent and significance of reading skills in pre-school children with Down syndrome'. Paper presented at the British Psychological Society Conference.

Buckley, S., (2001). *Reading and writing development for children with down syndrome: An overview*. The Down Syndrome Educational Trust: Downsed.org

Burroughs, J. (1989). 'The acquisition of contrasting symbol systems by language delay in children'. Paper presented at the Annual Conference of the American Speech-Language-Hearing Association.

Byrne, B. (1993). 'Learning to read in the absence of phonemic awareness? A comment on Cossu, Rossini and Marshall'. *Cognition, 48,* 285–288.

Carpenter, B. (1987). *A formative evaluation of a Makaton-based reading programme.* University of Nottingham, Nottingham, UK.

Carpenter, B., & Detheridge, T. (1994). 'Writing with symbols'. *Support For Learning, 9,* 27–32.

Carr, D. & Felce, D. (2000). 'Application of stimulus equivalence to language intervention for individuals with severe linguistic disabilities'. *Journal of Intellectual and Developmental Disability 25,* 181–205.

Chadwick, O., Cuddy, M., Kusel, Y., & Taylor, E. (2005). 'Handicaps and the development of skills between childhood and early adolescence in young people with severe intellectual disabilities'. *Journal of Intellectual Disability Research. 49,* 877–888.

Chu, M.M. & Leung, M. (2005). 'Reading strategy of Hong Kong school-aged children: The development of word-level and character-level processing'. *Applied Psycholinguistics, 26,* 505–520.

Clifford, V., & Miles, M. (1998). 'Information and Communications Technology'. *Educational Psychology in Practice, 14,* 183.

Cossu, G., Rossini, F., & Marshall, J.C. (1993). 'When reading is acquired but phonemic awareness is not: a study of literacy in Down's Syndrome'. *Cognition 46,* 129–138.

Crowder, R.G. (1982). *The psychology of reading.* Oxford: Oxford University Press.

Daly, I., Chafouleas, S.M., Persampieri, M., Bonfiglio, C.M., & Detheridge, T. (1993). 'Symbolic significance'. Special Needs. *The Times Educational Supplement,* pp. 30–31.

Daly, I.., Chafouleas, S.M., Persampieri, M., Bonfiglio, C.M., & LaFleur, K. (2004). 'Teaching phoneme segmenting and blending as critical early literacy skills: An experimental analysis of minimal textual repertoires'. *Journal of Behavioral Education, 13,* 3.

Detheridge, T. (1993). 'Symbolic significance. Special needs'. *The Times Educational Supplement,* pp. 30–31.

Duckett, P. (2003). 'Envisioning story: The eye movements of beginning readers'. *Literacy Teaching and Learning, 7,* 77–89.

Ehri, L.C. (2002). 'Phases of acquisition in learning to read words and implications for teaching'. *British Journal of Educational Psychology: Monograph Series, 1,* 7.

Ellis, A.W. (2003). *Reading, writing and dyslexia: A cognitive analysis* (2nd edn)'. London: LEA.

Evans, R. (1994). 'Phonological awareness in children with Down syndrome'. *Down Syndrome Research and Practice, 2,* 102–105.

Flaherty, M., & Moran, A. (2004). 'Deaf signers who know Japanese remember words and numbers more effectively than deaf signers who know English'. *American Annals of the Deaf, 149,* 39–45.

Frith, U. (1985). 'Beneath the surface of developmental dyslexia'. In M. Coltheart, K.E. Patterson, & J.C. Marshall (eds), *Surface dyslexia.* London: Routledge & Kegan Paul.

Fukuda, T. (1992). 'Visual capability to receive character information'. Part 1. How many characters can be recognised at a glance. *Ergonomics, 35,* 367–371.

Gates, A., & Boeker, E. (1923). 'A study of initial stages in reading by pre-school children'. *Teachers College Record, 24,* 469–488.

Goswami, U. (2007). 'Typical reading development and developmental dyslexia across languages'. In D. Coch, & K.W. Fischer (eds), *Human behavior, learning, and the developing brain* (pp. 145–167). New York: Guilford Press.

Goswami, U. and Bryant, P. (1990). *Phonological skills and learning to read*. Hove (Sussex): LEA.

Gough, P.B. (1993). 'The beginning of decoding'. *Reading and Writing, 5*, 181–192.

Hempenstall, K. (2004). 'How might a stage model of reading development be helpful in the classroom?' *Educational Psychology, 24*, 728–751.

House, B.J., Hanley, M.J., & Magid, D.F. (1980). 'Logographic reading by TMR adults'. *American Journal of Mental Deficiency, 85*, 161–170.

Jones, F.W., Long, K., &, Finlay, W.M.L. (2007). 'Symbols can improve the reading comprehension of adults with learning disabilities?' *Journal of Intellectual Disability Research, 51*, 545–550.

Jones, P.R., & Cregan, A. (1986). *Sign and symbol communication for mentally handicapped people*. London: Croom Helm.

Lacey, P., Layton, L., Miller, A. Goldbart, J., & Lawson, H. (2007). 'What is literacy for students with severe learning difficulties? Exploring conventional and inclusive literacy'. *Journal of Research in Special Educational Needs, 7*, 149–160.

Laws, G., & Gunn, D. (2002). 'Relationships between reading, phonological skills and language development in individuals with Down syndrome: A five-year follow-up study'. *Reading and Writing, 15*, 527–548.

McDowell, E.E. (1982). 'Specific aspects of prompting and fading procedures in teaching beginning reading'. *Perceptual and Motor Skills, 55*, 1103–1108.

Makaton Vocabulary Development Project (MVDP) (2007). 'Using symbols and signs: including the word under a symbol or sign'. http://www.makaton.org/about/ss_word.htm (accessed 15 October 2008).

Marchbanks, G., & Levin, H. (1965). 'Cues by which children recognise words'. *Journal of Educational Psychology, 52*, 57–61.

Marsh, G., Friedman, M., Welch, D., & Desberg, P. (1981). 'A cognitive-developmental theory of reading acquisition'. In W.T.G. MacKinnon (ed.), *Reading research: Advances in theory and practice* (Vol. 4). New York: Academic Press.

Muter, P., & Johns, E.J. (1985). 'Learning logographies and alphabetic codes'. *Human Learning, 4*, 105–125.

Nazir, T.A., Heller, D., & Sussman, C. (1992). 'Letter visibility and word recognition: The optimal viewing position in printed words'. *Memory and Cognition, 15*, 133–140.

O'Brien, G. (2004). 'Learning disability'. *Medicine*, 58–60

Olson, D. (1993). 'How writing represents speech'. *Language and Communication, 1*, 1–17.

Qi, S., & O'Connor, R. (2000). 'Comparison of phonological training procedures in kindergarten classrooms'. *Journal of Educational Research, 93*, 226.

Rose, T.L., & Furr, P.M. (1984). 'Negative effects of illustrations as word cues'. *Journal of Learning Disabilities, 17*, 334–337.

Rozin, P., Poritsky, S., & Sotsky, R. (1971). 'American children with reading problems can easily learn to read English represented by Chinese characters'. *Science, 71*, 1264–1267.

Rusted, J., & Coltheart, V. (1979). 'The effect of pictures on the retention of novel words and prose passages'. *Journal of Experimental Child Psychology, 28*, 516–524.

Saunders, K.J. (2007). 'Word-attack skills in individuals with mental retardation'. *Mental Retardation and Developmental Disabilities Research Reviews, 13*, 78–84.

Saunders, K.J. and DeFulio, A. (2007). 'Phonological awareness and rapid naming predict word attack and word identification in adults with mild mental retardation'. *American Journal on Mental Retardation, 112*, 155–166.

Saunders, R., & Solman, R.T. (1984). 'The effect of pictures on the acquisition of a small vocabulary of similar sight words'. *British Journal of Educational Psychology, 54*, 265–275.

Seymour, P.H.K. (2007). 'Continuity and discontinuity in the development of single-word reading: theoretical speculations'. In E.L. Grigorenko & A.J. Naples (eds), *Single-word reading: Behavioral and biological perspectives*. London: LEA.

Seymour, P.H.K., & MacGregor, C.J. (1984). 'Developmental dyslexia, cognitive experimental analysis of phonological, morphemic and visual impairments'. *Cognitive Neuropsychology, 1*, 43–83.

Seymour, P.H.K., & Elder, L. (1986). 'Beginning reading without phonology'. *Cognitive Neuropsychology, 3*, 1–36.

Sheehy, K. (1995). 'Teaching word recognition to children with severe learning disabilities'. In G. Shiel, U. Ni Dhalaigh, & B. O'Reilly (eds), *Reading development to age 15: Overcoming difficulties*. Reading Association of Ireland (pp. 64–70). Dublin: Blackrock.

—— (2002a). 'Overcoming failure to begin word recognition using a local feature strategy: The handle technique and children with severe learning difficulties'. *Journal of the Irish Learning Support Association, 24*, 78–87.

—— (2002b). 'The effective use of symbols in teaching word recognition to children with severe learning difficulties: A comparison of word alone, integrated picture cueing and the handle technique'. *International Journal of Disability, Development & Education, 49*, 47–59.

—— (2005). 'Morphing images: A potential tool for teaching word recognition to children with severe learning difficulties'. *British Journal of Educational Technology, 36*, 293–301.

Sheehy, K., & Howe, M.J. (2001). 'Teaching non-readers with severe learning difficulties to recognise words: The effective use of symbols in a new technique'. *Westminster Studies in Education, 24*, 61–71.

Solman, R.T., & Singh, N.N. (1992). 'Pictures block the learning of sight words'. *Educational Psychology, 2*, 143–153.

Solman, R.T., & Wu, H.M. (1995). 'Pictures as feedback in single word learning'. *Educational Psychology, 15*, 227–244.

Sprenger-Charolles, L., Siegel, L.S., & Bonnet, P. (1998). 'Reading and spelling acquisition in French: The role of phonological mediation and orthographic knowledge'. *Journal of Experimental Child Psychology, 68*, 134.

Stuart, M., & Coltheart, M. (1988). 'Does reading develop in a series of stages?' *Cognition 30*, 139–181.

Tabe, N., & Jackson, M. (1989). 'Teaching sight vocabulary to children with developmental disabilities'. *Australian and New Zealand Journal of Developmental Disabilities, 15*, 27–39.

Torrey, J.W. (1979). 'Reading that comes naturally: The early reader'. In T.G. Walker & G.E. MacKinnon (eds), *Reading research: Advances in theory and practice*. New York: Academic Press.

Treiman, R., & Hirsch-Pasek, K. (1985). 'Are there qualitative differences in reading between dyslexic and normal readers?' *Memory and Cognition, 13*, 357–364.

Van Oosterom, J., & Devereux, K. (1982). 'Rebus at Rees Thomas School'. *Special Education: Forward Trends, 9*, 31–33.

Verucci, L., Menghini, D., & Vicari, S. (2006). 'Reading skills and phonological awareness acquisition in Down syndrome'. *Journal of Intellectual Disability Research, 50*, 477–491.

Walker, M., Cousins, S., Parsons, F., & Carpenter, B. (1985). *Symbols for Makaton*. Camberley, Surrey: Makaton Vocabulary Development Project.

Wolf, P., & Levin, J.R. (1972). 'The role of overt activity in children's imagery production'. *Child Development, 43*, 537–547.

Worrall, N., & Singh, Y. (1983). 'Teaching TMR children to read using integrated picture cueing'. *American Journal of Mental Deficiency, 87*, 422–429.

Wu, H.M., & Solman, R.T. (1993). 'Effective use of pictures as extra-stimulus prompts'. *British Journal of Educational Psychology, 63*, 144–160.

Index